Supercharged Python

Supercharged Python

Brian Overland

John Bennett

Addison-Wesley

Boston • Columbus • New York • San Francisco • Amsterdam • Cape Town
Dubai • London • Madrid • Milan • Munich • Paris • Montreal • Toronto • Delhi • Mexico City
São Paulo • Sydney • Hong Kong • Seoul • Singapore • Taipei • Tokyo

Chapter 2 *Advanced String Capabilities*   33

Appendix A   *Python Operator Precedence Table*   547

Appendix B   *Built-In Python Functions*   549

Preface

Books on Python aimed for the absolute beginner have become a cottage industry these days. Everyone and their dog, it seems, wants to chase the Python.

We're a little biased, but one book we especially recommend is *Python Without Fear*. It takes you by the hand and explains the major features one at a time. But what do you do after you know a little of the language but not enough to call yourself an "expert"? How do you learn enough to get a job or to write major applications?

That's what this book is for: to be the *second* book you ever buy on Python and possibly the last.

What Makes Python Special?

It's safe to say that many people are attracted to Python because it looks easier than C++. That may be (at least in the beginning), but underneath this so-called easy language is a tool of great power, with many shortcuts and software libraries called "packages" that—in some cases—do most of the work for you. These let you create some really impressive software, outputting beautiful graphs and manipulating large amounts of data.

For most people, it may take years to learn all the shortcuts and advanced features. This book is written for people who want to get that knowledge now, to get closer to being a Python expert much faster.

What You'll Learn

The list of topics in this book that are not in *Python Without Fear* or other "beginner" texts is a long one, but here is a partial list of some of the major areas:

▶ List, set, and dictionary comprehension.

▶ Regular expressions and advanced formatting techniques; how to use them in lexical analysis.

▶ Packages: the use of Python's advanced numeric and plotting software. Also, special types such as `Decimal` and `Fraction`.

▶ Mastering all the ways of using binary file operations in Python, as well as text operations.

▶ How to use multiple modules in Python while avoiding the "gotchas."

▶ Fine points of object-oriented programming, especially all the "magic methods," their quirks, their special features, and their uses.

Have Fun

When you master some or all of the techniques of this book, you should make a delightful discovery: Python often enables you to do a great deal with a relatively small amount of code. That's why it's dramatically increasing in popularity every day. Because Python is not just a time-saving device, it's fun to be able to program this way . . . to see a few lines of code do so much.

We wish you the joy of that discovery.

Register your copy of *Supercharged Python* on the InformIT site for convenient access to updates and/or corrections as they become available. To start the registration process, go to informit.com/register and log in or create an account. Enter the product ISBN (9780135159941) and click Submit. Look on the Registered Products tab for an Access Bonus Content link next to this product, and follow that link to access any available bonus materials. If you would like to be notified of exclusive offers on new editions and updates, please check the box to receive email from us.

Acknowledgments

From Brian

I want to thank my coauthor, John Bennett. This book is the result of close collaboration between the two of us over half a year, in which John was there every step of the way to contribute ideas, content, and sample code, so his presence is there throughout the book. I also want to thank Greg Doench, acquisitions editor, who was a driving force behind the concept, purpose, and marketing of this book.

This book also had a wonderful supporting editorial team, including Rachel Paul and Julie Nahil. But I want to especially thank copy editor Betsy Hardinger, who showed exceptional competence, cooperation, and professionalism in getting the book ready for publication.

From John

I want to thank my coauthor, Brian Overland, for inviting me to join him on this book. This allows me to pass on many of the things I had to work hard to find documentation for or figure out by brute-force experimentation. Hopefully this will save readers a lot of work dealing with the problems I ran into.

About the Authors

Brian Overland started as a professional programmer back in his twenties, but also worked as a computer science, English, and math tutor. He enjoys picking up new languages, but his specialty is explaining them to others, as well as using programming to do games, puzzles, simulations, and math problems. Now he's the author of over a dozen books on programming.

In his ten years at Microsoft he was a software tester, programmer/writer, and manager, but his greatest achievement was in presenting Visual Basic 1.0, as lead writer and overall documentation project lead. He believes that project changed the world by getting people to develop for Windows, and one of the keys to its success was showing it could be fun and easy.

He's also a playwright and actor, which has come in handy as an instructor in online classes. As a novelist, he's twice been a finalist in the Pacific Northwest Literary Contest but is still looking for a publisher.

John Bennett was a senior software engineer at Proximity Technology, Franklin Electronic Publishing, and Microsoft Corporation. More recently, he's developed new programming languages using Python as a prototyping tool. He holds nine U.S. patents, and his projects include a handheld spell checker and East Asian handwriting recognition software.

Review of the Fundamentals

You and Python could be the start of a beautiful friendship. You may have heard that Python is easy to use, that it makes you productive fast. It's true. You may also find that it's fun. You can start programming without worrying about elaborate setups or declarations.

Although this book was written primarily for people who've already had an introduction to Python, this chapter can be your starting point to an exciting new journey. To download Python, go to **python.org**.

If you're familiar with all the basic concepts in Python, you can skip this chapter. You might want to take a look at the **global** statement at the end of this chapter, however, if you're not familiar with it. Many people fail to understand this keyword.

1.1 Python Quick Start

Start the Python interactive development environment (IDLE). At the prompt, you can enter statements, which are executed; and expressions, which Python evaluates and prints the value of.

You can follow along with this sample session, which shows input for you to enter in bold. The nonbold characters represent text printed by the environment.

```
>>> a = 10
>>> b = 20
>>> c = 30
>>> a + b + c
60
```

This "program" places the values 10, 20, and 30 into three variables and adds them together. So far, so good, but not amazing.

If it helps you in the beginning, you can think of variables as storage locations into which to place values, even though that's not precisely what Python does.

What Python really does is make a, b, and c into names for the values 10, 20, and 30. By this we mean "names" in the ordinary sense of the word. These names are looked up in a symbol table; they do not correspond to fixed places in memory! The difference doesn't matter now, but it will later, when we get to functions and global variables. These statements, which create a, b, and c as names, are *assignments*.

In any case, you can assign new values to a variable once it's created. So in the following example, it looks as if we're incrementing a value stored in a magical box (even though we're really not doing that).

```
>>> n = 5
>>> n = n + 1
>>> n = n + 1
>>> n
7
```

What's really going on is that we're repeatedly reassigning n as a name for an increasingly higher value. Each time, the old association is broken and n refers to a new value.

Assignments create variables, and you can't use a variable name that hasn't yet been created. IDLE complains if you attempt the following:

```
>>> a = 5
>>> b = a + x            # ERROR!
```

Because x has not yet been assigned a value, Python isn't happy. The solution is to assign a value to x before it's used on the right side of an assignment. In the next example, referring to x no longer causes an error, because it's been assigned a value in the second line.

```
>>> a = 5
>>> x = 2.5
>>> b = a + x
>>> b
7.5
```

Python has no data declarations. Let us repeat that: *There are no data declarations*. Instead, a variable is *created by an assignment*. There are some other ways to create variables (function arguments and **for** loops), but for the most part, a variable must appear on the left of an assignment before it appears on the right.

You can run Python programs as scripts. From within IDLE, do the following:

▶ From the Files menu, choose New File.

▶ Enter the program text. For this next example, enter the following:

```
side1 = 5
side2 = 12
hyp = (side1 * side1 + side2 * side2) ** 0.5
print(hyp)
```

Then choose Run Module from the Run menu. When you're prompted to save the file, click OK and enter the program name as hyp.py. The program then runs and prints the results in the main IDLE window (or "shell").

Alternatively, you could enter this program directly into the IDLE environment, one statement at a time, in which case the sample session should look like this:

```
>>> side1 = 5
>>> side2 = 12
>>> hyp = (side1 * side1 + side2 * side2) ** 0.5
>>> hyp
13.0
```

Let's step through this example a statement or two at a time. First, the values 5 and 12 are assigned to variables side1 and side2. Then the hypotenuse of a right triangle is calculated by squaring both values, adding them together, and taking the square root of the result. That's what ** 0.5 does. It raises a value to the power 0.5, which is the same as taking its square root.

(That last factoid is a tidbit you get from not falling asleep in algebra class.)

The answer printed by the program should be 13.0. It would be nice to write a program that calculated the hypotenuse for any two values entered by the user; but we'll get that soon enough by examining the **input** statement.

Before moving on, you should know about Python comments. A comment is text that's ignored by Python itself, but you can use it to put in information helpful to yourself or other programmers who may need to maintain the program.

All text from a hashtag (#) to the end of the line is a comment. This is text ignored by Python itself that still may be helpful for human readability's sake. For example:

```
side1 = 5          # Initialize one side.
side2 = 12         # Initialize the other.
hyp = (side1 * side1 + side2 * side2) ** 0.5
print(hyp)         # Print results.
```

1.2 Variables and Naming Names

Although Python gives you some latitude in choosing variable names, there are some rules.

▶ The first character must be a letter or an underscore (_), but the remaining characters can be any combination of underscores, letters, and digits.

▶ However, names with leading underscores are intended to be private to a class, and names starting with double underscores may have special meaning, such as **__init__** or **__add__**, so avoid using names that start with double underscores.

▶ Avoid any name that is a keyword, such as **if**, **else**, **elif**, **and**, **or**, **not**, **class**, **while**, **break**, **continue**, **yield**, **import**, and **def**.

▶ Also, although you can use capitals if you want (names are case-sensitive), initial-all-capped names are generally reserved for special types, such as class names. The universal Python convention is to stick to all-lowercase for most variable names.

Within these rules, there is still a lot of leeway. For example, instead of using boring names like a, b, and c, we can use i, thou, and a jug_of_wine—because it's more fun (with apologies to Omar Khayyam).

```
i = 10
thou = 20
a_jug_of_wine = 30
loaf_of_bread = 40
inspiration = i + thou + a_jug_of_wine + loaf_of_bread
print(inspiration, 'percent good')
```

This prints the following:

```
100 percent good
```

1.3 Combined Assignment Operators

From the ideas in the previous section, you should be able to see that the following statements are valid.

```
n = 10          # n is a name for 10.
n = n + 1       # n is a name for 11.
n = n + 1       # n is a name for 12.
```

A statement such as n = n + 1 is extremely common, so much so that Python offers a shortcut, just as C and C++ do. Python provides shortcut *assignment ops* for many combinations of different operators within an assignment.

```
n = 0         # n must exist before being modified.
n += 1        # Equivalent to n = n + 1
n += 10       # Equivalent to n = n + 10
n *= 2        # Equivalent to n = n * 2
n -= 1        # Equivalent to n = n - 1
n /= 3        # Equivalent to n = n / 3
```

The effect of these statements is to start n at the value 0. Then they add 1 to n, then add 10, and then double that, resulting in the value 22, after which 1 is subtracted, producing 21. Finally, n is divided by 3, producing a final result of n set to 7.0.

1.4 Summary of Python Arithmetic Operators

Table 1.1 summarizes Python arithmetic operators, shown by precedence, alongside the corresponding shortcut (a combined assignment operation).

Table 1.1. Summary of Arithmetic Operators

SYNTAX	DESCRIPTION	ASSIGNMENT OP	PRECEDENCE
a ** b	Exponentiation	**=	1
a * b	Multiplication	*=	2
a / b	Division	/=	2
a // b	Ground division	//=	2
a % b	Remainder division	%=	2
a + b	Addition	+=	3
a - b	Subtraction	-=	3

Table 1.1 shows that exponentiation has a higher precedence than the multiplication, division, and remainder operations, which in turn have a higher precedence than addition and subtraction.

Consequently, parentheses are required in the following statement to produce the desired result:

```
hypot = (a * a + b * b) ** 0.5
```

This statement adds a squared to b squared and then takes the square root of the sum.

1.5 Elementary Data Types: Integer and Floating Point

Because Python has no data declarations, a variable's type is whatever type the associated data object is.

For example, the following assignment makes x a name for 5, which has **int** type. This is the integer type, which is a number that has no decimal point.

```
x = 5          # x names an integer.
```

But after the following reassignment, x names a floating-point number, thereby changing the variable's type to **float**.

```
x = 7.3        # x names a floating-pt value.
```

As in other languages, putting a decimal point after a number gives it floating-point type, even the digit following the decimal point is 0:

```
x = 5.0
```

Python integers are "infinite integers," in that Python supports arbitrarily large integers, subject only to the physical limitations of the system. For example, you can store 10 to the 100th power, so Python can handle this:

```
google = 10 ** 100    # Raise 10 to the power of 100.
```

Integers store quantities precisely. Unlike floating-point values, they don't have rounding errors.

But system capacities ultimately impose limitations. A googleplex is 10 raised to the power of a google (!). That's too big even for Python. If every 0 were painted on a wooden cube one centimeter in length, the physical universe would be far too small to contain a printout of the number.

(As for attempting to create a googleplex; well, as they say on television, "Don't try this at home." You'll have to hit Ctrl+C to stop Python from hanging. It's like when Captain Kirk said to the computer, "Calculate pi to the last digit.")

The way that Python interprets integer and floating-point division (/) depends on the version of Python in use.

In Python 3.0, the rules for division are as follows:

▶ Division of any two numbers (integer and/or floating point) always results in a floating-point result. For example:

```
4 / 2        # Result is 2.0
7 / 4        # Result is 1.75
```

▶ If you want to divide one integer by another and get an integer result, use *ground division* (//). This also works with floating-point values.

```
4 // 2       # Result is 2
7 // 4       # Result is 1
23 // 5      # Result is 4
8.0 // 2.5   # Result is 3.0
```

▶ You can get the remainder using *remainder* (or *modulus)* division.

```
23 % 5       # Result is 3
```

Note that in remainder division, a division is carried out first and the quotient is thrown away. The result is whatever is left over after division. So 5 goes into 23 four times but results in a remainder of 3.

In Python 2.0, the rules are as follows:

▶ Division between two integers is automatically ground division, so the remainder is thrown away:

```
7 / 2           # Result is 3 (in Python 2.0)
```

▶ To force a floating-point result, convert one of the operands to floating-point format.

```
7 / 2.0       # Result is 3.5
7 / float(2)  # Ditto
```

▶ Remember that you can always use modulus division (%) to get the remainder.

Python also supports a **divmod** function that returns quotient and remainder as a *tuple* (that is, an ordered group) of two values. For example:

```
quot, rem = divmod(23, 10)
```

The values returned in quot and rem, in this case, will be 2 and 3 after execution. This means that 10 divides into 23 two times and leaves a remainder of 3.

1.6 Basic Input and Output

Earlier, in Section 1.1, we promised to show how to prompt the user for the values used as inputs to a formula. Now we're going to make good on that promise. (You didn't think we were lying, did you?)

The Python **input** function is an easy-to-use input mechanism that includes an optional prompt. The text typed by the user is returned as a string.

In Python 2.0, the **input** function works differently: it instead evaluates the string entered as if it were a Python statement. To achieve the same result as the Python 3.0 **input** statement, use the **raw_input** function in Python 2.0.

The **input** function prints the prompt string, if specified; then it returns the string the user entered. The input string is returned as soon as the user presses the Enter key; but no newline is appended.

input(*prompt_string*)

To store the string returned as a number, you need to convert to integer (**int**) or floating-point (**float**) format. For example, to get an integer use this code:

```
n = int(input('Enter integer here: '))
```

Or use this to get a floating-point number:

```
x = float(input('Enter floating pt value here: '))
```

The prompt is printed without an added space, so you typically need to provide that space yourself.

Why is an **int** or **float** conversion necessary? Remember that they are necessary when you want to get a number. When you get any input by using the **input** function, you get back a string, such as "5." Such a string is fine for many purposes, but you cannot perform arithmetic on it without performing the conversion first.

Python 3.0 also supports a **print** function that—in its simplest form—prints all its arguments in the order given, putting a space between each.

print(*arguments*)

Python 2.0 has a **print** statement that does the same thing but does not use parentheses.

The **print** function has some special arguments that can be entered by using the name.

▶ **sep=***string* specifies a separator string to be used instead of the default separator, which is one space. This can be an empty string if you choose: sep=''.

▶ **end=***string* specifies what, if anything, to print after the last argument is printed. The default is a newline. If you don't want a newline to be printed, set this argument to an empty string or some other string, as in end=''.

Given these elementary functions—**input** and **print**—you can create a Python script that's a complete program. For example, you can enter the following statements into a text file and run it as a script.

```
side1 = float(input('Enter length of a side: '))
side2 = float(input('Enter another length: '))
hyp = ((side1 * side1) + (side2 * side2)) ** 0.5
print('Length of hypotenuse is:', hyp)
```

1.7 Function Definitions

Within the Python interactive development environment, you can more easily enter a program if you first enter it as a function definition, such as **main**. Then call that function. Python provides the **def** keyword for defining functions.

```
def main():
    side1 = float(input('Enter length of a side: '))
    side2 = float(input('Enter another length: '))
    hyp = (side1 * side1 + side2 * side2) ** 0.5
    print('Length of hypotenuse is: ', hyp)
```

Note that you must enter the first line as follows. The **def** keyword, parentheses, and colon (**:**) are strictly required.

```
def main():
```

If you enter this correctly from within IDLE, the environment automatically indents the next lines for you. Maintain this indentation. If you enter the function as part of a script, then you must choose an indentation scheme, and it must be consistent. Indentation of four spaces is recommended when you have a choice.

Note ▶ Mixing tab characters with actual spaces can cause errors even though it might not look wrong. So be careful with tabs!

◀ Note

Because there is no "begin block" and "end block" syntax, Python relies on indentation to know where statement blocks begin and end. The critical rule is this:

✱ Within any given block of code, the indentation of all statements (that is, at the same level of nesting) must be the same.

For example, the following block is invalid and needs to be revised.

```
def main():
        side1 = float(input('Enter length of a side: '))
       side2 = float(input('Enter another length: '))
      hyp = (side1 * side1 + side2 * side2) ** 0.5
      print('Length of hypotenuse is: ', hyp)
```

If you have a nested block inside a nested block, the indentation of each level must be consistent. Here's an example:

```
def main():
    age = int(input('Enter your age: '))
    name = input('Enter your name: ')
    if age < 30:
        print('Hello', name)
        print('I see you are less than 30.')
        print('You are so young.')
```

The first three statements inside this function definition are all at the same level of nesting; the last three statements are at a deeper level. But each is consistent.

Even though we haven't gotten to the **if** statement yet (we're just about to), you should be able to see that the flow of control in the next example is different from the previous example.

```
def main():
    age = int(input('Enter your age: '))
    name = input('Enter your name: ')
    if age < 30:
        print('Hello', name)
    print('I see you are less than 30.')
    print('You are so young.')
```

Hopefully you can see the difference: In *this* version of the function, the last two lines do not depend on your age being less than 30. That's because Python uses indentation to determine the flow of control.

Because the last two statements make sense only if the age is less than 30, it's reasonable to conclude that this version has a bug. The correction would be to indent the last two statements so that they line up with the first **print** statement.

After a function is defined, you can call that function—which means to make it execute—by using the function name, followed by parentheses. (If you *don't* include the parentheses, you will not successfully execute the function!)

```
main()
```

So let's review. To define a function, which means to create a kind of mini-program unto itself, you enter the **def** statement and keep entering lines in the function until you're done—after which, enter a blank line. Then run the function by typing its name followed by parentheses. Once a function is defined, you can execute it as often as you want.

So the following sample session, in the IDLE environment, shows the process of defining a function and calling it twice. For clarity, user input is in bold.

```
>>> def main():
        side1 = float(input('Enter length of a side: '))
        side2 = float(input('Enter another length: '))
        hyp = (side1 * side1 + side2 * side2) ** 0.5
        print('Length of hypotenuse is: ', hyp)

>>> main()
Enter length of a side: 3
Enter another length: 4
Length of hypotenuse is: 5.0
>>> main()
Enter length of a side: 30
Enter another length: 40
Length of hypotenuse is: 50.0
```

As you can see, once a function is defined, you can call it (causing it to execute) as many times as you like.

The Python philosophy is this: Because you should do this indentation anyway, why shouldn't Python rely on the indentation and thereby save you the extra work of putting in curly braces? This is why Python doesn't have any "begin block" or "end block" syntax but relies on indentation.

1.8 The Python "if" Statement

As with all Python control structures, indentation matters in an **if** statement, as does the colon at the end of the first line.

```
if a > b:
    print('a is greater than b')
    c = 10
```

The **if** statement has a variation that includes an optional **else** clause.

```
if a > b:
    print('a is greater than b')
    c = 10
```

```
else:
    print('a is not greater than b')
    c = -10
```

An **if** statement can also have any number of optional **elif** clauses. Although the following example has statement blocks of one line each, they can be larger.

```
age = int(input('Enter age: '))
if age < 13:
    print('You are a preteen.')
elif age < 20:
    print('You are a teenager.')
elif age <= 30:
    print('You are still young.')
else:
    print('You are one of the oldies.')
```

You cannot have empty statement blocks; to have a statement block that does nothing, use the **pass** keyword.

Here's the syntax summary, in which square brackets indicate optional items, and the ellipses indicate a part of the syntax that can be repeated any number of times.

```
if condition:
    indented_statements
[ elif condition:
    indented_statements ]...
[ else:
    indented_statements ]
```

1.9 The Python "while" Statement

Python has a **while** statement with one basic structure. (There is no "do while" version, although there is an optional **else** clause, as mentioned in Chapter 4.)

This limitation helps keep the syntax simple. The **while** keyword creates a loop, which tests a condition just as an **if** statement does. But after the indented statements are executed, program control returns to the top of the loop and the *condition* is tested again.

```
while condition:
    indented_statements
```

Here's a simple example that prints all the numbers from 1 to 10.

```
n = 10        # This may be set to any positive integer.
i = 1
while i <= n:
    print(i, end=' ')
    i += 1
```

Let's try entering these statements in a function. But this time, the function takes an argument, n. Each time it's executed, the function can take a different value for n.

```
>>> def print_nums(n):
    i = 1
    while i <= n:
        print(i, end=' ')
        i += 1

>>> print_nums(3)
1  2  3
>>> print_nums(7)
1  2  3  4  5  6  7
>>> print_nums(8)
1  2  3  4  5  6  7  8
```

It should be clear how this function works. The variable i starts as 1, and it's increased by 1 each time the loop is executed. The loop is executed again as long as i is equal to or less than n. When i exceeds n, the loop stops, and no further values are printed.

Optionally, the **break** statement can be used to exit from the nearest enclosing loop. And the **continue** statement can be used to continue to the next iteration of the loop immediately (going to the top of the loop) but not exiting as **break** does.

Key Syntax

break

For example, you can use **break** to exit from an otherwise infinite loop. **True** is a keyword that, like all words in Python, is case-sensitive. Capitalization matters.

```
n = 10        # Set n to any positive integer.
i = 1
while True:   # Always executes!
    print(i)
```

```
    if i >= n:
        break
    i += 1
```

Note the use of i += 1. If you've been paying attention, this means the same as the following:

```
i = i + 1      # Add 1 to the current value and reassign.
```

1.10 A Couple of Cool Little Apps

At this point, you may be wondering, what's the use of all this syntax if it doesn't do anything? But if you've been following along, you already know enough to do a good deal. This section shows two great little applications that do something impressive . . . although we need to add a couple of features.

Here's a function that prints any number of the famous Fibonacci sequence:

```
def pr_fibo(n):
    a, b = 1, 0
    while a < n:
        print(a, sep=' ')
        a, b = a + b, a
```

You can make this a complete program by running it from within IDLE or by adding these module-level lines below it:

```
n = int(input('Input n: '))
pr_fibo(n)
```

New features, by the way, are contained in these lines of the function definition:

```
a, b = 1, 0
a, b = a + b, a
```

These two statements are examples of *tuple assignment*, which we return to in later chapters. In essence, it enables a list of values to be used as inputs, and a list of variables to be used as outputs, without one assignment interfering with the other. These assignments could have been written as

```
a = 1
b = 0
...
temp = a
a = a + b
b = temp
```

Simply put, a and b are initialized to 1 and 0, respectively. Then, later, a is set to the total a + b, while simultaneously, b is set to the old value of a.

The second app (try it yourself!) is a complete computer game. It secretly selects a random number between 1 and 50 and then requires you, the player, to try to find the answer through repeated guesses.

The program begins by using the **random** package; we present more information about that package in Chapter 11. For now, enter the first two lines as shown, knowing they will be explained later in the book.

```python
from random import randint
n = randint(1, 50)
while True:
    ans = int(input('Enter a guess: '))
    if ans > n:
        print('Too high! Guess again. ')
    elif ans < n:
        print('Too low! Guess again. ')
    else:
        print('Congrats! You got it!')
        break
```

To run, enter all this in a Python script (choose New from the File menu), and then choose Run Module from the Run menu, as usual. Have fun.

1.11 Summary of Python Boolean Operators

The Boolean operators return the special value **True** or **False**. Note that the logic operators **and** and **or** use short-circuit logic. Table 1.2 summarizes these operators.

Table 1.2. Python Boolean and Comparison Operators

OPERATOR	MEANING	EVALUATES TO
==	Test for equality	True or False
!=	Test for inequality	True or False
>	Greater than	True or False
<	Less than	True or False
>=	Greater than or equal to	True or False
<=	Less than or equal to	True or False
and	Logical "and"	Value of first or second operand

▼ continued on next page

Table 1.2. Python Boolean and Comparison Operators (*continued*)

OPERATOR	MEANING	EVALUATES TO
or	Logical "or"	Value of first or second operand
not	Logical "not"	True or False, reversing value of its single operand

All the operators in Table 1.2 are binary—that is, they take two operands—except **not**, which takes a single operand and reverses its logical value. Here's an example:

```
if not (age > 12 and age < 20):
    print('You are not a teenager.')
```

By the way, another way to write this—using a Python shortcut—is to write the following:

```
if not (12 < age < 20):
    print('You are not a teenager.')
```

This is, as far as we know, a unique Python coding shortcut. In Python 3.0, at least, this example not only works but doesn't even require parentheses right after the **if** and **not** keywords, because logical **not** has low precedence as an operator.

1.12 Function Arguments and Return Values

Function syntax is flexible enough to support multiple arguments and multiple return values.

```
def function_name(arguments):
    indented_statements
```

In this syntax, *arguments* is a list of argument names, separated by commas if there's more than one. Here's the syntax of the **return** statement:

```
return value
```

You can also return multiple values:

```
return value, value ...
```

Finally, you can omit the return value. If you do, the effect is the same as the statement **return None**.

```
return      # Same effect as return None
```

Execution of a **return** statement causes immediate exit and return to the caller of the function. Reaching the end of a function causes an implicit return—returning **None** by default. (Therefore, using **return** at all is optional.)

Technically speaking, Python argument passing is closer to "pass by reference" than "pass by value"; however, it isn't exactly either. When a value is passed to a Python function, that function receives a reference to the named data. However, whenever the function assigns a new value to the argument variable, it breaks the connection to the original variable that was passed.

Therefore, the following function does not do what you might expect. It does not change the value of the variable passed to it.

```python
def double_it(n):
    n = n * 2


x = 10
double_it(x)
print(x)          # x is still 10!
```

This may at first seem a limitation, because sometimes a programmer needs to create multiple "out" parameters. However, you can do that in Python by returning multiple values directly. The calling statement must expect the values.

```python
def set_values():
    return 10, 20, 30
a, b, c = set_values()
```

The variables a, b, and c are set to 10, 20, and 30, respectively.

Because Python has no concept of data declarations, an argument list in Python is just a series of comma-separated names—except that each may optionally be given a default value. Here is an example of a function definition with two arguments but no default values:

```python
def calc_hyp(a, b):
    hyp = (a * a + b * b) ** 0.5
    return hyp
```

These arguments are listed without type declaration; Python functions do no type checking except the type checking you do yourself! (However, you can check a variable's type by using the **type** or **isinstance** function.)

Although arguments have no type, they may be given default values.

The use of default values enables you to write a function in which not all arguments have to be specified during every function call. A default argument has the following form:

argument_name = default_value

For example, the following function prints a value multiple times, but the default number of times is 1:

```
def print_nums(n, rep=1):
    i = 1
    while i <= rep:
        print(n)
        i += 1
```

Here, the default value of rep is 1; so if no value is given for the last argument, it's given the value 1. Therefore this function call prints the number 5 one time:

```
print_nums(5)
```

The output looks like this:

```
5
```

Note ▶ Because the function just shown uses n as an argument name, it's natural to assume that n must be a number. However, because Python has no variable or argument declarations, there's nothing enforcing that; n could just as easily be passed a string.

But there are repercussions to data types in Python. In this case, a problem can arise if you pass a nonnumber to the second argument, rep. The value passed here is repeatedly compared to a number, so this value, if given, needs to be numeric. Otherwise, an exception, representing a runtime error, is raised.

◀ Note

Default arguments, if they appear in the function definition, must come after all other arguments.

Another special feature is the use of named arguments. These should not be confused with default values, which is a separate issue. Default arguments are specified *in a function definition*. Named arguments are specified during a function *call*.

Some examples should clarify. Normally, argument values are assigned to arguments in the order given. For example, suppose a function is defined to have three arguments:

```
def a_func(a, b, c):
    return (a + b) * c
```

But the following function call specifies c and b directly, leaving the first argument to be assigned to a, by virtue of its position.

```
print(a_func(4, c = 3, b = 2))
```

The result of this function call is to print the value 18. The values 3, 4, and 2 are assigned out of order, so that a, b, and c, respectively get 4, 2, and 3.

Named arguments, if used, must come at the end of the list of arguments.

1.13 The Forward Reference Problem

In most computer languages, there's an annoying problem every programmer has to deal with: the *forward reference problem*. The problem is this: In what order do I define my functions?

It's a problem because the general rule is that a function must exist before you call it. In a way, it's parallel to the rule for variables, which is that a variable must exist before you use it to calculate a value.

So how do you ensure that every function exists— meaning it must be defined—before you call it? And what if, God forbid, you have two functions that need to call each other? The problem is easily solved if you follow two rules:

▶ Define all your functions before you call any of them.

▶ Then, at the very end of the source file, put in your first module-level function call. (*Module-level code* is code that is outside any function.)

This solution works because a **def** statement creates a function as a callable object but does not yet execute it. Therefore, if funcA calls funcB, you can define funcA first—as long as when you get around to executing funcA, funcB is also defined.

1.14 Python Strings

Python has a text string class, **str**, which enables you to use characters of printable text. The class has many built-in capabilities. If you want to get a list of them, type the following into IDLE:

```
>>> help(str)
```

You can specify Python strings using a variety of quotation marks. The only rule is that they must match. Internally, the quotation marks are not stored as part of the string itself. This is a coding issue; what's the easiest way to represent certain strings?

```
s1 = 'This is a string.'

s2 = "This is also a string."
```

```
s3 = '''This is a special literal
   quotation string.'''
```

The last form—using three consecutive quotation marks to delimit the string—creates a literal quotation string. You can also repeat three double quotation marks to achieve the same effect.

```
s3 = """This is a special literal
   quotation string."""
```

If a string is delimited by single quotation marks, you can easily embed double quotation marks.

```
s1 = 'Shakespeare wrote "To be or not to be."'
```

But if a string is delimited by double quotation marks, you can easily embed single quotation marks.

```
s2 = "It's not true, it just ain't!"
```

You can print these two strings.

```
print(s1)
print(s2)
```

This produces the following:

```
Shakespeare wrote "To be or not to be."
It's not true, it just ain't!
```

The benefit of the literal quotation syntax is that it enables you to embed both kinds of quotation marks, as well as embed newlines.

```
'''You can't get it at "Alice's Restaurant."'''
```

Alternatively, you can place embedded quotation marks into a string by using the backslash (\) as an escape character.

```
s2 = 'It\'s not true, it just ain\'t!'
```

Chapter 2, "Advanced String Capabilities," provides a nearly exhaustive tour of string capabilities.

You can deconstruct strings in Python, just as you can in Basic or C, by indexing individual characters, using indexes running from 0 to N–1, where N is the length of the string. Here's an example:

```
s = 'Hello'
s[0]
```

This produces

```
'H'
```

However, you cannot assign new values to characters within existing strings, because Python strings are *immutable:* They cannot be changed.

How, then, can new strings be constructed? You do that by using a combination of concatenation and assignment. Here's an example:

```
s1 = 'Abe'
s2 = 'Lincoln'
s1 = s1 + ' ' + s2
```

In this example, the string s1 started with the value `'Abe'`, but then it ends up containing `'Abe Lincoln'`.

This operation is permitted because a variable is only a name.

Therefore, you can "modify" a string through concatenation without actually violating the immutability of strings. Why? It's because each assignment creates a new association between the variable and the data. Here's an example:

```
my_str = 'a'
my_str += 'b'
my_str += 'c'
```

The effect of these statements is to create the string `'abc'` and to assign it (or rather, reassign it) to the variable `my_str`. No string data was actually modified, despite appearances. What's really going on in this example is that the name `my_str` is used and reused, to name an ever-larger string.

You can think of it this way: With every statement, a larger string is created and then assigned to the name `my_str`.

In dealing with Python strings, there's another important rule to keep in mind: Indexing a string in Python produces a single character. In Python, a single character is not a separate type (as it is in C or C++), but is merely a string of length 1. The choice of quotation marks used has no effect on this rule.

1.15 Python Lists (and a Cool Sorting App)

Python's most frequently used collection class is called the *list* collection, and it's incredibly flexible and powerful.

```
[ items ]
```

Here the square brackets are intended literally, and *items* is a list of zero or more items, separated by commas if there are more than one. Here's an example, representing a series of high temperatures, in Fahrenheit, over a summer weekend:

```
[78, 81, 81]
```

Lists can contain any kind of object (including other lists!) and, unlike C or C++, Python lets you mix the types. For example, you can have lists of strings:

```
['John', 'Paul', 'George', 'Ringo' ]
```

And you can have lists that mix up the types:

```
['John', 9, 'Paul', 64 ]
```

However, lists that have mixed types cannot be automatically sorted in Python 3.0, and sorting is an important feature.

Unlike some other Python collection classes (dictionaries and sets), order is significant in a list, and duplicate values are allowed. But it's the long list of built-in capabilities (all covered in Chapter 3) that makes Python lists really impressive. In this section we use two: **append**, which adds an element to a list dynamically, and the aforementioned **sort** capability.

Here's a slick little program that showcases the Python list-sorting capability. Type the following into a Python script and run it.

```
a_list = []

while True:
    s = input('Enter name: ')
    if not s:
        break
    a_list.append(s)
a_list.sort()
print(a_list)
```

Wow, that's incredibly short! But does it work? Here's a sample session:

```
Enter name: John
Enter name: Paul
Enter name: George
Enter name: Ringo
Enter name: Brian
Enter name:
['Brian', 'George', 'John', 'Paul', 'Ringo']
```

See what happened? Brian (who was the manager, I believe) got added to the group and now all are printed in alphabetical order.

This little program, you should see, prompts the user to enter one name at a time; as each is entered, it's added to the list through the **append** method. Finally, when an empty string is entered, the loop breaks. After that, it's sorted and printed.

1.16 The "for" Statement and Ranges

When you look at the application in the previous section, you may wonder whether there is a refined way, or at least a more flexible way, to print the contents of a list. Yes, there is. In Python, that's the central (although not exclusive) purpose of the **for** statement: to iterate through a collection and perform the same operation on each element.

One such use is to print each element. The last line of the application in the previous section could be replaced by the following, giving you more control over how to print the output.

```
for name in a_list:
    print(name)
```

Now the output is

```
Brian
George
John
Paul
Ringo
```

In the sample **for** statement, *iterable* is most often a collection, such as a list, but can also be a call to the **range** function, which is a generator that produces an iteration through a series of values. (You'll learn more about generators in Chapter 4.)

```
for var in iterable:
    indented_statements
```

Notice again the importance of indenting, as well the colon (**:**).

Values are sent to a **for** loop in a way similar to function-argument passing. Consequently, assigning a value to a loop variable has no effect on the original data.

```
my_lst = [10, 15, 25]
for thing in my_lst:
    thing *= 2
```

It may seem that this loop should double each element of my_lst, but it does not. To process a list in this way, changing values in place, it's necessary to use indexing.

```
my_lst = [10, 15, 25]
for i in [0, 1, 2]:
    my_lst[i] *= 2
```

This has the intended effect: doubling each individual element of my_lst, so that now the list data is [20, 30, 50].

To index into a list this way, you need to create a sequence of indexes of the form

```
0, 1, 2, ... N-1
```

in which N is the length of the list. You can automate the production of such sequences of indexes by using the **range** function. For example, to double every element of an array of length 5, use this code:

```
my_lst = [100, 102, 50, 25, 72]
for i in range(5):
    my_lst[i] *= 2
```

This code fragment is not optimal because it hard-codes the length of the list, that length being 5, into the code. Here is a better way to write this loop:

```
my_lst = [100, 102, 50, 25, 72]
for i in range(len(my_lst)):
    my_lst[i] *= 2
```

After this loop is executed, my_lst contains [200, 204, 100, 50, 144].

The **range** function produces a sequence of integers as shown in Table 1.3, depending on whether you specify one, two, or three arguments.

Table 1.3. Effects of the Range Function

SYNTAX	EFFECT
range(*end*)	Produces a sequence beginning with 0, up to but not including *end*.
range(*beg*, *end*)	Produces a sequence beginning with *beg*, up to but not including *end*.
range(*beg*, *end*, *step*)	Produces a sequence beginning with *beg*, up to but not including *end*; however, the elements are increased by the value of *step* each time. If *step* is negative, then the range counts backward.

Another use of **range** is to create a loop that iterates through a series of integers. For example, the following loop calculates a factorial number.

```
n = int(input('Enter a positive integer: '))
prod = 1
for i in range(1, n + 1):
        prod *= i
print(prod)
```

This loop works because range(1, n + 1) produces integers beginning with 1 *up to but not including* n + 1. This loop therefore has the effect of doing the following calculation:

```
1 * 2 * 3 * ... n
```

1.17 Tuples

The Python concept of *tuple* is closely related to that of lists; if anything, the concept of tuple is even more fundamental. The following code returns a list of integers:

```
def my_func():
        return [10, 20, 5]
```

This function returns values as a list.

```
my_lst = my_func()
```

But the following code, returning a simple series of values, actually returns a tuple:

```
def a_func():
        return 10, 20, 5
```

It can be called as follows:

```
a, b, c = a_func()
```

Note that a tuple is a tuple even if it's grouped within parentheses for clarity's sake.

```
        return (10, 20, 5)   # Parens have no effect in
                             #  this case.
```

The basic properties of a tuple and a list are almost the same: Each is an ordered collection, in which any number of repeated values are allowed.

However, unlike a list, a tuple is immutable; tuple values cannot be changed in place. Tuples do not support all the methods or functions supported by lists; in particular, tuples do not support any methods that modify the contents of the tuple.

1.18 Dictionaries

A Python *dictionary* is a collection that contains a series of associations between key-value pairs. Unlike lists, dictionaries are specified with curly braces, not square brackets.

```
{ key1: value1, key2: value2, ...}
```

In plain English, a dictionary is like a flat, two-column table in a database. It lacks the advanced features of modern database management systems; it's only a table. But it can still serve as a rich data-storage object in your Python programs.

The keys for a dictionary are a series of unique values; keys cannot be duplicated. For each key there's an associated data object, called a *value*. For example, you can create a dictionary for grading a class of students as follows:

```
grade_dict = { 'Bob':3.9, 'Sue':3.9, 'Dick':2.5 }
```

This statement creates a dictionary with three entries—the strings "Bob," "Sue," and "Dick"—which have the associated values 3.9, 3.9, and 2.5, respectively. Note it's perfectly fine to duplicate the value 3.9, because it's not a key.

As usual, `grade_dict` is only a name, and you can give a dictionary almost any name you want (as long as the name obeys the rules listed earlier). I've chosen the name `grade_dict`, because it is suggestive of what this object is.

After a dictionary is created, you can always add a value through a statement such as this:

```
grade_dict['Bill G'] = 4.0
```

This statement adds the key "Bill G" and associates it with the value 4.0. That data is added to the dictionary named `grade_dict`. If the key "Bill G" already exists, the statement is still valid; but it has the effect of replacing the value associated with "Bill G" rather than adding Bill as a new entry.

You can print, or otherwise refer to, a value in the dictionary by using a statement such as the following. Note what it does: It uses a string ("Bill G") as a key, a kind of index value, to find the data associated with that key.

```
print(grade_dict['Bill G'])    # Print the value 4.0
```

Note that you can start with an empty dictionary and then add data to it.

```
grade_dict = { }
```

Additional rules apply to selecting types for use in dictionaries:

▶ In Python version 3.0, all the keys must share the same type, or at least a compatible type, such as integers and floating point, that can be compared.

▶ The key type should be immutable (data you cannot change "in place"). Strings and tuples are immutable, but lists are not.

▶ Therefore, lists such as `[1, 2]` cannot be used for keys, but tuples, such as `(1, 2)`, can.

▶ The values may be of any type; however, it is often a good idea to use the same type, if possible, for all the value objects.

There's a caution you should keep in mind. If you attempt to get the value for a particular key and if that key does not exist, Python raises an exception. To avoid this, use the **get** method to ensure that the specified key exists.

$$dictionary.\textbf{get}(key\ [,default\_value])$$

In this syntax, the square brackets indicate an optional item. If the *key* exists, its corresponding value in the dictionary is returned. Otherwise, the *default_value* is returned, if specified; or **None** is returned if there is no such default value. This second argument enables you to write efficient histogram code such as the following, which counts frequencies of words.

```
s = (input('Enter a string: ')).split()
wrd_counter = {}
for wrd in s:
    wrd_counter[wrd] = wrd_counter.get(wrd, 0) + 1
```

What this example does is the following: When it finds a new word, that word is entered into the dictionary with the value 0 + 1, or just 1. If it finds an existing word, that word frequency is returned by **get**, and then 1 is added to it. So if a word is found, its frequency count is incremented by 1. If the word is not found, it's added to the dictionary with a starting count of 1. Which is what we want.

In this example, the **split** method of the string class is used to divide a string into a list of individual words. For more information on **split**, see Section 2.12, "Breaking Up Input Using 'split'."

1.19 Sets

Sets are similar to dictionaries, but they lack associated values. A set, in effect, is only a set of unique keys, which has the effect of making a set different from a list in the following ways:

▶ All its members must be unique. An attempt to add an existing value to a set is simply ignored.

▶ All its members should be immutable, as with dictionary keys.

▶ Order is never significant.

For example, consider the following two set definitions:

```
b_set1 = { 'John', 'Paul', 'George', 'Pete' }
b_set2 = { 'John', 'George', 'Pete', 'Paul' }
```

These two sets are considered fully equal to each other, as are the following two sets:

```
set1 = {1, 2, 3, 4, 5}
set2 = {5, 4, 3, 2, 1}
```

Once a set is created, you can manipulate contents by using the **add** and **remove** methods. For example:

```
b_set1.remove('Pete')
b_set1.add('Ringo')
```

(Don't you always feel sorry for Pete?)

Note that when creating a new set, you cannot simply use a pair of empty curly braces, because that syntax is used to create empty dictionaries. Instead, use the following syntax:

```
my_set = set()
```

Set collections also support the **union** and **intersection** methods, as well as use of the following operators:

```
setA = {1, 2, 3, 4}
setB = {3, 4, 5}
setUnion = setA | setB        # Assign {1, 2, 3, 4, 5}
setIntersect = setA & setB    # Assign {3, 4}
setXOR = setA ^ setB          # Assign {1, 2, 5}
setSub = setA - setB          # Assign {1, 2}
```

In these examples, setUnion and setIntersect are the results of union and intersection operations, respectively. setXOR is the result of an either/or operation; it has all those elements that appear in one set or the other but not both. setSub contains elements that are in the first set (setA in this case) but not the second (setB).

Appendix C, "Set Methods," lists all the methods supported by the **set** class, along with examples for most of them.

1.20 *Global and Local Variables*

Python variables can be global or local, just as in other languages. Some programmers discourage the use of global variables, but when you need them, you need them.

What is a *global variable?* It's a variable that retains its value between function calls and is visible to all functions. So a change to my_global_var in one function reflects the value of my_global_var in another.

If a variable x is referred to within a function definition, then the local version of x is used—provided such a variable exists at the local level. Otherwise, a global version of the variable is used if it exists.

Local scope, as opposed to global, means that changes to the variable have no effect on variables having the same name outside the function definition. The variable in that case is private. But a global variable is visible everywhere.

For example, the following statements create two versions of count: a local version and a global one. But by default, the function uses its own (local) version of the variable.

```
count = 10
def funcA():
    count = 20
    print(count)    # Prints 20, a local value.

def funcB():
    print(count)    # Prints 10, the global value.
```

Do you see how this works? The first function in this example uses its own local version of count, because such a variable was created within that function.

But the second function, funcB, created no such variable. Therefore, it uses the global version, which was created in the first line of the example (count = 10).

The difficulty occurs when you want to refer to a global version of a variable, but you make it the target of an assignment statement. Python has no concept of data declarations, so adding an assignment statement has the effect of creating a new variable. And that's a problem, because when it creates a variable, then by default the variable will be local if it's inside a function.

For example, suppose you have funcB change the value of count. You can do so, but now funcB refers *only to its own private copy* of count. If you were relying on the function to change the value of count recognized everywhere, you're out of luck.

```
def funcB():
    count = 100    # count now is local, no effect
                   #  on global version of count.
    print(count)   # Prints 100, the local value.
```

The solution is to use the **global** statement. This statement tells Python to avoid using a local version of the variable; it therefore must refer to the global version, assuming it exists. Here's an example:

```
count = 10            # Variable created as global.

def my_func():
    global count
    count += 1

my_func()        # Call my_func.
print(count)     # Prints 11.
```

Now, calling my_func causes the value of count to be changed, and this affects program code outside the function itself, as you can see. If my_func had referred to a local copy of count, then it would have no effect on count outside the function.

The **global** statement itself does not create anything; you need an assignment to do that. In the previous example, count was created in the statement preceding the function definition.

Module-level code, which consists of all statements outside function and class definitions, enables you to create global variables. But so does the following code, which—upon being executed—creates a variable foo if it does not already exist.

```
def my_func():
    global foo
    foo = 5    # Create foo if it does not already
               #  exist (as a global).
    print(foo)
```

Assuming `foo` does not already exist, the effect of this function is to create `foo` and set it to 5. It cannot be created as a local—because of the statement **`global foo`**—and therefore `foo` is created as a global variable. This works even though the assignment to `foo` is not part of module-level code.

In general, there is a golden rule about global and local variables in Python. It's simply this:

> **✱** If there's any chance that a function might attempt to assign a value to a global variable, use the **`global`** statement so that it's not treated as local.

Chapter 1   *Summary*

Chapter 1 covers the fundamentals of Python except for class definitions, advanced operations on collections, and specialized parts of the library such as file operations. The information presented here is enough to write many Python programs.

So congratulations! If you understand everything in this chapter, you are already well on the way to becoming a fluent Python programmer. The next couple of chapters plunge into the fine points of lists and strings, the two most important kinds of collections.

Chapter 3 covers called something called "comprehension" in Python (not to be confused with artificial intelligence) and explains how comprehension applies not only to lists but also to sets, dictionaries, and other collections. It also shows you how to use lambda functions.

Chapter 1   *Review Questions*

1 Considering that there are no data declarations in Python, is it even theoretically possible to have uninitialized data?

2 In what sense are Python integers "infinite," and in what sense are they not infinite at all?

3 Is a class having infinite range even theoretically possible?

4 How exactly is indentation in Python more critical than in most other programming languages?

5 The best policy is to use a completely consistent indentation scheme throughout a Python program, but does Python give you some leeway? Exactly where must indentation be consistent in a program? Where can it differ? Show examples if you can.

6 Explain precisely why tab characters can cause a problem with the indentations used in a Python program (and thereby introduce syntax errors)?

7 What is the advantage of having to rely so much on indentation in Python?

8 How many different values can a Python function return to the caller?

9 Recount this chapter's solution to the forward reference problem for functions. How can such an issue arise in the first place?

10 When you're writing a Python text string, what, if anything, should guide your choice of what kind of quotation marks to use (single, double, or triple)?

11 Name at least one way in which Python lists are different from arrays in other languages, such as C, which are contiguously stored collections of a single base type.

Chapter 1   *Suggested Problems*

1 Write a little program that asks for your name, age, and address, and then prints all the information you just entered. However, instead of placing it in a function called `main`, place it in a function called `test_func`. Then call `test_func` to run it.

2 Write a program that gets the radius of a sphere, calculates the volume, and then prints the answer. If necessary, look up the volume formula online.

Advanced String Capabilities

How does a computer communicate messages to humans? Through hand-waving, smoke signals, or (as in sci-fi movies of the 1950s) a blinking red light?

No. Even programs that utilize voice or voice recognition (somewhat outside the scope of this book) depend on groups of printable characters called *text strings,* or just *strings*. Every programmer needs to manage the art of prompting for, searching, and printing these strings. Fortunately, Python excels at this task.

Even if you've used Python text strings before, you'll likely want to peruse this chapter to make sure that you're using all the built-in capabilities of Python strings.

2.1 Strings Are Immutable

Data types in Python are either mutable (changeable) or immutable.

The advantage of mutable types is clear. The data can be changed "in place," meaning you don't have to reconstruct an object from scratch every time you make a change. Mutable types include lists, dictionaries, and sets.

The advantage of immutable types is less obvious but important. An immutable type can be used as a key for a dictionary; such keys are frequently strings. For example, you might have a ratings dictionary to list average ratings from a group of critics.

```
movie_dict = { 'Star Bores': 5.0,
               'The Oddfather': 4.5,
               'Piranha: The Revenge': 2.0 }
```

Another advantage of immutable types is that because they cannot be changed, their usage is optimized internally. Using tuples, for example, is somewhat more efficient than using lists.

The limitation of immutable types is that such data cannot be changed in place. The following statements, for example, are not valid.

```
my_str = 'hello, Dave, this is Hal.'
my_str[0] = 'H'        # ERROR!
```

The second statement in this example is invalid because it attempts to take the string created in the first statement and modify the data itself. As a result, Python raises a **TypeError** exception.

But the following statements are valid.

```
my_str = 'hello'
my_str = 'Hello'
```

These statements are valid because each time, a completely new string is created, and the name my_str is reassigned.

In Python, a variable is nothing more than a name, and it may be reused, over and over. That's why these last statements might seem to violate immutability of strings but in fact do not. No existing string is altered in this last example; rather, two different strings are created and the name my_str is reused.

This behavior follows from the nature of assignment in Python and its lack of data declarations. You can reuse a name as often as you want.

2.2 *Numeric Conversions, Including Binary*

Type names in Python implicitly invoke type conversions wherever such conversions are supported.

```
type(data_object)
```

The action is to take the specified *data_object* and produce the result after converting it to the specified *type*—if the appropriate conversion exists. If not, Python raises a **ValueError** exception.

Here are some examples:

```
s = '45'
n = int(s)
x = float(s)
```

If you then print n and x, you get the following:

```
45
45.0
```

The **int** conversion, unlike most conversions, takes an optional second argument. This argument enables you to convert a string to a number while interpreting it in a different radix, such as binary. Here's an example:

```
n = int('10001', 2)     # Interpret in binary radix.
```

Printing n reveals it was assigned the decimal value 17.

Likewise, you can use other bases with the **int** conversion. The following code uses octal (8) and hexadecimal (16) bases.

```
n1 = int('775', 8)
n2 = int('1E', 16)
print('775 octal and 16 hex:', n1, n2)
```

These statements print the following results:

```
775 octal and 1E hex: 509 30
```

We can therefore summarize the **int** conversion as taking an optional second argument, which has a default value of 10, indicating decimal radix.

```
int(data_object, radix=10)
```

The **int** and **float** conversions are necessary when you get input from the keyboard—usually by using the **input** statement—or get input from a text file, and you need to convert the digit characters into an actual numeric value.

A **str** conversion works in the opposite direction. It converts a number into its string representation. In fact, it works on any type of data for which the type defines a string representation.

Converting a number to a string enables you to do operations such as counting the number of printable digits or counting the number of times a specific digit occurs. For example, the following statements print the length of the number 1007.

```
n = 1007
s = str(n)    # Convert to '1007'
print('The length of', n, 'is', len(s), 'digits.')
```

This example prints the following output:

```
The length of 1007 is 4 digits.
```

There are other ways to get this same information. You could, for example, use the mathematical operation that takes the base-10 logarithm. But this example suggests what you can do by converting a number to its string representation.

Note ▶ Converting a number to its string representation is not the same as converting a number to its ASCII or Unicode number. That's a different operation, and it must be done one character at a time by using the **ord** function.

◀ Note

2.3 *String Operators (+, =, *, >, etc.)*

The string type, **str**, supports some of the same operators that numeric types do, but interprets them differently. For example, addition (+) becomes string concatenation when applied to strings rather than numbers.

Here's an example of some valid string operators: assignment and test for equality.

```
dog1_str = 'Rover'        # Assignment
dog2_str = dog1_str       # Create alias for.

dog1_str == dog2_str      # True!
dog1_str == 'Rover'       # True!
```

In this example, the second statement creates a reference, or alias, for the same data that dog1_str refers to. (If, however, dog1_str is later assigned to new data, dog2_str still refers to 'Rover'.) Because dog1_str and dog2_str refer to the same data, the first test for equality must produce the value **True**.

But the second test for equality also returns **True**. As long as two strings have the same content, they are considered equal. They do not necessarily have to be aliases for the same data in memory.

All operator-based comparisons with Python strings are case-sensitive. There are several ways to ignore case. You can convert both operands to uppercase or both to lowercase (by using the **upper** or **lower** string method), and that will work fine with strings that contain ASCII characters only.

However, if you're working with strings that use the wider Unicode character set, the safest way to do case-insensitive comparisons is to use the **casefold** method, provided specifically for this purpose.

```
def compare_no_case(str1, str2):
    return str1.casefold() == str2.casefold()

print(compare_no_case('cat', 'CAT'))  # Return True.
```

Table 2.1 lists the operators available with the **str** type.

Table 2.1. String Operators

OPERATOR SYNTAX	DESCRIPTION
name = str	Assigns the string data to the specified variable name.
str1 == *str2*	Returns **True** if *str1* and *str2* have the same contents. (As with all comparison ops, this is case-sensitive.)
str1 != *str2*	Returns **True** if *str1* and *str2* have different contents.
str1 < *str2*	Returns **True** if *str1* is earlier in alphabetical ordering than *str2*. For example, 'abc' < 'def' returns **True**, but 'abc' < 'aaa' returns **False**. (See the note about ordering.)
str1 > *str2*	Returns **True** if *str1* is later in alphabetical ordering than *str2*. For example, 'def' > 'abc' returns **True**, but 'def' > 'xyz' returns **False**.
str1 <= *str2*	Returns **True** if *str1* is earlier than *str2* in alphabetical ordering or if the strings have the same content.
str1 >= *str2*	Returns **True** if *str1* is later than *str2* in alphabetical ordering or if the strings have the same content.
str1 + *str2*	Produces the concatenation of the two strings, which is the result of simply gluing *str2* contents onto the end of *str1*. For example, 'Big' + 'Deal' produces the concatenated string 'BigDeal'.
str1 * n	Produces the result of a string concatenated onto itself n times, where n is an integer. For example, 'Goo' * 3 produces 'GooGooGoo'.
n * *str1*	Same effect as *str1* * n.
str1 **in** *str2*	Produces **True** if the substring *str1*, in its entirety, is contained in *str2*.
str1 **not in** str2	Produces **True** if the substring *str1* is not contained in *str2*.
str **is** *obj*	Returns **True** if *str* and *obj* refer to the same object in memory; sometimes necessary for comparisons to **None** or to an unknown object type.
str **is not** *obj*	Returns **True** if *str* and *obj* do not refer to the same object in memory.

Note ▶ When strings are compared, Python uses a form of alphabetical order; more specifically, it uses *code point* order, which looks at ASCII or Unicode values of the characters. In this order, all uppercase letters precede all lowercase letters, but otherwise letters involve alphabetical comparisons, as you'd expect. Digit comparisons also work as you'd expect, so that '1' is less than '2'.

◀ Note

The concatenation operator (+) for strings may be familiar, because it is supported in many languages that have some kind of string class.

Concatenation does not automatically add a space between two words. You have to do that yourself. But all strings, including literal strings such as ' ', have the same type, **str**, so Python has no problem carrying out the following:

```
first = 'Will'
last = 'Shakespeare'
full_name = first + ' ' + last
print(full_name)
```

This example prints

```
Will Shakespeare
```

The string-multiplication operator (*****) can be useful when you're doing character-oriented graphics and want to initialize a long line—a divider, for example.

```
divider_str = '_' * 30
print(divider_str)
```

This prints the following:

```
_____
```

The result of this operation, '_' * 30, is a string made up of 30 underscores.

Performance Tip ▶ There are other ways of creating a string containing 30 underscores in a row, but the use of the multiplication operator (*****) is by far the most efficient.

◀ Performance Tip

Be careful not to abuse the **is** and **is not** operators. These operators test for whether or not two values are *the same object in memory*. You could have two string variables, for example, which both contain the value "cat". Testing them for equality (**==**) will always return **True** in this situation, but obj1 is obj2 might not.

When should you use **is** or **is not**? You should use them primarily when you're comparing objects of different types, for which the appropriate test for equality (**==**) might not be defined. One such case is testing to see whether some value is equal to the special value **None**, which is unique and therefore appropriate to test using **is**.

2.4 *Indexing and Slicing*

Two of the ways to extract data from strings include indexing and slicing:

▶ *Indexing* uses a number to refer to an individual character, according to its place within the string.

▶ *Slicing* is an ability more unique to Python. It enables you to refer to an entire substring of characters by using a compact syntax.

Lists support similar abilities, so Chapter 3, "Advanced List Capabilities," should look similar. However, there are some differences. The biggest one is this:

✱ **You cannot use indexing, slicing, or any other operation to change values of a string "in place," because strings are immutable.**

You can use both positive (nonnegative) and negative indexes in any combination. Figure 2.1 illustrates how positive indexes run from 0 to N−1, where N is the length of the string.

This figure also illustrates negative indexes, which run backward from −1 (indicating the last character) to −N.

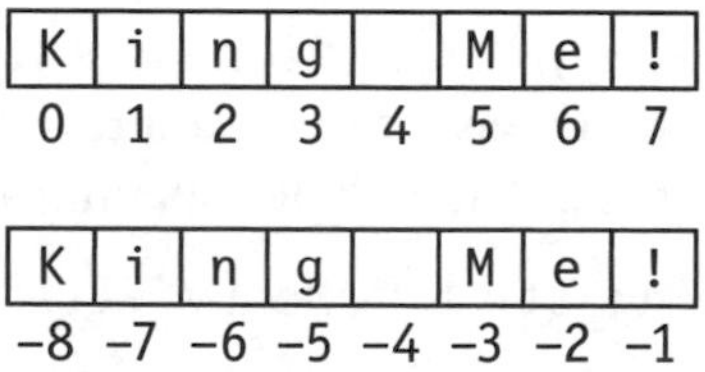

K	i	n	g		M	e	!
0	1	2	3	4	5	6	7

K	i	n	g		M	e	!
−8	−7	−6	−5	−4	−3	−2	−1

Figure 2.1. String indexing in Python

Aside from immutability, there's another difference between strings and lists. Indexing a string always produces a one-character string, assuming the index is valid. A one-character string has **str** type, just as a larger string does.

So, for example, suppose you index the first character of 'Hello'; the result is the string 'H'. Although its length is 1, it's still a string.

```
s = 'Hello'
ch = s[0]
print(type(ch))
```

This code, if executed, prints the following results—demonstrating that ch, though it only contains one character, still has type **str**:

```
<class 'str'>
```

Python has no separate "character" type.

Slicing is a special ability shared by Python strings, lists, and tuples. Table 2.2 summarizes the syntax supported for slicing of strings, which produces substrings. Remember that you can't assign *into* a slice of a string.

Table 2.2. Slicing Syntax for Python Strings

SYNTAX	GETS THIS SUBSTRING
string[*beg*: *end*]	All characters starting with *beg*, up to but not including *end*.
string[:*end*]	All characters from the beginning of the string up to but not including *end*.
string[*beg*:]	All elements from *beg* forward to the end of the string.
string[:]	All characters in the string; this operation copies the entire string.
string[*beg*: *end*: *step*]	All characters starting with *beg*, up to but not including *end*, moving through the string *step* items at a time.

Suppose you want to remove the beginning and last characters from a string. In this case, you'll want to combine positive and negative indexes. Start with a string that includes opening and closing double quotation marks.

```
king_str = '"Henry VIII"'
```

If you print this string directly, you get the following:

```
"Henry VIII"
```

But what if you want to print the string without the quotation marks? An easy way to do that is by executing the following code:

```
new_str = king_str[1:-1]
print(new_str)
```

The output is now

```
Henry VIII
```

Figure 2.2 illustrates how this works. In slicing operations, the slice begins with the first argument, *up to but not including the second argument.*

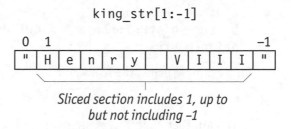

Figure 2.2. String slicing example 1

Here's another example. Suppose we'd like to extract the second word, "Bad," from the phrase "The Bad Dog." As Figure 2.3 illustrates, the correct slice would begin with index 4 and extend to all the characters *up to but not including index 7*. The string could therefore be accessed as `string[4:7]`.

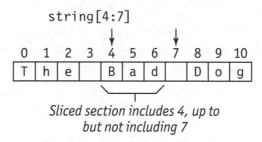

Figure 2.3. String slicing example 2

The rules for slicing have some interesting consequences.

▶ If both *beg* and *end* are positive indexes, *beg-end* gives the maximum length of the slice.

▶ To get a string containing the first N characters of a string, use `string[:N]`.

▶ To get a string containing the last N characters of a string, use `string[-N:]`.

▶ To cause a complete copy of the string to be made, use `string[:]`.

Slicing permits a third, and optional, `step` argument. When positive, the `step` argument specifies how many characters to move ahead at a time. A `step` argument of 2 means "Get every other character." A `step` argument of 3 means "Get every third character." For example, the following statements start with the second character in `'RoboCop'` and then step through the string two characters at a time.

```
a_str = 'RoboCop'
b_str = a_str[1::2]      # Get every other character.
print(b_str)
```

This example prints the following:

```
ooo
```

Here's another example. A step value of 3 means "Get every third character." This time the slice, by default, starts in the first position.

```
a_str = 'AbcDefGhiJklNop'
b_str = a_str[::3]        # Get every third character.
print(b_str)
```

This example prints the following:

```
ADGJN
```

You can even use a negative *step* value, which causes the slicing to be performed backward through the string. For example, the following function
returns the exact reverse of the string fed to it as an argument.

```
def reverse_str(s):
    return s[::-1]

print(reverse_str('Wow Bob wow!'))
print(reverse_str('Racecar'))
```

This example prints the following:

```
!wow boB woW
racecaR
```

When slicing, Python does not raise an exception for out-of-range indexes.
It simply gets as much input as it can. In some cases, that may result in an
empty string.

```
a_str = 'cat'
b_str = a_str[10:20]  # b_str assigned an empty string.
```

2.5 Single-Character Functions (Character Codes)

There are two functions intended to be used with strings of length 1. In effect,
these are single-character functions, even though they operate on strings.

```
ord(str)    # Returns a numeric code
chr(n)      # Converts ASCII/Unicode to a one-char str.
```

The **ord** function expects a string argument but raises a **TypeError** exception if the string is greater than 1. You can use this function to return the ASCII or Unicode value corresponding to a character. For example, the following example confirms that the ASCII code for the letter *A* is decimal 65.

```
print(ord('A'))   # Print 65.
```

The **chr** function is the inverse of the **ord** function. It takes a character code and returns its ASCII or Unicode equivalent, as a string of length 1. Calling **chr** with an argument of 65 should therefore print a letter *A*, which it does.

```
print(chr(65))    # Print 'A'
```

The **in** and **not in** operators, although not limited to use with one-character strings, often are used that way. For example, the following statements test whether the first character of a string is a vowel:

```
s = 'elephant'
if s[0] in 'aeiou':
    print('First char. is a vowel.')
```

Conversely, you could write a consonant test.

```
s = 'Helephant'
if s[0] not in 'aeiou':
    print('First char. is a consonant.')
```

One obvious drawback is that these examples do not correctly work on uppercase letters. Here's one way to fix that:

```
if s[0] in 'aeiouAEIOU':
    print('First char. is a vowel.')
```

Alternatively, you can convert a character to uppercase before testing it; that has the effect of creating a case-insensitive comparison.

```
s = 'elephant'
if s[0].upper() in 'AEIOU':
    print('First char. is a vowel.')
```

You can also use **in** and **not in** to test substrings that contain more than one character. In that case, the entire substring must be found to produce **True**.

```
'bad' in 'a bad dog'     # True!
```

Is there bad in a bad dog? Yes, there is.

Notice that the **in** operator, if tested, always responds as if all strings include the empty string, `''`, which differs from the way lists work. Python does not return **True** if you ask whether a list contains the empty list.

```
print('' in 'cat')        # Prints True
print([] in [1, 2, 3])    # Prints False
```

Another area in which single-character operations are important is in the area of **for** loops and iteration. If you iterate through a list, you get access to each list element. But if you iterate through a string, you get individual characters: again, these are each strings of length 1 rather than objects of a separate "character" type.

```
s = 'Cat'
for ch in s:
    print(ch, ',  type:', type(ch))
```

This code prints the following:

```
C,  type: <class 'str'>
a,  type: <class 'str'>
t,  type: <class 'str'>
```

Because each of these characters is a string of length 1, we can print the corresponding ASCII values:

```
s = 'Cat'
for ch in s:
    print(ord(ch), end='  ')
```

This example prints the following:

```
67  97  116
```

2.6 Building Strings Using "join"

Considering that strings are immutable, you might well ask the following question: How do you construct or build new strings?

Once again, the special nature of Python assignment comes to the rescue. For example, the following statements build the string "Big Bad John":

```
a_str = 'Big '
a_str = a_str + 'Bad '
a_str = a_str + 'John'
```

These are perfectly valid statements. They reuse the name `a_str`, each time assigning a new string to the name. The end result is to create the following string:

'Big Bad John'

The following statements are also valid, and even if they seem to violate immutability, they actually do not.

```
a_str = 'Big '
a_str += 'Bad '
a_str += 'John'
```

This technique, of using =, +, and += to build strings, is adequate for simple cases involving a few objects. For example, you could build a string containing all the letters of the alphabet as follows, using the **ord** and **chr** functions introduced in Section 2.5, "Single-Character Operations (Character Codes)."

```
n = ord('A')
s = ''
for i in range(n, n + 26):
    s += chr(i)
```

This example has the virtue of brevity. But it causes Python to create entirely new strings in memory, over and over again.

An alternative, which is slightly better, is to use the **join** method.

separator_string.**join**(*list*)

This method joins together all the strings in *list* to form one large string. If this list has more than one element, the text of *separator_string* is placed between each consecutive pair of strings. An empty list is a valid separator string; in that case, all the strings in the list are simply joined together.

Use of **join** is usually more efficient at run time than concatenation, although you probably won't see the difference in execution time unless there are a great many elements.

```
n = ord('A')
a_lst = [ ]
for i in range(n, n + 26):
    a_lst.append(chr(i))
s = ''.join(a_lst)
```

The **join** method concatenates all the strings in `a_lst`, a list of strings, into one large string. The separator string is empty in this case.

Performance Tip ▶ The advantage of **join** over simple concatenation can be seen in large cases involving thousands of operations. The drawback of concatenation in such cases is that Python has to create thousands of strings of increasing size, which are used once and then thrown away, through "garbage collection." But garbage collection exacts a cost in execution time, assuming it is run often enough to make a difference.

◀ Performance Tip

Here's a case in which the approach of using **join** is superior: Suppose you want to write a function that takes a list of names and prints them one at a time, nicely separated by commas. Here's the hard way to write the code:

```python
def print_nice(a_lst):
    s = ''
    for item in a_lst:
        s += item + ', '
    if len(s) > 0:          # Get rid of trailing
                            # comma+space
        s = s[:-2]
    print(s)
```

Given this function definition, we can call it on a list of strings.

```python
print_nice(['John', 'Paul', 'George', 'Ringo'])
```

This example prints the following:

```
John, Paul, George, Ringo
```

Here's the version using the **join** method:

```python
def print_nice(a_lst):
    print(', '.join(a_lst))
```

That's quite a bit less code!

2.7 Important String Functions

Many of the "functions" described in this chapter are actually *methods*: member functions of the class that are called with the "dot" syntax.

But in addition to methods, the Python language has some important built-in functions that are implemented for use with the fundamental types of the language. The ones listed here apply especially well to strings.

Key Syntax

```
input(prompt_str)      # Prompt user for input string.
len(str)               # Return num. of chars in str.
max(str)               # Return char with highest code val.
min(str)               # Return char with lowest code val.
reversed(str)          # Return iter with reversed str.
sorted(str)            # Return list with sorted str.
```

One of the most important functions is **len**, which can be used with any of the standard collection classes to determine the number of elements. In the case of strings, this function returns the number of characters. Here's an example:

```
dog1 = 'Jaxx'
dog2 = 'Cutie Pie'
print(dog1, 'has', len(dog1), 'letters.')
print(dog2, 'has', len(dog2), 'letters.')
```

This prints the following strings. Note that "Cutie Pie" has nine letters because it counts the space.

```
Jaxx has 4 letters.
Cutie Pie has 9 letters.
```

The **reversed** and **sorted** functions produce an iterator and a list, respectively, rather than strings. However, the output from these data objects can be converted back into strings by using the **join** method. Here's an example:

```
a_str = ''.join(reversed('Wow,Bob,wow!'))
print(a_str)
b_str = ''.join(sorted('Wow,Bob,wow!'))
print(b_str)
```

This prints the following:

```
!wow,boB,woW
!,,BWbooowww
```

2.8 Binary, Hex, and Octal Conversion Functions

In addition to the **str** conversion function, Python supports three functions that take numeric input and produce a string result. Each of these functions produces a digit string in the appropriate base (2, 16, and 8, corresponding to binary, hexadecimal, and octal).

```
      bin(n)    # Returns a string containing n in binary:
                #    For example, bin(15) -> '0b1111'
      hex(n)    # Returns a string containing n in hex:
                #    For example, hex(15) -> '0xf'
      oct(n)    # Returns a string containing n in octal:
                #    For example, oct(15) -> '0o17'
```

Here's another example, this one showing how 10 decimal is printed in binary, octal, and hexadecimal.

```
print(bin(10), oct(10), hex(10))
```

This prints the following:

```
0b1010 0o12 0xa
```

As you can see, these three functions automatically use the prefixes "0b," "0o," and "0x."

2.9 Simple Boolean ("is") Methods

These methods—all of which begin with the word "is" in their name—return either **True** or **False**. They are often used with single-character strings but can also be used on longer strings; in that case, they return **True** if and only if every character in the string passes the test. Table 2.3 shows the Boolean methods of strings.

Table 2.3. Boolean Methods of Strings

METHOD NAME/SYNTAX	RETURNS TRUE IF STRING PASSES THIS TEST
str.isalnum()	All characters are alphanumeric—a letter or digit—and there is at least one character.
str.isalpha()	All characters are letters of the alphabet, and there is at least one character.
str.isdecimal()	All characters are decimal digits, and there is at least one character. Similar to **isdigit** but intended to be used with Unicode characters.
str.isdigit()	All characters are decimal digits, and there is at least one character.
str.isidentifier()	The string contains a valid Python identifier (symbolic) name. The first character must be a letter or underscore; each other character must be a letter, digit, or underscore.
str.islower()	All letters in the string are lowercase, and there is at least one letter. (There may, however, be nonalphabetic characters.)
str.isprintable()	All characters in the string, if any, are printable characters. This excludes special characters such as \n and \t.

Table 2.3. Boolean Methods of Strings (*continued*)

METHOD NAME/SYNTAX	RETURNS TRUE IF STRING PASSES THIS TEST
str.**isspace()**	All characters in the string are "whitespace" characters, and there is at least one character.
str.**istitle()**	Every word in the string is a valid title, and there is at least one character. This requires that each word be capitalized and that no uppercase letter appear anywhere but at the beginning of a word. There may be whitespace and punctuation characters in between words.
str.**isupper()**	All letters in the string are uppercase, and there is at least one letter. (There may, however, be nonalphabetic characters.)

These functions are valid for use with single-character strings as well as longer strings. The following code illustrates the use of both.

```
h_str = 'Hello'
if h_str[0].isupper():
    print('First letter is uppercase.')
if h_str.isupper():
    print('All chars are uppercase.')
else:
    print('Not all chars are uppercase.')
```

This example prints the following:

```
First letter is uppercase.
Not all chars are uppercase.
```

This string would also pass the test for being a title, because the first letter is uppercase and the rest are not.

```
if h_str.istitle():
    print('Qualifies as a title.')
```

2.10 Case Conversion Methods

The methods in the previous section test for uppercase versus lowercase letters. The methods in this section perform conversion to produce a new string.

```
str.lower()      # Produce all-lowercase string
str.upper()      # Produce all-uppercase string
str.title()      # 'foo foo'.title() => 'Foo Foo'
str.swapcase()   # Upper to lower, and vice versa
```

The effects of the **lower** and **upper** methods are straightforward. The first converts each uppercase letter in a string to a lowercase letter; the second does the converse, converting each lowercase letter to an uppercase letter. Nonletter characters are not altered but kept in the string as is.

The result, after conversion, is then returned as a new string. The original string data, being immutable, isn't changed "in place." But the following statements do what you'd expect.

```
my_str = "I'm Henry VIII, I am!"
new_str = my_str.upper()
my_str = new_str
```

The last two steps can be efficiently merged:

```
my_str = my_str.upper()
```

If you then print my_str, you get the following:

```
I'M HENRY VIII, I AM!
```

The **swapcase** method is used only rarely. The string it produces has an uppercase letter where the source string had a lowercase latter, and vice versa. For example:

```
my_str = my_str.swapcase()
print(my_str)
```

This prints the following:

```
i'M hENRY viii, i AM!
```

2.11 Search-and-Replace Methods

The search-and-replace methods are among the most useful of the **str** class methods. In this section, we first look at **startswith** and **endswith**, and then present the other search-and-replace functions.

```
str.startswith(substr)    # Return True if prefix found.
str.endswith(substr)      # Return True if suffix found.
```

One of the authors wrote an earlier book, *Python Without Fear* (Addison-Wesley, 2018), which features a program that converts Roman numerals to decimal. It has to check for certain combinations of letters at the beginning of the input string—starting with any number of Roman numeral Ms.

```
while romstr.startswith('M'):
    amt += 1000            # Add 1,000 to running total.
    romstr = romstr[1:]    # Strip off first character.
```

The **endswith** method, conversely, looks for the presence of a target substring as the suffix. For example:

```
me_str = 'John Bennett, PhD'
is_doc = me_str.endswith('PhD')
```

These methods, **startswith** and **endswith**, can be used on an empty string without raising an error. If the substring is empty, the return value is always **True**.

Now let's look at other search-and-replace methods of Python strings.

```
str.count(substr [, beg [, end]])
str.find(substr [, beg [, end]])
str.index()   # Like find, but raises exception
str.rfind()   # Like find, but starts from end
str.replace(old, new [, count]) # count is optional; limits
                                #  no. of replacements
```

In this syntax, the brackets are not intended literally but represent optional items.

The **count** method reports the number of occurrences of a target substring. Here's how it works.

```
frank_str = 'doo be doo be doo...'

n = frank_str.count('doo')
print(n)                                  # Print 3.
```

You can optionally use the *start* and *end* arguments with this same method call.

```
print(frank_str.count('doo', 1))     # Print 2
print(frank_str.count('doo', 1, 10)) # Print 1
```

A *start* argument of 1 specifies that counting begins with the second character. If *start* and *end* are both used, then counting happens over a target string beginning with *start* position up to but not including the *end* position. These arguments are zero-based indexes, as usual.

If either or both of the arguments (*begin*, *end*) are out of range, the **count** method does not raise an exception but works on as many characters as it can.

Similar rules apply to the **find** method. A simple call to this method finds the first occurrence of the substring argument and returns the nonnegative index of that instance; it returns −1 if the substring isn't found.

```
frank_str = 'doo be doo be doo...'

print(frank_str.find('doo'))   # Print 0
print(frank_str.find('doob'))  # Print -1
```

If you want to find the positions of all occurrences of a substring, you can call the **find** method in a loop, as in the following example.

```
frank_str = 'doo be doo be doo...'
n = -1
while True:
    n = frank_str.find('doo', n + 1)
    if n == -1:
        break
    print(n, end=' ')
```

This example prints every index at which an instance of **'doo'** can be found.

```
0 7 14
```

This example works by taking advantage of the *start* argument. After each successful call to the **find** method, the initial searching position, n, is set to the previous successful find index and then is adjusted upward by 1. This guarantees that the next call to the **find** method must look for a new instance of the substring.

If the **find** operation fails to find any occurrences, it returns a value of −1.

The **index** and **rfind** methods are almost identical to the **find** method, with a few differences. The **index** function does not return −1 when it fails to find an occurrence of the substring. Instead it raises a **ValueError** exception.

The **rfind** method searches for the last occurrence of the substring argument. By default, this method starts at the end and searches to the left. However, this does not mean it looks for a reverse of the substring. Instead, it searches for a regular copy of the substring, and it returns the starting index number of the last occurrence—that is, where the last occurrence starts.

```
frank_str = 'doo be doo be doo...'
print(frank_str.rfind('doo'))   # Prints 14.
```

The example prints 14 because the rightmost occurrence of **'doo'** starts in zero-based position 14.

2

Finally, the **replace** method replaces each and every occurrence of an old substring with a new substring. This method, as usual, produces the resulting string, because it cannot change the original string in place.

For example, let's say we have a set of book titles but want to change the spelling of the word "Grey" to "Gray." Here's an example:

```
title = '25 Hues of Grey'
new_title = title.replace('Grey', 'Gray')
```

Printing `new_title` produces this:

```
25 Hues of Gray
```

The next example illustrates how **replace** works on multiple occurrences of the same substring.

```
title = 'Greyer Into Grey'
new_title = title.replace('Grey', 'Gray')
```

The new string is now

```
Grayer Into Gray
```

2.12 *Breaking Up Input Using "split"*

One of the most common programming tasks when dealing with character input is *tokenizing*—breaking down a line of input into individual words, phrases, and numbers. Python's **split** method provides an easy and convenient way to perform this task.

input_str.**split(***delim_string***=None)**

The call to this method returns a list of substrings taken from *input_string*. The *delim_string* specifies a string that serves as the delimiter; this is a substring used to separate one token from another.

If *delim_string* is omitted or is **None**, then the behavior of **split** is to, in effect, use any sequence of one or more whitespace characters (spaces, tabs, and newlines) to distinguish one token from the next.

For example, the **split** method—using the default delimiter of a space—can be used to break up a string containing several names.

```
stooge_list = 'Moe Larry Curly Shemp'.split()
```

The resulting list, if printed, is as follows:

```
['Moe', 'Larry', 'Curly', 'Shemp']
```

The behavior of **split** with a **None** or default argument uses *any number* of white spaces in a row as the delimiter. Here's an example:

```
stooge_list = 'Moe    Larry Curly  Shemp'.split()
```

If, however, a delimiter string is specified, it must be matched precisely to recognize a divider between one character and the next.

```
stooge_list = 'Moe    Larry Curly  Shemp'.split(' ')
```

In this case, the **split** method recognizes an extra string—although it is empty—wherever there's an extra space. That might not be the behavior you want. The example just shown would produce the following:

```
['Moe', '', '', '', 'Larry', 'Curly', '', 'Shemp']
```

Another common delimiter string is a comma, or possibly a comma combined with a space. In the latter case, the delimiter string must be matched exactly. Here's an example:

```
stooge_list = 'Moe, Larry, Curly, Shemp'.split(', ')
```

In contrast, the following example uses a simple comma as delimiter. This example causes the tokens to contain the extra spaces.

```
stooge_list = 'Moe, Larry, Curly, Shemp'.split(',')
```

The result in this case includes a leading space in the last three of the four string elements:

```
['Moe', ' Larry', ' Curly', ' Shemp']
```

If you don't want those leading spaces, an easy solution is to use stripping, as shown next.

2.13 Stripping

Once you retrieve input from the user or from a text file, you may want to place it in the correct format by stripping leading and trailing spaces. You might also want to strip leading and trailing "0" digits or other characters. The **str** class provides several methods to let you perform this stripping.

```
str.strip(extra_chars=' ')    # Strip leading & trailing.
str.lstrip(extra_chars=' ')   # String leading chars.
str.rstrip(extra_chars=' ')   # String trailing chars.
```

Each of these method calls produces a string that has trailing or leading characters (or both) to be stripped out.

The **lstrip** method strips only leading characters, and the **rstrip** method strips only trailing characters, but otherwise all three methods perform the same job. The **strip** method strips both leading and trailing characters.

With each method, if the *extra_chars* argument is specified, the method strips all occurrences of each and every character in the *extra_chars* string. For example, if the string contains *+0, then the method strips all leading or trailing asterisks (*) as well as all leading or trailing "0" digits and plus signs (+).

Internal instances of the character to be stripped are left alone. For example, the following statement strips leading and trailing spaces but not the space in the middle.

```
name_str = '   Will Shakes   '
new_str = name_str.strip()
```

Figure 2.4 illustrates how this method call works.

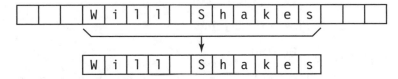

Figure 2.4. Python stripping operations

2.14 Justification Methods

When you need to do sophisticated text formatting, you generally should use the techniques described in Chapter 5, "Formatting Text Precisely." However, the **str** class itself comes with rudimentary techniques for justifying text: either left justifying, right justifying, or centering text within a print field.

```
str.ljust(width [, fillchar])    # Left justify
str.rjust(width [, fillchar])    # Right justify
str.center(width [, fillchar])   # Center the text.
digit_str.zfill(width)           # Pad with 0's.
```

In the syntax of these methods, each pair of square brackets indicates an optional item not intended to be interpreted literally. These methods return a string formatted as follows:

▶ The text of *str* is placed in a larger print field of size specified by *width*.

▶ If the string text is shorter than the specified length, the text is justified left, right, or centered, as appropriate. The **center** method slightly favors left justification if it cannot be centered perfectly.

▶ The rest of the result is padded with the fill character. If this fill character is not specified, then the default value is a white space.

Here's an example:

```
new_str = 'Help!'.center(10, '#')
print(new_str)
```

This example prints

```
##Help!###
```

Another common fill character (other than a space) is the digit character "0". Number strings are typically right justified rather than left justified. Here's an example:

```
new_str = '750'.rjust(6, '0')
print(new_str)
```

This example prints

```
000750
```

The **zfill** method provides a shorter, more compact way of doing the same thing: padding a string of digits with leading "0" characters.

```
s = '12'
print(s.zfill(7))
```

But the **zfill** method is not just a shortcut for **rjust**; instead, with **zfill**, the zero padding becomes part of the number itself, so the zeros are printed between the number and the sign:

```
>>> '-3'.zfill(5)
'-0003'
>>> '-3'.rjust(5, '0')
'000-3'
```

Chapter 2   *Summary*

The Python string type (**str**) is an exceptionally powerful data type, even in comparison to strings in other languages. String methods include the abilities to tokenize input (splitting); remove leading and trailing spaces (stripping); convert to numeric formats; and print numeric expressions in any radix.

The built-in search abilities include methods for counting and finding substrings (**count**, **find**, and **index**) as well as the ability to do text replacement.

And yet there's a great deal more you can do with strings. Chapter 5, "Formatting Text Precisely," explores the fine points of using formatting characters as well as the format method for the sophisticated printing of output.

Chapter 6, "Regular Expressions, Part I" goes even farther in matching, searching, and replacing text patterns, so that you can carry out flexible searches by specifying patterns of any degree of complexity.

Chapter 2 *Review Questions*

1 Does assignment to an indexed character of a string violate Python's immutability for strings?

2 Does string concatenation, using the **+=** operator, violate Python's immutability for strings? Why or why not?

3 How many ways are there in Python to index a given character?

4 How, precisely, are indexing and slicing related?

5 What is the exact data type of an indexed character? What is the data type of a substring produced from slicing?

6 In Python, what is the relationship between the string and character "types"?

7 Name at least two operators and one method that enable you to build a larger string out of one or more smaller strings.

8 If you are going to use the **index** method to locate a substring, what is the advantage of first testing the target string by using **in** or **not in**?

9 Which built-in string methods, and which operators, produce a simple Boolean (true/false) results?

Chapter 2 *Suggested Problems*

1 Write a program that prompts for a string and counts the number of vowels and consonants, printing the results. (Hint: use the **in** and **not in** operators to reduce the amount of code you might otherwise have to write.)

2 Write a function that efficiently strips the first two characters of a string and the last two characters of a string. Returning an empty string should be an acceptable return value. Test this function with a series of different inputs.

3 *Advanced List Capabilities*

"I've got a little list . . . "
—Gilbert and Sullivan, *The Mikado*

To paraphrase the Lord High Executioner in *The Mikado*, we've got a little list. . . . Actually, in Python we've got quite a few of them. One of the foundations of a strong programming language is the concept of *arrays* or *lists*—objects that hold potentially large numbers of other objects, all held together in a collection.

Python's most basic collection class is the list, which does everything an array does in other languages, but much more. This chapter explores the basic, intermediate, and advanced features of Python lists.

3.1 Creating and Using Python Lists

Python has no data declarations. How, then, do you create collections such as a list? You do so in the same way you create other data.

▶ Specify the data on the right side of an assignment. This is where a list is actually created, or built.

▶ On the left side, put a variable name, just as you would for any other assignment, so that you have a way to refer to the list.

Variables have no type except through assignment. In theory, the same variable could refer first to an integer and then to a list.

```
x = 5
x = [1, 2, 3]
```

But it's much better to use a variable to represent only one type of data and stick to it. We also recommend using suggestive variable names. For example, it's a good idea to use a "list" suffix when you give a name to list collections.

```
my_int_list = [5, -20, 5, -69]
```

Here's a statement that creates a list of strings and names it beat_list:

```
beat_list = [ 'John', 'Paul', 'George', 'Ringo' ]
```

You can even create lists that mix numeric and string data.

```
mixed_list = [10, 'John', 5, 'Paul' ]
```

But you should mostly avoid mixing data types inside lists. In Python 3.0, mixing data types prevents you from using the **sort** method on the list. Integer and floating-point data, however, can be freely mixed.

```
num_list = [3, 2, 17, 2.5]
num_list.sort()  # Sorts into [2, 2.5, 3, 17]
```

Another technique you can use for building a collection is to append one element at a time to an empty list.

```
my_list = []             # Must do this before you append!
my_list.append(1)
my_list.append(2)
my_list.append(3)
```

These statements have the same effect as initializing a list all at once, as here:

```
my_list = [1, 2, 3]
```

You can also remove list items.

```
my_list.remove(1)     # List is now [2, 3]
```

The result of this statement is to remove the first instance of an element equal to 1. If there is no such value in the list, Python raises a **ValueError** exception.

List order is meaningful, as are duplicate values. For example, to store a series of judge's ratings, you might use the following statement, which indicates that three different judges all assigned the score 1.0, but the third judge assigned 9.8.

```
the_scores = [1.0, 1.0, 9.8, 1.0]
```

The following statement removes only the first instance of 1.0.

```
the_scores.remove(1.0) # List now equals [1.0, 9.8, 1.0]
```

3.2 Copying Lists Versus Copying List Variables

In Python, variables are more like references in C++ than they are like "value" variables. In practical terms, this means that copying from one collection to another requires a little extra work.

What do you think the following does?

```
a_list = [2, 5, 10]
b_list = a_list
```

The first statement creates a list by building it on the right side of the assignment (=). But the second statement in this example creates no data. It just does the following action:

> Make "b_list" an alias for whatever "a_list" refers to.

The variable b_list therefore becomes an alias for whatever a_list refers to. Consequently, if changes are made to either variable, both reflect that change.

```
b_list.append(100)
a_list.append(200)
b_list.append(1)
print(a_list)     # This prints [2, 5, 10, 100, 200, 1]
```

If instead you want to create a separate copy of all the elements of a list, you need to perform a member-by-member copy. The simplest way to do that is to use slicing.

```
my_list = [1, 10, 5]
yr_list = my_list[:]    # Perform member-by-member copy.
```

Now, because my_list and yr_list refer to separate copies of [1, 10, 5], you can change one of the lists without changing the other.

3.3 Indexing

Python supports both nonnegative and negative indexes.

The nonnegative indexes are zero-based, so in the following example, list_name[0] refers to the first element. (Section 3.3.2 covers negative indexes.)

```
my_list = [100, 500, 1000]
print(my_list[0])       # Print 100.
```

Because lists are mutable, they can be changed "in place" without creating an entirely new list. Consequently, you can change individual elements by making one of those elements the target of an assignment—something you can't do with strings.

```
my_list[1] = 55          # Set second element to 55.
```

3.3.1 Positive Indexes

Positive (nonnegative) index numbers are like those used in other languages, such as C++. Index 0 denotes the first element in the list, 1 denotes the second, and so on. These indexes run from 0 to N–1, where N is the number of elements.

For example, assume the following statement has been executed, creating a list.

```
a_list = [100, 200, 300, 400, 500, 600]
```

These elements are indexed by the number 0 through 5, as shown in Figure 3.1.

0	1	2	3	4	5
100	200	300	400	500	600

Figure 3.1. Nonnegative indexes

The following examples use nonnegative indexes to access individual elements.

```
print(a_list[0])      # Prints 100.
print(a_list[1])      # Prints 200.
print(a_list[2])      # Prints 300.
```

Although lists can grow without limit, an index number must be in range at the time it's used. Otherwise, Python raises an **IndexError** exception.

Performance Tip ▶ Here, as elsewhere, we've used separate calls to the **print** function because it's convenient for illustration purposes. But remember that repeated calls to **print** slow down your program, at least within IDLE. A faster way to print these values is to use only one call to **print**.

```
print(a_list[0], a_list[1], a_list[2], sep='\n')
```

◀ Performance Tip

3.3.2 Negative Indexes

You can also refer to items in a list by using negative indexes, which refer to an element by its distance from the end of the list.

An index value of −1 denotes the last element in a list, and −2 denotes the next-to -last element, and so on. The value −N denotes the first element in the list. Negative indexes run from −1 to −N, in which N is the length of the list.

The list in the previous section can be indexed as illustrated in Figure 3.2.

```
 -6   -5   -4   -3   -2   -1
┌────┬────┬────┬────┬────┬────┐
│100 │200 │300 │400 │500 │600 │
└────┴────┴────┴────┴────┴────┘
```

Figure 3.2. Negative indexes

The following examples demonstrate negative indexing.

```
a_list = [100, 200, 300, 400, 500, 600]
print(a_list[-1])     # Prints 600.
print(a_list[-3])     # Prints 400.
```

Out-of-range negative indexes can raise an **IndexError** exception, just as nonnegative indexes can.

3.3.3 Generating Index Numbers Using "enumerate"

The "Pythonic" way is to avoid the **range** function except where it's needed. Here's the correct way to write a loop that prints elements of a list:

```
a_list = ['Tom', 'Dick', 'Jane']

for s in a_list:
    print(s)
```

This prints the following:

```
Tom
Dick
Jane
```

This approach is more natural and efficient than relying on indexing, which would be inefficient and slower.

```
for i in range(len(a_list)):
    print(a_list[i])
```

But what if you want to list the items next to numbers? You can do that by using index numbers (plus 1, if you want the indexing to be 1-based), but a better technique is to use the **enumerate** function.

```
enumerate(iter, start=0)
```

In this syntax, *start* is optional. Its default value is 0.

This function takes an iterable, such as a list, and produces another iterable, which is a series of tuples. Each of those tuples has the form

```
(num, item)
```

In which *num* is an integer in a series beginning with *start*. The following statement shows an example, using a_list from the previous example and starting the series at 1:

```
list(enumerate(a_list, 1))
```

This produces the following:

```
[(1, 'Tom'), (2, 'Dick'), (3, 'Jane')]
```

We can put this together with a **for** loop to produce the desired result.

```
for item_num, name_str in enumerate(a_list, 1):
    print(item_num, '. ', name_str, sep='')
```

This loop calls the **enumerate** function to produce tuples of the form (*num, item*). Each iteration prints the number followed by a period (".") and an element.

```
1. Tom
2. Dick
3. Jane
```

3.4 Getting Data from Slices

Whereas indexing refers to one element at a time, the technique of *slicing* produces a sublist from a specified range. The sublist can range in size from an empty list to a new list having all the contents of the original list.

Table 3.1 shows the various ways you can use slicing.

Table 3.1 Slicing Lists in Python

SYNTAX	PRODUCES THIS NEW LIST
list[*beg*:*end*]	All list elements starting with *beg*, up to but not including *end*.
list[:*end*]	All elements from the beginning of the list, up to but not including *end*.
list[*beg*:]	All elements from *beg* forward to the end of the list.
list[:]	All elements in the list; this operation copies the entire list, element by element.
list[*beg*: *end*: *step*]	All elements starting with *beg*, up to but not including *end*; but movement through the list is *step* items at a time.
	With this syntax, any or all of the three values may be omitted. Each has a reasonable default value; the default value of *step* is 1.

Here are some examples of list slicing:

```
a_list = [1, 2, 5, 10, 20, 30]

b_list = a_list[1:3]        # Produces [2, 5]
c_list = a_list[4:]         # Produces [20, 30]
```

These examples use positive indexing, in which index numbers run from 0 to N–1. You can just as easily use negative indexing to help specify a slice. Here's an example:

```
d_list = a_list[-4:-1]      # Produces [5, 10, 20]
e_list = a_list[-1:]        # Produces [30]
```

An important principle in either case is that the *end* argument specifies the end of the slice as follows: Copy elements *up to but not including* the *end* argument. Positive and negative index numbers can be mixed together.

Note ▶ When Python carries out a slicing operation, which always includes at least one colon (:) between the square brackets, the index specifications are not required to be in range. Python copies as many elements as it can. If it fails to copy any elements at all, the result is simply an empty list.

◀ Note

Figure 3.3 shows an example of how slicing works. Remember that Python selects elements starting with *beg*, up to but not including the element referred to by *end*. Therefore, the slice a_list[2:5] copies the sublist [300, 400, 500].

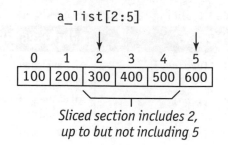

Figure 3.3 Slicing example

Finally, specifying a value for *step*, the third argument, can affect the data produced. For example, a value of 2 causes Python to get every *other* element from the range [2:5].

```
a_list = [100, 200, 300, 400, 500, 600]
b_list = a_list[2:5:2]     # Produces [300, 500]
```

A negative *step* value reverses the direction in which list elements are accessed. So a step value of –1 produces values in the slice by going backward through the list one item at a time. A step value of –2 produces values in the slice by going backward through the list two items at a time.

The following example starts with the last element and works backwards; it therefore produces an exact copy of the list—with all elements reversed!

```
rev_list = a_list[::-1]
```

Here's an example:

```
a_list = [100, 200, 300]
rev_list = a_list[::-1]
print(rev_list)            # Prints [300, 200, 100]
```

The *step* argument can be positive or negative but cannot be 0. If *step* is negative, then the defaults for the other values change as follows:

▶ The default value of *beg* becomes the last element in the list (indexed as –1).

▶ The default value of *end* becomes the beginning of the list.

Therefore, the slice expression [::-1] produces a reversal of the original list.

3.5 Assigning into Slices

Because lists are mutable, you can assign to elements in place. This extends to slicing. Here's an example:

```
my_list = [10, 20, 30, 40, 50, 60]
my_list[1:4] = [707, 777]
```

This example has the effect of deleting the range [20, 30, 40] and inserting the list [707, 777] in its place. The resulting list is

```
[10, 707, 777, 50, 60]
```

You may even assign into a position of length 0. The effect is to insert new list items without deleting existing ones. Here's an example:

```
my_list = [1, 2, 3, 4]
my_list[0:0] = [-50, -40]
print(my_list)       # prints [-50, -40, 1, 2, 3, 4]
```

The following restrictions apply to this ability to assign into slices:

▶ When you assign to a slice of a list, the source of the assignment must be another list or collection, even if it has zero or one element.

▶ If you include a *step* argument in the slice to be assigned to, the sizes of the two collections—the slice assigned to and the sequence providing the data— must match in size. If *step* is not specified, the sizes do not need to match.

3.6 List Operators

Table 3.2 summarizes the built-in operators applying to lists.

Table 3.2. List Operators in Python

OPERATOR/SYNTAX	DESCRIPTION
list1 + *list2*	Produces a new list containing the contents of both *list1* and *list2* by performing concatenation.
list1 * *n*, or *n* * *list1*	Produces a list containing the contents of *list1*, repeated *n* times. For example, [0] * 3 produces [0, 0, 0].
list[*n*]	Indexing. See Section 3.3.

▼ *continued on next page*

You'd probably expect none of these assignments to affect a_list, because that's a separate collection from b_list. But if you print a_list, here's what you get:

```
>>> print(a_list)
[1, 2, [0, 0]]
```

This may seem impossible, because a_list had the last element set to [5, 10]. Changes to b_list shouldn't have any effect on the contents of a_list, but now the latter's last element is [0, 0]! What happened?

The member-by-member copy, carried out earlier, copied the values 1 and 2, followed by a reference to the list-within-a-list. Consequently, changes made to b_list can affect a_list if they involve the second level.

Figure 3.4 illustrates the concept. Shallow copying makes new copies of top-level data only.

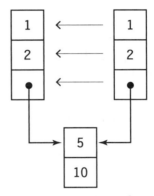

Figure 3.4. Shallow copying

And now you can see the problem. A member-by-member copy was carried out, but the list within the list was a *reference,* so both lists ended up referring to the same data in the final position.

The solution is simple. You need to do a *deep copy* to get the expected behavior. To get a deep copy, in which even embedded list items get copied, import the **copy** package and use **copy.deepcopy**.

```
import copy

a_list = [1, 2, [5, 10]]
b_list = copy.deepcopy(a_list)  # Create a DEEP COPY.
```

After these statements are executed, b_list becomes a new list completely unconnected to a_list. The result is illustrated in Figure 3.5, in which each list gets its own, separate copy of the list-within-a-list.

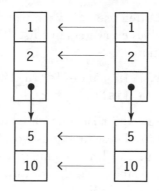

Figure 3.5. Deep copying

With deep copying, the depth of copying extends to every level. You could have collections within collections to any level of complexity.

If changes are now made to b_list after being copied to a_list, they will have no further effect on a_list. The last element of a_list will remain set to [5,10] until changed directly. All this functionality is thanks to deep copying.

3.8   List Functions

When you work with lists, there are several Python functions you'll find useful: These include **len**, **max**, and **min**, as well as **sorted**, **reversed**, and **sum**.

These are functions, not methods. The main difference is that methods use the dot (.) syntax; the other difference is that methods represent built-in abilities, whereas the functions here implement abilities that are useful with collections generally. Admittedly, this is sometimes a very fine distinction.

```
len(collection)        # Return length of the collection
max(collection)        # Return the elem with maximum
                       #  value.
min(collection)        # Return the elem with minimum
                       #  value.
reversed(collection)   # Produce iter in reversed order.
sorted(collection)     # Produce list in sorted order.
sum(collection)        # Adds up all the elements, which
                       #  must be numeric.
```

The **len** function returns the number of elements in a collection. This includes lists, strings, and other Python collection types. In the case of dictionaries, it returns the number of keys.

You'll often use **len** when working with lists. For example, the following loop doubles every item in a list. It's necessary to use **len** to make this a general solution.

```
for i in range(len(a_list)):
    a_list[i] *= 2
```

The **max** and **min** functions produce maximum and minimum elements, respectively. These functions work only on lists that have elements with compatible types, such as all numeric elements or all string elements. In the case of strings, alphabetical order (or rather, *code point* order) enables comparisons.

Here's an example:

```
a_list = [100, -3, -5, 120]
print('Length of the list is', len(a_list))
print('Max and min are', max(a_list), min(a_list))
```

This prints the following:

```
Length of the list is 4
Max and min are 120 -5
```

The **sorted** and **reversed** functions are similar to the **sort** and **reverse** methods, presented in Section 3.11. But whereas those methods reorganize a list in place, these functions produce new lists.

These functions work on tuples and strings as well as lists, but the **sorted** function always produces a list. Here's an example:

```
a_tup = (30, 55, 15, 45)
print(sorted(a_tup))    # Print [15, 30, 45, 55]
```

The **reversed** function is unusual because it produces an iterable but not a collection. In simple terms, this means you need a **for** loop to print it or else use a **list** or **tuple** conversion. Here's an example:

```
a_tup = (1, 3, 5, 0)
for i in reversed(a_tup):
    print(i, end=' ')
```

This prints

```
0 5 3 1
```

Alternatively, you can use the following:

```
print(tuple(reversed(a_tup)))
```

This produces

```
(0, 5, 3, 1)
```

Finally, there is the **sum** function, which is extremely convenient. You could write a loop yourself to perform this function, but it's nice not to have to do so. The **sum** function is supported for those arrays that are made up only of numeric types, such as **int** and **float**.

One possible use is to quickly and easily figure the average for any list of numbers. Here's an example:

```
>>> num_list = [2.45, 1, -10, 55.5, 100.03, 40, -3]
>>> print('The average is ', sum(num_list) / len(num_list))
The average is  26.56857142857143
```

3.9 List Methods: Modifying a List

The largest single group of list methods includes those that modify list data in place, modifying data in place rather than creating a new list.

```
list.append(value)        # Append a value
list.clear()              # Remove all contents
list.extend(iterable)     # Append a series of values
list.insert(index, value) # At index, insert value
list.remove(value)        # Remove first instance of
                          #  value
```

The **append** and **extend** methods have a similar purpose: to add data to the end of a list. The difference is that the **append** method adds a single element to the end of the list in question, whereas the **extend** method appends a series of elements from a collection or iterable.

```
a_list = [1, 2, 3]

a_list.append(4)
a_list.extend([4])        # This has the same effect.

a_list.extend([4, 5, 6])  # Adds 3 elements to the list.
```

The **insert** method has a purpose similar to **append**. However, **insert** places a value at the position indicated by the *index* argument; that is, the method places the new value just before whichever element is specified by the *index* argument.

If the index is out of range, the method places the new value at the end of the list if the index is too high to be in range, and it inserts the new value at the beginning of the list if the index is too low. Here's an example:

```
a_list = [10, 20, 40]   # Missing 30.
a_list.insert(2, 30 )   # At index 2 (third), insert 30.
print(a_list)           # Prints [10, 20, 30, 40]
a_list.insert(100, 33)
print(a_list)           # Prints [10, 20, 30, 40, 33]
a_list.insert(-100, 44)
print(a_list)           # Prints [44, 10, 20, 30, 40, 33]
```

The **remove** method removes the first occurrence of the specified argument from the list. There must be at least one occurrence of this value, or Python raises a **ValueError** exception.

```
my_list = [15, 25, 15, 25]
my_list.remove(25)
print(my_list)          # Prints [15, 15, 25]
```

You may want to use **in**, **not in**, or the **count** method to verify that a value is in a list before attempting to remove it.

Here's a practical example that combines these methods.

In competitive gymnastics, winners are determined by a panel of judges, each of whom submits a score. The highest and lowest scores are thrown out, and then the average of the remaining scores is taken. The following function performs these tasks:

```
def eval_scores(a_list):
    a_list.remove(max(a_list))
    a_list.remove(min(a_list))
    return sum(a_list) / len(a_list)
```

Here's a sample session. Suppose that `the_scores` contains the judges' ratings.

```
the_scores = [8.5, 6.0, 8.5, 8.7, 9.9, 9.0]
```

The `eval_scores` function throws out the low and high values (6.0 and 9.9); then it calculates the average of the rest, producing 8.675.

```
print(eval_scores(the_scores))
```

3.10 *List Methods: Getting Information on Contents*

The next set of list methods returns information about a list. The first two of these, **count** and **index**, do not alter contents and are also supported by tuples.

```
list.count(value)              # Get no. of
                               #   instances.

list.index(value[, beg [, end]])  # Get index of value.
list.pop([index])              # Return and remove
                               #   indexed item: use
                               #   last by default.
```

In this syntax, brackets are not intended literally but instead indicate optional items.

The **count** method returns the number of occurrences of the specified element. It returns the number of matching items at the top level only. Here's an example:

```
yr_list = [1, 2, 1, 1,[3, 4]]
print(yr_list.count(1))        # Prints 3
print(yr_list.count(2))        # Prints 1
print(yr_list.count(3))        # Prints 0
print(yr_list.count([3, 4]))   # Prints 1
```

The **index** method returns the zero-based index of the first occurrence of a specified value. You may optionally specify *start* and *end* indexes; the searching happens in a subrange beginning with the *start* position, up to but not including the *end* position. An exception is raised if the item is not found.

For example, the following call to the **index** method returns 3, signifying the fourth element.

```
beat_list = ['John', 'Paul', 'George', 'Ringo']
print(beat_list.index('Ringo'))    # Print 3.
```

But 3 is also printed if the list is defined as

```
beat_list = ['John', 'Paul', 'George', 'Ringo', 'Ringo']
```

3.11 *List Methods: Reorganizing*

The last two list methods in this chapter modify a list by changing the order of the elements in place.

```
list.sort([key=None] [, reverse=False])
list.reverse()       # Reverse existing order.
```

Each of these methods changes the ordering of all the elements in place. In Python 3.0, all the elements of the list—in the case of either method—must have compatible types, such as all strings or all numbers. The **sort** method places all the elements in lowest-to-highest order by default—or by highest-to-lowest if *reverse* is specified and set to **True**. If the list consists of strings, the strings are placed in alphabetical (code point) order.

The following example program prompts the user for a series of strings, until the user enters an empty string by pressing Enter without any other input. The program then prints the strings in alphabetical order.

```python
def main():
    my_list = []        # Start with empty list
    while True:
        s = input('Enter next name: ')
        if len(s) == 0:
            break
        my_list.append(s)
    my_list.sort()     # Place all elems in order.
    print('Here is the sorted list:')
    for a_word in my_list:
        print(a_word, end=' ')

main()
```

Here's a sample session of this program, showing user input in bold.

```
Enter next name: John
Enter next name: Paul
Enter next name: George
Enter next name: Ringo
Enter next name: Brian
Enter next name:
Here is the sorted list:
Brian George John Paul Ringo
```

The **sort** method has some optional arguments. The first is the **key** argument, which by default is set to **None**. This argument, if specified, is a function (a *callable*) that's run on each element to get that element's *key value*. Those keys are compared to determine the new order. So, for example, if a three-member list produced key values of 15, 1, and 7, they would be sorted as middle-last-first.

For example, suppose you want a list of strings to be ordered according to case-insensitive comparisons. An easy way to do that is to write a function that returns strings that are all uppercase, all lowercase, or converted with the **casefold** method, which essentially performs the same action (converting to all lowercase).

```
def ignore_case(s):
    return s.casefold()

a_list = [ 'john', 'paul', 'George', 'brian', 'Ringo' ]
b_list = a_list[:]
a_list.sort()
b_list.sort(key=ignore_case)
```

If you now print `a_list` and `b_list` in an IDLE session, you get the following results (with user input shown in bold):

```
>>> a_list
['George', 'Ringo', 'brian', 'john', 'paul']
>>> b_list
['brian', 'George', 'john', 'paul', 'Ringo']
```

Notice how `a_list` and `b_list`, which started with identical contents, are sorted. The first was sorted by ordinary, case-sensitive comparisons, in which all uppercase letters are "less than" compared to lowercase letters. The second list was sorted by case-insensitive comparisons, pushing poor old `'Ringo'` to the end.

The second argument is the *reversed* argument, which by default is **False**. If this argument is included and is **True**, elements are sorted in high-to-low order.

The **reverse** method changes the ordering of the list, as you'd expect, but without sorting anything. Here's an example:

```
my_list = ['Brian', 'John', 'Paul', 'George', 'Ringo']
my_list.reverse()     # Reverse elems in place.
for a_word in my_list:
    print(a_word, end=' ')
```

Calling **reverse** has the effect of producing a reverse sort: the last shall be first, and the first shall be last. Now Ringo becomes the frontman.

```
Ringo Paul John George Brian
```

Note ▶ Using the *keys* argument, as just explained, is a good candidate for the use of lambda functions, as explained later in Section 3.14.

◀ Note

3.12 Lists as Stacks: RPN Application

The **append** and **pop** methods have a special use. You can use these methods on a list as if the list were a stack mechanism, a last-in-first-out (LIFO) device.

Figure 3.6 illustrates the operation of a stack, using the visual image of a stack of plates or numbered blocks. Notice how it functions as a last-in-first-out mechanism.

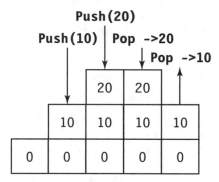

Figure 3.6. Operation of a hypothetical stack

The **push** and **pop** functions on a traditional stack are replaced by the **append** and **pop** methods of a Python list.

The key change that needs to be made—conceptually, at any rate—is to think of operating on the last element to be added to the end of the list, rather than to the literal top of a stack.

This end-of-the-list approach is functionally equivalent to a stack. Figure 3.7 illustrates 10 and 20 being pushed on, and then popped off, a list used as a stack. The result is that the items are popped off in reverse order.

0			
0	10		`stk.append(10)`
0	10	20	`stk.append(20)`
0	10	20	`stk.pop() -> 20`
0	10		`stk.pop() -> 10`

Figure 3.7. Stack operation with a Python list

One of the most useful demonstrations of a stack device is an interpreter for the Reverse Polish Notation (RPN) language. We develop a sophisticated language interpreter by the end of this book, but for now we start with a simple calculator.

The RPN language evaluates operators in a *postfix* language, in which two expressions are followed by an operator. Most languages use an *infix* notation. In postfix, the operands appear first and are followed by the operator. For example, to add 7 and 3, you write the numbers first and *then* write an addition sign (+).

```
7 3 +
```

This adds 7 to 3, which produces 10. Or, to multiply 10 by 5, producing 50, you use this:

```
10 5 *
```

Then—and here is why RPN is so useful—you can put these two expressions together in a clear, unambiguous way, without any need for parentheses:

```
10 5 * 7 3 + /
```

This expression is equivalent to the following standard notation, which produces 5.0:

```
(10 * 5) / (7 + 3)
```

Here's another example:

```
1 2 / 3 4 / +
```

This example translates into (1/2) + (3/4) and therefore produces 1.25. Here's another example:

```
2 4 2 3 7 + + + *
```

This translates into

```
2 * (4 + (2 + (3 + 7)))
```

which evaluates to 32. The beauty of an RPN expression is that parentheses are never needed. The best part is that the interpreter follows only a few simple rules:

▶ If the next item is a number, push it on the stack.

▶ If the next item is an operator, pop the top two items off the stack, apply the operation, and then push the result.

Here's the pseudocode for the application:

Get an input string.
Split it into tokens and store in a list.
For each item in the list,
    If item is an operator,
        Pop stack into op2
        Pop stack into op1
        Carry out operation and push the result onto the stack.
    Else
        Push item onto the stack as a float value.
Pop stack and print the value.

Here's the Python code that implements this program logic:

```python
the_stack = []

def push(v):
    the_stack.append(v)

def pop():
    return the_stack.pop()

def main():
    s = input('Enter RPN string: ')
    a_list = s.split()
    for item in a_list:
        if item in '+-*/':
            op2 = pop()
            op1 = pop()
            if item == '+':
                push(op1 + op2)
            elif item == '-':
                push(op1 - op2)
            elif item == '*':
                push(op1 * op2)
            else:
                push(op1 / op2)
```

```
        else:
             push(float(item))
    print(pop())

 main()
```

This application, although not long, could be more compact. We've included dedicated push and pop functions operating on a global variable, `the_stack`. A few lines could have been saved by using methods of `the_stack` directly.

```
op1 = the_stack.pop()
...
the_stack.append(op1 + op2)   # Push op1 + op2.
```

Revising the example so that it uses these methods directly is left as an exercise. Note also that there is currently no error checking, such as checking to make sure that the stack is at least two elements in length before an operation is carried out. Error checking is also left as an exercise.

Performance Tip ▶ The following tip saves you seven lines of code. Instead of testing for each operator separately, you can use the **eval** function to take a Python command string and execute it. You would then need only one function call to carry out any arithmetic operation in this app.

```
push(eval(str(op1) + item + str(op2)))
```

Be careful, however, because the **eval** function can easily be misused. In this application, it should be called only if the item is one of the four operators: +, *, −, or /.

◀ Performance Tip

3.13 The "reduce" Function

One of the more interesting features of Python lists is the ability to use customized functions to process all the elements of a list. This includes the **map** and **filter** list methods. The **map** method produces a new list by transforming all elements in a source list. The **filter** function produces a new list that is a sublist of the source, based on a specified condition (such as selecting positive numbers only).

However, list comprehension (discussed at length in Section 3.15, "List Comprehension") usually does a better job of what **map** and **filter** do.

But the **functools** package provides a reason to use list-processing mini-functions. To use the **functools** package, begin by importing it.

```
import functools
```

You can then use the **functools.reduce** function to apply a function of your choosing to operate on all the elements of an array.

functools.reduce(*function, list***)**

The action of **reduce** is to apply the specified *function* to each successive pair of neighboring elements in *list*, accumulating the result, passing it along, and finally returning the overall answer. The *function* argument—a callable—must itself take two arguments and produce a result. Assuming that a list (or other sequence) has at least four elements, the effect is as follows.

▶ Take the first two elements as arguments to the function. Remember the result.

▶ Take the result from step 1 and the third element as arguments to the function. Remember this result.

▶ Take the result from step 2 and the fourth element as arguments to the function.

▶ Continue to the end of the list in this manner.

The result is easy to understand in the case of addition and multiplication.

```
import functools

def add_func(a, b):
    return a + b

def mul_func(a, b):
    return a * b

n = 5
a_list = list(range(1, n + 1))

triangle_num = functools.reduce(add_func, a_list)
fact_num     = functools.reduce(mul_func, a_list)
```

If you remember how the **range** function works, then you'll see that a_list is equal to the following sequence, as long as n is set to 5.

```
1, 2, 3, 4, 5
```

The example calculates the *triangle* number of n, which is the sum of all the numbers in the sequence; and the *factorial* number of n, which is the product of all the numbers in the sequence.

```
triangle_num = 1 + 2 + 3 + 4 + 5
fact_num     = 1 * 2 * 3 * 4 * 5
```

Note ▶ This result—producing triangle numbers by calculating a sum—is more easily achieved by calling the **sum** function, as pointed out in Section 3.8, "List Functions."

◀ Note

3

Applying a subtraction function would be a strange thing to do in this example, but legal. It would produce the following.

```
(((1 - 2) - 3) - 4) - 5
```

Likewise, applying a division function would produce the following:

```
(((1 / 2) / 3) / 4) / 5
```

3.14 *Lambda Functions*

When you operate on a list as shown in the previous section, you may want to employ a simple function intended for a one-time use.

That's what a *lambda function* is: a function that's created on the fly, typically for one use. A lambda is a function that has no name, unless you choose to assign it to a variable.

Key Syntax

```
lambda arguments: return_value
```

In this syntax, *arguments* consists of zero or more variable names to be used as arguments to the function, separated by commas if there are more than one.

The result is a callable that cannot be either saved or used directly in an expression accepting a callable. Here's an example of saving a lambda by giving it a name:

```
my_f = lambda x, y: x + y
```

Given this assignment, which makes my_f a name for this minifunction, the name can now be used as a callable. Here's an example:

```
sum1 = my_f(3, 7)
print(sum1)          # Print 10.
sum2 = my_f(10, 15)
print(sum2)          # Print 25.
```

But this usage, while interesting to note, is not usually how a lambda is used. A more practical use is with the **reduce** function. For example, here's how to calculate the triangle number for 5:

```
t5 = functools.reduce(lambda x, y: x + y, [1,2,3,4,5])
```

Here's how to calculate the factorial of 5:

```
f5 = functools.reduce(lambda x, y: x * y, [1,2,3,4,5])
```

Programs create data dynamically, at run time, and assign names to data objects if you want to refer to them again. The same thing happens with functions (callables); they are created at run time and are either assigned names—if you want to refer to them again—or used anonymously, as in the last two examples.

3.15 List Comprehension

One of the most important features Python introduced with version 2.0 is *list comprehension*. It provides a compact way of using **for** syntax to generate a series of values from a list. It can also be applied to dictionaries, sets, and other collections.

The simplest illustration of list comprehension copies all the elements in a member-by-member copy.

The following statement uses slicing to create a copy:

```
b_list = a_list[:]
```

Here's another way to get a member-by-member copy:

```
b_list = []
for i in a_list:
    b_list.append(i)
```

Code like this is so common that Python 2.0 introduced a compact way of doing the same thing. (I've used spacing to make it easier to understand.)

```
b_list = [i    for i in a_list]
```

This example shows the two parts of the list-comprehension expression clearly, but once you understand it, you'll probably want to write it without the extra spaces.

```
b_list = [i for i in a_list]
```

Here's a variation. Suppose you want to create a list that contains the squares of each of the elements in a_list:

```
b_list = [ ]
for i in a_list:
    b_list.append(i * i)
```

If a_list contains [1, 2, 3], then the result of these statements is to create a list containing [1, 4, 9] and assign this list to the variable b_list. The corresponding list-comprehension expression in this case is shown here:

```
b_list = [i * i    for i in a_list]
```

Perhaps by now you can see the pattern. In this second example, the elements inside the square brackets can be broken down as follows:

▶ The *value* expression i * i, which is the value to be generated and placed in the new list; i * i specifies that the square of each element should be put in the new list.

▶ The **for** statement header, for i in a_list, supplies the series of values to operate on. Therefore, the source of the values is a_list.

Figure 3.8 illustrates this list-comprehension syntax.

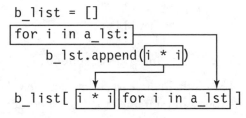

Figure 3.8. List comprehension

Syntactically, list compression is a way of creating a list by using a value expression, followed immediately by a **for** statement header that supplies a sequence of data. Remember, however, that the **for** statement header is used in the list-comprehension expression without its terminating colon (:).

```
[ value   for_statement_header ]
```

The *for_statement_header* can be taken from nested loops to any level. Here is an example involving two such loops:

```
mult_list = [ ]
for i in range(3):
    for j in range(3):
        mult_list.append(i * j)
```

This nested loop produces the list [0, 0, 0, 0, 1, 2, 0, 2, 4]. This loop is equivalent to the following list-comprehension statement:

```
mult_list = [i * j  for i in range(3) for j in range(3)]
```

In this case, i * j is the *value* produced by each iteration of the loops, and the rest of the line consists of the headers of the nested loops.

List comprehension has another, optional, feature. Syntactically, it's placed at the end of the expression but before the closing square bracket.

[*value   for_statement_header   if_expression*]

As a simple example, suppose you want to select only the elements of a list that are positive. If you wrote out the loop by hand, you could write it this way:

```
my_list = [10, -10, -1, 12, -500, 13, 15, -3]

new_list = []
for i in my_list:
    if i > 0:
        new_list.append(i)
```

The result, in this case, is to place the values [10, 12, 13, 15] in new_list. The following statement, using list comprehension, does the same thing:

```
new_list = [i    for i in my_list   if i > 0 ]
```

The list-comprehension statement on the right, within the square brackets, breaks down into three pieces in this case:

▶ The *value* expression i; takes a value directly from the list.

▶ The **for** statement header, for i in my_list, supplies the sequence of values to operate on.

▶ Finally, the **if** condition, if i > 0, selects which items get included.

Again, once you understand how this works, it's customary to write it without the extra spaces I used for clarity.

```
new_list = [i for i in my_list if i > 0 ]
```

The following example, in contrast, creates a list consisting only of negative values.

```
my_list = [1, 2, -10, -500, 33, 21, -1]
neg_list = [i for i in my_list if i < 0 ]
```

The result in this case is to produce the following list and give it the name neg_list:

```
[-10, -500, -1]
```

3.16 Dictionary and Set Comprehension

The principles of list comprehension extend to sets and dictionaries. It's easiest to see this with sets, because a set is a simple collection of values in which duplicates are ignored and order doesn't matter.

For example, suppose we want to get only the positive values from a_list and place them in a set rather than a list. You could write this using an ordinary loop:

```
a_list = [5, 5, 5, -20, 2, -1, 2]
my_set = set( )
for i in a_list:
    if i > 0:
        my_set.add(i)
```

You can also do this through set comprehension, by using set braces ("curly braces") rather than square brackets.

```
my_set = {i for i in a_list if i > 0}
```

The result, in either case, is to create the set {5, 2} and assign it to the variable my_set. There are no duplicate values. The elimination of duplicates happens automatically because you're producing a set.

Note here that set comprehension is being performed (creating a set), because curly braces ("set braces") are used instead of square brackets, which would have created a list.

Alternatively, suppose you want to produce the same set, but have it consist of the *squares* of positive values from a_list, resulting in {25, 4}. In that case, you could use the following statement:

```
my_set = {i * i  for i in a_list if i > 0}
```

Dictionary comprehension is a little more complicated, because in order to work, it's necessary to create a loop that generates key-value pairs, using this syntax:

```
key : value
```

Suppose you have a list of tuples that you'd like to be the basis for a data dictionary.

```
vals_list = [ ('pi', 3.14), ('phi', 1.618) ]
```

A dictionary could be created as follows:

```
my_dict = { i[0]: i[1] for i in vals_list }
```

Note the use of the colon (:) in the key-value expression, i[0] : i[1]. You can verify that a dictionary was successfully produced by referring to or printing the following expression, which should produce the number 3.14:

```
my_dict['pi']   # Produces 3.14.
```

Here's another example, which combines data from two lists into a dictionary. It assumes that these two lists are the same length.

```
keys = ['Bob', 'Carol', 'Ted', 'Alice' ]
vals = [4.0, 4.0, 3.75, 3.9]
grade_dict = { keys[i]: vals[i] for i in range(len(keys)) }
```

This example creates a dictionary initialized as follows:

```
grade_dict = { 'Bob':4.0, 'Carol':4.0, 'Ted':3.75,
    'Alice':3.9 }
```

Performance Tip ▶ You can improve the performance of the code in this last example by using the built-in **zip** function to merge the lists. The comprehension then is as follows:

```
grade_dict = { key: val for key, val in zip(keys, vals)}
```

◀ Performance Tip

In summary, the following syntax produces a set:

```
{ value   for_statement_header   optional_if_cond }
```

The following syntax produces a dictionary:

```
{ key : value   for_statement_header   optional_if_cond }
```

One of the cleverest ways to use dictionary comprehension is to invert a dictionary. For example, you might want to take a phone book, in which a name is used to look up a number, and invert it so that you can use a number to look up a name.

```
idict = {v : k for k, v in phone_dict.items() }
```

The **items** method of data dictionaries produces a list of k, v pairs, in which k is a key and v is a value. For each such pair, the value expression v:k inverts the key-value relationship in producing the new dictionary, idict.

3.17 Passing Arguments Through a List

Argument values in Python are not exactly passed either by reference or by value. Instead, Python arguments are passed as data-dictionary entries, in which an argument name is associated with the value at the time of the function call.

In practical terms, this means that you cannot simply give a variable name as an argument and write a function that modifies that variable.

```
double_it(n)
```

Let's assume that when double_it executes, the value passed to n is 10. The function receives the key-value pair n:10. But new assignments to n—treated as if it were a local variable—have no effect on the value of n outside the function, because such assignments would break the connection between n and the data.

You can, however, pass a list to a function and write the function in such a way that the function modifies some or all of the values in that list. This is possible because lists (in contrast to strings and tuples) are mutable. Here's an example:

```
def set_list_vals(list_arg):
    list_arg[0] = 100
    list_arg[1] = 200
    list_arg[2] = 150
```

```
a_list = [0, 0, 0]
set_list_vals(a_list)
print(a_list)              # Prints [100, 200, 150]
```

This approach works because the values of the list are changed in place, without creating a new list and requiring variable reassignment. But the following example fails to change the list passed to it.

```
def set_list_vals(list_arg):
    list_arg = [100, 200, 150]

a_list = [0, 0, 0]
set_list_vals(a_list)
print(a_list)              # Prints [0, 0, 0]
```

With this approach, the values of the list, a_list, were not changed after the function returned. What happened?

The answer is that the list argument, list_arg, was reassigned to refer to a completely new list. The association between the variable list_arg and the original data, [0, 0, 0], was broken.

However, slicing and indexing are different. Assigning into an indexed item or a slice of a list does not change what the name refers to; it still refers to the same list, but the first element of that list is modified.

```
my_list[0] = new_data    # This really changes list data.
```

3.18 Multidimensional Lists

List elements can themselves be lists. So you can write code like the following:

```
weird_list = [ [1, 2, 3], 'John', 'George' ]
```

But much more common is the true *multidimensional list*, or *matrix*. The following assignment creates a 3 × 3 list and assigns it to the variable mat:

```
mat = [[10, 11, 21], [20, 21, 22], [25, 15, 15]]
```

The right side of this assignment creates three rows, and each has three values:

```
[10, 11, 12],
[20, 21, 22],
[25, 15, 15]
```

You can index an individual element within this two-dimensional list as follows:

```
list_name[row_index][column_index]
```

As usual, indexes in Python run from 0 to N–1, where N is the length of the dimension. You can use negative indexes, as usual. Therefore, `mat[1][2]` (second row, third column) produces the value 22.

Note ▶ This chapter describes how to use the core Python language to create multidimensional lists. Chapter 12 describes the use of the **numpy** package, which enables the use of highly optimized routines for manipulating multidimensional arrays, especially arrays (or matrixes) of numbers.

◀ Note

3.18.1 Unbalanced Matrixes

Although you'll probably most often create matrixes that are rectangular, you can use Python to create *unbalanced matrixes*. Here's an example:

```
weird_mat = [[1, 2, 3, 4], [0, 5], [9, 8, 3]]
```

Program code can determine the exact size and shape of a Python matrix through inspection. Taking the length of such a list (in this case, a matrix) gets the number of elements at the top level. Here's an example:

```
len(weird_mat)      # Equal to 3.
```

This result tells you that there are three rows. You can then get the length of each of these rows, within the matrix, as follows:

```
len(weird_mat[0])   # Equal to 4.
len(weird_mat[1])   # Equal to 2.
len(weird_mat[2])   # Equal to 3.
```

This process can be repeated to any depth.

3.18.2 Creating Arbitrarily Large Matrixes

Creating an arbitrarily large multidimensional list is a challenge in Python. Fortunately, this section provides the simplest solution (other than using the dedicated **numpy** package described in Chapter 12).

Remember, Python has no concept of data declaration. Therefore, Python matrixes cannot be declared; they must be built.

It might seem that list multiplication would solve the problem. It does, in the case of one-dimensional lists.

```
big_list = [0] * 100    # Create a list of 100 elements
                        #  each initialized to 0.
```

This works so well, you might be tempted to just generalize to a second dimension.

```
mat = [[0] * 100] * 200
```

But although this statement is legal, it doesn't do what you want. The inner expression, [0] * 100, creates a list of 100 elements. But the code repeats that data 200 times—not by creating 200 separate rows but instead by creating 200 *references to the same row*.

The effect is to create 200 rows that aren't separate. This is a shallow copy; you get 200 redundant references to the same row. This is frustrating. The way around it is to append each of the 200 rows one at a time, which you can do in a **for** loop:

```
mat = [ ]
for i in range(200):
    mat.append([0] * 100)
```

In this example, `mat` starts out as an empty list, just like any other.

Each time through the loop, a row containing 100 zeros is appended. After this loop is executed, `mat` will refer to a true two-dimensional matrix made up of 20,000 fully independent cells. It can then be indexed as high as `mat[199]` `[99]`. Here's an example:

```
mat[150][87] = 3.141592
```

As with other **for** loops that append data to a list, the previous example is a great candidate for list comprehension.

```
mat = [ [0] * 100  for i in range(200) ]
```

The expression [0] * 100 is the *value* part of this list-comprehension expression; it specifies a one-dimensional list (or "row") that consists of 100 elements, each set to 0. This expression should not be placed in an additional pair of brackets, by the way, or the effect would be to create an extra, and unnecessary, level of indexing.

The expression `for i in range(200)` causes Python to create, and append, such a row . . . 200 times.

```
matrix_name = [[init] * ncols for var in range(nrows)]
```

In this syntax display, *init* is the initial value you want to assign each element to, and *ncols* and *nrows* are the number of columns and rows, respectively.

Because *var* isn't important and need not be used again, you can replace it with the trivial name "_" (just an underscore), which is basically a placeholder. For example, to declare a 30 × 25 matrix, you would use this statement:

```
mat2 = [ [0] * 25 for _ in range(30) ]
```

You can use this technique to build matrixes of even higher dimensions, each time adding a level of list comprehension. Here is a 30 × 20 × 25 three-dimensional list:

```
mat2 = [[ [0] * 25 for _ in range(20) ]
                   for _ in range(30) ]
```

And here is a 10 × 10 × 10 × 10 four-dimensional list:

```
mat2 = [[[ [0] * 10 for _ in range(10) ]
                    for _ in range(10) ]
                    for _ in range(10) ]
```

You can build matrixes of higher dimensions still, but remember that as dimensions increase, things get bigger—fast!

Chapter 3   *Summary*

This chapter has demonstrated just how powerful Python lists are. Many of these same abilities are realized in functions, such as **len**, **count**, and **index**, which apply to other collection classes as well, including strings and tuples. However, because lists are mutable, there are some list capabilities not supported by those other types, such as **sort** and **reverse**, which alter list data "in place."

This chapter also introduced some exotic abilities, such as the use of **functools** and lambda functions. It also explained techniques for creating multidimensional lists, an ability that Chapter 12 provides efficient and superior alternatives to; still, it's useful to know how to create multidimensional lists using the core language.

Chapter 3   *Review Questions*

1 Can you write a program, or a function, that uses both positive and negative indexing? Is there any penalty for doing so?

2 What's the most efficient way of creating a Python list that has 1,000 elements to start with? Assume every element should be initialized to the same value.

3 How do you use slicing to get every other element of a list, while ignoring the rest? (For example, you want to create a new list that has the first, third, fifth, seventh, and so on element.)

4 Describe some of the differences between indexing and slicing.

5 What happens when one of the indexes used in a slicing expression is out of range?

6 If you pass a list to a function, and if you want the function to be able to change the values of the list—so that the list is different after the function returns—what action should you avoid?

7 What is an unbalanced matrix?

8 Why does the creation of arbitrarily large matrixes require the use of either list comprehension or a loop?

Chapter 3   *Suggested Problems*

1 Use the **reduce** list-processing function to help get the average of a randomly chosen list of numbers. The correct answer should be no more than one or two lines of code. Then calculate the deviation of each element by subtracting each element from the average (also called the "mean") and squaring each result. Finally, return the resulting list.

2 Write a program that enables users to enter a list of numbers, in which the list is any length they want. Then find the *median* value, not the average or mean. The median value is the value that has just as many greater values as lesser values, in comparison to the rest of the list. If you order the entire list from lowest to highest, and if there are an even number of elements, then the median would be the average of the two values in the middle.

4 Shortcuts, Command Line, and Packages

Master crafters need many things, but, above all, they need to master the tools of the profession. This chapter introduces tools that, even if you're a fairly experienced Python programmer, you may not have yet learned. These tools will make you more productive as well as increase the efficiency of your programs.

So get ready to learn some new tips and tricks.

4.1 Overview

Python is unusually gifted with shortcuts and time-saving programming techniques. This chapter begins with a discussion of twenty-two of these techniques.

Another thing you can do to speed up certain programs is to take advantage of the many packages that are available with Python. Some of these—such as **re** (regular expressions), **system**, **random**, and **math**—come with the standard Python download, and all you have to do is to include an **import** statement. Other packages can be downloaded quite easily with the right tools.

4.2 Twenty-Two Programming Shortcuts

This section lists the most common techniques for shortening and tightening your Python code. Most of these are new in the book, although a few of them have been introduced before and are presented in greater depth here.

▶ Use Python line continuation as needed.

▶ Use **for** loops intelligently.

▶ Understand combined operator assignment (+= etc.).

▶ Use multiple assignment.

▶ Use tuple assignment.

▶ Use advanced tuple assignment.

▶ Use list and string "multiplication."

▶ Return multiple values.

▶ Use loops and the **else** keyword.

▶ Take advantage of Booleans and **not**.

▶ Treat strings as lists of characters.

▶ Eliminate characters by using **replace**.

▶ Don't write unnecessary loops.

▶ Use chained comparisons.

▶ Simulate "switch" with a table of functions.

▶ Use the **is** operator correctly.

▶ Use one-line **for** loops.

▶ Squeeze multiple statements onto a line.

▶ Write one-line if/then/else statements.

▶ Create Enum values with **range**.

▶ Reduce the inefficiency of the **print** function within IDLE.

▶ Place underscores inside large numbers.

Let's look at these ideas in detail.

4.2.1 Use Python Line Continuation as Needed

In Python, the normal statement terminator is just the end of a physical line (although note the exceptions in Section 3.18). This makes programming easier, because you can naturally assume that statements are one per line.

But what if you need to write a statement longer than one physical line? This dilemma can crop up in a number of ways. For example, you might have a string to print that you can't fit on one line. You could use literal quotations, but line wraps, in that case, are translated as newlines—something you might not want. The solution, first of all, is to recognize that literal strings positioned next to other literal strings are automatically concatenated.

```
>>> my_str = 'I am Hen-er-y the Eighth,' ' I am!'
>>> print(my_str)
I am Hen-er-y the Eighth, I am!
```

If these substrings are too long to put on a single physical line, you have a couple of choices. One is to use the line-continuation character, which is a backslash (\).

```
my_str = 'I am Hen-er-y the Eighth,' \
' I am!'
```

Another technique is to observe that any open—and so far unmatched—parenthesis, square bracket, or brace automatically causes continuation onto the next physical line. Consequently, you can enter as long a statement as you want—and you can enter a string of any length you want—without necessarily inserting newlines.

```
my_str = ('I am Hen-er-y the Eighth, '
'I am! I am not just any Henry VIII, '
'I really am!')
```

This statement places all this text in one string. You can likewise use open parentheses with other kinds of statements.

```
length_of_hypotenuse = ( (side1 * side1 + side2 * side2)
                         ** 0.5 )
```

A statement is not considered complete until all open parentheses [**(**] have been matched by closing parentheses [**)**]. The same is true for braces and square brackets. As a result, this statement will automatically continue to the next physical line.

4.2.2 Use "for" Loops Intelligently

If you come from the C/C++ world, you may tend to overuse the **range** function to print members of a list. Here's an example of the C way of writing a **for** loop, using **range** and an indexing operation.

```
beat_list = ['John', 'Paul', 'George', 'Ringo']
for i in range(len(beat_list)):
    print(beat_list[i])
```

If you ever write code like this, you should try to break the habit as soon as you can. It's better to print the contents of a list or iterator directly.

```
beat_list = ['John', 'Paul', 'George', 'Ringo']
for guy in beat_list:
    print(guy)
```

Even if you need access to a loop variable, it's better to use the **enumerate** function to generate such numbers. Here's an example:

```
beat_list = ['John', 'Paul', 'George', 'Ringo']
for i, name in enumerate(beat_list, 1):
    print(i, '. ', name, sep='')
```

This prints

```
1. John
2. Paul
3. George
4. Ringo
```

There are, of course, some cases in which it's necessary to use indexing. That happens most often when you are trying to change the contents of a list in place.

4.2.3   Understand Combined Operator Assignment (+= etc.)

The combined operator-assignment operators are introduced in Chapter 1 and so are reviewed only briefly here. Remember that assignment (=) can be combined with any of the following operators: **+, -, /, //, %, **, &, ^, |, <<, >>**.

The operators **&, |,** and **^** are bitwise "and," "or," and "exclusive or," respectively. The operators **<<** and **>>** perform bit shifts to the left and to the right.

This section covers some finer points of operator-assignment usage. First, any assignment operator has low precedence and is carried out last.

Second, an assignment operator may or may not be in place, depending on whether the type operated on is mutable. *In place* refers to operations that work on existing data in memory rather than creating a completely new object. Such operations are faster and more efficient.

Integers, floating-point numbers, and strings are immutable. Assignment operators, used with these types, do not cause in-place assignment; they instead must produce a completely new object, which is reassigned to the variable. Here's an example:

```
s1 = s2 = 'A string.'
s1 += '...with more stuff!'
print('s1:', s1)
print('s2:', s2)
```

The **print** function, in this case, produces the following output:

```
s1: A string...with more stuff!
s2: A string.
```

When s1 was assigned a new value, it did not change the string data in place; it assigned a whole new string to s1. But s2 is a name that still refers to the original string data. This is why s1 and s2 now contain different strings.

But lists are mutable, and therefore changes to lists can occur in place.

```
a_list = b_list = [10, 20]
a_list += [30, 40]
print('a_list:', a_list)
print('b_list:', b_list)
```

This code prints

```
a_list: [10, 20, 30, 40]
b_list: [10, 20, 30, 40]
```

In this case, the change was made to the list in place, so there was no need to create a new list and reassign that list to the variable. Therefore, a_list was not assigned to a new list, and b_list, a variable that refers to the same data in memory, reflects the change as well.

In-place operations are almost always more efficient. In the case of lists, Python reserves some extra space to grow when allocating a list in memory, and that in turns permits **append** operations, as well as **+=**, to efficiently grow lists. However, occasionally lists exceed the reserved space and must be moved. Such memory management is seamless and has little or no impact on program behavior.

Non-in-place operations are less efficient, because a new object must be created. That's why it's advisable to use the **join** method to grow large strings rather than use the **+=** operator, especially if performance is important. Here's an example using the **join** method to create a list and join 26 characters together.

```
str_list = []
n = ord('a')
for i in range(n, n + 26):
    str_list += chr(i)
alphabet_str = ''.join(str_list)
```

Figures 4.1 and 4.2 illustrate the difference between in-place operations and non-in-place operations. In Figure 4.1, string data seems to be appended onto an existing string, but what the operation really does is to create a new string and then assign it to the variable—which now refers to a different place in memory.

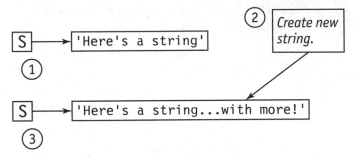

Figure 4.1. Appending to a string (not in-place)

But in Figure 4.2, list data is appended onto an existing list without the need to create a new list and reassign the variable.

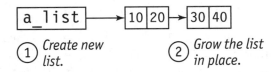

Figure 4.2. Appending to a list (in-place)

Here's a summary:

▶ Combined assignment operators such as **+=** cause in-place changes to data if the object is mutable (such as a list); otherwise, a whole new object is assigned to the variable on the left.

▶ In-place operations are faster and use space more efficiently, because they do not force creation of a new object. In the case of lists, Python usually allocates extra space so that the list can be grown more efficiently at run time.

4.2.4 Use Multiple Assignment

Multiple assignment is one of the most commonly used coding shortcuts in Python. You can, for example, create five different variables at once, assigning them all the same value—in this case, 0:

```
a = b = c = d = e = 0
```

Consequently, the following returns **True**:

```
a is b
```

This statement would no longer return **True** if either of these variables was later assigned to a different object.

Even though this coding technique may look like it is borrowed from C and C++, you should not assume that Python follows C syntax in most respects. Assignment in Python is a statement and not an expression, as it is in C.

4.2.5 Use Tuple Assignment

Multiple assignment is useful when you want to assign a group of variables the same initial value.

But what if you want to assign different values to different variables? For example, suppose you want to assign 1 to a, and 0 to b. The obvious way to do that is to use the following statements:

```
a = 1
b = 0
```

But through *tuple assignment,* you can combine these into a single statement.

```
a, b = 1, 0
```

In this form of assignment, you have a series of values on one side of the equals sign (=) and another on the right. They must match in number, with one exception: You can assign a tuple of any size to a single variable (which itself now represents a tuple as a result of this operation).

```
a = 4, 8, 12    # a is now a tuple containing three values.
```

Tuple assignment can be used to write some passages of code more compactly. Consider how compact a Fibonacci-generating function can be in Python.

```
def fibo(n):
    a, b = 1, 0
    while a <= n:
        print(a, end=' ')
        a, b = a + b, a
```

In the last statement, the variable a gets a new value: a + b; the variable b gets a new value—namely, the old value of a.

Most programming languages have no way to set a and b simultaneously. Setting the value of a changes what gets put into b, and vice versa. So normally, a temporary variable would be required. You could do that in Python, if you wanted to:

```
temp = a      # Preserve old value of a
a = a + b     # Set new value of a
b = temp      # Set b to old value of a
```

But with tuple assignment, there's no need for a temporary variable.

```
a, b = a + b, a
```

Here's an even simpler example of tuple assignment. Sometimes, it's useful to swap two values.

```
x, y = 1, 25
print(x, y)    # prints 1 25
x, y = y, x
print(x, y)    # prints 25 1
```

The interesting part of this example is the statement that performs the swap:

```
x, y = y, x
```

In another language, such an action would require three separate statements. But Python does not require this, because—as just shown—it can do the swap all at once. Here is what another language would require you to do:

```
temp = x
x = y
y = temp
```

4.2.6 Use Advanced Tuple Assignment

Tuple assignment has some refined features. For example, you can unpack a tuple to assign to multiple variables, as in the following example.

```
tup = 10, 20, 30
a, b, c = tup
print(a, b, c)    # Produces 10, 20, 30
```

It's important that the number of input variables on the left matches the size of the tuple on the right. The following statement would produce a runtime error.

```
tup = 10, 20, 30
a, b = tup    # Error: too many values to unpack
```

Another technique that's occasionally useful is creating a tuple that has one element. That would be easy to do with lists.

```
my_list = [3]
```

This is a list with one element, 3. But the same approach won't work with tuples.

```
my_tup = (3)
print(type(my_tup))
```

This **print** statement shows that my_tup, in this case, produced a simple integer.

```
<class 'int'>
```

This is not what was wanted in this case. The parentheses were treated as a no-op, as would any number of enclosing parentheses. But the following statement produces a tuple with one element, although, to be fair, a tuple with just one element isn't used very often.

```
my_tup = (3,)      # Assign tuple with one member, 3.
```

The use of an asterisk (*) provides a good deal of additional flexibility with tuple assignment. You can use it to split off parts of a tuple and have one (and only one) variable that becomes the default target for the remaining elements, which are then put into a list. Some examples should make this clear.

```
a, *b = 2, 4, 6, 8
```

In this example, a gets the value 2, and b is assigned to a list:

```
2
[4, 6, 8]
```

You can place the asterisk next to any variable on the left, but in no case more than one. The variable modified with the asterisk is assigned a list of whatever elements are left over. Here's an example:

```
a, *b, c = 10, 20, 30, 40, 50
```

In this case, a and c refer to 10 and 50, respectively, after this statement is executed, and b is assigned the list [20, 30, 40].

You can, of course, place the asterisk next to a variable at the end.

```
big, bigger, *many = 100, 200, 300, 400, 500, 600
```

Printing these variables produces the following:

```
>>> print(big, bigger, many, sep='\n')
100
200
[300, 400, 500, 600]
```

4.2.7   Use List and String "Multiplication"

Serious programs often deal with large data sets—for example, a collection of 10,000 integers all initialized to 0. In languages such as C and Java, the way to do this is to first declare an array with a large dimension.

Because there are no data declarations in Python, the only way to create a large list is to construct it on the right side of an assignment. But constructing a super-long list by hand is impractical. Imagine trying to construct a super-long list this way:

```
my_list = [0, 0, 0, 0, 0, 0, 0, 0...]
```

As you can imagine, entering 10,000 zeros into program code would be very time-consuming! And it would make your hands ache.

Applying the multiplication operator provides a more practical solution:

```
my_list = [0] * 10000
```

This example creates a list of 10,000 integers, all initialized to 0.

Such operations are well optimized in Python, so that even in the interactive development environment (IDLE), such interactions are handled quickly.

```
>>> my_list = [0] * 10000
>>> len(my_list)
10000
```

Note that the integer may be either the left or the right operand in such an expression.

```
>>> my_list = 1999 * [12]
>>> len(my_list)
1999
```

You can also "multiply" longer lists. For example, the following list is 300 elements long. It consists of the numbers 1, 2, 3, repeated over and over.

```
>>> trip_list = [1, 2, 3] * 100
>>> len(trip_list)
300
```

The multiplication sign (*) does not work with dictionaries and sets, which require unique keys. But it does work with the string class (**str**); for example, you can create a string consisting of 40 underscores, which you might use for display purposes:

```
divider_str = '_' * 40
```

Printing out this string produces the following:

```
_____
```

4.2.8 Return Multiple Values

You can't pass a simple variable to a Python function, change the value inside the function, and expect the original variable to reflect the change. Here's an example:

```
def double_me(n):
    n *= 2


a = 10
double_me(a)
print(a)          # Value of a did not get doubled!!
```

When n is assigned a new value, the association is broken between that variable and the value that was passed. In effect, n is a local variable that is now associated with a different place in memory. The variable passed to the function is unaffected.

But you can always use a return value this way:

```
def double_me(n):
    return n * 2


a = 10
a = double_me(a)
print(a)
```

Therefore, to get an *out* parameter, just return a value. But what if you want more than one out parameter?

In Python, you can return as many values as you want. For example, the following function performs the quadratic equation by returning two values.

```
def quad(a, b, c):
    determin = (b * b - 4 * a * c) ** .5
    x1 = (-b + determin) / (2 * a)
```

```
        x2 = (-b - determin) / (2 * a)
        return x1, x2
```

This function has three input arguments and two output variables. In calling the function, it's important to receive both arguments:

```
    x1, x2 = quad(1, -1, -1)
```

If you return multiple values to a single variable in this case, that variable will store the values as a tuple. Here's an example:

```
>>> x = quad(1, -1, -1)
>>> x
(1.618033988749895, -0.6180339887498949)
```

Note that this feature—returning multiple values—is actually an application of the use of tuples in Python.

4.2.9 Use Loops and the "else" Keyword

The **else** keyword is most frequently used in combination with the **if** keyword. But in Python, it can also be used with **try-except** syntax and with loops.

With loops, the **else** clause is executed if the loop has completed without an early exit, such as **break**. This feature applies to both **while** loops and **for** loops.

The following example tries to find an even divisor of n, up to and including the limit, **max**. If no such divisor is found, it reports that fact.

```
    def find_divisor(n, max):
        for i in range(2, max + 1):
            if n % i == 0:
                print(i, 'divides evenly into', n)
                break
        else:
            print('No divisor found')
```

Here's an example:

```
>>> find_divisor(49, 6)
No divisor found
>>> find_divisor(49, 7)
7 divides evenly into 49
```

4.2.10 Take Advantage of Boolean Values and "not"

Every object in Python evaluates to **True** or **False**. For example, every empty collection in Python evaluates to **False** if tested as a Boolean value; so does the special value **None**. Here's one way of testing a string for being length zero:

```
if len(my_str) == 0:
    break
```

However, you can instead test for an input string this way:

```
if not s:
    break
```

Here are the general guidelines for Boolean conversions.

▶ Nonempty collections and nonempty strings evaluate as **True**; so do nonzero numeric values.

▶ Zero-length collections and zero-length strings evaluate to **False**; so does any number equal to 0, as well as the special value **None**.

4.2.11 Treat Strings as Lists of Characters

When you're doing complicated operations on individual characters and building a string, it's sometimes more efficient to build a list of characters (each being a string of length 1) and use list comprehension plus **join** to put it all together.

For example, to test whether a string is a palindrome, it's useful to omit all punctuation and space characters and convert the rest of the string to either all-uppercase or all-lowercase. List comprehension does this efficiently.

```
test_str = input('Enter test string: ')
a_list = [c.upper() for c in test_str if c.isalnum()]
print(a_list == a_list[::-1])
```

The second line in this example uses list comprehension, which was introduced in Section 3.15, "List Comprehension."

The third line in this example uses slicing to get the reverse of the list. Now we can test whether test_str is a palindrome by comparing it to its own reverse. These three lines of code have to be the shortest possible program for testing whether a string is a palindrome. Talk about compaction!

```
Enter test string: A man, a plan, a canal, Panama!
True
```

4.2.12 Eliminate Characters by Using "replace"

To quickly remove all instances of a particular character from a string, use **replace** and specify the empty string as the replacement.

For example, a code sample in Chapter 10 asks users to enter strings that represent fractions, such as "1/2". But if the user puts extra spaces in, as in "1 / 2", this could cause a problem. Here's some code that takes an input string, s, and quickly rids it of all spaces wherever they are found (so it goes beyond stripping):

```
s = s.replace(' ', '')
```

Using similar code, you can quickly get rid of all offending characters or substrings in the same way—but only one at a time. Suppose, however, that you want to get rid of all vowels in one pass. List comprehension, in that case, comes to your aid.

```
a_list = [c for c in s if c not in 'aeiou']
s = ''.join(a_list)
```

4.2.13 Don't Write Unnecessary Loops

Make sure that you don't overlook all of Python's built-in abilities, especially when you're working with lists and strings. With most computer languages, you'd probably have to write a loop to get the sum of all the numbers in a list. But Python performs summation directly. For example, the following function calculates $1 + 2 + 3 ... + N$:

```
def calc_triangle_num(n):
    return sum(range(n+1))
```

Another way to use the **sum** function is to quickly get the average (the mean) of any list of numbers.

```
def get_avg(a_list):
    return sum(a_list) / len(a_list)
```

4.2.14 Use Chained Comparisons (n < x < m)

This is a slick little shortcut that can save you a bit of work now and then, as well as making your code more readable.

It's common to write **if** conditions such as the following:

```
if 0 < x and x < 100:
    print('x is in range.')
```

But in this case, you can save a few keystrokes by instead using this:

```
if 0 < x < 100:         # Use 'chained' comparisons.
    print('x is in range.')
```

This ability potentially goes further. You can chain together any number of comparisons, and you can include any of the standard comparison operators, including **==**, **<**, **<=**, **>**, and **>=**. The arrows don't even have to point in the same direction or even be combined in any order! So you can do things like this:

```
a, b, c = 5, 10, 15
if 0 < a <= c > b > 1:
    print('All these comparisons are true!')
    print('c is equal or greater than all the rest!')
```

You can even use this technique to test a series of variables for equality. Here's an example:

```
a = b = c = d = e = 100
if a == b == c == d == e:
    print('All the variables are equal to each other.')
```

For larger data sets, there are ways to achieve these results more efficiently. Any list, no matter how large, can be tested to see whether all the elements are equal this way:

```
if min(a_list) == max(a_list):
    print('All the elements are equal to each other.')
```

However, when you just want to test a few variables for equality or perform a combination of comparisons on a single line, the techniques shown in this section are a nice convenience with Python. Yay, Python!

4.2.15 Simulate "switch" with a Table of Functions

This next technique is nice because it can potentially save a number of lines of code.

Section 15.12 offers the user a menu of choices, prompts for an integer, and then uses that integer to decide which of several functions to call. The obvious way to implement this logic is with a series of **if**/**elif** statements, because Python has no "switch" statement.

```
if n == 1:
    do_plot(stockdf)
elif n == 2:
    do_highlow_plot(stockdf)
```

```
    elif n == 3:
        do_volume_subplot(stockdf)
    elif n == 4:
        do_movingavg_plot(stockdf)
```

Code like this is verbose. It will work, but it's longer than it needs to be. But Python functions are objects, and they can be placed in a list just like any other kind of objects. You can therefore get a reference to one of the functions and call it.

```
    fn = [do_plot, do_highlow_plot, do_volume_subplot,
          do_movingavg_plot][n-1]
    fn(stockdf)                     # Call the function
```

For example, n-1 is evaluated, and if that value is 0 (that is, n is equal to 1), the first function listed, do_plot, is executed.

This code creates a compact version of a C++ switch statement by calling a different function depending on the value of n. (By the way, the value 0 is excluded in this case, because that value is used to exit.)

You can create a more flexible control structure by using a dictionary combined with functions. For example, suppose that "load," "save," "update," and "exit" are all menu functions. We might implement the equivalent of a switch statement this way:

```
    menu_dict = {'load':load_fn, 'save':save_fn,
                 'exit':exit_fn, 'update':update_fn}
    (menu_dict[selector])()        # Call the function
```

Now the appropriate function will be called, depending on the string contained in selector, which presumably contains 'load', 'save', 'update', or 'exit'.

4.2.16 Use the "is" Operator Correctly

Python supports both a test-for-equality operator (==) and an **is** operator. These tests sometimes return the same result, and sometimes they don't. If two strings have the same value, a test for equality always produces **True**.

```
    a = 'cat'
    b = 'cat'
    a == b    # This must produce True.
```

But the **is** operator isn't guaranteed to produce **True** in string comparisons, and it's risky to rely upon. A constructed string isn't guaranteed to match another string if you use **is** rather than test-for-equality (**==**). For example:

```
>>> s1 = 'I am what I am and that is all that I am.'
>>> s2 = 'I am what I am' + ' and that is all that I am.'
>>> s1 == s2
True
>>> s1 is s2
False
```

What this example demonstrates is that just because two strings have identical contents does not mean that they correspond to the same object in memory, and therefore the **is** operator produces **False**.

If the **is** operator is unreliable in such cases, why is it in the language at all? The answer is that Python has some unique objects, such as **None**, **True**, and **False**. When you're certain that you're comparing a value to a unique object, then the **is** keyword works reliably; moreover, it's preferable in those situations because such a comparison is more efficient.

```
a_value = my_function()
if a_value is None:
    # Take special action if None is returned.
```

4.2.17 Use One-Line "for" Loops

If a **for** loop is short enough, with only one statement inside the loop (that is, the statement *body*), you can squeeze the entire **for** loop onto a single physical line.

for *var* **in** *sequence***:** *statement*

Not all programmers favor this programming style. However, it's useful as a way of making your program more compact. For example, the following one-line statement prints all the numbers from 0 to 9:

```
>>> for i in range(10): print(i, end=' ')

0 1 2 3 4 5 6 7 8 9
```

Notice that when you're within IDLE, this **for** loop is like any other: You need to type an extra blank line in order to terminate it.

4.2.18 Squeeze Multiple Statements onto a Line

If you have a lot of statements you want to squeeze onto the same line, you can do it—if you're determined and the statements are short enough.

The technique is to use a semicolon (;) to separate one statement on a physical line from another. Here's an example:

```
>>> for i in range(5): n=i*2; m = 5; print(n+m, end=' ')

5 7 9 11 13
```

You can squeeze other kinds of loops onto a line in this way. Also, you don't have to use loops but can place any statements on a line that you can manage to fit there.

```
>>> a = 1; b = 2; c = a + b; print(c)
3
```

At this point, some people may object, "But with those semicolons, this looks like C code!" (Oh, no—anything but that!)

Maybe it does, but it saves space. Keep in mind that the semicolons are statement separators and not terminators, as in the old Pascal language.

4.2.19 Write One-Line if/then/else Statements

This feature is also called an *in line* **if** conditional. Consider the following if/else statement, which is not uncommon:

```
turn = 0
...
if turn % 2:
    cell = 'X'
else:
    cell = 'O'
```

The book *Python Without Fear* uses this program logic to help operate a tic-tac-toe game. On alternate turns, the cell to be added was either an "X" or an "O". The turn counter, advanced by 1 each time, caused a switch back and forth (a *toggle*) between the two players, "X" and "O."

That book replaced the if/else block just shown with the more compact version:

```
cell = 'X' if turn % 2 else 'O'
```

true_expr **if** *conditional* **else** *false_expr*

If the *conditional* is true, then the *true_expr* is evaluated and returned; otherwise the *false_expr* is evaluated and returned.

4.2.20 Create Enum Values with "range"

Many programmers like to use enumerated (or "enum") types in place of so-called magic numbers. For example, if you have a `color_indicator` variable, in which the values 1 through 5 represent the values red, green, blue, back, and white, the code becomes more readable if you can use the color names instead of using the literal numbers 1 through 5.

You could make this possible by assigning a number to each variable name.

```
red   = 0
blue  = 1
green = 2
black = 3
white = 4
```

This works fine, but it would be nice to find a way to automate this code. There is a simple trick in Python that allows you to do that, creating an enumeration. You can take advantage of multiple assignment along with use of the **range** function:

```
red, blue, green, black, white = range(5)
```

The number passed to **range** in this case is the number of settings. Or, if you want to start the numbering at 1 instead of 0, you can use the following:

```
red, blue, green, black, white = range(1, 6)
```

Note ▶ For more sophisticated control over the creation and specification of enumerated types, you can import and examine the **enum** package.

```
import enum
help(enum)
```

You can find information on this feature at

https://docs.python.org/3/library/enum.html.

◀ Note

4.2.21 Reduce the Inefficiency of the "print" Function Within IDLE

Within IDLE, calls to the **print** statement are incredibly slow. If you run programs from within the environment, you can speed up performance dramatically by reducing the number of separate calls to **print**.

For example, suppose you want to print a 40 × 20 block of asterisks (*). The slowest way to do this, by far, is to print each character individually. Within IDLE, this code is painfully slowly.

```
for i in range(20):
    for j in range(40):
        print('*', end='')
    print()
```

You can get much better performance by printing a full row of asterisks at a time.

```
row_of_asterisks = '*' * 40
for i in range(20):
    print(row_of_asterisks)
```

But the best performance is achieved by revising the code so that it calls the **print** function only once, after having assembled a large, multiline output string.

```
row_of_asterisks = '*' * 40
s = ''
for i in range(20):
    s += row_of_asterisks + '\n'
print(s)
```

This example can be improved even further by utilizing the string class **join** method. The reason this code is better is that it uses in-place appending of a list rather than appending to a string, which must create a new string each time.

```
row_of_asterisks = '*' * 40
list_of_str = []
for i in range(20):
    list_of_str.append(row_of_asterisks)
print('\n'.join(list_of_str))
```

Better yet, here is a one-line version of the code!

```
print('\n'.join(['*' * 40] * 20))
```

4.2.22 Place Underscores Inside Large Numbers

In programming, you sometimes have to deal with large numeric literals. Here's an example:

```
CEO_salary = 1500000
```

Such numbers are difficult to read in programming code. You might like to use commas as separators, but commas are reserved for other purposes, such as creating lists. Fortunately, Python provides another technique: You can use underscores (_) inside a numeric literal.

```
CEO_salary = 1_500_000
```

Subject to the following rules, the underscores can be placed anywhere inside the number. The effect is for Python to read the number as if no underscores were present. This technique involves several rules.

▶ You can't use two underscores in a row.

▶ You can't use a leading or trailing underscore. If you use a leading underscore (as in _1), the figure is treated as a variable name.

▶ You *can* use underscores on either side of a decimal point.

This technique affects only how numbers appear in the code itself and not how anything is printed. To print a number with thousands-place separators, use the **format** function or method as described in Chapter 5, "Formatting Text Precisely."

4.3 Running Python from the Command Line

If you've been running Python programs from within IDLE—either as commands entered one at a time or as scripts—one way to improve execution speed is to run programs from a command line instead; in particular, doing so greatly speeds up the time it takes to execute calls to the **print** function.

Some of the quirks of command-line operation depend on which operating system you're using. This section covers the two most common operating systems: Windows and Macintosh.

4.3.1 Running on a Windows-Based System

Windows systems, unlike Macintosh, usually do not come with a version of Python 2.0 preloaded, a practice that actually saves you a good deal of fuss as long as you install Python 3 yourself.

To use Python from the command line, first start the DOS Box application, which is present as a major application on all Windows systems. Python should be easily available because it should be placed in a directory that is part of the PATH setting. Checking this setting is easy to do while you're running a Windows DOS Box.

In Windows, you can also check the PATH setting by opening the Control Panel, choose Systems, and select the Advanced tab. Then click Environment Variables.

You then should be able to run Python programs directly as long as they're in your PATH. To run a program from the command line, enter **python** and the name of the source file (the main module), including the **.py** extension.

```
python test.py
```

4.3.2 Running on a Macintosh System

Macintosh systems often come with a version of Python already installed; unfortunately, on recent systems, the version is Python 2.0 and not Python 3.0.

To determine which version has been installed for command-line use, first bring up the Terminal application on your Macintosh system. You may need to first click the Launchpad icon.

You should find yourself in your default directory, whatever it is. You can determine which command-line version of Python you have by using the following command:

```
python -V
```

If the version of Python is 2.0+, you'll get a message such as the following:

```
python 2.7.10
```

But if you've downloaded some version of Python 3.0, you should have that version of Python loaded as well. However, to run it, you'll have to use the command **python3** rather than **python**.

If you do have **python3** loaded, you can verify the exact version from the command line as follows:

```
python3 -V
python 3.7.0
```

For example, if the file test.py is in the current directory, and you want to compile it as a Python 3.0 program, then use the following command:

```
python3 test.py
```

The Python command (whether **python** or **python3**) has some useful variations. If you enter it with **-h**, the "help" flag, you get a printout on all the possible flags that you can use with the command, as well as relevant environment variables.

```
python3 -h
```

4.3.3 Using pip or pip3 to Download Packages

Some of the packages in this book require that you download and install the packages from the Internet before you use those packages. The first chapter that requires that is Chapter 12, which introduces the **numpy** package.

All the packages mentioned in this book are completely free of charge (as most packages for Python are). Even better, the **pip** utility—which is included with the Python 3 download—goes out and finds the package that you name; thus all you should need is an Internet connection!

On Windows-based systems, use the following command to download and install a desired package.

```
pip install package_name
```

The package name, incidentally, uses no file extension:

```
pip install numpy
```

On Macintosh systems, you may need to use the **pip3** utility, which is download with Python 3 when you install it on your computer. (You may also have inherited a version of pip, but it will likely be out-of-date and unusable.)

```
pip3 install package_name
```

4.4 Writing and Using Doc Strings

Python *doc strings* enable you to leverage the work you do writing comments to get free online help. That help is then available to you while running IDLE, as well as from the command line, when you use the **pydoc** utility.

You can write doc strings for both functions and classes. Although this book has not yet introduced how to write classes, the principles are the same. Here's an example with a function, showcasing a doc string.

```
def quad(a, b, c):
    '''Quadratic Formula function.

    This function applies the Quadratic Formula
    to determine the roots of x in a quadratic
    equation of the form ax^2 + bx + c = 0.
    '''
```

```
determin = (b * b - 4 * a * c) ** .5
x1 = (-b + determin) / (2 * a)
x2 = (-b - determin) / (2 * a)
return x1, x2
```

When this doc string is entered in a function definition, you can get help from within IDLE:

```
>>> help(quad)
Help on function quad in module __main__:

quad(a, b, c)
    Quadratic Formula function.

    This function applies the Quadratic Formula
    to determine the roots of x in a quadratic
    equation of the form ax^2 + bx + c = 0.
```

The mechanics of writing a doc string follow a number of rules.

▶ The doc string itself must immediately follow the heading of the function.

▶ It must be a literal string utilizing the triple-quote feature. (You can actually use any style quote, but you need a literal quotation if you want to span multiple lines.)

▶ The doc string must also be aligned with the "level-1" indentation under the function heading: For example, if the statements immediately under the function heading are indented four spaces, then the beginning of the doc string must also be indented four spaces.

▶ Subsequent lines of the doc string may be indented as you choose, because the string is a literal string. You can place the subsequent lines flush left or continue the indentation you began with the doc string. In either case, Python online help will line up the text in a helpful way.

This last point needs some clarification. The doc string shown in the previous example could have been written this way:

```
def quad(a, b, c):
    '''Quadratic Formula function.

This function applies the Quadratic Formula
to determine the roots of x in a quadratic
equation of the form ax^2 + bx + c = 0.
'''
```

```
determin = (b * b - 4 * a * c) ** .5
x1 = (-b + determin) / (2 * a)
x2 = (-b - determin) / (2 * a)
return x1, x2
```

You might expect this doc string to produce the desired behavior—to print help text that lines up—and you'd be right. But you can also put in extra spaces so that the lines also align *within program code*. It might seem this shouldn't work, but it does.

For stylistic reasons, programmers are encouraged to write the doc string this way, in which the subsequent lines in the quote line up with the beginning of the quoted string instead of starting flush left in column 1:

```
def quad(a, b, c):
    '''Quadratic Formula function.

    This function applies the Quadratic Formula
    to determine the roots of x in a quadratic
    equation of the form ax^2 + bx + c = 0.
    '''
```

As part of the stylistic guidelines, it's recommended that you put in a brief summary of the function, followed by a blank line, followed by more detailed description.

When running Python from the command line, you can use the **pydoc** utility to get this same online help shown earlier. For example, you could get help on the module named queens.py. The **pydoc** utility responds by printing a help summary for every function. Note that "py" is *not* entered as part of the module name in this case.

```
python -m pydoc queens
```

4.5 Importing Packages

Later sections in this chapter, as well as later chapters in the book, make use of packages to extend the capabilities of the Python language.

A *package* is essentially a software library of objects and functions that perform services. Packages come in two varieties:

▶ Packages included with the Python download itself. This includes **math**, **random**, **sys**, **os**, **time**, **datetime**, and **os.path**. These packages are especially convenient, because no additional downloading is necessary.

▶ Packages you can download from the Internet.

The syntax shown here is the recommended way to an import a package. There are a few variations on this syntax, as we'll show later.

```
import package_name
```

For example:

```
import math
```

Once a package is imported, you can, within IDLE, get help on its contents. Here's an example:

```
>>> import math
>>> help(math)
```

If you type these commands from within IDLE, you'll see that the math package supports a great many functions.

But with this approach, each of the functions needs to be qualified using the dot (.) syntax. For example, one of the functions supported is **sqrt** (square root), which takes an integer or floating-point input.

```
>>> math.sqrt(2)
1.4142135623730951
```

You can use the **math** package, if you choose, to calculate the value of **pi**. However, the math package also provides this number directly.

```
>>> math.atan(1) * 4
3.141592653589793
>>> math.pi
3.141592653589793
```

Let's look at one of the variations on the **import** statement.

```
import package_name [as new_name]
```

In this syntax, the brackets indicate that the **as** *new_name* clause is optional. You can use it, if you choose, to give the package another name, or *alias*, that is referred to in your source file.

This feature provides short names if the full package name is long. For example, Chapter 13 introduces the **matplotlib.pyplot** package.

```
import matplotlib.pyplot as plt
```

Now, do you want to use the prefix **matplotlib.pyplot**, or do you want to prefix a function name with **plt**? Good. We thought so.

Python supports other forms of syntax for the **import** statement. With both of these approaches, the need to use the package name and the dot syntax is removed.

```
from package_name import symbol_name
from package_name import *
```

In the first form of this syntax, only the *symbol_name* gets imported, and not the rest of the package. But the specified symbol (such as **pi** in this next example) can then be referred to without qualification.

```
>>> from math import pi
>>> print(pi)
3.141592653589793
```

This approach imports only one symbol—or a series of symbols separated by commas—but it enables the symbolic name to be used more directly. To import an entire package, while also gaining the ability to refer to all its objects and functions directly, use the last form of the syntax, which includes an asterisk (*).

```
>>> from math import *
>>> print(pi)
3.141592653589793
>>> print(sqrt(2))
1.4142135623730951
```

The drawback of using this version of **import** is that with very large and complex programs, it gets difficult to keep track of all the names you're using, and when you import packages without requiring a package-name qualifier, name conflicts can arise.

So, unless you know what you're doing or are importing a really small package, it's more advisable to import specific symbols than use the asterisk (*****).

4.6 A Guided Tour of Python Packages

Thousands of other packages are available if you go to **python.org**, and they are all free to use. The group of packages in Table 4.1 is among the most useful of all packages available for use with Python, so you should be sure to look them over.

The **re**, **math**, **random**, **array**, **decimal**, and **fractions** packages are all included with the standard Python 3 download, so you don't need to download them separately.

The **numpy**, **matplotlib**, and **pandas** packages need to be installed separately by using the **pip** or **pip3** utility. Later chapters, starting with Chapter 12, cover those utilities in depth.

Table 4.1. Python Packages Covered in This Book

NAME TO IMPORT	DESCRIPTION
`re`	Regular-expression package. This package lets you create text patterns that can match many different words, phrases, or sentences. This pattern-specification language can do sophisticated searches with high efficiency. This package is so important that it's explored in both Chapters 6 and 7.
`math`	Math package. Contains helpful and standard math functions so that you don't have to write them yourself. These include trigonometric, hyperbolic, exponential, and logarithmic functions, as well as the constants **e** and **pi**. This package is explored in Chapter 11.
`random`	A set of functions for producing pseudo-random values. Pseudo-random numbers behave as if random—meaning, among other things, it's a practical impossibility for a user to predict them. This random-number generation package includes the ability to produce random integers from a requested range, as well as floating-point numbers and normal distributions. The latter cluster around a mean value to form a "bell curve" of frequencies. This package is explored in Chapter 11.
`decimal`	This package supports the **Decimal** data type, which (unlike the **float** type) enables you to represent dollars-and-cents figures precisely without any possibility of rounding errors. **Decimal** is often preferred for use in accounting and financial applications. This package is explored in Chapter 10.
`fractions`	This package supports the **Fraction** data type, which stores any fractional number with absolute precision, provided it can be represented as the ratio of two integers. So, for example, this data type can represent the ratio 1/3 absolutely, something that neither the **float** nor **Decimal** type can do without rounding errors. This package is explored in Chapter 10.
`array`	This package supports the **array** class, which differs from lists in that it holds raw data in contiguous storage. This isn't always faster, but sometimes it's necessary to pack your data into contiguous storage so as to interact with other processes. However, the benefits of this package are far exceeded by the **numpy** package, which gives you the same ability, but much more. This package is briefly covered in Chapter 12.
`numpy`	This package supports the **numpy** (numeric Python) class, which in turn supports high-speed batch operations on one-, two-, and higher-dimensional arrays. The class is useful not only in itself, as a way of supercharging programs that handle large amounts of data, but also as the basis for work with other classes. This package is explored in Chapters 12 and 13. **numpy** needs to be installed with **pip** or **pip3**.

Table 4.1. Python Packages Covered in This Book (*continued*)

NAME TO IMPORT	DESCRIPTION
`numpy.random`	Similar to **random**, but designed especially for use with **numpy**, and ideally suited to situations in which you need to generate a large quantity of random numbers quickly. In head-to-head tests with the standard **random** class, the **numpy** random class is several times faster when you need to create an array of such numbers. This package is also explored in Chapter 12.
`matplotlib.pyplot`	This package supports sophisticated plotting routines for Python. Using these routines, you can create beautiful looking charts and figures—even three-dimensional ones. This package is explored in Chapter 13. It needs to be installed with **pip** or **pip3**.
`pandas`	This package supports *data frames*, which are tables that can hold a variety of information, as well as routines for going out and grabbing information from the Internet and loading it. Such information can then be combined with the **numpy** and plotting routines to create impressive-looking graphs. This package is explored in Chapter 15. It also needs to be downloaded.

4.7 Functions as First-Class Objects

Another productivity tool—which may be useful in debugging, profiling, and related tasks—is to treat Python functions as *first-class* objects. That means taking advantage of how you can get information about a function at run time. For example, suppose you've defined a function called `avg`.

```
def avg(a_list):
    '''This function finds the average val in a list.'''
    x = (sum(a_list) / len(a_list))
    print('The average is:', x)
    return x
```

The name `avg` is a symbolic name that refers to a function, which in Python lingo is also a callable. There are a number of things you can do with `avg`, such as verify its type, which is **function**. Here's an example:

```
>>> type(avg)
<class 'function'>
```

We already know that `avg` names a function, so this is not new information. But one of the interesting things you can do with an object is assign it to a new name. You can also assign a different function altogether to the symbolic name, avg.

```
def new_func(a_list):
    return (sum(a_list) / len(a_list))

old_avg = avg
avg = new_func
```

The symbolic name old_avg now refers to the older, and longer, function we defined before. The symbolic name avg now refers to the newer function just defined.

The name old_avg now refers to our first averaging function, and we can call it, just as we used to call avg.

```
>>> old_avg([4, 6])
The average is 5.0
5.0
```

The next function shown (which we might loosely term a "metafunction," although it's really quite ordinary) prints information about another function—specifically, the function argument passed to it.

```
def func_info(func):
    print('Function name:', func.__name__)
    print('Function documentation:')
    help(func)
```

If we run this function on old_avg, which has been assigned to our first averaging function at the beginning of this section, we get this result:

```
Function name: avg
Function documentation:
Help on function avg in module __main__:
```

```
avg(a_list)
    This function finds the average val in a list.
```

We're currently using the symbolic name old_avg to refer to the first function that was defined in this section. Notice that when we get the function's name, the information printed uses the name that *the function was originally defined with*.

All of these operations will become important when we get to the topic of "decorating" in Section 4.9, "Decorators and Function Profilers."

4.8 Variable-Length Argument Lists

One of the most versatile features of Python is the ability to access variable-length argument lists. With this capability, your functions can, if you choose, handle any number of arguments—much as the built-in **print** function does.

The variable-length argument ability extends to the use of named arguments, also called "keyword arguments."

4.8.1 The *args List

The ***args** syntax can be used to access argument lists of any length.

```
def func_name([ordinary_args,] *args):
    statements
```

The brackets are used in this case to show that ***args** may optionally be preceded by any number of ordinary positional arguments, represented here as *ordinary_args*. The use of such arguments is always optional.

In this syntax, the name **args** can actually be any symbolic name you want. By convention, Python programs use the name **args** for this purpose.

The symbolic name **args** is then interpreted as a Python list like any other; you expand it by indexing it or using it in a **for** loop. You can also take its length as needed. Here's an example:

```
def my_var_func(*args):
    print('The number of args is', len(args))
    for item in args:
        print(items)
```

This function, my_var_func, can be used with argument lists of any length.

```
>>> my_var_func(10, 20, 30, 40)
The number of args is 4
10
20
30
40
```

A more useful function would be one that took any number of numeric arguments and returned the average. Here's an easy way to write that function.

```
def avg(*args):
    return sum(args)/len(args)
```

Now we can call the function with a different number of arguments each time.

```
>>> avg(11, 22, 33)
22.0
>>> avg(1, 2)
1.5
```

The advantage of writing the function this way is that no brackets are needed when you call this function. The arguments are interpreted as if they were elements of a list, but you pass these arguments without list syntax.

What about the ordinary arguments we mentioned earlier? Additional arguments, not included in the list ***args**, must either precede ***args** in the argument list or be keyword arguments.

For example, let's revisit the avg example. Suppose we want a separate argument that specifies what units we're using. Because units is not a keyword argument, it must appear at the beginning of the list, in front of ***args**.

```
def avg(units, *args):
    print (sum(args)/len(args), units)
```

Here's a sample use:

```
>>> avg('inches', 11, 22, 33)
22.0 inches
```

This function is valid because the ordinary argument, units, precedes the argument list, ***args**.

Note ▶ The asterisk (*) has a number of uses in Python. In this context, it's called the *splat* or the *positional expansion* operator. Its basic use is to represent an "unpacked list"; more specifically, it replaces a list with a simple sequence of separate items.

The limitation on such an entity as ***args** is that there isn't much you can do with it. One thing you can do (which will be important in Section 4.9, "Decorators and Function Profilers") is pass it along to a function. Here's an example:

```
>>> ls = [1, 2, 3]    # Unpacked list.
>>> print(*ls)        # Print unpacked version
1 2 3
>>> print(ls)         # Print packed (ordinary list).
[1, 2, 3]
```

The other thing you can do with ***args** or *ls is to pack it (or rather, *repack* it) into a standard Python list; you do that by dropping the asterisk. At that point, it can be manipulated with all the standard list-handling abilities in Python.

◄ Note

4.8.2 The "**kwargs" List

The more complete syntax supports keyword arguments, which are named arguments during a function call. For example, in the following call to the **print** function, the **end** and **sep** arguments are named.

```
print(10, 20, 30, end='.', sep=',')
```

The more complete function syntax recognizes both unnamed and named arguments.

> **def** *func_name*([*ordinary_args*,] **args*, ***kwargs*):
>   *statements*

As with the symbolic name **args**, the symbolic name **kwargs** can actually be any name, but by convention, Python programmers use **kwargs**.

Within the function definition, **kwargs** refers to a dictionary in which each key-value pair is a string containing a named argument (as the key) and a value, which is the argument value passed.

An example should clarify. Assume you define a function as follows:

```
def pr_named_vals(**kwargs):
    for k in kwargs:
        print(k, ':', kwargs[k])
```

This function cycles through the dictionary represented by **kwargs**, printing both the key values (corresponding to argument names) and the corresponding values, which have been passed to the arguments.

For example:

```
>>> pr_named_vals(a=10, b=20, c=30)
a : 10
b : 20
c : 30
```

A function definition may combine any number of named arguments, referred to by **kwargs**, with any number of arguments that are not named, referred to by **args**. Here is a function definition that does exactly that.

The following example defines such a function and then calls it.

```
def pr_vals_2(*args, **kwargs):
    for i in args:
        print(i)
    for k in kwargs:
        print(k, ':', kwargs[k])

pr_vals_2(1, 2, 3, -4, a=100, b=200)
```

This miniprogram, when run as a script, prints the following:

```
1
2
3
-4
a : 100
b : 200
```

Note ▶ Although **args** and **kwargs** are expanded into a list and a dictionary, respectively, these symbols can be passed along to another function, as shown in the next section.

◀ Note

4.9 Decorators and Function Profilers

When you start refining your Python programs, one of the most useful things to do is to time how fast individual functions run. You might want to know how many seconds and fractions of a second elapse while your program executes a function generating a thousand random numbers.

Decorated functions can profile the speed of your code, as well as provide other information, because functions are first-class objects. Central to the concept of decoration is a *wrapper* function, which does everything the original function does but also adds other statements to be executed.

Here's an example, illustrated by Figure 4.3. The decorator takes a function F1 as input and returns another function, F2, as output. This second function, F2, is produced by including a call to F1 but adding other statements as well. F2 is a wrapper function.

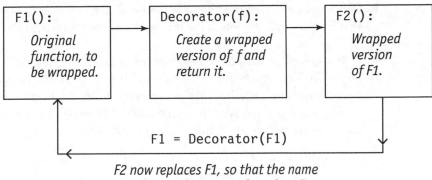

F2 now replaces F1, so that the name
F1 refers to the wrapped version, F2.

Figure 4.3. How decorators work (high-level view)

Here's an example of a decorator function that takes a function as argument and wraps it by adding calls to the **time.time** function. Note that **time** is a package, and it must be imported before **time.time** is called.

```
import time

def make_timer(func):
    def wrapper():
        t1 = time.time()
        ret_val = func()
        t2 = time.time()
        print('Time elapsed was', t2 - t1)
        return ret_val
    return wrapper
```

There are several functions involved with this simple example (which, by the way, is not yet complete!), so let's review.

▶ There is a function to be given as input; let's call this the *original* function (F1 in this case). We'd like to be able to input any function we want, and have it decorated—that is, acquire some additional statements.

▶ The *wrapper* function is the result of adding these additional statements to the original function. In this case, these added statements report the number of seconds the original function took to execute.

▶ The *decorator* is the function that performs the work of creating the wrapper function and returning it. The decorator is able to do this because it internally uses the **def** keyword to define a new function.

▶ Ultimately, the wrapped version is intended to replace the original version, as you'll see in this section. This is done by reassigning the function name.

If you look at this decorator function, you should notice it has an important omission: The arguments to the original function, *func*, are ignored. The wrapper function, as a result, will not correctly call *func* if arguments are involved.

The solution involves the ***args** and ****kwargs** language features, introduced in the previous section. Here's the full decorator:

```
import time

def make_timer(func):
    def wrapper(*args, **kwargs):
        t1 = time.time()
        ret_val = func(*args, **kwargs)
        t2 = time.time()
        print('Time elapsed was', t2 - t1)
        return ret_val
    return wrapper
```

The new function, remember, will be wrapper. It is wrapper (or rather, the function temporarily named wrapper) that will eventually be called in place of func; this wrapper function therefore must be able to take any number of arguments, including any number of keyword arguments. The correct action is to pass along all these arguments to the original function, func. Here's how:

```
ret_val = func(*args, **kwargs)
```

Returning a value is also handled here; the wrapper returns the same value as func, as it should. What if func returns no value? That's not a problem, because Python functions return **None** by default. So the value **None**, in that case, is simply passed along. (You don't have to test for the existence of a return value; there always is one!)

Having defined this decorator, make_timer, we can take any function and produce a wrapped version of it. Then—and this is almost the final trick—we reassign the function name so that it refers to the wrapped version of the function.

```
def count_nums(n):
    for i in range(n):
        for j in range(1000):
            pass

count_nums = make_timer(count_nums)
```

The wrapper function produced by make_timer is defined as follows (except that the identifier func will be reassigned, as you'll see in a moment).

```
def wrapper(*args, **kwargs):
    t1 = time.time()
    ret_val = func(*args, **kwargs)
    t2 = time.time()
    print('Time elapsed was', t2 - t1)
    return ret_val
```

We now reassign the name count_nums so that it refers to *this* function—wrapper—which will call the original count_nums function but also does other things.

Confused yet? Admittedly, it's a brain twister at first. But all that's going on is that (1) a more elaborate version of the original function is being created at run time, and (2) this more elaborate version is what the name, count_nums, will hereafter refer to. Python symbols can refer to any object, including functions (callable objects). Therefore, we can reassign function names all we want.

```
count_nums = wrapper
```

Or, more accurately,

```
count_nums = make_timer(count_nums)
```

So now, when you run count_nums (which now refers to the wrapped version of the function), you'll get output like this, reporting execution time in seconds.

```
>>> count_nums(33000)
Time elapsed was 1.063697338104248
```

The original version of count_nums did nothing except do some counting; this wrapped version reports the passage of time in addition to calling the original version of count_nums.

As a final step, Python provides a small but convenient bit of syntax to automate the reassignment of the function name.

```
@decorator
def func(args):
    statements
```

This syntax is translated into the following:

```
def func(args):
    statements
func = decorator(func)
```

In either case, it's assumed that *decorator* is a function that has already been defined. This decorator must take a function as its argument and return a wrapped version of the function. Assuming all this has been done correctly, here's a complete example utilizing the **@** sign.

```
@make_timer
def count_nums(n):
    for i in range(n):
        for j in range(1000):
            pass
```

After this definition is executed by Python, `count_num` can then be called, and it will execute `count_num` as defined, but it will also add (as part of the wrapper) a **print** statement telling the number of elapsed seconds.

Remember that this part of the trick (the final trick, actually) is to get the name `count_nums` to refer to the *new* version of `count_nums`, after the new statements have been added through the process of decoration.

4.10 Generators

There's no subject in Python about which more confusion abounds than generators. It's not a difficult feature once you understand it. Explaining it's the hard part.

But first, what does a generator do? The answer: It enables you to deal with a sequence one element at a time.

Suppose you need to deal with a sequence of elements that would take a long time to produce if you had to store it all in memory at the same time. For example, you want to examine all the Fibonacci numbers up to 10 to the 50th power. It would take a lot of time and space to calculate the entire sequence. Or you may want to deal with an infinite sequence, such as all even numbers.

The advantage of a generator is that it enables you to deal with one member of a sequence at a time. This creates a kind of "virtual sequence."

4.10.1 What's an Iterator?

One of the central concepts in Python is that of *iterator* (sometimes confused with *iterable)*. An iterator is an object that produces a stream of values, one at a time.

All lists can be iterated, but not all iterators are lists. There are many functions, such as **reversed**, that produce iterators that are not lists. These cannot be indexed or printed in a useful way, at least not directly. Here's an example:

```
>>> iter1 = reversed([1, 2, 3, 4])
>>> print(iter1)
<list_reverseiterator object at 0x1111d7f28>
```

However, you can convert an iterator to a list and then print it, index it, or slice it:

```
>>> print(list(iter1))
[4, 3, 2, 1]
```

Iterators in Python work with **for** statements. For example, because iter1 is an iterator, the following lines of code work perfectly well.

```
>>> iter1 = reversed([1, 2, 3, 4])
>>> for i in iter1:
        print(i, end=' ')

4  3  2  1
```

Iterators have *state information*; after reaching the end of its series, an iterator is exhausted. If we used iter1 again without resetting it, it would produce no more values.

4.10.2 Introducing Generators

A generator is one of the easiest ways to produce an iterator. But the generator function is not itself an iterator. Here's the basic procedure.

▶ Write a generator function. You do this by using a **yield** statement anywhere in the definition.

▶ Call the function you completed in step 1 to get an iterator object.

▶ The iterator created in step 2 is what yields values in response to the **next** function. This object contains state information and can be reset as needed.

Figure 4.4 illustrates the process.

A generator function is really a generator factory!

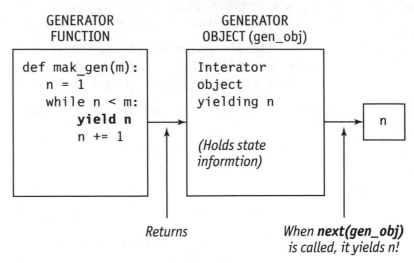

Figure 4.4. Returning a generator from a function

Here's what almost everybody gets wrong when trying to explain this process: It looks as if the **yield** statement, placed in the generator function (the thing on the left in Figure 4.4), is doing the yielding. That's "sort of" true, but it's not really what's going on.

The generator function defines the behavior of the iterator. But the iterator object, the thing to its right in Figure 4.4, is what actually executes this behavior.

When you include one or more **yield** statements in a function, the function is no longer an ordinary Python function; **yield** describes a behavior in which the function does not return a value but sends a value back to the caller of **next**. State information is saved, so when **next** is called again, the iterator advances to the next value in the series without starting over. This part, everyone seems to understand.

But—and this is where people get confused—it isn't the generator function that performs these actions, even though that's where the behavior is *defined*. Fortunately, you don't need to understand it; you just need to use it. Let's start with a function that prints even numbers from 2 to 10:

```
def print_evens():
    for n in range(2, 11, 2):
        print(n)
```

Now replace print(n) with the statement yield n. Doing so changes the nature of what the function does. While we're at it, let's change the name to make_evens_gen to have a more accurate description.

```
def make_evens_gen():
    for n in range(2, 11, 2):
        yield n
```

The first thing you might say is "This function no longer returns anything; instead, it yields the value n, suspending its execution and saving its internal state."

But this revised function, make_evens_gen, does indeed have a return value! As shown in Figure 4.4, the value returned is not n; the return value is an iterator object, also called a "generator object." Look what happens if you call make_evens_gen and examine the return value.

```
>>> make_evens_gen()
<generator object make_evens_gen at 0x1068bd410>
```

What did the function do? Yield a value for n? No! Instead, it returned an iterator object, and that's the object that yields a value. We can save the iterator object (or generator object) and then pass it to **next**.

```
>>> my_gen = make_evens_gen()
>>> next(my_gen)
2
>>> next(my_gen)
4
>>> next(my_gen)
6
```

Eventually, calling **next** exhausts the series, and a **StopIteration** exception is raised. But what if you want to reset the sequence of values to the beginning? Easy. You can do that by calling make_evens_gen again, producing a new instance of the iterator. This has the effect of starting over.

```
>>> my_gen = make_evens_gen()    # Start over
>>> next(my_gen)
2
>>> next(my_gen)
4
>>> next(my_gen)
6
>>> my_gen = make_evens_gen()    # Start over
>>> next(my_gen)
2
>>> next(my_gen)
4
>>> next(my_gen)
6
```

What happens if you call make_evens_gen every time? In that case, you keep starting over, because each time you're creating a new generator object. This is most certainly not what you want.

```
>>> next(make_evens_gen())
2
>>> next(make_evens_gen())
2
>>> next(make_evens_gen())
2
```

Generators can be used in **for** statements, and that's one of the most frequent uses. For example, we can call make_evens_gen as follows:

```
for i in make_evens_gen():
    print(i, end=' ')
```

This block of code produces the result you'd expect:

```
2   4   6   8   10
```

But let's take a look at what's really happening. The **for** block calls make_evens_gen one time. The result of the call is to get a generator object. That object then provides the values in the **for** loop. The same effect is achieved by the following code, which breaks the function call onto an earlier line.

```
>>> my_gen = make_evens_gen()
>>> for i in my_gen:
        print(i, end=' ')
```

Remember that my_gen is an iterator object. If you instead referred to make_evens_gen directly, Python would raise an exception.

```
for i in make_evens_gen:          # ERROR! Not an iterable!
    print(i, end=' ')
```

Once you understand that the object returned by the generator function is the generator object, also called the iterator, you can call it anywhere an *iterable* or *iterator* is accepted in the syntax. For example, you can convert a generator object to a list, as follows.

```
>>> my_gen = make_evens_gen()
>>> a_list = list(my_gen)
>>> a_list
[2, 4, 6, 8, 10]
```

```
>>> a_list = list(my_gen)        # Oops! No reset!
>>> a_list
[]
```

The problem with the last few statements in this example is that each time you iterate through a sequence using a generator object, the iteration is exhausted and needs to be reset.

```
>>> my_gen = make_evens_gen()    # Reset!
>>> a_list = list(my_gen)
>>> a_list
[2, 4, 6, 8, 10]
```

You can of course combine the function call and the **list** conversion. The list itself is stable and (unlike a generator object) will retain its values.

```
>>> a_list = list(make_evens_gen())
>>> a_list
[2, 4, 6, 8, 10]
```

One of the most practical uses of an iterator is with the **in** and **not in** keywords. We can, for example, generate an iterator that produces Fibonacci numbers up to and including N, but not larger than N.

```
def make_fibo_gen(n):
    a, b = 1, 1
    while a <= n:
        yield a
        a, b = a + b, a
```

The **yield** statement changes this function from an ordinary function to a generator function, so it returns a generator object (iterator). We can now determine whether a number is a Fibonacci by using the following test:

```
n = int(input('Enter number: '))
if n in make_fibo_gen(n):
    print('number is a Fibonacci. ')
else:
    print('number is not a Fibonacci. ')
```

This example works because the iterator produced does not yield an infinite sequence, something that would cause a problem. Instead, the iterator terminates if n is reached without being confirmed as a Fibonacci.

Remember—and we state this one last time—by putting **yield** into the function make_fibo_gen, it becomes a generator function and it returns the generator object we need. The previous example could have been written as follows, so that the function call is made in a separate statement. The effect is the same.

```
n = int(input('Enter number: '))
my_fibo_gen = make_fibo_gen(n)
if n in my_fibo_gen:
    print('number is a Fibonacci. ')
else:
    print('number is not a Fibonacci. ')
```

As always, remember that a generator function (which contains the **yield** statement) is not a generator object at all, but rather a generator factory. This is confusing, but you just have to get used to it. In any case, Figure 4.4 shows what's really going on, and you should refer to it often.

4.11 Accessing Command-Line Arguments

Running a program from the command lets you provide the program an extra degree of flexibility. You can let the user specify *command-line arguments*; these are optional arguments that give information directly to the program on start-up. Alternatively, you can let the program prompt the user for the information needed. But use of command-line arguments is typically more efficient.

Command-line arguments are always stored in the form of strings. So—just as with data returned by the input function—you may need to convert this string data to numeric format.

To access command-line arguments from within a Python program, first import the **sys** package.

```
import sys
```

You can then refer to the full set of command-line arguments, including the function name itself, by referring to a list named **argv**.

```
argv        # If 'import sys.argv' used
sys.argv    # If sys imported as 'import sys'
```

In either case, **argv** refers to a list of command-line arguments, all stored as strings. The first element in the list is always the name of the program itself. That element is indexed as **argv[0]**, because Python uses zero-based indexing.

For example, suppose that you are running quad (a quadratic-equation evaluator) and input the following command line:

```
python quad.py -1 -1 1
```

In this case, **argv** will be realized as a list of four strings.

Figure 4.5 illustrates how these strings are stored, emphasizing that the first element, **argv[0]**, refers to a string containing the program name.

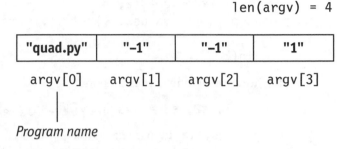

Figure 4.5. Command-line arguments and argv

In most cases, you'll probably ignore the program name and focus on the other arguments. For example, here is a program named silly.py that does nothing but print all the arguments given to it, including the program name.

```
import sys
for thing in sys.argv:
    print(thing, end=' ')
```

Now suppose we enter this command line:

```
python  silly.py  arg1  arg2  arg3
```

The Terminal program (in Mac) or the DOS Box prints the following:

```
silly.py  arg1  arg2  arg3
```

The following example gives a more sophisticated way to use these strings, by converting them to floating-point format and passing the numbers to the quad function.

```
import sys

def quad(a, b, c):
    '''Quadratic Formula function.'''

    determin = (b * b - 4 * a * c) ** .5
    x1 = (-b + determin) / (2 * a)
```

```
    x2 = (-b - determin) / (2 * a)
    return x1, x2

def main():
    '''Get argument values, convert, call quad.'''

    s1, s2, s3 = sys.argv[1], sys.argv[2], sys.argv[3]
    a, b, c = float(s1), float(s2), float(s3)
    x1, x2 = quad(a, b, c)
    print('x values: {}, {}.'.format(x1, x2))

main()
```

The interesting line here is this one:

```
    s1, s2, s3 = sys.argv[1], sys.argv[2], sys.argv[3]
```

Again, the **sys.argv** list is zero-based, like any other Python list, but the program name, referred to as **sys.arg[0]**, typically isn't used in the program code. Presumably you already know what the name of your program is, so you don't need to look it up.

Of course, from within the program you can't always be sure that argument values were specified on the command line. If they were not specified, you may want to provide an alternative, such as prompting the user for these same values.

Remember that the length of the argument list is always N+1, where N is the number of command-line arguments—beyond the program name, of course.

Therefore, we could revise the previous example as follows:

```
import sys

def quad(a, b, c):
    '''Quadratic Formula function.'''

    determin = (b * b - 4 * a * c) ** .5
    x1 = (-b + determin) / (2 * a)
    x2 = (-b - determin) / (2 * a)
    return x1, x2

def main():
    '''Get argument values, convert, call quad.'''
```

```
if len(sys.argv) > 3:
    s1, s2, s3 = sys.argv[1], sys.argv[2], sys.argv[3]
else:
    s1 = input('Enter a: ')
    s2 = input('Enter b: ')
    s3 = input('Enter c: ')
a, b, c = float(s1), float(s2), float(s3)
x1, x2 = quad(a, b, c)
print('x values: {}, {}.'.format(x1, x2))

main()
```

The key lines in this version are in the following **if** statement:

```
if len(sys.argv) > 3:
    s1, s2, s3 = sys.argv[1], sys.argv[2], sys.argv[3]
else:
    s1 = input('Enter a: ')
    s2 = input('Enter b: ')
    s3 = input('Enter c: ')
a, b, c = float(s1), float(s2), float(s3)
```

If there are at least four elements in **sys.argv** (and therefore three command-line arguments beyond the program name itself), the program uses those strings. Otherwise, the program prompts for the values.

So, from the command line, you'll be able to run the following:

```
python quad.py 1 -9 20
```

The program then prints these results:

```
x values: 4.0 5.0
```

Chapter 4 *Summary*

A large part of this chapter presented ways to improve your efficiency through writing better and more efficient Python code. Beyond that, you can make your Python programs run faster if you call the **print** function as rarely as possible from within IDLE—or else run programs from the command line only.

A technique helpful in making your code more efficient is to profile it by using the **time** and **datetime** packages to compute the relative speed of the code, given different algorithms. Writing decorators is helpful in this respect, because you can use them to profile function performance.

One of the best ways of supercharging your applications, in many cases, is to use one of the many free packages available for use with Python. Some of these are built in; others, like the **numpy** package, you'll need to download.

Chapter 4 *Questions for Review*

1 Is an assignment operator such as **+=** only a convenience? Can it actually result in faster performance at run time?

2 In most computer languages, what is the minimum number of statements you'd need to write instead of the Python statement a, b = a + b, a?

3 What's the most efficient way to initialize a list of 100 integers to 0 in Python?

4 What's the most efficient way of initializing a list of 99 integers with the pattern 1, 2, 3 repeated? Show precisely how to do that, if possible.

5 If you're running a Python program from within IDLE, describe how to most efficiently print a multidimensional list.

6 Can you use list comprehension on a string? If so, how?

7 How can you get help on a user-written Python program from the command line? From within IDLE?

8 Functions are said to be "first-class objects" in Python but not in most other languages, such as C++ or Java. What is something you can do with a Python function (callable object) that you cannot do in C or C++?

9 What's the difference between a wrapper, a wrapped function, and a decorator?

10 When a function is a generator function, what does it return, if anything?

11 From the standpoint of the Python language, what is the one change that needs to be made to a function to turn it into a generator function?

12 Name at least one advantage of generators.

Chapter 4 *Suggested Problems*

1 Print a matrix of 20 × 20 stars or asterisks (*). From within IDLE, demonstrate the slowest possible means of doing this task and the fastest possible means. (Hint: Does the fastest way utilize string concatenation of the **join**

method?) Compare and contrast. Then use a decorator to profile the speeds of the two ways of printing the asterisks.

2 Write a generator to print all the perfect squares of integers, up to a specified limit. Then write a function to determine whether an integer argument is a perfect square if it falls into this sequence—that is, if n is an integer argument, the phrase n in square_iter(n) should yield **True** or **False**.

Formatting Text Precisely

When programming for business and professional use, you want to format text to create beautiful-looking tables and presentations. In this area, Python has an embarrassment of riches. It has several ways to modify and enhance the printing of information in text-character form.

This chapter presents all three approaches in detail, beginning with the string-formatting operator, **%s**, which typically provides the quickest, easiest solution. For the most complete control, you may want to use the **format** function or **format** method, which support many options, even letting you print large numbers with the thousands-place separator (**,**).

5.1 Formatting with the Percent Sign Operator (%)

Here's a simple problem in formatting output. Suppose you want to print a sentence in the following form, in which a, b, and c are currently equal to 25, 75, and 100, but they could have any values. You want to get the following result by referring to the variables.

```
25 plus 75 equals 100.
```

This should be easy. But if you use the **print** function, it puts a space between the number 100 and the dot (.), so you get the following:

```
25 plus 75 equals 100 .
```

What do you do about that unwanted space? The **print** function lets you turn off the default placing of a space between print fields by setting the **sep** argument to an empty space. But in that case, you have to put in all the spaces yourself.

```
print(a, ' plus ', b, ' equals ', c, '.', sep='')
```

This works, but it's ugly.

A better approach is to use the **str** class formatting operator (%) to format the output, using format specifiers like those used by the C-language "printf" function. Here's how you'd revise the example:

```
print('%d plus %d equals %d.' % (a, b, c))
```

Isn't that better?

The expression (a, b, c) is actually a tuple containing three arguments, each corresponding to a separate occurrence of **%d** within the format string. The parentheses in (a, b, c) are strictly required—although they are not required if there is only one argument.

```
>>> 'Here is a number: %d.' % 100
'Here is a number: 100.'
```

These elements can be broken up programmatically, of course. Here's an example:

```
n = 25 + 75
fmt_str = 'The sum is %d.'
print(fmt_str % n)
```

This example prints the following:

```
The sum is 100.
```

The string formatting operator, %, can appear in either of these two versions.

```
format_str % value        # Single value
format_str % (values)     # One or more values
```

If there is more than one *value* argument, the arguments corresponding to print fields (which are marked by a type character and a percent sign, %) must be placed inside a tuple. Both of the following statements are valid:

```
print('n is %d' % n)
print('n is %d and m is %d' % (n, m))
```

The next example also works, because it organizes three numbers into a tuple.

```
tup = 10, 20, 30
print('Answers are %d, %d, and %d.' % tup)
```

These statements print the following:

```
Answers are 10, 20, and 30.
```

5.2 Percent Sign (%) Format Specifiers

The format specifier **%d** stands for decimal integer. It's a common format, but the formatting operator (%) works with other formats, as shown in Table 5.1.

Table 5.1. Percent-Sign Specifiers

SPECIFIER	MEANING	EXAMPLE OF OUTPUT
%d	Decimal integer.	199
%i	Integer. Same meaning as **%d**.	199
%s	Standard string representation of the input. This field says, "Produce a string," but it can be used to print the standard string representation of any data object. So this can actually be used with integers if you choose.	Thomas
%r	Standard %r representation of the input, which is often the same as %s but uses the canonical representation of the object as it appears in Python code. (For more information, see Section 5.7, "'Repr' Versus String Conversion.")	'Bob'
%x	Hexadecimal integer.	ff09a
%X	Same as **%x**, but letter digits A–F are uppercase.	FF09A
%o	Octal integer.	177
%u	Unsigned integer. (But note that this doesn't reliably change signed integers into their unsigned equivalent, as you'd expect.)	257
%f	Floating-point number to be printed in fixed-point format	3.1400
%F	Same as **%f**.	33.1400
%e	Floating-point number, printing exponent sign (e).	3.140000e+00
%E	Same as **%e** but uses uppercase E.	3.140000E+00
%g	Floating point, using shortest canonical representation.	7e-06
%G	Same as **%g** but uses uppercase E if printing an exponent.	7E-06
%%	A literal percent sign (%).	%

Here's an example that uses the **int** conversion, along with hexadecimal output, to add two hexadecimal numbers: e9 and 10.

```python
h1 = int('e9', 16)
h2 = int('10', 16)
print('The result is %x.' % (h1 + h2))
```

The example prints

```
The result is f9.
```

Therefore, adding hexadecimal e9 and hexadecimal 10 produces hexadecimal f9, which is correct.

The parentheses around h1 and h2 are necessary in this example. Otherwise, the example creates a formatted string by using h1 as the data, and then it attempts to concatenate *that* string with a number, h2, causing an error.

```
print('The result is %x.' % h1 + h2)    # ERROR!
```

When you're printing a hexadecimal or octal number, the formatting operator (%) puts no prefix in front of the number. If you want to print hexadecimal numbers with prefixes, you need to specify them yourself.

```
print('The result is 0x%x.' % (h1 + h2))
```

That statement prints the following:

```
The result is 0xf9.
```

Printing a substring (%s) inside a larger string is another common usage for the formatting operator. Here's an example:

```
s = 'We is %s, %s, & %s.' % ('Moe', 'Curly', 'Larry')
print(s)
```

This prints

```
We is Moe, Curly, & Larry.
```

The behavior of these formats can be altered by the use of width and precision numbers. Each print field has the format shown here, in which **c** represents one of the format characters in Table 5.1.

```
%[-][width][.precision]c
```

In this syntax, the square brackets indicate optional items and are not intended literally. The minus sign (–) specifies left justification within the print field. With this technology, the default is right justification for all data types.

But the following example uses left justification, which is not the default, by including the minus sign (–) as part of the specifier.

```
>>> 'This is a number: %-6d.' % 255
'This is a number: 255   .'
```

As for the rest of the syntax, a format specifier can take any of the following formats.

```
%c
%widthc
%width.precisionc
%.precisionc
```

In the case of string values, the text is placed into a print field of size *width*, if specified. The substring is right justified (by default) and padded with spaces. If the print field is smaller than the length of the substring, *width* is ignored. The *precision*, if included, specifies a maximum size for the string, which will be truncated if longer.

Here's an example of the use of a 10-space print-field width.

```
print('My name is %10s.' % 'John')
```

This prints the following, including six spaces of padding.

```
My name is       John.
```

In the case of integers to be printed, the *width* number is interpreted in the same way. But in addition, the *precision* specifies a smaller field, within which the number is right justified and padded with leading zeros. Here's an example:

```
print('Amount is %10d.' % 25)
print('Amount is %.5d.' % 25)
print('Amount is %10.5d.' % 25)
```

These statements print

```
Amount is         25.
Amount is 00025.
Amount is      00025.
```

Finally, the *width* and *precision* fields control print-field width and precision in a floating-point number. The precision is the number of digits to the right of the decimal point; this number contains trailing zeros if necessary.

Here's an example:

```
print('result:%12.5f' % 3.14)
print('result:%12.5f' % 333.14)
```

These statements print the following:

```
result:     3.14000
result:   333.14000
```

In this case, the number 3.14 is padded with trailing zeros, because a precision of 5 digits was specified. When the precision field is smaller than the precision of the value to be printed, the number is rounded up or down as appropriate.

```
print('%.4f' % 3.141592)
```

This function call prints the following—in this case with 4 digits of precision, produced through rounding:

```
3.1416
```

Use of the **%s** and **%r** format characters enables you to work with any classes of data. These specifiers result in the calling of one of the internal methods from those classes supporting string representation of the class, as explained in Chapter 9, "Classes and Magic Methods."

In many cases, there's no difference in effect between the **%s** and **%r** specifiers. For example, either one, used with an **int** or **float** object, will result in that number being translated into the string representation you'd expect.

You can see those results in the following IDLE session, in which user input is in bold.

```
>>> 'The number is %s.' % 10
The number is 10.
>>> 'The number is %r.' % 10
The number is 10.
```

From these examples, you can see that both the **%s** and the **%r** just print the standard string representation of an integer.

In some cases, there is a difference between the string representation indicated by **%s** and by **%r**. The latter is intended to get the canonical representation of the object as it appears in Python code.

One of the principal differences between the two forms of representation is that the **%r** representation includes quotation marks around strings, whereas **%s** does not.

```
>>> print('My name is %r.' % 'Sam')
My name is 'Sam'.
>>> print('My name is %s.' % 'Sam')
My name is Sam.
```

5.3 Percent Sign (%) Variable-Length Print Fields

After you've been using the format operator (**%**) for a while, you may wonder whether there's a way to create variable-length widths for print fields. For example, you might want to print a table after determining the maximum width needed, set this as the desired width (say, N = 6, where N is the maximum size needed), and then give every print field the same size.

Fortunately, the percent sign formatting (%) provides an easy way to do this. To create a variable-width field, place an asterisk (*) where you'd normally place an integer specifying a fixed width. Here's an example:

```
>>> 'Here is a number: %*d' % (3, 6)
'Here is a number:   6'
```

Each asterisk used in this way creates the need for an extra argument. That argument appears first, before the data object it's being applied to. So the order of the two arguments within the tuple is (1) print field width and (2) data to be printed.

You can print other kinds of data, such as strings.

```
>>> 'Here is a number: %*s' % (3, 'VI')
'Here is a number:  VI'
```

Again, the first argument is the print-field width—in this case, 3. The second argument is the data to be printed—in this case, the string 'VI'.

You can include multiple uses of a variable-width print field within a format string. Remember that for each asterisk that appears in the format string, there must be an additional argument. So if you want to format *two* such data objects at once, you'd need to have *four* arguments altogether. Here's an example:

```
>>> 'Item 1: %*s, Item 2: %*s' % (8, 'Bob', 8, 'Suzanne')
'Item 1:      Bob, Item 2:  Suzanne'
```

The arguments—all placed in the tuple following the argument (with parentheses required, by the way)—are 8, 'Bob', 8, and 'Suzanne'.

The meaning of these four arguments is as follows:

▶ The first print-field width is 8.

▶ The first data object to be printed is 'Bob' (that is, print the string as is).

▶ The second print-field width is 8.

▶ The second data object to be printed is 'Suzanne'.

As indicated earlier, this number can be a variable whose value is determined at run time. Here's an example:

```
>>> n = 8
>>> 'Item 1: %*s, Item 2: %*s' % (n, 'Bob', n, 'Suzanne')
'Item 1:      Bob, Item 2:  Suzanne'
```

All the arguments—including the field-width arguments (n in this example)—are placed in a tuple that follows the percent operator (%).

The variable-length width feature can be combined with other features. For example, you can use the %r specifier instead of %s; this has no effect on numbers to be printed, but it causes strings to be printed with quotation marks.

```
>>> n = 9
>>> 'Item 1: %*r, Item 2: %*r' % (n, 'Bob', n, 'Suzanne')
"Item 1:       'Bob', Item 2: 'Suzanne'"
```

You can also create variable-length precision indicators. The general rule with the format operator (%) is this:

> ✱ **Where you'd normally put an integer as a formatting code, you can instead place an asterisk (*); and for each such asterisk, you must place a corresponding integer expression in the argument list.**

For example, the following statement formats a number as if the specifier were '%8.3f':

```
>>> '%*.*f' % (8, 3, 3.141592)
'   3.142'
```

5.4 The Global "format" Function

Two closely related features of Python give you even greater control over specifications. The global **format** function enables specification of one print field. For example, it provides an easy way to add commas as thousands place separators.

```
>>> big_n = 10 ** 12    # big_n is 10 to 12th power
>>> format(big_n, ',')
'1,000,000,000,000'
```

This is only a hint of what you can do with the **format** function. This section provides only an introduction to this function's capabilities. Section 5.8, "The 'spec' Field of the 'format' Function and Method," describes other syntactic elements of a format specification (or *spec*) that you can use with this function.

The **format** function is closely related to the **format** method of the string class (**str**).

When the **format** method processes a string, it analyzes format specifiers, along with the data objects used as input. It carries out this analysis by calling the global **format** function for each individual field.

The **format** function then calls the **__format__** method for the data object's class, as explained in Chapter 9. This process has the virtue of letting every type, including any new classes you might write, interact with all the format specifier syntax—or choose to ignore it.

Figure 5.1 shows the flow of control between the various functions involved: the **format** method of the string class, the global **format** function, and finally the **__format__** method within each class.

The class may or may not choose to handle this method directly. By default, the **__str__** method of that class is called if **__format__** is not defined.

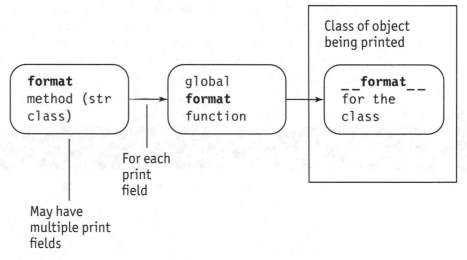

Figure 5.1. Flow of control between formatting routines

format(*data*, *spec*)

This function returns a string after evaluating the data and then formatting according to the specification string, *spec*. The latter argument is a string containing the specification for printing one item.

The syntax shown next provides a simplified view of *spec* grammar. It omits some features such as the fill and align characters, as well as the use of 0 in right justifying and padding a number. To see the complete syntax of *spec*, see Section 5.8, "The 'spec' Field of the 'format' Method."

[*width*] [*,*] [*.precision*] [*type*]

In this syntax, the brackets are not intended literally but signify optional items. Here is a summary of the meaning.

The function attempts to place the string representation of the data into a print field of *width* size, justifying text if necessary by padding with spaces. Numeric data is right justified by default; string data is left justified by default.

The comma (**,**) indicates insertion of commas as thousands place separators. This is legal only with numeric data; otherwise, an exception is raised.

The *precision* indicates the total number of digits to print with a floating-point number, or, if the data is not numeric, a maximum length for string data. It is not supported for use with integers. If the *type_char* is **f**, then the precision indicates a fixed number of digits to print to the right of the decimal point.

The *type_char* is sometimes a radix indicator, such as **b** or **x** (binary or hexadecimal), but more often it is a floating-point specifier such as **f**, which indicates fixed-point format, or **e** and **g**, as described later in Table 5.5.

Table 5.2 gives some examples of using this specification. You can figure out most of the syntax by studying these examples.

Table 5.2. Sample Format Specifiers for the "format" Function

FORMAT SPECIFICATION	MEANING
`','`	Displays thousands place separators as part of a number—for example, displaying 1000000 as 1,000,000.
`'5'`	Specifies a minimum print-field width of 5 characters. If the information to be displayed is smaller in size, it is justified by being padded. Numbers are right justified by default; strings are left justified by default.
`'10'`	Specifies a minimum print-field width of 10 characters. If the representation of the object is smaller than 10 characters, it is justified within a field that wide.
`'10,'`	Specifies a minimum print-field width of 10 characters and also displays thousands place separators.
`'10.5'`	Specifies a minimum print-field width of 10. If the data is a string, 5 characters is a print-field maximum and anything larger is truncated. If the data is floating point, the field displays at most 5 digits total to the left and right of the decimal point; rounding is performed, but if the display size still exceeds the space allowed, the number is displayed in exponential format, such as 3+010e. The precision field (5 in this case) is not valid for integers.
`'8.4'`	Same as above, but print-field width is 8 and precision is 4.
`'10,.7'`	Specifies a minimum print-field width of 10 and precision of 7 (total number of digits to the left and right), *and* it displays thousands place separators.
`'10.3f'`	Fixed-point display. Uses a print-field width of 10 and displays exactly 3 digits to the right of the decimal point. Rounding up or down, or putting in trailing zeros, is performed as needed to make the number of digits come out exactly right.

Table 5.2. Sample Format Specifiers for the "format" Function (*continued*)

FORMAT SPECIFICATION	MEANING
`'10.5f'`	Uses a print-field width of 10 and displays exactly 5 digits to the right of the decimal point.
`'.3f'`	Displays exactly 3 digits to the right of the decimal point. There is no minimum width in this case.
`'b'`	Uses binary radix.
`'6b'`	Uses binary radix; right justifies numbers within a field of 6 characters.
`'x'`	Uses hexadecimal radix.
`'5x'`	Uses hexadecimal radix; right justifies numbers within a field of 5 characters.
`'o'`	Uses octal radix.
`'5o'`	Uses octal radix; right justifies numbers within a field of 5 characters.

The remainder of this section discusses the features in more detail, particularly width and precision fields.

The thousands place separator is fairly self-explanatory but works only with numbers. Python raises an exception if this specifier is used with data that isn't numeric.

You might use it to format a large number such as 150 million.

```
>>> n = 150000000
>>> print(format(n, ','))
150,000,000
```

The width character is used consistently, always specifying a minimum print-field width. The string representation is padded—with spaces by default—and uses a default of left justification for strings and right justification for numbers. Both the padding character and justification can be altered, however, as explained later in this chapter, in Section 5.8.2, "Text Justification: 'fill' and 'align' Characters."

Here are examples of justification, padding, and print fields. The single quotation marks implicitly show the extent of the print fields. Remember that numeric data (150 and 99, in this case) are right justified by default, but other data is not.

```
>>> format('Bob', '10')
'Bob       '
>>> format('Suzie', '7')
'Suzie  '
```

```
>>> format(150, '8')
'     150'
>>> format(99, '5')
'   99'
```

The width is always a print-field minimum, not a maximum. A width field does not cause truncation.

The precision specifier works differently, depending on the kind of data it's applied to. With string data, the precision is a print-field maximum, and it can cause truncation. With floating-point fields, precision specifies the maximum number of total characters to the left and right of the decimal point—not counting the decimal point itself—and thereby rounds up or down as needed. Here's an example:

```
>>> format('Bobby K.', '6.3')
'Bob   '
>>> format(3.141592, '6.3')
'  3.14'
```

But if the **f** type specifier is also used, it specifies fixed-point display format, and that changes the rules for floating point. With fixed-point format, the precision specifies the number of digits to the right of the decimal point, unconditionally.

The **format** function uses rounding or padding with trailing zeros, as needed, to achieve the fixed number of digits to the right of the decimal point. Here's an example:

```
>>> format(3.141592, '9.3f')
'    3.142'
>>> format(100.7, '9.3f')
'  100.700'
```

As you can see, the fixed-point format is useful for placing numbers in columns in which the decimal point lines up nicely.

As mentioned earlier, Section 5.8 discusses the complete syntax for *spec*, which is used by both the global **format** function and the **format** method.

5.5 Introduction to the "format" Method

To get the most complete control over formatting, use the **format** method. This technique contains all the power of the global **format** function but is more flexible because of its ability to handle multiple print fields.

Let's return to the example that started this chapter. Suppose you have three integer variables (a, b, and c) and you want to print them in a sentence that reads as follows:

```
25 plus 75 equals 100.
```

The **format** method provides a smooth, readable way to produce this print string.

```
print('{} plus {} equals {}.'.format(25, 75, 100))
```

Each occurrence of {} in the format string is filled in with the string representation of the corresponding argument.

format_specifying_str.**format(***args***)**

Let's break down the syntax a little. This expression passes through all the text in *format_specifying_str* (or just "format string"), except where there's a print field. Print fields are denoted as "{}." Within each print field, the value of one of the *args* is printed.

If you want to print data objects and are not worried about the finer issues of formatting, just use a pair of curly braces, {}, for each argument. Strings are printed as strings, integers are printed as integers, and so on, for any type of data. Here's an example:

```
fss = '{} said, I want {} slices of {}.'

name = 'Pythagoras'
pi = 3.141592
print(fss.format(name, 2, pi))
```

This prints

```
Pythagoras said, I want 2 slices of 3.141592.
```

The *arg* values, of course, either can be constants or can be supplied by variables (such as name and pi in this case).

Curly braces are special characters in this context. To print *literal* curly braces, not interpreted as field delimiters, use {{ and }}. Here's an example:

```
print('Set = {{{}, {}}}'.format(1, 2))
```

This prints

```
Set = {1, 2}
```

This example is a little hard to read, but the following may be clearer. Remember that double open curly braces, **{{**, and double closed curly braces, **}}**, cause a literal curly brace to be printed.

```
fss = 'Set = {{ {}, {}, {} }}'
print(fss.format(15, 35, 25))
```

This prints

```
Set = { 15, 35, 25 }
```

Of course, as long as you have room on a line, you can put everything together:

```
print('Set = {{ {}, {}, {} }}'.format(15, 35, 25))
```

This prints the same output. Remember that each pair of braces defines a print field and therefore causes an argument to be printed, but **{{** and **}}** cause printing of literal braces.

5.6 Ordering by Position (Name or Number)

```
{ [position] [!r|s|a] [: spec ] }
```

In the syntax for print fields within a **format** string, the square brackets are not intended literally but indicate optional items. With the second item, the syntax indicates an exclamation mark followed by **r**, **s**, or **a**, but not more than one of these; we look at that syntax in the next section.

The *spec* is a potentially complex series of formatting parameters. This chapter focuses on *spec* beginning in Section 5.8 and explains all the possible subfields.

One of the simplest applications of this syntax is to use a lone *position* indicator.

```
{ position }
```

The *position* indicates which argument is being referred to by using either a number or a name. Using a *position* indicator lets you to refer to arguments out of order.

The *position* indicator, in turn, is either an index number or a named position:

```
pos_index | pos_name
```

We'll consider each of these in turn. A position index is a number referring to an item in the **format** method argument list according to its zero-based index. A position name needs to be matched by named arguments, which we'll return to. First, let's look at position indexes, because these are fairly easy to understand.

The general rule about arguments to the **format** method is this:

> A call to the format method must have at least as many arguments as the format-specification string has print fields, unless fields are repeated as shown at the end of this section. But if more arguments than print fields appear, the excess arguments (the last ones given) are ignored.

So, for example, consider the following **print** statement:

```
print('{}; {}; {}!'.format(10, 20, 30))
```

This prints

```
10; 20; 30!
```

You can use integer constants in the position field to print in reverse order. These are zero-based indexes, so they are numbered 0, 1, and 2.

```
print('The items are {2}, {1}, {0}.'.format(10, 20, 30))
```

This statement prints

```
The items are 30, 20, 10.
```

You can also use zero-based index numbers to refer to excess arguments, in which there are more arguments than print fields. Here's an example:

```
fss = 'The items are {3}, {1}, {0}.'
print(fss.format(10, 20, 30, 40))
```

These statements print

```
The items are 40, 20, 10.
```

Note that referring to an out-of-range argument raises an error. In this example there are four arguments, so they are indexed as 0, 1, 2, and 3. No index number was an out-of-range reference in this case.

Print fields can also be matched to arguments according to argument names. Here's an example:

```
fss = 'a equals {a}, b equals{b}, c equals {c}.'
print(fss.format(a=10, c=100, b=50))
```

This example prints

```
a equals 10, b equals 50, c equals 100.
```

You can also use the positioning techniques to repeat values in your output. Here's an example:

```
print('{0}, {0}, {1}, {1}'.format(100, 200))
```

This example prints

```
100, 100, 200, 200
```

Position ordering has an advanced feature that's occasionally useful for certain applications. By changing the format string itself, you can change which parts of an argument get selected for inclusion in the print string.

For example, {0[0]:} means "Select the first element of the first argument." {0[1]:} means "Select the second element of the first argument." And so on.

Here's a more complete example. Remember that zero-based indexing is used, as usual.

```
>>> a_list = [100, 200, 300]
>>> '{0[1]:}, {0[2]:}'.format(a_list)
'200, 300'
```

This technology works with named positions as well.

```
>>> '{a[1]:}, {a[2]:}'.format(a=a_list)
'200, 300'
```

So what is the point of maintaining this control over position ordering? Many applications will never need it, but it enables you to use a format string to reorder data as needed. This is particularly useful, for example, when you're translating to another natural language and reordering may be mandated by the language grammar.

One case of this might involve the Japanese language, as in this example:

```
if current_lang == 'JPN':
    fss = '{0}はいつ{2}の{1}と会うのだろうか？'
else:
    fss = "When will {0} meet {1} at {2}'s?"
print(fss.format('Fred', 'Sam', 'Joe'))
```

Depending on the value of current_lang, this may print the following:

```
When will Fred meet Sam at Joe's?
```

Or else it will print the following. Notice that the position of the names has changed, in line with Japanese grammar, which changes the order of some of the names.

Fredはいつ Joe の Sam と会うのだろうか？

5.7 *"Repr" Versus String Conversion*

In Python, every type may have up to two different string representations. This may seem like overkill, but occasionally it's useful. It stems from Python being an interpreted language.

This section discusses the difference between **str** and **repr** conversions. However, all the information here is equally applicable to other uses of **str** and **repr**, such as the **%s** and **%r** formatting specifiers.

When you apply a **str** conversion, that conversion returns the string equivalent of the data exactly as it would be printed by the **print** function.

```
print(10)          # This prints 10.
print(str(10))     # So does this!
```

But for some types of data, there is a separate **repr** conversion that is not the same as **str**. The **repr** conversion translates a data object into its *canonical representation in source code*—that is, how it would look inside a Python program.

Here's an example:

```
print(repr(10))     # This ALSO prints 10.
```

In this case, there's no difference in what gets printed. But there is a difference with strings. Strings are stored in memory without quotation marks; such marks are delimiters that usually appear only in source code. Furthermore, escape sequences such as \n (a newline) are translated into special characters when they are stored; again \n is a source-code representation, not the actual storage.

Take the following string, test_str:

```
test_str = 'Here is a \n newline! '
```

Printing this string directly causes the following to be displayed:

```
Here is a
 newline!
```

But applying **repr** to the string and then printing it produces a different result, essentially saying, "Show the canonical source-code representation."

This includes quotation marks, even though they are not part of the string itself unless they're embedded. But the **repr** function includes quotation marks because they are part of what would appear in Python source code to represent the string.

```
print(repr(test_str))
```

This statement prints

```
'Here is a \n newline.'
```

The **%s** and **%r** formatting specifiers, as well as the **format** method, enable you to control which style of representation to use. Printing a string argument without **repr** has the same effect as printing it directly. Here's an example:

```
>>> print('{}'.format(test_str))
Here is a
 newline!
```

Using the **!r** modifier causes a **repr** version of the argument to be used—that is, the **repr** conversion is applied to the data.

```
>>> print('{!r}'.format(test_str))
'Here is a \n newline! '
```

The use of **!r** is orthogonal with regard to position ordering. Either may be used without interfering with the other. So can you see what the following example does?

```
>>> print('{1!r} loves {0!r}'.format('Joanie', 'ChaCha'))
'ChaCha' loves 'Joanie'
```

The formatting characters inside the curly braces do two things in this case. First, they use position indexes to reverse "Joanie loves ChaCha"; then the **!r** format causes the two names to be printed with quotation marks, part of the canonical representation within Python code.

> **Note ▶** Where **!s** or **!r** would normally appear, you can also use **!a**, which is similar to **!s** but returns an ASCII-only string.
>
> ◀ Note

5.8   The "spec" Field of the "format" Function and Method

This section and all its subsections apply to both the global **format** function and the **format** method. However, most of the examples in the remainder of the chapter assume the use of the **format** method, which is why they show *spec* in the context of a print field, **{}**, and a colon (**:**).

The syntax of the *spec*, the format specifier, is the most complex part of **format** method grammar. Each part is optional, but if used, it must observe the order shown. (The square brackets indicate that each of these items is optional.)

$$[[fill]align][sign][\#][0][width][,][.prec][type]$$

The items here are mostly independent of each other. Python interprets each item according to placement and context. For example, *prec* (precision) appears right after a decimal point (.) if it appears at all.

When looking at the examples, remember that curly braces and colons are used only when you use *spec* with the global **format** function and not the **format** method. With the **format** function, you might include *align*, *sign*, **0**, *width*, *precision*, and *type* specifiers, but no curly braces or colon. Here's an example:

```
s = format(32.3, '<+08.3f')
```

5.8.1 Print-Field Width

One of the commonly used items is print-field *width*, specified as an integer. The text to be printed is displayed in a field of this size. If the text is shorter than this width, it's justified and extra spaces are padded with blank spaces by default.

Placement: As you can see from the syntax display, the *width* item is in the middle of the *spec* syntax. When used with the **format** method, *width* always follows a colon (:), as does the rest of the *spec* syntax.

The following example shows how width specification works on two numbers: 777 and 999. The example uses asterisks (*) to help illustrate where the print fields begin and end, but otherwise these asterisks are just literal characters thrown in for the sake of illustration.

```
n1, n2 = 777, 999
print('**{:10}**{:2}**'.format(n1, n2))
```

This prints

```
**       777**999**
```

The numeral 777 is right justified within a large print field (10). This is because, by default, numeric data is right justified and string data is left justified.

The numeral **999** exceeds its print-field size (2) in length, so it is simply printed as is. No truncation is performed.

Width specification is frequently useful with tables. For example, suppose you want to print a table of integers, but you want them to line up.

```
   10
 2001
    2
   55
  144
 2525
 1984
```

It's easy to print a table like this. Just use the **format** method with a print-field width that's wider than the longest number you expect. Because the data is numeric, it's right justified by default.

```
'{:5}'.format(n)
```

Print-field width is orthogonal with most of the other capabilities. The "ChaCha loves Joanie" example from the previous section could be revised:

```
fss = '{1!r:10} loves {0!r:10}!!'
print(fss.format('Joanie', 'ChaCha'))
```

This prints

```
'ChaCha'    loves 'Joanie'  !!
```

The output here is similar output to the earlier "ChaCha and Joanie" example but adds a print-field width of 10 for both arguments. Remember that a width specification must appear to the right of the colon; otherwise it would function as a position number.

5.8.2 Text Justification: "fill" and "align" Characters

The *fill* and *align* characters are optional, but the *fill* character can appear only if the *align* character does.

```
[[fill]align]
```

Placement: these items, if they appear within a print-field specification, precede all other parts of the syntax, including *width*. Here's an example containing *fill*, *align*, and *width*:

```
{:->24}
```

The next example uses this specification in context:

```
print('{:->24}'.format('Hey Bill G, pick me!'))
```

This prints

```
----Hey Bill G, pick me!
```

Let's examine each part of this print field, `{:->24}`. Here's the breakdown.

▸ The colon (:) is the first item to appear inside the print-field spec when you're working with the **format** method (but not the global **format** function).

▸ After the colon, a *fill* and an *align* character appear. The minus sign (-) is the fill character here, and the alignment is right justification (>).

▸ After *fill* and *align* are specified, the print-field *width* of 24 is given.

Because the argument to be printed ('Hey Bill G, pick me!') is 20 characters in length but the print-field width is 24 characters, four copies of the fill character, a minus sign in this case, are used for padding.

The fill character can be any character other than a curly brace. Note that if you want to pad a number with zeros, you can alternatively use the '0' specifier described in Section 5.8.4, "The Leading Zero Character (0)."

The *align* character must be one of the four values listed in Table 5.3.

Table 5.3. "Align" Characters Used in Formatting

ALIGN CHARACTER	MEANING
<	Left justify. This is the default for string data.
>	Right justify. This is the default for numbers.
^	Center the text in the middle of the print field. (This slightly favors left justification when the text can't be centered perfectly.)
=	Place all padding characters between the sign character (+ or −) and the number to be printed. This specification is valid only for numeric data.

A fill (or padding) character is recognized as such only if there is an *align* character just after it (<, >, ^, or =).

```
print('{:>7}'.format('Tom'))      # Print '    Tom'
print('{:@>7}'.format('Lady'))    # Print '@@@Lady'
print('{:*>7}'.format('Bill'))    # Print '***Bill'
```

In the first of these examples, no *fill* character is specified, so a default value of a blank space is used to pad the print field. In the second and third cases, fill characters of an ampersand (@) and an asterisk (*) are used.

If we were to instead use < to specify left justification, padding would be placed on the right (although note that left justification is the default for strings). So the previous examples would be revised:

```
print('{:<7}'.format('Tom'))    # Print 'Tom    '
print('{:@<7}'.format('Lady'))  # Print 'Lady@@@'
print('{:*<7}'.format('Bill'))  # Print 'Bill***'
```

The next few examples demonstrate the use of ^ to specify centering of the data; padding appears on either side of the text.

```
fss = '{:^10}Jones'
print(fss.format('Tom'))    # Print '   Tom    Jones'
fss = '{:@^10}'
print(fss.format('Lady'))   # Print '@@@Lady@@@'
fss = '{:*^10}'
print(fss.format('Bill'))   # Print '***Bill***'
```

Finally, the next examples show the use of = to specify padding between a sign character (+ or -) and numeric data. The second case uses a zero as a fill character.

```
print('{:=8}'.format(-1250))   # Print '-   1250'
print('{:0=8}'.format(-1250))  # Print '-0001250'
```

> **Note** ▶ Remember (and sorry if we're getting a little redundant about this), all the examples for the *spec* grammar apply to the global **format** function as well. But the **format** function, as opposed to the **format** method, does not use curly braces to create multiple print fields. It works on only one print field at a time.
>
> Here's an example:
>
> ```
> print(format('Lady', '@<7'))   # Print 'Lady@@@'
> ```

5.8.3 The "sign" Character

The *sign* character, which is usually a plus sign (+) if used at all, helps determine whether or not a plus or minus sign is printed in a numeric field.

Placement: The *sign* character comes after the *fill* and *align* characters, if included, but before other parts of *spec*. In particular, it precedes the *width*. Table 5.4 lists the possible values for this character.

Table 5.4. "Sign" Characters for the "format" Method

CHARACTER	MEANING
+	Prints a plus sign (+) for nonnegative numbers; prints a minus sign (–) for negative numbers, as usual.
-	Prints a minus sign for negative numbers only. This is the default behavior.
(blank space)	Prints a blank space where a plus sign would go, for nonnegative numbers; prints a minus sign for negative numbers, as usual. This is useful for getting numbers to line up nicely in tabs, whether or not a negative sign is present.

A simple example illustrates the use of the sign character.

```
print('results>{: },{:+},{:-}'.format(25, 25, 25))
```

This example prints

```
results> 25,+25,25
```

Notice how there's an extra space in front of the first occurrence of 25, even though it's nonnegative; however, if the print fields had definite widths assigned—which they do not in this case—that character would produce no difference.

This next example applies the same formatting to three negative values (–25).

```
print('results>{: },{:+},{:-}'.format(-25, -25, -25))
```

This example prints the following output, illustrating that negative numbers are always printed with a minus sign.

```
results>-25,-25,-25
```

5.8.4 The Leading-Zero Character (0)

This character specifies padding a 0 digit character for numbers, causing a "0" to be used instead of spaces. Although you can achieve similar effects by specifying align and fill characters, this technique is slightly less verbose.

Placement: This character, if used, immediately precedes the *width* specification. Essentially, it amounts to adding a leading-zero prefix (0) to the width itself.

For example, the following statement causes leading zeros to be printed whenever the text to be displayed is smaller than the print-field width.

```
i, j = 125, 25156
print('{:07}  {:010}.'.format(i, j))
```

This prints

```
0000125  0000025156.
```

Here's another example:

```
print('{:08}'.format(375))   # This prints 00000375
```

The same results could have been achieved by using *fill* and *align* characters, but because you can't specify *fill* without also explicitly specifying *align*, that approach is slightly more verbose.

```
fss = '{:0>7}  {:0>10}'
```

Although these two approaches—specifying 0 as fill character and specifying a leading zero—are often identical in effect, there are situations in which the two cause different results. A fill character is not part of the number itself and is therefore not affected by the comma, described in the next section.

There's also interaction with the plus/minus sign. If you try the following, you'll see a difference in the location where the plus sign (+) gets printed.

```
print('{:0>+10} {:+010}'.format(25, 25))
```

This example prints

```
0000000+25 +000000025
```

5.8.5 Thousands Place Separator

One of the most convenient features of the **format** method is the ability to use a thousands place separator with numeric output. How often have you seen output like the following?

```
The US owes 21035786433031 dollars.
```

How much is this really? One's eyes glaze over, which probably is a happy result for most politicians. It just looks like "a big number."

This number is much more readable if printed as follows—although it's still too large for most mortals to comprehend. But if you have a little numeric aptitude, you'll see that this is not just 21 million or 21 billion, but rather *21 trillion*.

```
The US owes 21,035,786,433,031 dollars.
```

Placement: The comma follows the *width* specifier and precedes the *precision* specifier, it if appears. The comma should be the last item other than *precision* and *type*, if they appear.

You may want to refer to the syntax display at the beginning of Section 5.8.1.

The following examples use a {:,} print field. This is a simple specification because it just involves a comma to the immediate right of the colon—all inside a print field.

```
fss1 = 'The USA owes {:,} dollars.'
print(fss1.format(21000000000))
fss2 = 'The sun is {:,} miles away.'
print(fss2.format(93000000))
```

These statements print

```
The USA owes 21,000,000,000,000 dollars.
The sun is 93,000,000 miles away.
```

The next example uses the comma in combination with *fill* and *align* characters * and >, respectively. The *width* specifier is 12. Notice that the comma (,) appears just after *width*; it's the last item before the closing curly brace.

```
n = 4500000
print('The amount on the check was ${:*>12,}'.format(n))
```

This example prints

```
The amount on the check was $***4,500,000
```

The print width of 12 includes room for the number that was printed, including the commas (a total of nine characters); therefore, this example uses three fill characters. The fill character in this case is an asterisk (*). The dollar sign ($) is not part of this calculation because it is a literal character and is printed as is.

If there is a leading-zero character as described in Section 5.8.4 (as opposed to a 0 fill character), the zeros are also grouped with commas. Here's an example:

```
print('The amount is {:011,}'.format(13000))
```

This example prints

```
The amount is 000,013,000
```

In this case, the leading zeros are grouped with commas, because all the zeros are considered part of the number itself.

A print-field size of 12 (or any other multiple of 4), creates a conflict with the comma, because an initial comma cannot be part of a valid number. Therefore, Python adds an additional leading zero in that special case.

```
n = 13000
print('The amount is {:012,}'.format(n))
```

This prints

```
The amount is 0,000,013,000
```

But if 0 is specified as a fill character instead of as a leading zero, the zeros are not considered part of the number and are not grouped with commas. Note the placement of the 0 here relative to the right justify (>) sign. This time it's just to the *left* of this sign.

```
print('The amount is {:0>11,}'.format(n))
```

This prints

```
The amount is 0000013,000
```

5.8.6 Controlling Precision

The *precision* specifier is a number provided primarily for use with floating-point values, although it can also be used with strings. It causes rounding and truncation. The precision of a floating-point number is the maximum number of digits to be printed, both to the right and to the left of the decimal point.

Precision can also be used, in the case of fixed-point format (which has an **f** type specifier), to ensure that an exact number of digits are always printed to the *right* of the decimal point, helping floating-point values to line up in a table.

Placement: Precision is always a number to the immediate right of a decimal point (.). It's the last item in a *spec* field, with the exception of the one-letter *type* specifier described in the next section.

```
.precision
```

Here are some simple examples in which precision is used to limit the total number of digits printed.

```
pi = 3.14159265
phi = 1.618

fss = '{:.2} + {:.2} = {:.2}'
print(fss.format(pi, phi, pi + phi))
```

These statements print the following results. Note that each number has exactly two total digits:

```
3.1 + 1.6 = 4.8
```

This statement looks inaccurate, due to rounding errors. For each number, only two digits total are printed. Printing three digits for each number yields better results.

```
pi = 3.14159265
phi = 1.618

fss = '{:.3} + {:.3} = {:.3}'
print(fss.format(pi, phi, pi + phi))
```

This prints

```
3.14 + 1.62 = 4.76
```

The last digit to appear, in all cases of limited precision, is rounded as appropriate.

If you want to use *precision* to print numbers in fixed-point format, combine *width* and *precision* with an **f** type specifier at the end of the print field. Here's an example:

```
fss = '  {:10.3f}\n  {:10.3f}'
print(fss.format(22.1, 1000.007))
```

This prints

```
    22.100
  1000.007
```

Notice how well things line up in this case. In this context (with the **f** type specifier) the precision specifies not the total number of digits but *the number of digits just to the right of the decimal point*—which are padded with trailing zeros if needed.

The example can be combined with other features, such as the thousands separator, which comes after the width but before precision. Therefore, in this example, each comma comes right after 10, the width specifier.

```
fss = '  {:10,.3f}\n  {:10,.3f}'
print(fss.format(22333.1, 1000.007))
```

This example prints

```
  22,333.100
   1,000.007
```

The fixed-point format **f**, in combination with *width* and *precision*, is useful for creating tables in which the numbers line up. Here's an example:

```
fss = '  {:10.2f}'
for x in [22.7, 3.1415, 555.5, 29, 1010.013]:
    print(fss.format(x))
```

This example prints

```
  22.70
   3.14
 555.50
  29.00
1010.01
```

5.8.7 "Precision" Used with Strings (Truncation)

When used with strings, the *precision* specifier potentially causes truncation. If the length of the string to be printed is greater than the *precision*, the text is truncated. Here's an example:

```
print('{:.5}'.format('Superannuated.'))   # Prints 'Super'
print('{:.5}'.format('Excellent!'))       # Prints 'Excel'
print('{:.5}'.format('Sam'))              # Prints 'Sam'
```

In these examples, if the string to be printed is shorter than the *precision*, there is no effect. But the next examples use a combination of *fill* character, *alignment*, *width*, and *precision*.

```
fss = '{:*<6.6}'
```

Let's break down what these symbols mean.

▶ The *fill* and *align* characters are * and <, respectively. The < symbol specifies left justification, so asterisks are used for padding on the right, if needed.

▶ The *width* character is 6, so any string shorter than 6 characters in length is padded after being left justified.

▶ The *precision* (the character after the dot) is also 6, so any string longer than 6 characters is truncated.

Let's apply this format to several strings.

```
print(fss.format('Tom'))
print(fss.format('Mike'))
print(fss.format('Rodney'))
print(fss.format('Hannibal'))
print(fss.format('Mortimer'))
```

These statements could have easily been written by using the global **format** function. Notice the similarities as well as the differences; the previous examples involved the format string '{:*<6.6}'.

```
print(format('Tom', '*<6.6'))
print(format('Mike', '*<6.6'))
print(format('Rodney', '*<6.6'))
print(format('Hannibal', '*<6.6'))
print(format('Mortimer', '*<6.6'))
```

In either case—that is, for either block of code just shown—the output is

```
Tom***
Mike**
Rodney
Hannib
Mortim
```

The *width* and *precision* need not be the same. For example, the following format specifies a width of 5, so any string shorter than 5 is padded; but the precision is 10, so any string longer than 10 is truncated.

```
fss = '{:*<5.10}'
```

5.8.8 "Type" Specifiers

The last item in the *spec* syntax is the *type* specifier, which influences how the data to be printed is interpreted. It's limited to one character and has one of the values listed in Table 5.5.

Placement: When the *type* specifier is used, it's the very last item in the *spec* syntax.

Table 5.5. "Type" Specifiers Recognized by the Format Method

TYPE CHARACTER	DESCRIPTION
b	Display number in binary.
c	Translate a number into its ASCII or Unicode character.
d	Display number in decimal format (the default).
e	Display a floating-point value using exponential format, with lowercase e—for example, 12e+20.
E	Same as **e**, but display with an uppercase E—for example, 12E+20.
f or **F**	Display number in fixed-point format.
g	Use format **e** or **f**, whichever is shorter.
G	Same as **g**, but use uppercase E.

▼ *continued on next page*

Table 5.5. "Type" Specifiers Recognized by the Format Method (*continued*)

TYPE CHARACTER	DESCRIPTION
n	Use the local format for displaying numbers. For example, instead of printing 1,200.34, the American format, use the European format: 1.200,34.
o	Display integer in octal format (base 8).
x	Display integer in hexadecimal format, using lowercase letters to represent digits greater than 9.
X	Same as **x**, but uses uppercase letters for hex digits.
%	Displays a number as a percentage: Multiply by 100 and then add a percent sign (%).

The next five sections illustrate specific uses of the *type* specifier.

5.8.9 Displaying in Binary Radix

To print an integer in binary radix (base 2), use the **b** specifier. The result is a series of 1's and 0's. For example, the following statement displays 5, 6, and 16 in binary radix:

```
print('{:b}  {:b}  {:b}'.format(5, 6, 16))
```

This prints the following:

```
101  110  10000
```

You can optionally use the **#** specifier to automatically put in radix prefixes, such as **0b** for binary. This formatting character is placed after the *fill*, *align*, and *sign* characters if they appear but before the *type* specifier. (It also precedes *width* and *precision*.) Here's an example:

```
print('{:#b}'.format(7))
```

This prints

```
0b111
```

5.8.10 Displaying in Octal and Hex Radix

The octal (base 8) and hexadecimal (base 16) radixes are specified by the **o**, **x**, and **X** type specifiers. The last two specify lowercase and uppercase hexadecimal, respectively, for digits greater than 9.

The following example illustrates how each format displays decimal 63:

```
print('{:o}, {:x}, {:X}'.format(63, 63, 63))
```

This could also be written as

```
print('{0:o}, {0:x}, {0:X}'.format(63))
```

In either case, this prints

```
77, 3f, 3F
```

Again, you can have the **format** method automatically insert a radix prefix by using the # specifier, which is placed after the *fill*, *align*, and *sign* characters if they appear. Here's an example:

```
print('{0:#o}, {0:#x}, {0:#X}'.format(63))
```

This statement prints

```
0o77, 0x3f, 0X3F
```

5.8.11 *Displaying Percentages*

A common use of formatting is to turn a number into a percentage—for example, displaying 0.5 as 50% and displaying 1.25 as 125%. You can perform that task yourself, but the % type specifier automates the process.

The percent format character (%) multiplies the value by 100 and then appends a percent sign. Here's an example:

```
print('You own {:%} of the shares.'.format(.517))
```

This example prints

```
You own 51.700000% of the shares.
```

If a *precision* is used in combination with the % type specifier, the *precision* controls the number of digits to the right of the decimal point as usual—but after first multiplying by 100. Here's an example:

```
print('{:.2%} of {:.2%} of 40...'.format(0.231, 0.5))
```

This prints

```
23.10% of 50.00% of 40...
```

As with fixed-point format, if you want to print percentages so that they line up nicely in a table, then specify both *width* and *precision* specifiers.

5.8.12 Binary Radix Example

The **format** method provides the tools to print numeric output in binary, octal, or hex radix. You can combine that capability with **int** conversions to create a binary calculator that uses both binary input and output—that is to say, its input and output features strings of 1's and 0's.

This next example performs binary addition, displaying results in both decimal and binary.

```
def calc_binary():
    print('Enter values in binary only!')
    b1 = int(input('Enter b1:'), 2)
    b2 = int(input('Enter b2:'), 2)
    print('Total is: {:#b}'.format(b1 + b2))
    print('{} + {} = {}'.format(b1, b2, b1 + b2))
```

Here's a sample session with user input in bold.

```
>>> calc_binary()
Enter values in binary only!
Enter b1: 101
Enter b2: 1010
Total is: 0b1111
5 + 10 = 15
```

The key format-specification string is in the following statement:

```
print('Total is: {:#b}'.format(b1 + b2))
```

To the right of the colon are two characters: the pound sign (**#**), which causes the radix symbol, 0b, to be printed; and the type specifier, **b**, which causes the use of binary radix—that is, base 2.

```
'{:#b}'
```

The second output line uses simple print fields, which default to decimal output.

```
'{} + {} = {}'
```

5.9 Variable-Size Fields

Section 5.3 explained how to use variable-width print fields with the formatting operator (**%**). The **format** method provides the same, or more, flexibility. You can leave any part of the specifier syntax open to be filled in later.

The general rule for variable fields within the **format** method is to place a nested pair of curly braces, {}, *within* a print field, where you would ordinarily put a fixed value. The method then scans the format string and performs a substitution, replacing a nested {} minifield with the corresponding item from the argument list. Finally, the string is applied to formatting as usual.

The value to be filled in is read from the argument list.

```
>>> 'Here is a num: {:{}.{}}'.format(1.2345, 10, 4)
'Here is a num:      1.234'
```

This example works as if it were written as follows, with the numbers 10 and 4 substituting for the two inner sets of curly braces (so the previous example has the same effect as this):

```
'Here is a num: {:10.4}'.format(1.2345)
```

The arguments in this case are integer expressions, so the variable-length example could have been written with variable references:

```
a, b = 10, 4
'Here is a num: {:{}.{}}'.format(1.2345, a, b)
```

The way in which arguments are applied with this method is slightly different from the way they work with the formatting operator (Section 5.3).

The difference is this: When you use the **format** method this way, the data object comes *first* in the list of arguments; the expressions that alter formatting come immediately after. This is true even with multiple print fields. For example:

```
>>> '{:{}}  {:{}}!'.format('Hi', 3, 'there', 7)
'Hi   there  !'
```

Note that with this technology, strings are left justified by default.

The use of position numbers to clarify order is recommended. Use of these numbers helps keep the meaning of the expressions clearer and more predictable. The example just shown could well be revised so that it uses the following expression:

```
>>> '{0:{1}}  {2:{3}}!'.format('Hi', 3, 'there', 7)
'Hi   there  !'
```

The meaning of the format is easier to interpret with the position numbers. By looking at the placement of the numbers in this example, you should be able to see that position indexes 0 and 2 (corresponding to first and third argument positions, respectively) refer to the first and third arguments to **format**.

Meanwhile, position indexes 1 and 3 (corresponding to second and fourth arguments) refer to the integer expressions 3 and 7, which become the print-field widths of the respective fields.

Similarly, the following example shows the use of position indexes to display the number 3.141592, using a print-field width of 8 and a fixed-point display of 3 digits to the right of the decimal point. Note that numbers are right justified by default.

```
>>> 'Pi is approx. {0:{1}.{2}f}'.format(3.141592, 8, 3)
'Pi is approx.    3.142'
```

Remember that both 8 and 3, in this case, could be replaced by any integer expressions, including variables, which is really the whole point of this feature.

```
>>> a, b = 8, 3
>>> 'Pi is approx. {0:{1}.{2}f}'.format(3.141592, a, b)
'Pi is approx.    3.142'
```

This example is equivalent to the following in its effects:

```
'Pi is approx. {0:8.3f}'.format(3.141592)
```

Position names are also very useful in this context, as a way of making the intent of the formatting especially clear. Here's an example:

```
>>> 'Pi is {pi:{fill}{align}{width}.{prec}f}'.format(
        pi=3.141592, width=8, prec=3, fill='0', align='>')
```

Again, the values of the arguments can be filled in with numeric and string variables, which in turn allow adjustment of these values during execution of the code.

Chapter 5 *Summary*

The Python core language provides three techniques for formatting output strings. One is to use the string-class formatting operator (%) on display strings; these strings contain print-field specifiers similar to those used in the C language, with "printf" functions.

The second technique involves the **format** function. This approach allows you to specify not only things such as width and precision, but also thousands place grouping and handling of percentages.

The third technique, the **format** method of the string class, builds on the global **format** function but provides the most flexibility of all with multiple print fields.

The next two chapters take text-handling capabilities to a higher level still by utilizing the regular expression package.

Chapter 5   *Review Questions*

1 What, if any, are the advantages of using the first major technique—the string-class format operator (**%**)?

2 What, if any, are the advantages of using the global **format** function?

3 What advantage does the **format** method of the string class have, if any, compared to use of the global **format** function?

4 How exactly are these two techniques—**format** function and the **format** method of the string class—related, if at all?

5 How, in turn do these two techniques involve the **__format__** methods of individual classes, if at all?

6 What features of the format operator (**%**) do you need, at minimum, to print a table that lines up floating-point numbers in a nice column?

7 What features of the **format** method do you need, at minimum, to print a table that lines up floating-point numbers in a nice column?

8 Cite at least one example in which **repr** and **str** provide a different representation of a piece of data. Why does the **repr** version print more characters?

9 The **format** method enables you to specify a zero (0) as a fill character *or* as a leading zero to numeric expressions. Is this entirely redundant syntax? Or can you give at least one example in which the result might be different?

10 Of the three techniques—**format** operator (**%**), global **format** function, and **format** method of the **string** class—which support the specification of variable-length print fields?

Chapter 5   *Suggested Problems*

1 Write a hexadecimal calculator program that takes any number of hexadecimal numbers—breaking only when the user enters an empty string—and then outputs the sum, again, in hexadecimal numbers. (Hint: Remember that the **int** conversion, as explained in Chapter 1, "Review of the Fundamentals," enables conversion of strings using hexadecimal radix.)

2 Write a two-dimensional array program that does the following: Take integer input in the form of five rows of five columns each. Then, by looking at the maximum print width needed by the entire set (that is, the number of digits in the biggest number), determine the ideal print width for every cell in the table. This should be a uniform width, but one that contains the largest entry in the table. Use variable-length print fields to print this table.

3 Do the same application just described but for floating-point numbers. The printing of the table should output all the numbers in nice-looking columns.

6 Regular Expressions, Part I

Increasingly, the most sophisticated computer software deals with *patterns*—for example, speech patterns and the recognition of images. This chapter deals with the former: how to recognize patterns of words and characters. Although you can't construct a human language translator with these techniques alone, they are a start.

That's what regular expressions are for. A *regular expression* is a pattern you specify, using special characters to represent combinations of specified characters, digits, and words. It amounts to learning a new language, but it's a relatively simple one, and once you learn it, this technology lets you to do a great deal in a small space—sometimes only a statement or two—that would otherwise require many lines.

Note ▶ Regular expression syntax has a variety of flavors. The Python regular-expression package conforms to the Perl standard, which is an advanced and flexible version.

◀ Note

6.1 Introduction to Regular Expressions

A regular expression can be as simple as a series of characters that match a given word. For example, the following pattern matches the word "cat"; no surprise there.

```
cat
```

But what if you wanted to match a larger set of words? For example, let's say you wanted to match the following combination of letters:

▶ Match a "c" character.

▶ Match any number of "a" characters, but at least one.

▶ Match a "t" character.

Here's the regular expression that implements these criteria:

```
ca+t
```

With regular expressions (as with formatting specifiers in the previous chapter), there's a fundamental difference between *literal* and *special* characters.

Literal characters, such as "c" and "t" in this example, must be matched exactly, or the result is failure to match. Most characters are literal characters, and you should assume that a character is literal unless a special character changes its meaning. All letters and digits are, by themselves, literal characters; in contrast, punctuation characters are usually special; they change the meaning of nearby characters.

The plus sign (+) is a special character. It does not cause the regular-expression processor to look for a plus sign. Instead, it forms a subexpression, together with "a" that says, "Match one or more 'a' characters."

The pattern ca+t therefore matches any of the following:

```
cat
caat
caaat
caaaat
```

What if you wanted to match an *actual* plus sign? In that case, you'd use a backslash (\) to create an escape sequence. One of the functions of escape sequences is to turn a special character back into a literal character.

So the following regular expression matches ca+t exactly:

```
ca\+t
```

Another important operator is the multiplication sign (*), which means "*zero or more* occurrences of the preceding expression." Therefore, the expression ca*t matches any of the following:

```
ct
cat
caat
caaaaaat
```

Notably, this pattern matches "ct". It's important to keep in mind that the asterisk is an expression modifier and should not be evaluated separately. Instead, observe this rule.

> The asterisk (*****) modifies the meaning of the expression immediately preceding it, so the **a**, *together with the* *****, matches zero or more "a" characters.

You can break this down syntactically, as shown in Figure 6.1. The literal characters "c" and "t" each match a single character, but a***** forms a unit that says, "Match zero or more occurrences of 'a'."

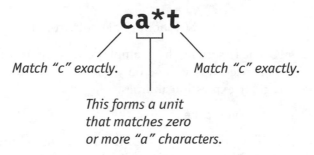

Match "c" exactly.

This forms a unit that matches zero or more "a" characters.

Match "c" exactly.

Figure 6.1. Parsing a simple expression

The plus sign (**+**), introduced earlier, works in a similar way. The plus sign, *together with the character or group that precedes it*, means "Match one or more instances of this expression."

6.2 A Practical Example: Phone Numbers

Suppose you want to write a verification function for phone numbers. We might think of the pattern as follows, in which **#** represents a digit:

```
###-###-####
```

With regular-expression syntax, you'd write the pattern this way:

```
\d\d\d-\d\d\d-\d\d\d\d
```

In this case, the backslash (****) continues to act as the escape character, but its action here is not to make "d" a literal character but to create a special meaning.

The subexpression \d means to match any one-digit character. Another way to express a digit character is to use the following subexpression:

```
[0-9]
```

However, \d is only two characters long instead of five and is therefore more succinct.

Here's a complete Python program that implements this regular-expression pattern for verifying a telephone number.

```
import re
pattern = r'\d\d\d-\d\d\d-\d\d\d\d'

s = input('Enter tel. number: ')
if re.match(pattern, s):
    print('Number accepted.')
else:
    print('Incorrect format.')
```

The first thing the example does is import the regular-expression package. This needs to be done only one time for each module (source file) that uses regular-expression abilities.

```
import re
```

Next, the example specifies the regular-expression pattern, coded as a *raw string*. With raw strings, Python itself does not translate any of the characters; it does not translate \n as a newline, for example, or \b by ringing a bell. Instead, all text in a raw string is passed directly along to the regular-expression evaluator.

```
r'string'    or
r"string"
```

After prompting the user for input, the program then calls the **match** function, which is qualified as **re.match** because it is imported from the **re** package.

```
re.match(pattern, s)
```

If the pattern argument matches the target string (s in this case), the function returns a match object; otherwise it returns the value **None**, which converts to the Boolean value **False**.

You can therefore use the value returned as if it were a Boolean value. If a match is confirmed, **True** is returned; otherwise, **False** is returned.

Note ▶ If you forget to include **r** (the raw-string indicator), this particular example still works, but your code will be more reliable if you always use the **r** when specifying regular-expression patterns. Python string interpretation does not work precisely the way C/C++ string interpretation does. In those languages, every backslash is automatically treated with special meaning unless you use a raw string. (Late versions of C++ also support a raw-string feature.) With Python, certain subexpressions, such as \n have special meaning. But otherwise, a backslash is accepted as a literal character.

Because Python sometimes interprets a backslash literally and sometimes doesn't, results can be unreliable and unpredictable, unless you get in the habit of always using raw strings. Therefore, the safe policy is to always place an **r** in front of regular-expression specification strings.

◀ Note

6.3 Refining Matches

Although the phone-number example featured in the previous section works, it has some limitations. The **re.match** function returns a "truc" value any time the pattern matches the beginning of the target string. It docs not have to match the entire string. So the code confirms a match for the following phone-number pattern:

```
555-123-5000
```

But it also matches the following:

```
555-345-5000000
```

If you want to restrict positive results to exact matches—so that the entire string has to match the pattern with nothing left over—you can add the special character **$**, which means "end of string." This character causes the match to fail if any additional text is detected beyond the specified pattern.

```
pattern = r'\d\d\d-\d\d\d-\d\d\d\d$'
```

There are other ways you might want to refine the regular-expression pattern. For example, you might want to permit input matching either of the following formats:

```
555-123-5000
555 123 5000
```

To accommodate both these patterns, you need to create a *character set*, which allows for more than one possible value in a particular position. For example, the following expression says to match either an "a" or a "b", but not both:

```
[ab]
```

It's possible to put many characters in a character set. But only one of the characters will be matched at a time. For example, the following range matches exactly one character: an "a", "b", "c", or "d" in the next position.

```
[abcd]
```

Likewise, the following expression says that either a space or a minus sign (–) can be matched—which is what we want in this case:

```
[ -]
```

In this context, the square brackets are the only special characters; the two characters inside are literal and at most one of them will be matched. The minus sign often has a special meaning within square brackets, but not when it appears in the very front or end of the characters inside the brackets.

Here's the full regular expression we need:

```
pattern = r'\d\d\d[ -]\d\d\d[ -]\d\d\d\d$'
```

Now, putting everything together with the refined pattern we've come up with in this section, here's the complete example:

```
import re
pattern = r'\d\d\d[ -]\d\d\d[ -]\d\d\d\d$'

s = input('Enter tel. number: ')
if re.match(pattern, s):
    print('Number accepted.')
else:
    print('Incorrect format.')
```

To review, here's what the Python regular-expression evaluator does, given this pattern.

- It attempts to match three digits: \d\d\d.

- It then reads the character set [-] and attempts to match either a space or a minus sign, but not both—that is, only one of these two characters will be matched here.

- It attempts to match three more digits: \d\d\d.

- Again, it attempts to match a space or a minus sign.

- It attempts to match four more digits : \d\d\d\d.

▶ It must match an end-of-string, $. This means there cannot be any more input in the target string after these last four digits are matched.

Another way to enforce an exact match, so that no trailing data is permitted, is to use the **re.fullmatch** method instead of **re.match**. You could use the following statements to match the telephone-number pattern; the use of **fullmatch** makes the end-of-string character unnecessary in this case.

```
import re

pattern = r'\d\d\d[ -]\d\d\d[ -]\d\d\d\d'

s = input('Enter tel. number: ')
if re.fullmatch(pattern, s):
    print('Number accepted.')
else:
    print('Incorrect format.')
```

So far, this chapter has only scratched the surface of what regular-expression syntax can do. Section 6.5 explains the syntax in greater detail. But in mastering this syntax, there are several principles to keep in mind.

▶ A number of characters have special meaning when placed in a regular-expression pattern. It's a good idea to become familiar with all of them. These include most punctuation characters, such as **+** and *****.

▶ Any characters that do not have special meaning to the Python regular-expression interpreter are considered literal characters. The regular-expression interpreter attempts to match these exactly.

▶ The backslash can be used to "escape" special characters, making them into literal characters. The backslash can also add special meaning to certain ordinary characters—for example, causing \d to mean "any digit" rather than a "d".

Admittedly, this might be a little confusing at first. If a character (such as *****) is special to begin with, escaping it (preceding it with a backslash) takes away that special meaning. But in other cases, escaping a character *gives* it special meaning.

Yes, both those things are true! But if you look at enough examples, it should make sense.

Here's a short program that tests for the validity of Social Security numbers. It's similar, but not identical, to that for checking the format of telephone numbers. This pattern looks for three digits, a minus sign, two digits, another minus sign, and then four digits.

```
import re

pattern = r'\d\d\d-\d\d-\d\d\d\d$'

s = input('Enter SSN: ')
if re.match(pattern, s):
    print('Number accepted.')
else:
    print('Incorrect format.')
```

6.4 How Regular Expressions Work: Compiling Versus Running

Regular expressions can seem like magic. But the implementation is a standard, if a relatively advanced, topic in computer science. The processing of regular expressions takes two major steps.

▶ A regular expression pattern is analyzed and then compiled into a series of data structures collectively called a *state machine*.

▶ The actual process of matching is considered "run time" for the regular-expression evaluator, as opposed to "compile time." During run time, the program traverses the state machine as it looks for a match.

Unless you're going to implement a regular-expression package yourself, it's not necessary to understand how to create these state machines, only what they do. But it's important to understand this dichotomy between compile time and runtime.

Let's take another simple example. Just as the modifier + means "Match one or more instances of the previous expression," the modifier * means "Match zero or more instances of the previous expression." So consider this:

```
ca*b
```

This expression matches "cb" as well as "cab", "caab", "caaab", and so on. When this regular expression is compiled, it produces the state machine shown in Figure 6.2.

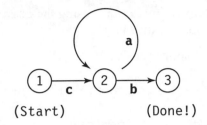

Figure 6.2. State machine for **ca*b**

The following list describes how the program traverses this state machine to find a match at run time. Position 1 is the starting point.

▶ A character is read. If it's a "c", the machine goes to state 2. Reading any other character causes failure.

▶ From state 2, either an "a" or a "b" can be read. If an "a" is read, the machine stays in state 2. It can do this any number of times. If a "b" is read, the machine transitions to state 3. Reading any other character causes failure.

▶ If the machine reaches state 3, it is finished, and success is reported.

This state machine illustrates some basic principles, simple though it is. In particular, a state machine has to be compiled and then later traversed at run time.

Note ▶ The state machine diagrams in this chapter assume DFAs (deterministic finite automata), whereas Python actually uses NFAs (nondeterministic finite automata). This makes no difference to you unless you're implementing a regular-expression evaluator, something you'll likely never need to do.

So if that's the case, you can ignore the difference between DFAs and NFAs! You're welcome.

◀ Note

Here's what you need to know: If you're going to use the same regular-expression pattern multiple times, it's a good idea to compile that pattern into a regular-expression object and then use that object repeatedly. The regex package provides a method for this purpose called **compile**.

```
regex_object_name = re.compile(pattern)
```

Here's a full example using the **compile** function to create a regular expression object called reg1.

```
import re

reg1 = re.compile(r'ca*b$')   # Compile the pattern!

def test_item(s):
    if re.match(reg1, s):
        print(s, 'is a match.')
    else:
        print(s, 'is not a match!')

test_item('caab')
test_item('caaxxb')
```

This little program prints the following:

```
caab is a match.
caaxxb is not a match!
```

You could perform these tasks without precompiling a regular-expression object. However, compiling can save execution time if you're going to use the same pattern more than once. Otherwise, Python may have to rebuild a state machine multiple times when it could have been built only once.

As a point of comparison, Figure 6.3 shows a state machine that implements the plus-sign (**+**), which means "one or more" rather than "zero or more."

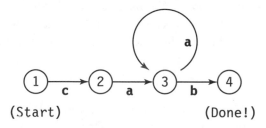

Figure 6.3. State machine for **ca+b**

Given this pattern, "cb" is not a successful match, but "cab", "caab", and "caaab" are. This state machine requires the reading of at least one "a". After that, matching further "a" characters is optional, but it can match as many instances of "a" in a row as it finds.

Another basic operator is the *alteration* operator (|), which means "either-or."

The following pattern matches an expression on either side of the bar. So what exactly do you think the following means?

ax|yz

The alteration operator, |, has about the lowest precedence of any part of the syntax. Therefore, this expression matches "ax" and "yz", but not "axyz". If no parentheses are used, the expression is evaluated as if written this way:

(ax)|(yz)

Figure 6.4 shows the state machine that implements this expression.

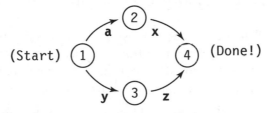

Figure 6.4. State machine for **(ax)|(yz)**

Now consider following expression, which uses parentheses to change the order of evaluation. With these parentheses, the alteration operator is interpreted to mean "either x or y but not both."

a(x|y)z

The parentheses and the | symbol are all special characters. Figure 6.5 illustrates the state machine that is compiled from the expression a(x|y)z.

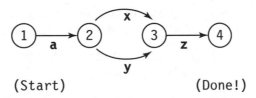

Figure 6.5. State machine for **a(x|y)z**

This behavior is the same as that for the following expression, which uses a character set rather than alteration:

```
a[xy]z
```

Is there a difference between alteration and a character set? Yes: A character set always matches one character of text (although it may be part of a more complex pattern, of course). Alteration, in contrast, may involve groups longer than a single character. For example, the following pattern matches either "cat" or "dog" in its entirety—but not "catdog":

```
cat|dog
```

6.5 Ignoring Case, and Other Function Flags

When a regular-expression pattern is compiled or being interpreted directly (through a call to a function such as **re.match**), you can combine a series of *regex* flags to influence behavior. A commonly used flag is the **re.IGNORECASE** flag. For example, the following code prints "Success."

```
if re.match('m*ack', 'Mack the Knife', re.IGNORECASE):
    print ('Success.')
```

The pattern 'm*ack' matches the word "Mack," because the flag tells Python to ignore the case of the letters. Watch out for Mack the Knife even if he doesn't know how to use uppercase!

The following does the same thing, because it uses the **I** abbreviation for the **IGNORECASE** flag, so **re.IGNORECASE** and **re.I** mean the same thing.

```
if re.match('m*ack', 'Mack the Knife', re.I):
    print ('Success.')
```

Binary flags may be combined using the binary OR operator (|). So you can turn on both the **I** and **DEBUG** flags as follows:

```
if re.match('m*ack', 'Mack the Knife', re.I | re.DEBUG):
    print ('Success.')
```

Table 6.1 summarizes the flags that can be used with regular-expression searching, matching, compiling, and so on.

Table 6.1. Regular-Expression Flags

FLAG	ABBREVIATION	DESCRIPTION
ASCII	A	Assume ASCII settings.
IGNORECASE	I	All searches and matches are case-insensitive.
DEBUG		When the operation is carried out within IDLE, debugging information is printed.
LOCALE	L	Causes matching of alphanumeric characters, word boundaries, and digits to recognize LOCALE settings.
MULTILINE	M	Causes the special characters ^ and $ to match beginnings and ends of lines as well as the beginning and end of the string.
DOTALL	S	The dot operator (.) matches all characters, including end of line (\n).
UNICODE	U	Causes matching of alphanumeric characters, word boundaries, and digits to recognize characters that UNICODE classifies as such.
VERBOSE	X	White space within patterns is ignored except when part of a character class. This enables the writing of prettier expressions in code.

6.6 Regular Expressions: Basic Syntax Summary

Learning regular-expression syntax is a little like learning a new language; but once you learn it, you'll be able to create patterns of endless variety. As powerful as this language is, it can be broken down into a few major elements.

▶ Meta characters: These are tools for specifying either a specific character or one of a number of characters, such as "any digit" or "any alphanumeric character." Each of these characters matches one character at a time.

▶ Character sets: This part of the syntax also matches one character at a time—in this case, giving a set of values from which to match.

▶ Expression quantifiers: These are operators that enable you to combine individual characters, including *wildcards*, into patterns of expressions that can be repeated any number of times.

▶ Groups: You can use parentheses to combine smaller expressions into larger ones.

6.6.1 Meta Characters

Table 6.2 lists meta characters, including wildcards that can be matched by any of a group, or range, of characters. For example, a dot (**.**) matches any one character, subject to a few limitations.

These meta characters match exactly one character at a time. Section 6.6.3, "Pattern Quantifiers," shows how to match a variable number of characters. The combination of wildcards, together with quantifiers, provides amazing flexibility.

Meta characters include not only those shown in the table but also the standard escape characters: These include **\t** (tab), **\n** (newline), **\r** (carriage return), **\f** (form feed), and **\v** (vertical tab).

Table 6.2. Regular-Expression Meta Characters

SPECIAL CHARACTER	NAME/DESCRIPTION
.	Dot. Matches any one character except a newline. If the **DOTALL** flag is enabled, it matches any character at all.
^	Caret. Matches the beginning of the string. If the **MULTILINE** flag is enabled, it also matches beginning of lines (any character after a newline).
$	Matches the end of a string. If the **MULTILINE** flag is enabled, it matches the end of a line (the last character before a newline or end of string).
\A	Matches beginning of a string.
\b	Word boundary. For example, r'ish\b' matches 'ish is' and 'ish)' but not 'ishmael'.
\B	Nonword boundary. Matches only if a new word does *not* begin at this point. For example, r'al\B' matches 'always' but not 'al '.
\d	Any digit character. This includes the digit characters 0 through 9. If the **UNICODE** flag is set, then Unicode characters classified as digits are also included.
\s	Any whitespace character; may be blank space or any of the following: \t, \n, \r, \f, or \v. **UNICODE** and **LOCALE** flags may have an effect on what is considered a whitespace character.
\S	Any character that is not a white space, as defined just above.
\w	Matches any alphanumeric character (letter or digit) or an underscore (_). The **UNICODE** and **LOCALE** flags may have an effect on what characters are considered to be alphanumeric.
\W	Matches any character that is not alphanumeric as described just above.
\z	Matches the end of a string.

For example, the following regular-expression pattern matches any string that begins with two digits:

```
r'\d\d'
```

The next example matches a string that consists of a two-digit string and nothing else:

```
r'\d\d$'
```

6.6.2 *Character Sets*

The character-set syntax of Python regular expressions provides even finer control over what character is to be matched next.

```
[char_set]    // Match any one character in the set.
[^char_set]   // Match any one character NOT in the set.
```

You can specify character sets by listing characters directly, as well as by ranges, covered a few paragraphs later. For example, the following expression matches any vowel (except, of course, for "y").

```
[aeiou]
```

For example, suppose you specify the following regular-expression pattern:

```
r'c[aeiou]t'
```

This matches any of the following:

```
cat
cet
cit
cot
cut
```

We can combine ranges with other operators, such as **+**, which retains its usual meaning outside the square brackets. So consider

```
c[aeiou]+t
```

This matches any of the following, as well as many other possible strings:

```
cat
ciot
ciiaaet
caaauuuut
ceeit
```

Within a range, the minus sign (-) enables you to specify ranges of characters when the minus sign appears between two other characters in a character range. Otherwise, it is treated as a literal character.

For example, the following range matches any character from lowercase "a" to lowercase "n":

```
[a-n]
```

This range therefore matches an "a", "b", "c", up to an "l", "m", or "n". If the **IGNORECASE** flag is enabled, it also matches uppercase versions of these letters.

The following matches any uppercase or lowercase letter, or digit. Unlike "\w," however, this character set does not match an underscore (_).

```
[A-Za-z0-9]
```

The following matches any hexadecimal digit: a digit from 0 to 9 or an uppercase or lowercase letter in the range "A", "B", "C", "D", "E", and "F".

```
[A-Fa-f0-9]
```

Character sets observe some special rules.

▶ Almost all characters within square brackets ([ ]) lose their special meaning, except where specifically mentioned here. Therefore, almost everything is interpreted literally.

▶ A closing square bracket has special meaning, terminating the character set; therefore, a closing bracket must be escaped with a backslash to be interpreted literally: "\]"

▶ The minus sign (-) has special meaning unless it occurs at the very beginning or end of the character set, in which case it is interpreted as a literal minus sign. Likewise, a caret (^) has special meaning at the beginning of a range but not elsewhere.

▶ The backslash (\), even in this context, must be escaped to be represented literally. Use "\\" to represent a backslash.

For example, outside a character-set specification, the arithmetic operators + and * have special meaning. Yet they lose their meaning within square brackets, so you can specify a range that matches any one of these characters:

```
[+*/-]
```

This range specification includes a minus sign (-), but it has no special meaning because it appears at the end of the character set rather than in the middle.

The following character-set specification uses a caret to match any character that is *not* one of the four operators +, *, /, or -. The caret has special meaning here because it appears at the beginning.

```
[^+*/-]
```

But the following specification, which features the caret (^) in a different position, matches any of five operators, ^, +, *, /, or -.

```
[+*^/-]
```

Therefore, the following Python code prints "Success!" when run.

```python
import re
if re.match(r'[+*^/-]', '^'):
    print('Success!')
```

However, the following Python code does not print "Success," because the caret at the beginning of the character set reverses the meaning of the character set.

```python
import re
if re.match(r'[^+*^/-]', '^'):
    print('Success!')
```

6.6.3 *Pattern Quantifiers*

All of the quantifiers in Table 6.3 are expression modifiers, and not expression extenders. Section 6.6.4, discusses in detail what the implications of "greedy" matching are.

Table 6.3. Regular-Expression Quantifiers (Greedy)

SYNTAX	DESCRIPTION
*expr***	Modifies meaning of expression *expr* so that it matches zero or more occurrences rather than one. For example, a* matches "a", "aa", and "aaa", as well as an empty string.
expr+	Modifies meaning of expression *expr* so that it matches one or more occurrences rather than only one. For example, a+ matches "a", "aa", and "aaa".
expr?	Modifies meaning of expression *expr* so that it matches zero or one occurrence of *expr*. For example, a? matches "a" or an empty string.
expr1 | *expr2*	Alternation. Matches a single occurrence of *expr1*, or a single occurrence of *expr2*, but not both. For example, a|b matches "a" or "b". Note that the precedence of this operator is very low, so cat|dog matches "cat" or "dog".

▼ *continued on next page*

Table 6.3. Regular-Expression Quantifiers (Greedy) (*continued*)

SYNTAX	DESCRIPTION
expr{*n*}	Modifies expression so that it matches exactly *n* occurrences of *expr*. For example, a{3} matches "aaa"; but although sa{3}d matches "saaad" it does not match "saaaaad".
expr{*m, n*}	Matches a minimum of *m* occurrences of *expr* and a maximum of *n*. For example, x{2,4}y matches "xxy", "xxxy", and "xxxxy" but not "xxxxxxy" or "xy".
expr{*m,*}	Matches a minimum of *m* occurrences of *expr* with no upper limit to how many can be matched. For example, x{3,} finds a match if it can match the pattern "xxx" anywhere. But it will match more than three if it can. Therefore zx(3,)y matches "zxxxxxy".
expr{*,n*}	Matches a minimum of zero, and a maximum of *n*, instances of the expression *expr*. For example, ca{,2}t matches "ct", "cat", and "caat" but not "caaat".
(*expr*)	Causes the regular-expression evaluator to look at all of *expr* as a single group. There are two major purposes for doing so. First, a quantifier applies to the expression immediately preceding it; but if that expression is a group, the entire group is referred to. For example, (ab)+ matches "ab", "abab", "ababab", and so on.
	Second, groups are significant because they can be referred to later, both in matching and text replacement.
n	Refers to a group that has already previously matched; the reference is to the text actually found at run time and not just a repeat of the pattern itself. \1 refers to the first group, \2 refers to the second group, and so on.

The next-to-last quantifier listed in Table 6.3 is the use of parentheses for creating groups. Grouping can dramatically affect the meaning of a pattern. Putting items in parentheses also creates tagged groups for later reference.

The use of the numeric quantifiers from Table 6.3 makes some expressions easier to render, or at least more compact. For example, consider the phone-number verification pattern introduced earlier.

```
r'\d\d\d-\d\d\d-\d\d\d\d'
```

This can be revised as

```
r'\d{3}-\d{3}-\d{4}'
```

This example saves a few keystrokes of typing, but other cases might save quite a bit more. Using these features also creates code that is more readable and easier to maintain.

Parentheses have a great deal of significance beyond mere clarity. Their most important role is in specifying groups, which in turn can affect how a pattern is parsed. For example, consider the following two patterns:

```
pat1 = r'cab+'
pat2 = r'c(ab)+'
```

The first pattern matches any of the following strings, in which the "b" is repeated.

```
cab
cabb
cabbb
cabbbb
```

But the second pattern—thanks to the virtues of grouping—matches any of the following strings. These strings repeat "ab" rather than "b".

```
cab
cabab
cababab
cabababab
```

In this case, grouping is highly significant. Figure 6.6 shows how the Python regular-expression evaluator interprets the meaning of the pattern differently because of the parentheses; specifically, it's the group "ab" that is repeated.

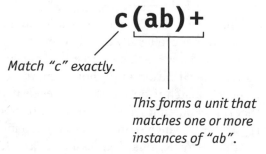

Match "c" exactly.

This forms a unit that matches one or more instances of "ab".

Figure 6.6. Parsing a group in a regular expression

6.6.4 Backtracking, Greedy, and Non-Greedy

Python regular expressions are flexible in many subtle ways. In particular, the regular-expression evaluator will always favor a match over a nonmatch, even if this requires a technique called *backtracking*.

Consider the following example.

```
import re
pat = r'c.*t'
if re.match(pat, 'cat'):
    print('Success!')
```

Ask yourself: Does the pattern c.*t match the target string, "cat"? It should, shouldn't it? Because "c" will match a "c", "t" will match a "t", and the pattern ".*" says, "Match any number of characters." So it should match "cat".

But wait a moment. If you take the ".*" pattern literally, shouldn't it do the following?

▶ Match the "c".

▶ Match the general pattern ".*" by matching all the remaining characters, namely "at".

▶ The end of the string is then reached. The regular-expression evaluator tries to match a "t" but it can't, because it's now at the end of the string. The result? It looks like failure.

Fortunately, the regular-expression evaluator is more sophisticated than that. Having failed to match the string, it will backtrack and try matching fewer characters based on ".*"; after backtracking one character, it finds that it does match the target string, "cat".

The point is that regular-expression syntax is flexible and correctly matches any pattern it can legally match, even if it has to use backtracking.

A related issue is that of greedy versus non-greedy quantifiers. All types of pattern specification in Python regular expressions follow the Golden Rule: Report a match if one is possible, even if you have to backtrack. But within that rule, sometimes multiple results are possible. "Greedy versus non-greedy" is an issue of which string to select when more than one is possible.

Chapter 7, "Regular Expressions, Part II," covers that issue in depth, listing the non-greedy quantifiers.

6.7 A Practical Regular-Expression Example

This section uses the elements shown earlier in a practical example. Suppose you're given the task of writing software that verifies whether a password is strong enough.

We're not talking about password encryption. That's a different topic. But before a password is accepted, you could test whether it has sufficient strength.

Some time ago, in the Wild West of software development, any word at least one character in size might be accepted. Such passwords proved easy to crack. Nowadays, only difficult-to-crack passwords are accepted. Otherwise the user is automatically prompted to reenter. Here are some typical criteria:

▶ Each and every character must be an uppercase or lowercase letter, digit, or underscore (_), or one of the following punctuation characters: **@, #, $, %, ^, &, *,** or **!**.

▶ The minimum length is eight characters total.

▶ It must contain at least one letter.

▶ It must contain at least one digit.

▶ It must contain one of the accepted punctuation characters.

Now let's say you're employed to write these tests. If you use regular expressions, this job will be easy for you—a delicious piece of cake.

The following verification function performs the necessary tests. We can implement the five rules by using four patterns and performing **re.match** with each.

```
import re

pat1 = r'(\w|[@#$%^&*!]){8,}$'
pat2 = r'.*\d'
pat3 = r'.*[a-zA-Z]'
pat4 = r'.*[@#$%^$*]'

def verify_passwd(s):
    b = (re.match(pat1, s) and re.match(pat2, s) and
            re.match(pat3, s) and re.match(pat4, s))
    return bool(b)
```

The verify_passwd function applies four different match criteria to a target string, s. The **re.match** function is called with each of four different patterns, pat1 through pat4. If all four matches succeed, the result is "true."

The first pattern accepts any character that is a letter, character, or underscore *or* a character in the range @#$%^&*! . . . and then it requires a match of eight or more of such characters.

The \w meta character means "Match any alphanumeric character." So when the expression inside parentheses is put together, it means "Match an alphanumeric character *or* one of the punctuation characters listed."

```
(\w|[@#$%^&*!]){8,}
```

Let's break this down a little bit. Inside the parentheses, we find this expression:

```
\w|[@#$%^&*!]
```

Alteration is used here, indicated by the vertical bar, |. This subpattern says, "Match \w *or* match a character in the set [@#$%^&*!]."

The characters within the square brackets lose the special meaning that they would otherwise have outside the brackets. Therefore, everything inside the range specification is treated literally rather than as a special character.

Putting this all together, the subexpression says, "Match either an alphanumeric character (\w), or match one of the punctuation characters listed." The next part of the pattern, {8,}, says to do this at least eight times.

Therefore, we match eight or more characters, in which each is alphanumeric or one of the punctuation characters shown.

Finally, there is an end-of-string indicator, $. Consequently, there cannot be, for example, any trailing spaces. Appending an end-of-line symbol, $, requires the string to terminate after reading the last character.

```
(\w|[@#$%^&*!]){8,}$
```

The rest of the tests implemented with **re.match**—each using a different string—check for the presence of a certain kind of character. For example, pat2 matches any number of characters of any kind (.*) and then matches a digit. As a regular-expression pattern, this says, "Match zero or more characters, and then match a digit."

```
.*\d
```

The next pattern, pat3, matches zero or more characters (.*) and then matches an uppercase or lowercase letter.

```
.*[a-zA-Z]
```

The final pattern matches zero or more characters and then matches a character in the range @#$%^$*!.

```
.*[@#$%^$*!]
```

The effect is to test for each of the following: a letter, a digit, and a punctuation character. There must be at least one of each. Having more than one of any of these characters (digit, letter, underscore, punctuation character), of course, is fine.

6.8 Using the Match Object

The **re.match** function returns either a **match** object, if it succeeds, or the special object **None**, if it fails. So far we've been using this value (object or **None**) as if it were a Boolean value (true/false), which is a valid technique in Python.

However, if you get back a **match** object, you can use it to get information about the match. For example, a regular-expression pattern may optionally be divided into subgroups by use of parentheses. A **match** object can be used to determine what text was matched in each subgroup.

For example, consider the following:

```
import re
pat = r'(a+)(b+)(c+)'
m = re.match(pat, 'abbcccee')
print(m.group(0))
print(m.group(1))
print(m.group(2))
print(m.group(3))
```

This example prints the following:

```
abbccc
a
bb
ccc
```

The **group** method, as you can see from this example, returns all or part of the matched text as follows.

▶ **group(0)** returns the entire text that was matched by the regular expression.

▶ **group(**n**)**, starting with 1, returns a matched group, in which a group is delimited by parentheses. The first such group can be accessed as group(1), the second as group(2), and so on.

Another attribute of **match** objects is **lastindex**. This is an integer containing the number of the last group found during the match. The previous example can therefore be written with a more general loop.

```
import re
pat = r'(a+)(b+)(c+)'
m = re.match(pat, 'abbcccee')
for i in range(m.lastindex + 1):
    print(i, '. ', m.group(i), sep='')
```

This example produces the following output:

```
0. abbccc
1. a
2. bb
3. ccc
```

In the code for this example, 1 had to be added to m.lastindex. That's because the **range** function produces an iterator beginning with 0, up to but not including the argument value. In this case, the groups are numbered 1, 2, 3, so the range needs to extend to 3; and the way you do that is by adding 1 to the end of the range.

Table 6.4 summarizes the attributes of a **match** object.

Table 6.4. Match Object Attributes

SYNTAX	DESCRIPTION
group(*n*)	Returns text corresponding to the specified group, beginning with 1 as the first group; the default value is 0, which returns the text of the entire matched string.
groups()	Returns a tuple containing all the groups within the matched text, beginning with group 1 (the first subgroup).
groupdict()	Returns a dictionary consisting of all named groups, in the format *name*:*text*.
start(*n*)	Returns the starting position, within the target string, of the group referred to by *n*. Positions within a string are zero-based, but the group numbering is 1-based, so start(1) returns the starting string index of the first group. start(0) returns the starting string index of all the matched text.
end(*n*)	Similar to **start(*n*)**, except that **end(*n*)** gets the ending position of the identified group, relative to the entire target string. Within this string, the text consists of all characters within the target string, beginning with the "start" index, up to but not including the "end" index. For example, start and end values of 0 and 3 means that the first three characters were matched.
span(*n*)	Returns the information provided by **start(*n*)** and **end(*n*)** but returns it in tuple form.
lastindex	The highest index number among the groups.

6.9 Searching a String for Patterns

Once you understand the basic regular-expression syntax, you can apply it in many useful ways. So far, we've used it to look for exact matches of a pattern.

But another basic usage for regular expressions is to do searches: not to require the entire string to match but only part of it. This section focuses on finding the first substring that matches a pattern. The **re.search** function performs this task.

$$match\_obj = \texttt{re.search}(pattern, target\_string, flags=0)$$

In this syntax, *pattern* is either a string containing a regular-expression pattern or a precompiled regular-expression object; *target_string* is the string to be searched. The *flags* argument is optional and has a default value of 0.

The function produces a **match** object if successful and **None** otherwise. This function is close to **re.match** in the way that it works, except it does not require the match to happen at the beginning of the string.

For example, the following code finds the first occurrence of a number that has at least two digits.

```
import re
m = re.search(r'\d{2,}', '1 set of 23 owls, 999 doves.')
print('"', m.group(), '" found at ', m.span(), sep='')
```

In this case, the search string specifies a simple pattern: two or more digits. This search pattern is easy to express in regular-expression syntax, using the special characters introduced earlier in this chapter.

```
\d{2,}
```

The rest of the code uses the resulting match object, assigning that object a variable name of m. Using the **group** and **span** methods of this object, as described in Section 6.8, "Using the Match Object," you can get information about what was matched and where in the target string the match occurred.

The code in this example prints the following:

```
"23" found at (9, 11)
```

This successfully reports that the substring "23" was found by the search: m.group() produced the substring that was matched, "23," while m.span() produced the starting and ending positions within the target string as the tuple (9, 11).

Here, as elsewhere, the starting position is a zero-based index into the target string, so the value 9 means that the substring was found starting at the tenth character. The substring occupies all positions *up to but not including* the ending position, 11.

6.10 Iterative Searching ("findall")

One of the most common search tasks is to find *all* substrings matching a particular pattern. This turns out to be easy, because there is such a function and it produces a Python list.

$$list = \texttt{re.findall}(pattern,\ target\_string,\ flags\texttt{=0})$$

In this syntax, most of the individual items have the meaning described in the previous section: *pattern* is a regular-expression string or precompiled object, *target_string* is the string to be searched, and *flags* is optional.

The return value of **re.findall** is a list of strings, each string containing one of the substrings found. These are returned in the order found.

Regular-expression searches are *non-overlapping*. This means, for example, that once the string "12345" is found, the search will not then find "2345," "345," "45," and so on. Furthermore, all the quantifiers in this chapter are greedy; each will find as long a string as it can.

An example should help clarify. Let's take an example from the previous section and search for all digit strings, and not only the first one. Also, let's look for digit strings that have at least one digit.

```
import re
s = '1 set of 23 owls, 999 doves.'
print(re.findall(r'\d+', s))
```

The code prints the following list of strings:

```
['1', '23', '999']
```

This is almost certainly the result you want. Because the search is both non-overlapping and greedy, each string of digits is fully read but read only once.

What if you want to extract a digit string that optionally contains any number of thousands place separators (a comma, in the American nomenclature), decimal points, or both? The easiest way to do this is to specify that the first character must be a digit, but it can be followed by another digit, a comma (,), or a dot(.)—and that such a character (digit, comma, or dot) can appear zero or more times.

```
import re
s = 'What is 1,000.5 times 3 times 2,000?'
print(re.findall(r'\d[0-9,.]*', s))
```

This example prints the following list:

```
['1,000.5', '3', '2,000']
```

In looking back at this example, keep in mind that the regular-expression pattern is

```
\d[0-9,.]*
```

This means "Match a digit (\d), followed by any character in the range [0-9,.], zero or more times."

Here's another example. Suppose we want to find all occurrences of words six or more characters in length. Here's some code that implements that search.

```
s = 'I do not use sophisticated, multisyllabic words!'
print(re.findall(r'\w{6,}', s))
```

This code prints the following list:

```
['sophisticated', 'multisyllabic']
```

In this case, the regular expression pattern is

```
\w{6,}
```

The special character \w matches any of the following: a letter, a digit, or an underscore. Therefore, the pattern matches any word at least six characters long.

Finally, let's write a function useful for the Reverse Polish Notation calculator introduced in Section 3.12. We'd like to break down input into a list of strings, but we'd like operators (+, *, /, −) to be recognized separately from numbers. In other words, suppose we have the input

```
12 15+3 100-*
```

We'd like 12, 15, 3, 100, and the three operators (+, −, and *) to each be recognized as separate substrings, or *tokens*. The space between "12" and "15" is necessary, but extra spaces shouldn't be required around the operators. An easy solution is to use the **re.findall** function.

```
import re
s = '12 15+3 100-*'
print(re.findall(r'[+*/-]|\w+', s))
```

This example prints the following:

```
['12', '15', '+', '3', '100', '-', '*']
```

This is exactly what we wanted.

This example has a subtlety. As explained in Section 6.6.2, "Character Sets," the minus sign (-) has a special meaning within square brackets *unless* it appears at the very beginning or end of the range, as is the case here. In this case, the minus sign is at the end of the range, so it's interpreted literally.

```
[+*/-]|\w+
```

What this pattern says is "First, match one of the four operator characters if possible (+, *, /, or -). Failing that, try to read a word, which is a series of one or more "w" characters: Each of these characters is a digit, letter, or underscore (_)." In this case, the strings "12," "15," "3," and "100" are each read as words.

But the previous expression used both the alternation operator and plus sign (| and +). How does precedence work in this case? The answer is that | has low priority, so the expression means "Match one of the operators *or* match any number of digit characters." That's why the return value is

```
['12', '15', '+', '3', '100', '-', '*']
```

Each of these substrings consists of either an operator or a word: the word ends when a white space or operator is read (because white spaces and operators are not matched by \w).

6.11 The "findall" Method and the Grouping Problem

The **re.findall** method has a quirk that, although it creates useful behavior, can also produce frustrating results if you don't anticipate it.

One of the most useful tools in regular-expression grammar is grouping. For example, the following regular-expression pattern captures all instances of well-formed numbers in the standard American format, including thousands place separators (,):

```
num_pat = r'\d{1,3}(,\d{3})*(\.\d*)?'
```

To summarize, this pattern looks for the following:

▶ Between one and three digits. Not optional.

▶ A group of characters beginning with a comma (,) followed by exactly three digits. This group can appear zero or more times.

▶ A decimal point (.) followed by zero or more digits. This group is optional.

You can use this pattern effectively to match valid digit strings, such as any of the following:

```
10.5
5,005
12,333,444.0007
```

But a problem occurs when you use this pattern to search for all occurrences of numbers. When the **re.findall** function is given a regular-expression pattern containing parenthesized groups, it returns a list of tuples in which each tuple contains all the text found in that subgroup.

Here's an example:

```
pat = r'\d{1,3}(,\d{3})*(\.\d*)?'
print(re.findall(pat, '12,000 monkeys and 55.5 cats.'))
```

These statements print the following:

```
[(',000', ''), ('', '.5')]
```

But this is not what we wanted!

What went wrong? The problem in this case is that if you use grouping in the search string, the **findall** function returns a list containing the subgroups found *within* each matched string, rather than returning strings that matched the overall pattern, which is what we wanted.

So the results, in this case, are wrong.

To get what was desired, use a two-part solution.

1 Put the entire expression in a grouping by putting the whole thing in parentheses.

2 Print the expression item[0].

Here is the code that implements this solution.

```
pat = r'(\d{1,3}(,\d{3})*(\.\d*)?)'
lst = re.findall(pat, '12,000 monkeys on 55.5 cats.')
for item in lst:
    print(item[0])
```

This produces

```
12,000
55.5
```

This is what we wanted.

6.12 Searching for Repeated Patterns

The most sophisticated patterns involve references to *tagged groups*. When a pattern inside parentheses gets a match, the regular expression notes the characters that were actually matched at run time and remembers them by *tagging* the group—that is, the actual characters that were matched.

An example should make this clear. One of the common mistakes writers make is to repeat words. For example, you write "the the" instead of "the" or write "it it" instead of "it".

Here's a search pattern that looks for a repeated word:

```
(w+) \1
```

This pattern matches a word, a series of one or more "w" characters (letter, digit, or underscore) followed by a space, followed by a repeat of those same characters.

This pattern does not match the following:

```
the dog
```

Although "the" and "dog" both match the word criterion (\w+), the second word is not identical to the first. The word "the" was tagged but not repeated in this case.

But the following does matches the pattern, because it repeats the tagged substring, "the":

```
the the
```

Here's the pattern used in a fuller context, which has "the the" in the target string.

```
import re

s = 'The cow jumped over the the moon.'
m = re.search(r'(\w+) \1', s)
print(m.group(), '...found at', m.span())
```

This code, when run, prints the following:

```
the the ...found at (20, 27)
```

The following pattern says, "Match a word made up of one or more alphanumeric characters. Tag them, then match a space, and then match a recurrence of the tagged characters."

```
(\w+) \1
```

Here's another example using this same pattern, applied to a string with "of of".

```
s = 'The United States of of America.'
m = re.search(r'(\w+) \1', s)
print(m.group(), '...found at', m.span())
```

This example prints the result

```
of of ...found at (18, 23)
```

As with all other regular-expression matches and searches, the Python implementation makes it easy to make comparisons case-insensitive, which can be useful in this case. Consider this text string:

```
s = 'The the cow jumped over the the moon.'
```

Can we do a search that indicates a repeated word at the beginning of this sentence, or not? Yes, because all we have to do is specify the **re.IGNORECASE** flag, or **re.I**, for short.

```
m = re.search(r'(\w+) \1', s, flags=re.I)
print(m.group(), '...found at', m.span())
```

This example prints

```
The the ...found at (0, 7)
```

The **re.search** function reports the first successful match that was found.

6.13 *Replacing Text*

Another tool is the ability to replace text—that is, text substitution. We might want to replace all occurrences of a pattern with some other pattern. This almost always involves group tagging, described in the previous section.

The **re.sub** function performs text substitution.

re.sub(*find_pattern*, *repl*, *target_str*, *count*=0, *flags*=0)

In this syntax, *find_pattern* is the pattern to look for, *repl* is the regular-expression replacement string, and *target_str* is the string to be searched. The last two arguments are both optional.

The return value is the new string, which consists of the target string after the requested replacements have been made.

Here is a trivial example, which replaces each occurrence of "dog" with "cat":

```
import re
s = 'Get me a new dog to befriend my dog.'
s2 = re.sub('dog', 'cat', s)
print(s2)
```

This example prints

```
Get me a new cat to befriend my cat.
```

However, this is not that interesting, because it does not use any regular-expression special characters. The next example does.

```
s = 'The the cow jumped over over the moon.'
s2 = re.sub(r'(\w+) \1', r'\1', s, flags=re.I)
print(s2)
```

This prints the following string, which fixes the repeated word problem—both occurrences, in fact, even though the first of them required the case-insensitive flag to be set.

```
The cow jumped over the moon.
```

In this output, "The the" has been replaced by "The" and "over over" has been replaced by "over". This works because the regular-expression search pattern specifies any repeated word. It's rendered here as a raw string:

```
r'(\w+) \1'
```

The next string, the replacement string, contains only a reference to the first half of that pattern. This is a tagged string, so this directs the regular-expression evaluator to note that tagged string and use it as the replacement string.

```
r'\1'
```

This example illustrates some critical points.

First, the replacement string should be specified as a raw string, just as the search string is. Python string handling attaches a special meaning to \1; therefore, if you don't specify the replacement text as a raw string, nothing works—unless you use the other way of specifying a literal backslash:

```
\\1
```

But it's easier to just stick to using raw strings.

Second, the repeated-word test on "The the" will fail unless the *flags* argument is set to **re.I** (or **re.IGNORECASE**). In this example, the *flags* argument must be specifically named.

```
s2 = re.sub(r'(\w+) \1', r'\1', s, flags=re.I)
```

Chapter 6   *Summary*

This chapter explored the basic capabilities of the Python regular-expression package: how you can use it to validate the format of data input, how to search for strings that match a specified pattern, how to break up input into tokens, and how to use regular expressions to do sophisticated search-and-replace operations.

Understanding the regular-expression syntax is a matter of understanding ranges and wildcards—which can match one character at a time—and understanding quantifiers, which say that you can match zero, one, or any number of repetitions of a group of characters. Combining these abilities enables you to use regular expressions to express patterns of unlimited complexity.

In the next chapter, we'll look at some more examples of regular-expression use, as well as looking at non-greedy operators and the Scanner interface, which builds on top of the Python regular-expression package.

Chapter 6   *Review Questions*

1 What are the minimum number of characters, and the maximum number of characters, that can be matched by the expression "x*"?

2 Explain the difference in results between "(ab)c+" and "a(bc)+". Which, if either, is equivalent to the unqualified pattern "abc+"?

3 When using regular expressions, precisely how often do you need to use the following statement?

```
import re
```

4 When you express a range using square brackets, exactly which characters have special meaning, and under what circumstances?

5 What are the advantages of compiling a regular-expression object?

6 What are some ways of using the match object returned by functions such as **re.match** and **re.search**?

7 What is the difference between using an alteration, which involves the vertical bar (|), and using a character set, which involves square brackets?

8 Why is it important to use the raw-string indicator (**r**) in regular-expression search patterns? In replacement strings?

9 Which characters, if any, have special meaning inside a replacement string?

Chapter 6   *Suggested Problems*

1 Write a verification function that recognizes phone numbers under the old format, in which the area code—the first three digits—was optional. (When omitted, the implication was that the phone number was local.)

2 Write another version of this phone-number verification program, but this time make an initial "1" digit optional. However, make sure that the one digit appears at the beginning only if the area code (first three digits) does as well.

3 Write a program that takes a target string as input and replaces all occurrences of multiple spaces (such as two or three spaces in a row) and then replaces each of these occurrences with a single space.

7 Regular Expressions, Part II

Regular expressions are such a big subject in Python that it's hard to cover it all in one chapter. This chapter explores the finer points of the Python regular-expression grammar.

One of the most useful advanced features of Python is the Scanner class. It's little known and little documented. The last couple of sections in this chapter explain the use of this feature at length. Once you understand it, you'll find it an extremely useful tool. It's a way of directing specific patterns to be associated with specific kinds of tokens and then taking the appropriate action.

7.1 Summary of Advanced RegEx Grammar

Table 7.1 summarizes the advanced grammar introduced in this chapter. The subsequent sections explain how each of these features works in more detail.

Table 7.1. Advanced Regular-Expression Grammar

SYNTAX	DESCRIPTION
(?:*expr*)	Nontagged group. Treat the *expr* as a single unit, but do not tag the characters matched at run time. The characters are recognized for the purpose of matching but not recorded as a group.
expr??	Non-greedy version of the **?** operator.
*expr**?	Match zero or more instances of *expr* using non-greedy matching. (So, for example, the pattern <.*?> stops matching at the first angle bracket it sees and not the last.)
expr+?	Match one or more instances of expr using non-greedy matching; given more than one valid way to match the target string, match as few characters as possible.

▼ *continued on next page*

Table 7.1. Advanced Regular-Expression Grammar (*continued*)

SYNTAX	DESCRIPTION
expr{*m*}? *expr*{*m*,*n*}?	Non-greedy versions of the {*m*} and {*m*,*n*} operators. A non-greedy version of the first syntax, *expr*{*m*}?, is unlikely to ever behave any differently from the greedy version, but it is included here for the sake of completeness.
(?=*expr*)	Positive look-ahead. The overall expression matches if *expr* matches the next characters to be read; however, these characters are neither "consumed" nor tagged; they are treated as if not yet read—meaning that the next regex operation will read them again.
(?!*expr*)	Negative look-ahead. The overall expression matches if *expr* fails to match the next characters to be read. However, these characters are neither consumed nor tagged, so they remain to be read by the next regex matching or searching operation.
(?<=*expr*)	Positive look-behind. The overall expression matches if immediately preceded by *expr*, which must be of fixed length. The effect is to temporarily back up the appropriate number of characters and reread them if possible. The characters reread this way are not tagged. For example, given the expression (?<=abc)def, the characters def within abcdef are matched; however, only the characters def are actually matched; the characters abc are not part of the match itself. The pattern says, "Match def but only if preceded by abc."
(?<!*expr*)	Negative look-behind. The overall expression matches if not immediately preceded by *expr*, which must be of fixed length. The effect is to temporarily back up the appropriate number of characters and reread them. The characters reread are not tagged.
(?P<*name*>*expr*)	Named group. The overall expression matches if *expr* matches. As a result, the group is tagged but also given a name so that it can be referred to in other expressions by that name.
(?P=*name*)	Test for a named group. This expression is a positive "match" if the named group has previously appeared and been matched.
(#*text*)	Comment. This text may appear within a regular expression, but it will be ignored by the regular-expression evaluator itself.
(?(*name*)yes_pat|no_pat) (?(*name*)yes_pat) (?(*id*)yes_pat|no_pat) (?(*id*)yes_pat)	Conditional matching. If the named group has previously appeared and been identified as such, then this expression will attempt to match the "yes" pattern, *yes_pat*; otherwise, it will attempt to match the "no" pattern, *no_pat*. An id is a number identifying a group.

In this table, *name* can be any nonconflicting name you choose, subject to the standard rules for forming symbolic names.

7.2 Noncapture Groups

One of the advanced regular-expression operations is to put expressions into groups without tagging them. There are many reasons you might want to put characters into groups. But *tagging*—the capturing of character groups matched at run time—is a separate ability. Sometimes you need to do one without the other.

7.2.1 The Canonical Number Example

An example near the end of Chapter 6, "Regular Expressions, Part I," showed how to create a pattern that accepts all valid numerals in the American format, including thousands group separators (,)—but rejects everything else.

```
r'\d{1,3}(,\d{3})*(\.\d*)?'
```

If you append an end-of-line symbol (**$**), this pattern correctly matches an individual number. At the same time, it rejects any string that does not contain a valid numeral.

```
r'\d{1,3}(,\d{3})*(\.\d*)?$'
```

Applying the **re.match** function with this pattern gets a positive (true) result for all these strings:

```
12,000,330
1,001
0.51
0.99999
```

But it does not return true for any of these:

```
1,00000
12,,1
0..5.7
```

To employ this regular-expression pattern successfully with **re.findall**, so that you can find multiple numbers, two things need to be done.

First, the pattern needs to end with a word boundary (**\b**). Otherwise, it matches two numerals stuck together, an outcome that, unfortunately, compromises one long number that is not valid.

```
1,20010
```

This number would be incorrectly accepted, because **findall** accepts 1,200 and then accepts 10, given the current pattern.

The solution is to use **\b**, the end-of-word meta character. To get a correct match, the regular-expression evaluator must find an end-of-word transition: This can be a space, a punctuation mark, end of line, or the end of the string.

There also remains the issue of tagged groups. The problem is that with the following string (which now includes the word boundary), grouping is necessary to express all the subpatterns.

```
r'\d{1,3}(,\d{3})*(\.\d*)?\b'
```

Let's review what this means.

▶ The characters \d{1,3} say, "Match between 1 and 3 digits."

▶ The characters (,\d{3})* say, "Match a comma followed by exactly three digits." This must be a group, because the whole expression, and not only a part, is matched zero or more times.

▶ The characters (\.\d*)? say, "Match a literal dot (.) followed by zero or more digits . . . but then make this entire group an optional match." That is to say, match this expression either zero or one time. It must also be a group.

7.2.2 Fixing the Tagging Problem

The problem is that grouping, by default, causes the characters matched at run time to be tagged. This is not usually a problem. But tagged groups of characters alter the behavior of **re.findall**.

One solution was shown near the end of Chapter 6: tagging the entire pattern. Another solution is to avoid tagging altogether.

```
(?:expr)
```

This syntax treats *expr* as a single unit but does not tag the characters when the pattern is matched.

Another way to look at this is to say, "To create a group without tagging it, keep everything the same but insert the characters **?:** right after the opening parentheses."

Here's how this nontagging syntax works with the number-recognition example:

```
pat = r'\d{1,3}(?:,\d{3})*(?:\.\d*)?\b'
```

In this example, the characters that need to be inserted are shown in bold for the sake of illustration. Everything else in the regular-expression pattern is the same.

Now, this nontagging pattern can be used smoothly with **re.findall**. Here's a complete example.

```
import re
pat = r'\d{1,3}(?:,\d{3})*(?:\.\d*)?\b'
s = '12,000 monkeys on 100 typewriters for 53.12 days.'
lst = re.findall(pat, s)
for item in lst:
    print(item)
```

This example prints

```
12,000
100
53.12
```

Performance Tip ▶ As explained in Chapter 6, if you're going to search or match with a particular regular-expression pattern multiple times, remember that it's more efficient to compile it using the **re.compile** function. You can then use the regex object produced rather than causing Python to recompile the regular-expression search string each time (which otherwise it would have to do):

```
regex1 = re.compile(r'\d{1,3}(?:,\d{3})*(?:\.\d*)?\b')
s = '12,000 monkeys on 100 typewriters for 53.12 days.'
lst = re.findall(regex1, s)
```

◀ Performance Tip

7.3 *Greedy Versus Non-Greedy Matching*

One of the subtleties in regular-expression syntax is the issue of greedy versus non-greedy matching. The second technique is also called "lazy." (Oh what a world, in which everyone is either greedy or lazy!)

The difference is illustrated by a simple example. Suppose we're searching or matching text in an HTML heading, and the regular-expression evaluator reaches a line of text such as the following:

```
the_line = '<h1>This is an HTML heading.</h1>'
```

Suppose, also, that we want to match a string of text enclosed by two angle brackets. Angle brackets are not special characters, so it should be easy to construct a regular-expression search pattern. Here's our first attempt.

```
pat = r'<.*>'
```

Now let's place this into a complete example and see if it works.

```
import re
pat = r'<.*>'
the_line = '<h1>This is an HTML heading.</h1>'
m = re.match(pat, the_line)
print(m.group())
```

What we might expect to be printed is the text <h1>. Instead here's what gets printed:

```
<h1>This is an HTML heading.</h1>
```

As you can see, the regular-expression operation matched the entire line of text! What happened? Why did the expression <.*> match the entire line of text rather than only the first four characters?

The answer is that the asterisk (*) matches zero or more characters and uses greedy rather than non-greedy (lazy) matching. Greedy matching says, "Given more than one way of successfully matching text, I will match as much text as I can."

Take another look at the target string.

```
'<h1>This is an HTML heading.</h1>'
```

The first character in the search pattern is <, a literal character, and it matches the first angle bracket in the target string. The rest of the expression then says, "Match any number of characters, after which match a closing angle bracket (>)."

But there are *two* valid ways to do that.

▶ Match all the characters on the line up to the last character, and then match the second and final closing angle bracket (>) (greedy).

▶ Match the two characters h1 and then the *first* closing angle bracket (>) (non-greedy).

In this case, both approaches to matching are successful. When only one match is possible, the regular-expression evaluator will either back up or continue until it finds a valid match. But when there is more than one matching substring, greedy and non-greedy matching have different effects.

Figure 7.1 illustrates how greedy matching tags the entire line of text in this example. It matches the first open angle bracket and doesn't stop matching characters until it reaches the last closing angle bracket.

Greedy: <.*>

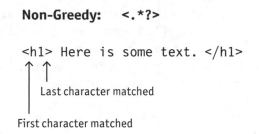

Figure 7.1. Greedy matching

The problem with greedy matching—although we've presented it as the more basic operation—is that it may match more characters than you intended, at least in this example.

Figure 7.2 illustrates how non-greedy matching works, tagging only four characters. As with greedy, it matches the first open angle bracket; but then it stops matching characters as soon as it reaches the first closing bracket.

Non-Greedy: <.*?>

```
<h1> Here is some text. </h1>
    ↑ ↑
      Last character matched

  First character matched
```

Figure 7.2. Non-Greedy matching

To specify non-greedy matching, use syntax that immediately follows the asterisk or plus sign with a question mark (**?**).

```
expr??    # Non-greedy zero-or-one matching
expr*?    # Non-greedy zero-or-more matching
expr+?    # Non-greedy one-or-more matching
```

For example, the pattern *expr***?** matches zero or more instances of the expression, *expr*, but uses non-greedy matching rather than greedy.

If you want non-greedy matching in this case, so that only four or five characters are matched rather than the entire string, the correct pattern is

```
pat = r'<.*?>'
```

Note the appearance of the question mark (**?**) just after the asterisk, placed in bold for illustration. Otherwise, it looks the same as the greedy match pattern.

Here's the example in context:

```
import re
pat = r'<.*?>'       # Use NON-GREEDY matching!
the_line = '<h1>This is an HTML heading.</h1>'
m = re.match(pat, the_line)
print(m.group())
```

This example (non-greedy) prints

```
<h1>
```

At this point, what difference does it make? Either way, the string matches. But there are many situations in which there is a practical difference. In cases when text is being tagged and replaced (for example, with **re.sub**), there is a significant difference in the final result. But differences can also arise merely in counting text patterns in a file.

Suppose you want to count the number of tags—expressions of the form *<text>* in an HTML text file. You could do this by setting the **DOTALL** flag, which enables the dot meta character (.) to read ends of lines as single characters rather than as ends of strings, and by using **re.findall** to scan all the text. The length of the list returned by the function gives you the number of HTML tags.

If you used greedy matching, the program would report back that the entire file had only one tag, no matter how many there actually were!

Here's an example. The following string uses both raw-string and literal-string conventions to represent multiline text-file contents.

```
s = r'''<h1>This is the first heading.</h1>
<h1>This is the second heading.</h1>
<b>This is in bold.</b>'''
```

Suppose we want to count the number of HTML tags. The way to do this is to use non-greedy matching with **re.findall**.

```
pat = r'<.*?>'            # Notice use of NON-GREEDY
                         #  because of the ?.
lst = re.findall(pat, s, flags=re.DOTALL)
print('There are', len(lst), 'tags.')
```

This example prints

```
There are 6 tags.
```

But notice what happens if we use standard (greedy) matching instead of non-greedy. Remember that greedy matching is enabled by using <.*> instead of <.*?>.

```
pat = r'<.*>'       # Notice use of GREEDY here!
lst = re.findall(pat, s, flags=re.DOTALL)
print('There are', len(lst), 'tags.')
```

This example prints

```
There are 1 tags.
```

That is not the correct answer. The regular expression matched the first opening angle bracket, **<**, and then kept matching characters until it got to the last and final closing bracket, **>**, because greedy matching was used.

As a final example in this section, you can use non-greedy matching to help count the number of sentences in a text file. To correctly count sentences, you need to match characters until you get to the nearest period (.) or other end-of-sentence punctuation.

Here's a sample string that represents the multiline contents of a text file that might have multiple sentences.

```
s = '''Here is a single sentence. Here is
  another sentence, ending in a period. And
  here is yet another.'''
```

In this example, we want to count three sentences. The following example code produces the correct result, because it searches for and counts sentences using non-greedy matching. (As in other examples, bold is used to emphasize the question mark that needs to be added to turn the greedy into non-greedy matching.)

```
pat = r'.*?[.?!]'    # Notice use of NON-GREEDY
                     #   because of the first "?".
lst = re.findall(pat, s, flags=re.DOTALL)
print('There are', len(lst), 'sentences.')
```

This example prints

```
There are 3 sentences.
```

If greedy finding had been used instead but the rest of the code was kept the same, the example would have reported that only 1 sentence was found.

The first question mark (**?**) in the regular-expression pattern indicated non-greedy rather than greedy matching. In contrast, the question mark inside the square brackets is interpreted as a literal character. As explained in Chapter 6, almost all special characters lose their special meaning when placed in a character set, which has the form

[*chars*]

Note ▶ The **re.DOTALL** flag causes the dot meta character (.) to recognize end-of-line characters (\n,) rather than interpret them as the end of a string. To make your code more concise, you can use the abbreviated version of the flag: **re.S**.

◀ Note

7.4 The Look-Ahead Feature

If you closely examine the sentence-counting example at the end of the previous section, you may notice that abbreviations could create a problem. Not all uses of the dot (.) indicate the end of a sentence; some are part of an abbreviation, as in the following example:

```
The U.S.A. has many people.
```

There is only one sentence present here, although the code at the end of the previous section would count this text as having four sentences! Another source of potential trouble is decimal points:

```
The U.S.A. has 310.5 million people.
```

We need a new set of criteria for reading patterns of characters as sentences. This criteria will use a *look-ahead* rule, without which it could not read sentences correctly.

(?=*expr*)

The regular-expression evaluator responds to the look-ahead pattern by comparing *expr* to the characters that immediately follow the current position. If *expr* matches those characters, there is a match. Otherwise, there is no match.

The characters in *expr* are not tagged. Moreover, they are not *consumed*; this means that they remain to be read again by the regular-expression evaluator, as if "put back" into the string data.

Here are the criteria we need to correctly read a sentence from a longer string of text.

First, begin reading characters by finding a capital letter.

Then read up to the next period, using non-greedy matching, provided that either one of the following conditions is true.

▶ This period is followed by a space and then another capital letter.

▶ It is followed by the end of the string.

If the regular-expression evaluator scans a period but neither of these conditions is true, then it should not conclude that it's reached the end of a sentence. The period is likely an abbreviation or decimal point. We need the look-ahead ability to implement this rule.

The correct regular-expression search pattern is therefore

```
r'[A-Z].*?[.!?](?= [A-Z]|$)'
```

This syntax is getting complex, so let's look at it one piece at a time.

The subexpression `[A-Z]` means that a capital letter must first be read. This will become the first character in the pattern—a sentence—that we're looking for.

The subexpression `.*?` says, "Match any number of characters." Because the question mark is added after `.*`, non-greedy matching is used. This means the sentence will be terminated as soon as possible.

The character set `[.!?]` specifies the end-of-sentence condition. The regular-expression evaluator stops reading a sentence at any one of these marks, subject to the look-ahead condition, considered next. Note that all of these characters lose their special meaning inside square brackets (a character set) and are interpreted as literal characters.

The final part of the pattern is the look-ahead condition: `(?= [A-Z]|$)`. If this condition is not met, the sentence is not complete, and the regular-expression evaluator keeps reading. This expression says, "The *next* character(s) after this one must consist of a space followed by a capital letter, *or* by the end of the line or the end of the string. Otherwise, we haven't reached the end of a sentence."

Note ▶ As you'll see in the upcoming examples, looking ahead for an end of line requires the **re.MULTILINE** flag to be correct in all cases.

◀ Note

There's an important difference between the last character read in a sentence (which will be a punctuation mark in this case), and the characters in the look-ahead condition. The latter do not become part of the sentence itself.

An example in context should illustrate how this works. Consider the following text string. Again, this might possibly be read from a text file.

```
s = '''See the U.S.A. today. It's right here, not
  a world away. Average temp. is 66.5.'''
```

Using the pattern we gave earlier—combining non-greedy matching with the look-ahead ability—this string can be searched to find and isolate each sentence.

```
import re
pat = r'[A-Z].*?[.!?](?= [A-Z]|$)'
m = re.findall(pat, s, flags=re.DOTALL | re.MULTILINE)
```

The variable m now contains a list of each sentence found. A convenient way to print it is this way:

```
for i in m:
    print('->', i)
```

This prints the following results:

```
-> See the U.S.A. today.
-> It's right here, not
a world away.
-> Average temp. is 66.5.
```

As we hoped, the result is that exactly three sentences are read, although one has an embedded newline. (There are, of course, ways of getting rid of that newline.) But other than that, the results are exactly what we hoped for.

Now, let's review the flag settings **re.DOTALL** and **re.MULTILINE**. The **DOTALL** flag says, "Match a newline as part of a '.' expression, as in '.*' or '.+'." The **MULTILINE** flag says "Enable $ to match a newline as well as an end-of-string condition." We set both flags so that a newline (\n) can match both conditions. If the **MULTILINE** flag is not set, then the pattern will fail to read complete sentences when a newline comes immediately after a period, as in the following:

```
To be or not to be.
That is the question.
So says the Bard.
```

Without the **MULTILINE** flag being set, the look-ahead condition would fail in this case. The look-ahead would mean, "Find a space followed by a capital letter after the end of a sentence or *match the end of the string*." The flag enables the look-ahead to match an end of line as well as end of string.

What if the final condition for ending a sentence had not been written as a look-ahead condition but rather as a normal regular-expression pattern? That is, what if the pattern had been written this way:

```
r'[A-Z].*?[.!?] [A-Z]|$'
```

This is the same pattern, except that the final part of this is not written as a look-ahead condition.

Here's the problem: Because the final condition (look for a space followed by a capital letter) is not a look-ahead condition, it was read as part of the sentence itself. Consider the beginning of this string:

```
See the U.S.A. today. It's right here, not
```

If look-ahead is not used, then *I* in *It's* will be read as part of the first sentence. It will not be put back into the sequence of characters to start the second sentence, causing everything to fail.

But enough theory; let's try it.

```
pat = r'[A-Z].*?[.!?] [A-Z]|$'
m = re.findall(pat, s, flags=re.DOTALL)
for i in m:
    print('->', i)
```

This example—which does not use look-ahead, remember—produces the following results:

```
-> See the U.S.A. today. I
->
```

When the first sentence is read, it ought to do a look-ahead to the space and capital letter that follows. Instead, these two characters—the space and the capital *I*—are considered part of the first sentence. These characters were *consumed*, so they did not remain to be read by the next attempt to find a sentence. This throws everything off. As a result, no further sentences are correctly read.

Therefore, there are cases in which you need to use the look-ahead feature. Look-ahead avoids consuming characters that you want to remain to be read.

7.5 Checking Multiple Patterns (Look-Ahead)

Some problems may require you to check for multiple conditions; for example, a string entered by a user might need to pass a series of tests. Only if it passes all the tests is the data entry validated.

Chapter 6 presented such a problem: testing for a sufficiently strong password. Only passwords that met all the criteria would be accepted. Let's note those criteria again. The password must have the following:

▶ Between 8 and 12 characters, in which each character is a letter, digit, or punctuation character.

▶ At least one of the characters must be a letter.

▶ At least one of the characters must be a digit.

▶ At least one of the characters must be a punctuation character.

The solution given in the previous chapter was to test each of these conditions through four separate calls to **re.match**, passing a different pattern each time.

While that approach is certainly workable, it's possible to use look-ahead to place multiple matching criteria in the same large pattern, which is more efficient. Then **re.match** needs to be called only once. Let's use the password-selection problem to illustrate.

First, we create regular-expression patterns for each of the four criteria. Then the patterns are glued together to create one long pattern.

```
pat1 = r'(\w|[!@#$%^&*+-]){8,12}$'
pat2 = r'(?=.*[a-zA-Z])'       # Must include a letter.
pat3 = r'(?=.*\d)'             # Must include a digit.
pat4 = r'(?=.*[!@#$%^&*+-])'   # Must include punc. char.

pat = pat2 + pat3 + pat4 + pat1
```

Every pattern except the first one uses look-ahead syntax. This syntax tries to match a pattern but does not consume the characters it examines. Therefore, if we place pat2, pat3, and pat4 at the beginning of the overall pattern, the regular-expression evaluator will check all these conditions.

Note ▶ Remember, the minus sign (–) has special meaning when placed inside square brackets, which create a character set, but not if this sign comes at the beginning or end of the set. Therefore, this example refers to a literal minus sign. ◀ Note

The various patterns are joined together to create one large pattern. Now we can test for password strength by a single call to **re.match**:

```
import re
passwd = 'HenryThe5!'
if re.match(pat, passwd):
    print('It passed the test!')
else:
    print('Insufficiently strong password.')
```

If you run this example, you'll find that 'HenryThe5!' passes the test for being a sufficiently strong password, because it contains letters, a digit, and a punctuation mark (!).

7.6 Negative Look-Ahead

An alternative to the look-ahead capability is the negative look-ahead capability.

The former says, "Consider this pattern a match only if the next characters to be read (ahead of the current position) match a certain subpattern; but in any case, don't consume those look-ahead characters but leave them to be read."

The *negative look-ahead* capability does the same thing but checks to see whether the next characters *fail* to match a certain subpattern. Only if there is a fail does the overall match succeed.

This is less complicated than it may sound.

(?!*expr*)

This negative look-ahead syntax says, "Permit a match only if the next characters to be read are not matched by *expr*; but in any case, do not consume the look-ahead characters but leave them to be read again by the next match attempt."

Here's a simple example. The following pattern matches *abc* but only if not followed by another instance of *abc*.

```
pat = r'abc(?!abc)'
```

If used with **re.findall** to search the following string, it will find exactly one copy of *abc*:

```
s = 'The magic of abcabc.'
```

In this case, the second instance of *abc* will be found but not the first. Note also that because this is a look-ahead operation, the second instance of *abc* is not consumed, but remains to be read; otherwise, that instance would not be found either.

Here's the code that implements the example:

```
import re
pat = r'abc(?!abc)'
s = 'The magic of abcabc.'
m = re.findall(pat, s)
print(m)
```

Remember what this (admittedly strange) pattern says: "Match 'abc' but only if it's not immediately followed by another instance of 'abc'."

As expected, this example prints a group with just one instance of "abc," not two.

```
['abc']
```

Here's an even clearer demonstration. We can distinguish between instances of *abc* by putting the second instance in capital letters and then turning on the **IGNORECASE** flag (**re.I**).

```
pat = r'abc(?!abc)'
s = 'The magic of abcABC.'
m = re.findall(pat, s, flags=re.I)
print(m)
```

Notice that the key characters, indicating negative look-ahead, are in bold.

The following text is printed, confirming that only the second instance of "abc" (this one in capital letters) is matched. The first group failed to match not because it was lowercase, but because there was a negative look-ahead condition ("Don't find another occurrence of 'abc' immediately after this one"). So this example prints

```
['ABC']
```

Now let's return to the use of positive look-ahead in the previous section and see how it's used to read complete sentences, while distinguishing between abbreviations and decimal points rather than mistaking them for full stops.

Here again is some sample test data that we need our sentence scanner to read correctly:

```
s = '''See the U.S.A. today. It's right here, not
a world away. Average temp. is 70.5.'''
```

Instead of reaching the end of a sentence and looking for a positive look-ahead condition, we can specify a negative condition to achieve similar results. To represent the end of a sentence, a period (.) must *not* be followed by either of these:

▶ A space and then a lowercase letter or digit

▶ Any alphanumeric character

A sentence pattern using a negative look-ahead condition could be written the following way, in which the key characters (indicating negative look-ahead) are bold:

```
r'[A-Z].*?[.!?](?! [a-z0-9]|\w)'
```

The negative look-ahead component of this pattern is `(?! [a-z0-9]|\w)`, which says, "Don't match a space followed by a lowercase letter or digit, and don't match any alphanumeric character, right after the current position."

We can use this pattern in the context of a complete example. To better test the pattern, we've added another sentence.

```
import re    # Use if you haven't put this in
            #  the source file yet.

pat = r'[A-Z].*?[.!?](?! [a-z]|\w)'
s = '''See the U.S.A. today. It's right here, not
 a world away. Average temp. is 70.5. It's fun!'''
m = re.findall(pat, s, flags=re.DOTALL)
for i in m:
    print('->', i)
```

This example prints the following results:

```
-> See the U.S.A. today.
-> It's right here, not
a world away.
-> Average temp. is 70.5.
-> It's fun!
```

These are the same results we'd get with positive look-ahead, although, of course, the look-ahead condition was phrased in a negative, rather than positive, way.

There are a number of ways available to get rid of the newline if it isn't desired. If you've just read all the text from a text file into a single string, for example, you can remove all the newlines with the following statement:

```
s = re.sub(r'\n', '', s)
```

If you remove newlines this way and run the example again, you'll get this output:

```
-> See the U.S.A. today.
-> It's right here, not a world away.
-> Average temp. is 70.5.
-> It's fun!
```

7.7 Named Groups

As we explained in Chapter 6, tagged groups are available by number. The overall string matched is available through the match object as

```
match_obj.group(0)
```

Individual tagged groups are available by using the numbers 1, 2, 3, and so on. For example, the following refers to the first tagged group:

```
match_obj.group(1)
```

But if you're dealing with a particularly complex regular expression, you may want to refer to tagged groups not by number but by name. In that case, you may want to use named groups.

```
(?P<name>expr)    # Tags the matching group, using name.
(?P=name)         # Attempt to match repeat of named group.
```

Let's look at an example that's practical but simple. A common action for a program is to take a name entered in one format and save it in another. For example, names might be entered as follows:

```
Brian R. Overland
John R. Bennett
John Q. Public
```

A common operation is to take these names and store them by last name (surname) rather than first, so you get

```
Overland, Brian R.
Bennett, John R.
Public, John Q.
```

It's then an easy matter to order them alphabetically by last name if desired. But what if someone enters a name without a middle initial?

```
Jane Austen
Mary Shelley
```

Ideally, we'd like to handle those as well. We'd like a pattern that smoothly handles both kinds of cases—middle initial present or not present.

```
Austen, Jane
Shelley, Mary
```

So let's start with the simple case: first and last name only. It's particularly convenient to tag two groups and give them the names first and last, as in the following pattern.

```
pat = r'(?P<first>\w+) (?P<last>\w+)'
```

We can successfully apply this pattern in a program in which a person enters their full name, to be broken down and analyzed.

```
import re
s = 'Jane Austen'
m = re.match(pat, s)
```

Having run this code, we can then print the two parts of the name. Note that the group name must be in string format—and therefore be delimited by single quotation marks—before being passed to the **print** function.

```
print('first name = ', m.group('first'))
print('last name = ', m.group('last'))
```

This prints

```
first name = Jane
last name = Austen
```

Given this division, it's easy to print or store the name in last-name-first order:

```
print(m.group('last') + ', ' + m.group('first'))
```

This prints

```
Austen, Jane
```

The pattern to recognize middle initials and place them in the right order is a little more complex. Let's make this middle initial optional.

```
pat = r'(?P<first>\w+) (?P<mid>\w\. )?(?P<last>\w+)'
```

Notice that a white space after the first name is mandatory, but the middle initial is followed by a space only if the middle name is matched. This pattern, if matched against a name, will optionally recognize a middle initial but not require it. So the following are all successfully matched:

```
Brian R. Overland
John R. Bennett
John Q. Public
Jane Austen
Mary Shelley
```

In every case, group(name) can be accessed, where name is 'first', 'mid', or 'last'. However, group('mid') in some cases—where there was no match of that named group—will return the special value **None**. But that can be tested for.

Therefore, we can write the following function to break down a name and reformat it.

```
pat = r'(?P<first>\w+) (?P<mid>\w\. )?(?P<last>\w+)'

def reorg_name(in_s):
    m = re.match(pat, in_s)
    s = m.group('last') + ', ' + m.group('first')
    if m.group('mid'):
        s += ' ' + m.group('mid')
    return s
```

By applying this function to each name entered, placing the result into a list, and then sorting the list, we can store all the names in alphabetical last-name-first format:

```
Austen, Jane
Bennett, John R.
Overland, Brian R.
Public, John Q.
Shelley, Mary
```

The use of named groups was helpful in this case, by giving us a way to refer to a group—the middle initial and dot—that might not be matched at all. In any case, being able to refer to the groups as "first," "mid," and "last" makes the code clearer and easier to maintain.

As a final example in this section, you can use named groups to require repeating of previously tagged sequences of characters. Chapter 6 showed how you can use numbers to refer to the repetition of named groups.

```
pat = r'(\w+) \1'
```

The named-group version of this pattern is

```
pat = r'(?P<word>\w+) (?P=word)'
```

This pattern gets a positive match in the following function call:

```
m = re.search(pat, 'The the dog.', flags=re.I)
```

7.8 The "re.split" Function

Consider the Reverse Polish Notation (RPN) interpreter introduced in previous chapters. Another way to invoke regular expressions to help analyze text into tokens is to use the **re.split** function.

list = **re.split**(*pattern, string, maxsplit=0, flags=0*)

In this syntax, *pattern* is a regular-expression pattern supporting all the grammar shown until now; however, it doesn't specify a pattern to find but to skip over. All the text in between is considered a token. So the *pattern* is really representative of token separators, and not the tokens themselves.

The *string*, as usual, is the target string to split into tokens.

The *maxsplit* argument specifies the maximum number of tokens to find. If this argument is set to 0, the default, then there is no maximum number.

The action of the **re.split** function is to return a list of strings, in which each string is a token, which in this case is a string of text that appears between occurrences of the indicated search pattern.

It's common to make the search pattern a space, a series of spaces, or a comma. One virtue of using regular expressions is that you can combine these:

```
pat = r', *| +'
```

This pattern, in effect, says, "A substring is a separator if it consists of a comma followed by zero or more spaces, or if it consists of one or more spaces." If you think about it, this condition creates a situation in which a separator can be any of the following: a comma, a series of at least one space, or both.

Let's try this pattern on a target string.

```
import re
lst = re.split(pat, '3, 5  7 8,10, 11')
```

If you now print the list, you get

```
['3', '5', '7', '8', '10', '11']
```

This is exactly what we'd hope to get. In this case, all the resulting tokens are numbers, but they could be any substrings that didn't contain commas or internal spaces.

Let's apply this pattern to the RPN interpreter. You can use the **re.split** function to split up text such as this:

```
s = '3 2 * 2 15 * + 4 +'
```

If you recall how RPN works, you'll recognize that this is RPN for the following:

```
(3 * 2) + (2 * 15) + 4
```

Let's apply the regular-expression function to the target string, s:

```
toks = re.split(pat, s)
```

Printing toks, a list of tokens, produces

```
['3', '2', '*', '2', '15', '*', '+', '4', '+']
```

This is what we'd expect.

But a problem occurs in tokenizing a string such as the following, which in some cases uses a number-to-operator transition to demarcate a token:

```
s = '3 2* 2 15*+ 4 +'
```

7.9 The Scanner Class and the RPN Project

Another way to analyze input for the RPN application is to use a convenient part of the Python regular expression package that is, as of this writing, documented in very few places.

The **re.Scanner** class enables you to create your own Scanner object. You need to initialize the object by giving it a series of tuples. Each tuple contains the following:

▶ A regular-expression pattern describing a token to search for.

▶ A function to be called in response to finding the token. The function itself is listed as if it were an object (it is; it's a callable object). But this function is not listed as a call, and arguments are not included. (However, two arguments will be passed when it is called.) The function can return any kind of object, and this is returned along with other tokens found.

When the scanner is then run on a target string by calling **scan**, it returns a series of objects as it was programmed to do. The beauty of this approach, as you'll see, is that you don't have to worry about separators; you just look for the tokens you want to find.

Here we summarize this part of the syntax. Unless you employ lambda functions, this part of the syntax should appear after the functions are defined.

Key Syntax

```
scanner_name = re.Scanner([
    (tok_pattern1, funct1),
    (tok_pattern2, funct2),
    ...
)]
```

In this syntax, each instance of *tok_pattern* is a regular expression describing some kind of token to recognize. Each *funct* is a previously defined callable or a lambda. If **None** is specified as the function, no action is taken for the associated pattern; it is skipped over.

Before we show how to write the token-processing functions, here's an example written for the RPN project:

```
scanner = re.Scanner ([
    (r'[*+/-]',    sc_oper),
    (r'\d+\.\d*', sc_float),
    (r'\d+',       sc_int),
    (r'\s+',       None)
    ])
```

This example says, "Recognize the three types of tokens—operators, integers, and floating point—and deal with each by calling the corresponding function."

Note ▶ In this example, it's important that the floating-point pattern is listed before the integer pattern. Otherwise, a floating-point number such as 11.502 will be read as an integer, 11, followed by a dot (.), followed by another integer.

◀ Note

Later, in Chapter 8, we'll add variable names (also called *identifiers* or *symbols*) to the RPN language. These are the variables within this RPN language.

```
scanner = re.Scanner ([
    (r'[a-zA-Z]\w*', sc_ident),
    (r'[*+/-]',        sc_oper),
    (r'\d+\.\d*',     sc_float),
    (r'\d+',            sc_int),
    (r'\s+',            None)
    ])
```

Now, let's look at how each of the functions is used.

function_name(*scanner*, *tok_str*)

The first argument, *scanner*, is a reference to the scanner object itself. You aren't required to do anything more with that argument, although it can be used to pass in additional information.

The second argument, *tok_str*, is a reference to the substring containing the token.

Here's a full example that creates a scanner for a simple RPN interpreter.

```
import re

def sc_oper(scanner, tok): return tok
def sc_int(scanner, tok): return int(tok)
def sc_float(scanner, tok): return float(tok)
```

```
scanner = re.Scanner ([
    (r'[*+/-]',   sc_oper),
    (r'\d+\.\d*', sc_float),
    (r'\d+',      sc_int),
    (r'\s+',      None)
    ])
```

With these definitions in place, we can now call the function `scanner.scan`. That function returns a tuple with two outputs: the first is a list of all the tokens returned by the functions; the second is a string containing text not successfully scanned. Here are some examples:

```
print(scanner.scan('3 3+'))
```

This prints

```
([3, 3, '+'], '')
```

Notice that the numbers are returned as integers, whereas the operator, *, is returned as a one-character string. Here's a more complex example:

```
print(scanner.scan('32 6.67+ 10 5- *'))
```

This prints

```
([32, 6.67, '+', 10, 5, '-', '*'], '')
```

The scanner object, as you can see, returns a list of tokens, each having the proper type. However, it does not yet evaluate an RPN string. We still have a little work to do. Remember that the logic of evaluating RPN is as follows:

If a token is integer or floating point,

   Place that number on top of the stack.

Else If the token is an operator,

   Pop the top two items into op2, op1 (in that order).

   Perform the appropriate operation.

   Place the result on top of the stack.

In the next section, we'll show how to best implement this program logic from within a Scanner object.

7.10 RPN: Doing Even More with Scanner

The previous section developed an **re.Scanner** object that recognizes integers, floating-point numbers, and operators. The Scanner portion of the application is

```
import re

scanner = re.Scanner ([
    (r'[*+/-]',   sc_oper),
    (r'\d+\.\d*', sc_float),
    (r'\d+',      sc_int),
    (r'\s+',      None)
    ])
```

To extend the RPN Interpreter application, we need to make each of the three functions, sc_oper, sc_float, and sc_int, do its part. The final two have to put numbers onto the stack. The sc_oper function, however, has to do more: It has to call a function that pops the top two operands, performs the operation, and pushes the result onto the stack.

Some of these functions can be made shorter by being written as lambda functions. Lambdas, first introduced in Chapter 3, are anonymously named functions created on the fly.

But the first line is going to require a more elaborate function that pops operands and carries out the operation; the function of this lambda is to call that more elaborate function, bin_op. So the code is now

```
scanner = re.Scanner ([
    (r'[*+/-]',   lambda s, t: bin_op(t)),
    (r'\d+\.\d*', lambda s, t: the_stk.append(float(t))),
    (r'\d+',      lambda s, t: the_stk.append(int(t))),
    (r'\s+',      None)
    ])

def bin_op(tok):
    op2, op1 = the_stk.pop(), the_stk.pop()
    if tok == '+':
        the_stk.append(op1 + op2)
    elif tok == '*':
        the_stk.append(op1 * op2)
```

```
    elif tok == '/':
        the_stk.append(op1 / op2)
    elif tok == '-':
        the_stk.append(op1 - op2)
```

The `bin_op` function is called by the top line of the scanner object whenever the scanner finds an operator: *****, **+**, **/**, or **-**. That operator is then passed as an argument (`tok`), which in turn is used to decide which of the four operations to carry out.

These lambda functions, it should be clear, do relatively little except call other functions. The top line (recognizing operator tokens) just calls the `bin_op` function, passing along the operator token itself. The second and third lines append an integer or floating point as appropriate.

There's a subtlety here. Each of the lambda functions gets called with two arguments, `s` and `t` (standing for the scanner and token, respectively), but each lambda function calls some other function while passing along one argument.

Now, armed with the appropriate Scanner object and a `bin_op` function to do much of the work, we just need a **main** function that gets a line of input, scans it, and finishes.

Here, then, is the completed application:

```
# File scanner_rpn.py -------------------------------

import re

the_stk = [ ]

scanner = re.Scanner ([
    (r'[*+/-]',    lambda s, t: bin_op(t)),
    (r'\d+\.\d*', lambda s, t: the_stk.append(float(t))),
    (r'\d+',       lambda s, t: the_stk.append(int(t))),
    (r'\s+',       None)
    ])

def bin_op(tok):
    op2, op1 = the_stk.pop(), the_stk.pop()
    if tok == '+':
        the_stk.append(op1 + op2)
    elif tok == '*':
        the_stk.append(op1 * op2)
```

```
    elif tok == '/':
        the_stk.append(op1 / op2)
    elif tok == '-':
        the_stk.append(op1 - op2)

def main():
    input_str = input('Enter RPN string: ')
    tokens, unknown = scanner.scan(input_str)
    if unknown:
        print('Unrecognized input:', unknown)
    else:
        print('Answer is', the_stk.pop())

main()
```

Here is the sequence of actions.

▶ The main function calls `scanner.scan`, which finds as many tokens (operators or numbers or both) as it can.

▶ Each time the Scanner object finds such a token, it calls the appropriate function: `bin_op` or the **append** method of `the_stk` (which is actually a list).

We can revise this code so that it is a little more concise and clear, by passing operations rather than carrying out each separately.

To understand what's going on in this version, it's important to remember that in Python, functions are first-class objects—that is, they are objects just like any other. They can therefore be passed directly as arguments.

We can take advantage of that fact by using function objects (callables) already defined for us in the **operator** package. To use these, we need to import the **operator** package itself.

```
import operator
```

We can then refer to callables that define addition, subtraction, and so on, for two binary operands. The operands are not part of the argument list, which contains only a single callable. Instead, the operands will be provided by the `bin_op` function—by popping values off the stack.

```
operator.add
operator.sub
operator.mul
operator.truediv
```

The revised application is now more streamlined and easier to maintain, even though it does exactly what it did before. Lines that are added or changed are shown here in bold.

```python
# File scanner_rpn2.py -----------------------------

import re
import operator

the_stk = [ ]

scanner = re.Scanner ([
    (r'[+]',      lambda s, t: bin_op(operator.add)),
    (r'[*]',      lambda s, t: bin_op(operator.mul)),
    (r'[-]',      lambda s, t: bin_op(operator.sub)),
    (r'[/]',      lambda s, t: bin_op(operator.truediv)),
    (r'\d+\.\d*', lambda s, t: the_stk.append(float(t))),
    (r'\d+',      lambda s, t: the_stk.append(int(t))),
    (r'\s+',      None)
    ])

def bin_op(oper):
    op2, op1 = the_stk.pop(), the_stk.pop()
    the_stk.append(oper(op1, op2))

def main():
    input_str = input('Enter RPN string: ')
    tokens, unknown = scanner.scan(input_str)
    if unknown:
        print('Unrecognized input:', unknown)
    else:
        print('Answer is', the_stk.pop())

main()
```

This last set of changes, you should be able to see, reduces the amount of code by several lines.

Let's review. By using this approach, adopting a Scanner object, what has been gained?

We could have just used the regular expression function, **re.findall**, to split up a line of input into tokens and then processed the tokens as part of a list, one at a time, examining the token and deciding what function to call.

By creating a Scanner object, we're doing something similar, but it gives us more control. This RPN Interpreter application is controlled by functions that the Scanner object calls directly in response to finding specific kinds of tokens.

Chapter 7   *Summary*

In this chapter, we've seen many uses for the advanced features of the Python regular-expression capability.

Two of the more useful features are nontagging groups and the look-ahead capability. Nontagging groups are useful when you want to form a grammatical unit (a group) but don't want to store the characters for later use. It turns out that the **re.findall** function is much easier to use, in some cases, if you don't tag the group. A nontagged group has this syntax:

> **(?:*expr*)**

The regular-expression look-ahead feature is useful in many situations. It provides a way to look at upcoming characters, match them or fail to match them, but not consume any of them. This simply means that the next regular-expression match attempt (after the look-ahead is completed) will start from the current position. The look-ahead characters are put back into the string to be read again.

This feature is so powerful that it enables you to use matching to check for multiple conditions using a single call to **re.match** or other matching function.

The look-ahead feature has the following syntax:

> **(?=*expr*)**

Finally, this chapter introduced the Scanner class. Use of this feature gives you maximum flexibility in reading tokens from a file or input string, transforming each one into the desired type of data.

In Chapter 8, "Text and Binary Files," we'll reuse much of this grammar in the context of the ongoing RPN interpreter project.

Chapter 7   *Review Questions*

1   In as few words as possible, state the difference between greedy syntax and non-greedy syntax, in visual terms. That is, what is the minimum effort you'd need to expend to change a greedy pattern into a non-greedy one? What characters or character do you need to change or add?

2 When exactly does greedy versus non-greedy make a difference? What if you're using non-greedy but the only possible match is a greedy one?

3 In a simple match of a string, which looks only for one match and does not do any replacement, is the use of a nontagged group likely to make any practical difference?

4 Describe a situation in which the use of a nontagged group *will* make a big difference in the results of your program.

5 A look-ahead condition behaves differently from a standard regex pattern in that a look-ahead does not consume the characters that it looks at. Describe a situation in which this could make a difference in the results of your program.

6 What precisely is the difference between positive look-ahead and negative look-ahead in regular expressions?

7 What is the advantage to using named groups in a regular expression instead of referring to groups only by number?

8 Can you use named groups to recognize repeated elements within a target string, such as in "The cow jumped over the the moon"?

9 What is at least one thing that the Scanner interface does for you when parsing a string that the **re.findall** function does not?

10 Does a scanner object have to be named **scanner**?

Chapter 7   *Suggested Problems*

1 The regular-expression examples in Section 7.4, "The Look-Ahead Feature," were developed to read multiple sentences—and determine the number of sentences—within complicated text. Revise this code to deal with even more complicated patterns, such as sentences with multiple spaces between them, and sentences that begin with numbers.

2 Revise such code further, so that if a newline (\n) is read, it's replaced by a single space.

 # Text and Binary Files

The earliest personal computers used old-fashioned, slow-winding cassette drives—the equivalent of a horse and buggy. But the world has changed.

What hasn't changed is the importance of files and devices, which are all about persistent storage. Python provides many ways to read and write files. *Python Without Fear* presented basic techniques for text I/O. This chapter builds on those techniques as well as exploring ways of reading and writing raw, or *binary,* data.

Prepare to enter the exciting world of persistent data! But first, a review of the basics: What's the difference between text and binary modes, as they apply to Python specifically?

8.1 Two Kinds of Files: Text and Binary

Python makes a major distinction between text and binary files, as you can see in Figure 8.1.

```
X0 FF 17 23
2E 4A 9B 02
78 62 5E 44
```

```
I walk the
journey of
1,000 miles.
```

Binary File
(Hex code representation)

Text File
(Character representation)

Figure 8.1. Binary and text files

First, there's a low-level difference in file-access modes. In text mode, a translation is automatically performed on newlines, substituting a newline-carriage-return pair (the order varies depending on the system). It's critical to use the right mode.

Second, while in text-file mode, Python requires reading and writing standard Python strings, which support both ASCII and Unicode encodings. But binary operations require use of the **bytes** class, which guarantees the use of raw bytes.

Finally, writing text involves conversion of numeric data to string format.

8.1.1 Text Files

A *text file* is a file in which all the data consists (for the most part) of characters of text. All the data—even numeric data—is intended to be viewed by, and editable in, a text editor.

That's not to say that you can't write numbers to such a file, but they're usually written out as printable digit characters.

The advantage of text files is that they conform to a relatively universal and simple format—lines of text separated by newlines—while binary files have no universally recognized format. Yet the latter has advantages in terms of performance.

Performance Tip ▶ If a data file has a large amount of data and if it's all numeric, then programs that use binary format to deal with it (as opposed to text format, the default) can frequently run several times faster. That's because they spend no time on costly numeric-to-text or text-to numeric conversions.

◀ Performance Tip

8.1.2 Binary Files

A binary file can contain printable data, but it doesn't have to. The biggest difference occurs when you read and write numbers.

As shown in Figure 8.2, text-file operations write out all data as human-readable characters, including numerals (that is, they are written out as decimal characters). So the number 1,000 is written out as the character "1" followed by three "0" characters.

In the oldest days of computer programming, when programmers assumed the use of the English language, it was common to assume strict ASCII format, which was one byte per character. In today's environment, it's common to use Unicode, which maps a character to two or more bytes rather than one, so that it can represent other human languages. This is why you can't assume one byte to a character any more.

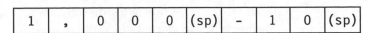

Text File: each byte contains a character.

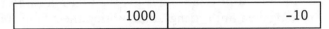

Binary File: structured into fixed-length interger fields.

Figure 8.2. Text versus binary operations

In binary mode, the number 1,000 is written directly as a numeric value—a four-byte integer, in this case. The human language has no effect on the binary representation.

The advantages of binary mode include increased speed and reduced size. However, operations on a binary file require understanding of the particular format in use.

8.2 Approaches to Binary Files: A Summary

Binary files can be problematic for the Python programmer, because Python deals in high-level objects, whereas binary files consist of raw data.

For example, the Python language can potentially store integers that are astronomical and take many bytes of storage. But when you write an integer to a file, you need to decide precisely how many bytes to write to the file. That's also an issue for text strings, and even floating-point values, which can use short or long formats.

Python provides packages that help solve these problems. There are at least four approaches to reading and writing binary files that don't require downloading any additional software. The packages all come with the standard Python download.

▶ Reading and writing bytes directly by encoding them into **bytes** strings.

▶ Using the **struct** package to standardize both number and string storage so that it can be consistently read and written.

▶ Using the **pickle** package to read and write items as high-level Python objects. (Try to say "Python pickle package" ten times fast.)

▶ Using the **shelve** package to treat the whole data file as one big data dictionary made up of Python objects.

You can read and write bytes directly, by using **bytes** strings containing embedded hex codes. This is analogous to doing machine-language programming.

Alternatively, you can use the **struct** package for converting common Python built-in types (integers, floating-point, and strings) into "C" types, placing them into strings, and writing them. This technique—unlike writing raw bytes—handles difficulties such as packing Python variables into data fields of specific sizes. In this way, when they are read back, the right number of bytes are read. This approach is useful when you're interacting with existing binary files.

When you create new binary files, to be read by other Python programs, you can use the **pickle** package to "pickle" Python objects. Then you let the package's routines worry about how precisely to represent the object when it's stored in a file.

Finally, you can use the **shelve** package, which is built on top of pickling and is even higher level. The shelving operation pickles data but treats an entire file as one big dictionary. The location of any desired object, according to its key, is looked up, and the object is found quickly through random access.

8.3 The File/Directory System

The Python download comes with an **os** (operating system) package that enables you to inspect the file/directory system as well as control processes. You can get a complete summary by importing the package and getting help for it.

```
import os
help(os)
```

The number of functions supported by the **os** package is large and too numerous to fully list or describe here. However, the following list provides an overview.

▶ Functions that start, end, or repeat processes: These include **spawn**, **kill**, **abort**, and **fork**. The **fork** function spawns a new process based on an existing one.

▶ Functions that make changes to, or navigate through, the file/directory system: These include **rename**, **removedirs**, **chroot**, **getwcd** (get current working directory), and **rmdir** (remove directory). Also included are **listdir**, **makedir**, and **mkdir**.

▶ Functions that modify file flags and other attributes: These include **chflags**, **chmod**, and **chown**.

▶ Functions that get or alter environment variables: These include **getenv**, **getenvb**, and **putenv**.

▶ Functions that execute new system commands: These include functions that start with the name **exec**.

▶ Functions that provide low-level access to file I/O: Python read/write functions are built on top of these. These include **open**, **read**, and **write**.

The **os** and **os.path** packages can effectively check for the existence of a file before you try to open it, as well as giving you the ability to delete files from the disk. You might want to use that one with care.

The following IDLE session checks the working directory, switches to the Documents subdirectory, and checks the current working directory again. Then it checks for the existence of a file named pythag.py, confirming that it exists. The session finally removes this file and confirms that the file has been removed.

```
>>> import os
>>> os.getcwd()
'/Users/brianoverland'
>>> os.chdir('Documents')
>>> os.path.isfile('pythag.py')
True
>>> os.remove('pythag.py')
>>> os.path.isfile('pythag.py')
False
```

Checking for the existence of a file by calling the **os.path.isfile** function is often a good idea. Another useful function is **os.listdir**, which returns a list of all the names of files in the current directory (by default) or of a specified directory.

```
os.listdir()
```

8.4 Handling File-Opening Exceptions

Whenever you open a file, a number of runtime errors (exceptions) can arise. Your programs will always be more professional and easy to use if you handle exceptions gracefully rather than letting the program "bomb out."

One of the most common exceptions is raised by the attempt to open a non-existent file for reading. That can easily happen because the user might mistype a character. The result is that the **FileNotFoundError** exception gets raised.

```
try:
    statement_block_1
except exception_class:
    statement_block_2
```

If, during execution of *statement_block_1*, an exception is raised, that exception causes the program to terminate abruptly unless the **except** clause catches the exception by specifying a matching *exception_class*. If you want the program to look for more than one type of exception, you can do so by using multiple **except** clauses.

```
try:
    statement_block_1
except exception_class_A:
    statement_block_A
[ except exception_class_B:
    statement_block_B ]...
```

In this case, the brackets are not intended literally but indicate optional items. The ellipses (. . .) indicate that there may be any number of such optional clauses.

There are also two more optional clauses: **else** and **finally**. You can use either one or both.

```
try:
    statement_block_1
except exception_class_A:
    statement_block_A
[ except exception_class_B:
    statement_block_B ]...
[ else:
    statement_block_2 ]
[ finally:
    statement_block_3 ]
```

The optional **else** clause is executed if the first statement block completes execution with no exceptions. The **finally** clause, if present, is executed after all the other blocks are, unconditionally.

Here's how you might use these features to open a file for reading, in text mode:

```
try:
    fname = input('Enter file to read:')
    f = open(fname, 'r')
    print(f.read())
except FileNotFoundError:
    print('File', fname, 'not found. Terminating.')
```

The use of **except** in this case handles the exception raised if the file can't be found. By handling this exception, you can terminate nicely or perform other actions. However, it doesn't automatically reprompt the user for the right name, which is usually what you'd want.

Therefore, you may want to set up a loop that does not terminate until (1) the user enters a file name that is successfully found, or (2) the user indicates he or she wants to quit by entering an empty string.

So, for more flexibility, you can combine **try/except** syntax with a **while** loop. The loop has **break** conditions and so is not truly infinite. It prompts the user until she either enters a valid file name or else she quits by entering an empty string.

```
while True:
    try:
        fname = input('Enter file name: ')
        if not fname:      # Quit on empty string.
            break
        f = open(fname)   # Attempt file open here.
        print(f.read())
        f.close()
        break
    except FileNotFoundError:
        print('File could not be found. Re-enter.')
```

Here's a version of this code that uses the **else** clause. This version calls the **close** function if and only if there were no exceptions raised. The behavior of the code at run time should be the same, but this version uses the keywords more selectively.

```
while True:
        fname = input('Enter file name: ')
        if not fname:
            break
```

```
try:
    f = open(fname)   # Attempt file open here.
except FileNotFoundError:
    print('File could not be found. Re-enter.')
else:
    print(f.read())
    f.close()
    break
```

8.5 Using the "with" Keyword

The most obvious way to do file operations is to open a file, perform file I/O, and close the file. But what if an exception is raised in the middle of a file I/O read? The program abruptly ends without tying up loose ends and politely closing down resources.

A nice shortcut is to employ a **with** statement. The action is to open a file and permit access through a variable. If, during execution of the block, an exception is raised, the file is automatically closed, so that no file handles remain open.

```
with open(filename, mode_str) as file_obj:
        statements
```

In this syntax, the *filename* and *mode_str* arguments have the same meaning they do in the **open** statement as described in the next section. The *file_obj* is a variable name that you supply; this variable gets assigned the file object returned by the **open** statement. The statements are then executed, until (of course) an exception is raised.

Here's an example that reads a text file using the **with** keyword:

```
with open('stuff.txt', 'r') as f:
    lst = f.readlines()
    for thing in lst:
        print(thing, end='')
```

8.6 Summary of Read/Write Operations

Table 8.1 summarizes the basic syntax for reading and writing to text, binary, and pickled files.

Table 8.1. Syntax for Reading and Writing to Files

FUNCTION OR METHOD	DESCRIPTION
file = **open(***name,* *mode***)**	Opens a file so that it can be written to or read. Common modes include text modes "w" and "r", as well as binary modes "wb" and "rb". Text-file mode (whether read or write) is the default. Also note that adding a plus sign (**+**) to the "r" or "w" mode specifies read/write mode.
str = *file*.**readline(***size* = -1**)**	Text-file read operation. Reads the next line of text by reading up to the newline and returning the string that was read. The trailing newline is read as part of the string returned; therefore at least a newline is returned, except for one situation: If and only if the end of file (EOF) has already been reached, this method returns an empty string.
	In the special case of reading the last line of the file, this function will return a string without a newline—unless of course a newline is present as the final character.
list = *file*.**readlines()**	Text-file read operation. Reads all the text in the file by returning a list, in which each member of the list is a string containing one line of text. You can assume that each line of text, with the possible exception of the last, will end with a newline.
str = *file*.**read(***size*=-1**)**	Binary-file read, but it can also be used with text files. Reads the contents of the file and returns as a string. The *size* argument controls the number of bytes read, but if set to −1 (the default), reads all the contents and returns them.
	In text mode, the *size* argument refers to number of characters, not bytes.
	In binary mode, the string returned should be viewed as a container of bytes, and not a true text string.
file.**write(***text***)**	Text or binary write operation. Returns the number of bytes written (or characters, in the case of text mode), which is always the length of the string.
	In binary mode, the string will often contain data that is not a byte string; such data must be converted to **bytes** string or **bytearray** format before being written.
	In text mode, neither this method nor **writelines** automatically appends newlines.
file.**writelines(***str_list***)**	Write operation used primarily with text mode. Writes a series of strings. The argument contains a list of text strings to write.
	This method does not append newlines to the data written out. Therefore, if you want each element of the list to be recognized as a separate line, you need to append newlines yourself.
file.**writable()**	Returns **True** if the file can be written to.

▼ *continued on next page*

8

Table 8.1. Syntax for Reading and Writing to Files (*continued*)

FUNCTION OR METHOD	DESCRIPTION
file.**seek**(*pos*, *orig*)	Moves the file pointer to indicated position in the file. If random access is supported, then this method moves the file pointer to a positive or negative offset (*pos*) relative to the origin (*orig*), which has one of three arguments: 0 – beginning of the file 1 – current position 2 – end of the file
file.**seekable**()	Returns **True** if the file system supports random access. Otherwise, use of **seek** or **tell** raises an **UnsupportedOperation** exception.
file.**tell**()	Returns the current file position: number of bytes from the beginning of the file.
file.**close**()	Closes the file and flushes the I/O buffer, so all pending read or write operations are realized in the file. Other programs and processes may now freely access the file.
pickle.dump(*obj*, *file*)	Used with pickling. This method creates a binary representation of *obj*, which is an object, and writes that representation to the specified file.
pickle.dumps(*obj*)	Used with pickling. This method returns the binary representation of *obj*, in byte form, that is used with the previous method, **pickle.dump**. This method doesn't actually write out the object, so its usefulness is limited.
pickle.load(*file*)	Used with pickling. This method returns an object previously written to the file with the **pickle.dump** method.

Note that the pickle functions require you to import the **pickle** package before using of its features.

```
import pickle
```

8.7 Text File Operations in Depth

After a text file is successfully opened, you can read or write it almost as if you were reading and writing text to the console.

Note ▶ Interaction with the console is supported by three special files—**sys.stdin**, **sys.stdout**, and **sys.stderr**—which never need to be opened. It usually isn't necessary to refer to these directly, but **input** and **print**

functions actually work by interacting with these files, even though you normally don't see it.

◀ Note

There are three methods available for reading from a file; all of them can be used with text files.

```
str = file.read(size=-1)
str = file.readline(size=-1)
list = file.readlines()
```

The **read** method reads in the entire contents of the file and returns it as a single string. That string can then be printed directly to the screen if desired. If there are newlines, they are embedded into this string.

A *size* can be specified as the maximum number of characters to read. The default value of –1 causes the method to read the entire file.

The **readline** method reads up to the first newline or until the *size*, if specified, has been reached. The newline itself, if read, is returned as part of the string.

Finally, the **readlines** method reads in all the lines of text in a file and returns them as a list of strings. As with **readline**, each string read contains a trailing newline, if present. (All strings would therefore have a newline, except maybe the last.)

There are two methods that can be used to write to text files.

```
file.write(str)
file.writelines(str | list_of_str)
```

The **write** and **writelines** methods do not automatically append newlines, so if you want to write the text into the files as a series of separate lines, you need to append those newlines yourself.

The difference between the two methods is that the **write** method returns the number of characters or bytes written. The **writelines** method takes two kinds of arguments: You can pass either a single string or a list of strings.

A simple example illustrates the interaction between file reading and writing.

```
with open('file.txt', 'w') as f:
    f.write('To be or not to be\n')
    f.write('That is the question.\n')
    f.write('Whether tis nobler in the mind\n')
    f.write('To suffer the slings and arrows\n')

with open('file.txt', 'r') as f:
    print(f.read())
```

This example writes out a series of strings as separate lines and then prints the contents directly, including the newlines.

```
To be or not to be
That is the question.
Whether tis nobler in the mind
To suffer the slings and arrows
```

Reading this same file with either **readline** or **readlines**—each of which recognizes newlines as separators—likewise reads in the newlines at the end of each string. Here's an example that reads in one line at a time and prints it.

```
with open('file.txt', 'r') as f:
    s = ' '   # Set to a blank space initially
    while s:
        s = f.readline()
        print(s)
```

The **readline** method returns the next line in the file, in which a "line" is defined as the text up to and including the next newline or end of file. It returns an empty string only if the end-of-file condition (EOF) has already been reached. But the **print** function automatically prints an extra newline unless you use the **end** argument to suppress that behavior. The output in this case is

```
To be or not to be

That is the question.

Whether tis nobler in the mind

To suffer the slings and arrows
```

A **print** function argument of end=' ' would avoid printing the extra newline. Alternatively, you can strip the newlines from the strings that are read, as follows.

```
with open('file.txt', 'r') as f:
    s = ' '          # Set to a blank space, initially
    while s:
        s = f.readline()
        s = s.rstrip('\n')
        print(s)
```

This is starting to look complicated, despite what should be a simple operation. A simpler solution may be to use the **readlines** method (note the use of the plural) to read the entire file into a list, which can then be read as such. This method also picks up the trailing newlines.

```
with open('file.txt', 'r') as f:
    str_list = f.readlines()
    for s in str_list:
        print(s, end='')
```

But the simplest solution—as long as you don't need to place the strings into a list—is to read the entire file at once, by making a simple call to the **read** method, and then print all the contents, as shown earlier.

8.8 Using the File Pointer ("seek")

If you open a file that supports random access, you can use the **seek** and **tell** methods to move to any position within the file.

```
file.seek(pos, orig)
file.seekable()
file.tell()
```

The **seekable** method is included in case you need to check on whether the file system or device supports random access operations. Most files do. Trying to use **seek** or **tell** without there being support for random access causes an exception to be raised.

The **seek** method is sometimes useful even in programs that don't use random access. When you read a file, in either text or binary mode, reading starts at the beginning and goes sequentially forward.

What if you want to read a file again, from the beginning? Usually you won't need to do that, but we've found it useful in testing, in which you want to rerun the file-read operations. You can always use **seek** to return to the beginning.

```
file_obj.seek(0, 0)    # Go back to beginning of the file.
```

This statement assumes that **file_obj** is a successfully opened file object. The first argument is an offset. The second argument specifies the origin value 0, which indicates the beginning of the file. Therefore, the effect of this statement is to reset the file pointer to the beginning of the file.

The possible values for *offset* are 0, 1, and 2, indicating the beginning, current position, and end of the file.

Moving the file pointer also affects writing operations, which could cause you to write over data you've already written. If you move to the end of the file, any writing operations effectively append data.

Otherwise, random access is often most useful in binary files that have a series of fixed-length records. In that case, you can directly access a record by using its zero-based index and multiplying by the record size:

```
file_obj.seek(rec_size * rec_num, 0)
```

The **tell** method is the converse of **seek**. It returns an offset number that tells the number of bytes from the beginning of the file. A value of 0 indicates that the beginning of the file is in fact your current position.

```
file_pointer = file_obj.tell()
```

8.9 Reading Text into the RPN Project

Armed with the ability to read and write text files, we can add a new capability to the Reverse Polish Notation (RPN) project. After the changes in this section, you'll be able to open a text file made up of RPN statements, execute each one of them, and print the results.

After adding the text-file read ability, we'll have taken a major step toward building a full-featured language interpreter.

8.9.1 The RPN Interpreter to Date

The current version of the program, inherited from Chapter 7, uses regular-expression syntax and a Scanner object to lexically analyze and parse RPN statements. The program evaluates RPN statements one at a time, exiting when it encounters a blank line.

In response to each line of RPN entered, the program inputs that line of code and prints the final numeric value of that one RPN statement.

```
import re
import operator

stack = []        # Stack to hold the values.

# Scanner object. Isolate each token and take
# appropriate action: push a numeric value, but perform
# operation on top two elements on stack if an operator
# is found.
```

```
scanner = re.Scanner([
    (r"[ \t\n]", lambda s, t: None),
    (r"-?(\d*\.)?\d+", lambda s, t:
        stack.append(float(t))),
    (r"\d+", lambda s, t: stack.append(int(t))),
    (r"[+]", lambda s, t: bin_op(operator.add)),
    (r"[-]", lambda s, t: bin_op(operator.sub)),
    (r"[*]", lambda s, t: bin_op(operator.mul)),
    (r"[/]", lambda s, t: bin_op(operator.truediv)),
    (r"[\^]", lambda s, t: bin_op(operator.pow)),
])

# Binary Operator function. Pop top two elements from
# stack and push the result back on the stack.

def bin_op(action):
    op2, op1 = stack.pop(), stack.pop()
    stack.append(action(op1, op2))

def main():
    while True:
        input_str = input('Enter RPN line: ')
        if not input_str:
            break
        try:
            tokens, unknown = scanner.scan(input_str)
            if unknown:
                print('Unrecognized input:', unknown)
            else:
                print(str(stack[-1]))
        except IndexError:
            print('Stack underflow.')

main()
```

Here is a sample session:

```
Enter RPN line: 25 4 *
100.0
Enter RPN line: 25 4 * 50.75-
49.25
Enter RPN line: 3 3* 4 4* + .5^
5.0
Enter RPN line:
```

Each of the lines of RPN code—although differently and inconsistently spaced—is correctly read and evaluated by the program. For example, the third line of input (in bold) is an example of the Pythagorean Theorem, as it is calculating the value of

```
square_root((3 * 3) + (4 * 4))
```

8.9.2 Reading RPN from a Text File

The next step is to get the program to open a text file and read RPN statements from that file. The "statements" can consist of a series of operators and numbers, like those shown in the previous example, but what should the program do after evaluating each one?

For now, let's adopt a simple rule: If a line of text in the file to be read is blank, do nothing. But if there is any input on the line, then execute that line of RPN code and print the result, which should be available as `stack[-1]` (the "top" of the stack).

The new version of the program follows. Note that the bold lines represent new or strongly altered lines. Moreover, the `open_rpn_file` definition is new.

```
import re
import operator

stack = []        # Stack to hold the values.

# Scanner object. Isolate each token and take
# appropriate action: push a numeric value, but perform
# operation on top two elements on stack if an operator
# is found.

scanner = re.Scanner([
    (r"[ \t\n]", lambda s, t: None),
    (r"-?(\d*\.)?\d+", lambda s, t:
        stack.append(float(t))),
    (r"\d+", lambda s, t: stack.append(int(t))),
    (r"[+]", lambda s, t: bin_op(operator.add)),
    (r"[-]", lambda s, t: bin_op(operator.sub)),
    (r"[*]", lambda s, t: bin_op(operator.mul)),
    (r"[/]", lambda s, t: bin_op(operator.truediv)),
    (r"[\^]", lambda s, t: bin_op(operator.pow)),
])
```

```
# Binary Operator function. Pop top two elements from
# stack and push the result back on the stack.

def bin_op(action):
    op2, op1 = stack.pop(), stack.pop()
    stack.append(action(op1, op2))

def main():
    a_list = open_rpn_file()
    if not a_list:
        print('Bye!')
        return

    for a_line in a_list:
        a_line = a_line.strip()
        if a_line:
            tokens, unknown = scanner.scan(a_line)
            if unknown:
                print('Unrecognized input:', unknown)
            else:
                print(str(stack[-1]))

def open_rpn_file():
    '''Open-source-file function. Open a named
    file and read lines into a list, which is
    returned.
    '''
    while True:
        try:
            fname = input('Enter RPN source: ')
            f = open(fname, 'r')
            if not f:
                return None
            else:
                break
        except:
            print('File not found. Re-enter.')
    a_list = f.readlines()
    return a_list

main()
```

Let's further assume that there is a file in the same directory that is named rpn.txt, which has the following contents:

```
3 3 * 4 4 * + .5 ^
1 1 * 1 1 * + .5 ^
```

Given this file and the new version of the RPN Interpreter program, here is a sample session.

```
Enter RPN source: rppn.txt
File not found. Re-enter.
Enter RPN source: rpn.txt
5.0
1.4142135623730951
```

The program behaved exactly as designed. When a file RPN file name was entered (rpn.txt), the program evaluated each of the lines as appropriate.

Notice that the first line of rpn.txt was left intentionally blank, as a test. The program simply skipped over it, as designed.

The basic action of this version of the program is to open a text file, which ideally contains syntactically correct statements in the RPN language. When it manages to open a valid text file, the open_rpn_file function returns a list of text lines. The main function then evaluates each member of this list, one at a time.

But we're just getting started. The next step is to expand the grammar of the RPN language so that it enables values to be assigned to variables, just as Python itself does.

8.9.3 Adding an Assignment Operator to RPN

The RPN "language" is about to become much more interesting. We're going to make it recognize and store symbolic names. How do we implement such a thing?

We need a *symbol table*. Python provides an especially convenient, fast, and easy way to do that: Use a data dictionary. Remember, you can create an empty dictionary by assigning { }.

```
sym_tab = { }
```

Now we can add entries to the symbol table. The following RPN syntax assigns a value; as in Python itself, the symbol is created if it does not yet exist. Otherwise, its value is replaced by the new value.

```
symbol expression =
```

Here are some examples:

```
x 35.5 =
x 2 2 + =
my_val 4 2.5 * 2 + =
x my_val +
```

The effect of these statements should be to place the value 35.5 in x, then place 4 (which is 2 + 2) into x, and then place the amount 12 into my_val. Finally, the effect would be to place the expression x my_val + on the top of the stack, which should cause the value 16 to be printed.

Thanks to Python's dictionary capabilities, it's easy to add a symbol to the table. For example, you can place the symbol x in the table with a value of 35.5.

```
sym_tab['x'] = 35.5
```

We can incorporate this action into the Scanner object, along with other operations.

```
scanner = re.Scanner([
    (r"[ \t\n]", lambda s, t: None),
    (r"[+-]*(\d*\.)?\d+", lambda s, t:
        stack.append(float(t))),
    (r"\d+", lambda s, t: stack.append(int(t))),
    (r"[a-zA-Z_][a-zA-Z_0-9]*", lambda s, t:
        stack.append(t)),
    (r"[+]", lambda s, t: bin_op(operator.add)),
    (r"[-]", lambda s, t: bin_op(operator.sub)),
    (r"[*]", lambda s, t: bin_op(operator.mul)),
    (r"[/]", lambda s, t: bin_op(operator.truediv)),
    (r"[\^]", lambda s, t: bin_op(operator.pow)),
    (r"[=]", lambda s, t: assign_op()),
])
```

In this new version of scanner, the following regular expression says, "Look for a pattern that starts with a lowercase letter, uppercase letter, or underscore (_) and then contains zero or more instances of one of those characters or a digit character."

That item is added to the stack, as a string. Note that Python lists may freely intermix strings and numbers. When such a symbol is added, it will be stored as just that: a string. As such it may be the target of an assignment. The assign_op function is defined as follows:

```
def assign_op():
    op2, op1 = stack.pop(), stack.pop()
```

```
    if type(op2) == str:      # Source may be another var!
        op2 = sym_tab[op2]
sym_tab[op1] = op2
```

Although op1 refers to a variable name (that is, a variable in the RPN language), op2 may refer to either a variable name or a numeric value. So, as with the next block of code, op2 must be looked up in the symbol table, sym_tab, if it's a string.

Note ▶ In the previous example, if op1 does not refer to a variable name, then it represents a syntax error.

◀ Note

In the case of other binary actions—addition, multiplication, etc.—each operand may be either a symbolic name (stored in a string) or a numeric value. Therefore, with the bin_op function, it's necessary to check the type of each operand and look up the value if it's a string.

```
def bin_op(action):
    op2, op1 = stack.pop(), stack.pop()
    if type(op1) == str:
        op1 = sym_tab[op1]
    if type(op2) == str:
        op2 = sym_tab[op2]
    stack.append(action(op1, op2))
```

We can now create the fully revised application. However, this raises a design issue. Should the program evaluate and print the result of every single line of RPN?

Probably it should not, because some RPN lines will do nothing more than assign values, and such an action will not place any value on top of the stack. Therefore, this version of the program does not print any result except the final one.

Other than input and error messages, this version of the application waits until the end of execution to print anything.

```
import re
import operator

# Provide a symbol table; values of variables will be
#    stored here.

sym_tab = { }
```

```
stack = []         # Stack to hold the values.

# Scanner: Add items to recognize variable names, which
#    are stored in the symbol table, and to perform
#    assignments, which enter values into the sym. table.

scanner = re.Scanner([
    (r"[ \t\n]", lambda s, t: None),
    (r"[+-]*(\d*\.)?\d+", lambda s, t:
        stack.append(float(t))),
    (r"[a-zA-Z_][a-zA-Z_0-9]*", lambda s, t:
        stack.append(t)),
    (r"\d+", lambda s, t: stack.append(int(t))),
    (r"[+]", lambda s, t: bin_op(operator.add)),
    (r"[-]", lambda s, t: bin_op(operator.sub)),
    (r"[*]", lambda s, t: bin_op(operator.mul)),
    (r"[/]", lambda s, t: bin_op(operator.truediv)),
    (r"[\^]", lambda s, t: bin_op(operator.pow)),
    (r"[=]", lambda s, t: assign_op()),
])


def assign_op():
    '''Assignment Operator function: Pop off a name
    and a value, and make a symbol-table entry. Remember
    to look up op2 in the symbol table if it is a string.
    '''
    op2, op1 = stack.pop(), stack.pop()
    if type(op2) == str:      # Source may be another var!
        op2 = sym_tab[op2]
    sym_tab[op1] = op2


def bin_op(action):
    '''Binary Operation evaluator: If an operand is
    a variable name, look it up in the symbol table
    and replace with the corresponding value, before
    being evaluated.
    '''
    op2, op1 = stack.pop(), stack.pop()
    if type(op1) == str:
        op1 = sym_tab[op1]
```

8

```
        if type(op2) == str:
            op2 = sym_tab[op2]
    stack.append(action(op1, op2))


def main():
    a_list = open_rpn_file()
    if not a_list:
        print('Bye!')
        return

    for a_line in a_list:
        a_line = a_line.strip()
        if a_line:
            tokens, unknown = scanner.scan(a_line)
            if unknown:
                print('Unrecognized input:', unknown)
    print(str(stack[-1]))

def open_rpn_file():
    '''Open-source-file function. Open a named
    file and read lines into a list, which is
    returned.
    '''
    while True:
        try:
            fname = input('Enter RPN source: ')
            if not fname:
                return None
            f = open(fname, 'r')
            break
        except:
            print('File not found. Re-enter.')
    a_list = f.readlines()
    return a_list


main()
```

Here's a sample session. Assume that the file `rpn2.txt` contains the following file:

```
side1 30 =
side2 40 =
sum side1 side1 * side2 side2 *+ =
sum 0.5 ^
```

The effect of these RPN statements, if correctly executed, is to apply the Pythagorean Theorem to the inputs 30 and 40, which ought to output 50.0. If this is the content of `rpn2.txt`, then the following session demonstrates how it is evaluated.

```
Enter RPN source: rpn2.txt
50.0
```

There are some limitations of this program. Not every kind of error is properly reported here. Also, if the last statement is an assignment, ideally the program should report the value assigned, but it does not.

We'll solve that problem in Chapter 14, by adding INPUT and PRINT statements to the RPN grammar.

Before leaving this topic, let's review how this Python program works. First, it sets up a Scanner object, the use of which was explained in Chapter 7, "Regular Expressions II." This object looks for individual items, or tokens, and takes action depending on what kind of token it is.

▶ If a numerical expression is found, it's converted to a true number and placed on the stack.

▶ If it's a symbolic name—that is, a variable—it's put on the stack as a string; later, as the result of an assignment, it can be added to the symbol table.

▶ If it's an operator, the two most recent operands are popped off the stack and evaluated, and the result is placed back on the stack. An exception is assignment (=), which doesn't place anything on the stack (although arguably, maybe it should).

And there's a new twist: If a variable name is popped off the stack, it's looked up in the symbol table, and the operand is replaced by the variable's value before being used as part of an operation.

Note ▶ If you look through the code in this application, you may notice that the symbol-look-up code is repetitive and could be replaced by a function call. The function would have to be written in a sufficiently general way that it would accommodate any operand, but that shouldn't be hard. This approach would only save a line here and there, but it's a reasonable use of *code refactoring,* which gathers similar operations and replaces them with a common function call. For example, right now the code uses

```
if type(op1) == str:
    op1 = sym_tab[op1]
```

This could be replaced by a common function call, as follows:

```
op1 = symbol_look_up(op1)
```

Of course, you would need to define the function.

◀ Note

8.10 *Direct Binary Read/Write*

For the rest of the chapter, we move onto the new horizon of reading and writing binary files.

When you open a file in binary mode, you can, if you choose, read and write bytes of data directly into the file. These operations deal with strings of type **bytes**.

Low-level binary read/write operations in Python use some of the same methods that are used with text-file operations, but with **bytes** data.

```
byte_str = file.read(size=-1)
file.write(byte_str)
```

A *byte_str* is a string having the special type **bytes**. In Python 3.0, it's necessary to use this type while doing low-level I/O in binary mode. This is a string guaranteed to be treated as a series of individual bytes rather than character codes, which may or may not be more than one byte long.

To code a byte string, use the **b** prefix before the opening quotation mark.

```
with open('my.dat', 'wb') as f:
    f.write(b'\x01\x02\x03\x10')
```

The effect of this example is to write four bytes into the file my.dat—specifically, the hexadecimal values 1, 2, 3, and 10, the last of which is equal to 16 decimal. Notice that this statement uses the "wb" format, a combination of write and binary modes.

You can also write out these bytes as a *list* of byte values, each value ranging between 0 and 255:

```
f.write(bytes([1, 2, 3, 0x10]))
```

The file can then be closed, and you can read back these same byte values.

```
with open('my.dat', 'rb') as f:
    bss = f.read()
    for i in bss:
        print(i, end=' ')
```

This example code prints

```
1 2 3 16
```

Most of the time, putting individual byte values into a file, one at a time, is not likely to be a good way to support Python applications or even examining existing file formats. Individual byte values range from 0 to 255. But larger values require combinations of bytes; there is no universal, clean correspondence between these values and Python objects, especially as factors such as "little endian" and data-field size change everything. This raises questions of portability.

Fortunately, the **struct**, **pickle**, and **shelve** packages all facilitate the transfer of data to and from binary files at a higher level of abstraction. You'll almost always want to use one of those packages.

8.11 Converting Data to Fixed-Length Fields ("struct")

If you're creating an application that needs to read and write new data files from scratch, you'll find that the pickling interface is the easiest to use, and you may want to go directly to the next section.

If, however, you need to interact with existing binary files not created with Python, you'll need a lower-level solution that enables you to read and write integers and floating-point numbers of various sizes, as well as strings. Although it's possible to do that by reading and writing one byte at a time—as in the previous section—that's a nonportable and difficult way to do things.

The **struct** package is an aid in packing and unpacking familiar built-in types into strings of bytes. It includes a number of function calls.

```
import struct
bytes_str = struct.pack(format_str, v1, v2, v3...)
v1, v2, v3... = struct.unpack(format_str, bytes_str)
struct.calcsize(format_str)
```

The **struct.pack** function takes a format string (see Table 8.2) and a series of one or more values. It returns a **bytes** string that can be written to a binary file.

The **struct.unpack** function does the reverse, taking a string of type **bytes** and returning a series of values, in a tuple. The number and type of values are controlled by the *format_str* argument.

The **calcsize** function returns the number of bytes required by the given format_str argument. Whereas *bytes_str* has type **bytes**, the format string is an ordinary Python string.

Table 8.2 lists the characters that can appear in a format string in this context (not to be confused with the formatting in Chapter 5).

Table 8.2. Common Data Formats for Packing and Unpacking

FORMAT SPECIFIER	C-LANG TYPE	PYTHON CLASS	SIZE
c	char	**bytes**	1
?	bool	**bool**	1
h	short	**int**	2
H	unsigned short	**int**	2
l	long	**int**	4
L	unsigned long	**int**	4
q	long long	**int**	8
Q	unsigned long	**int**	8
f	float	**float**	4
d	double	**float**	8
*int*s	char[ ]	**str**	*int* length
p	Pascal string type; see online help for more information.		

Table 8.2 lists C-language data types in the second column. Many other languages usually have a concept of short and long integers and short and long floating-point numbers that correspond to these types. (Python integers, however, have to be "packed," as shown in this section.)

Note ▶ The integer prefix can be applied to fields other than strings. For example, '3f' means the same as 'fff'.

◀ Note

To write to a binary file using the **struct** package, follow these steps.

▶ Open a file in binary write mode ('wb').

▶ If you're going to write a string, first convert it into a **bytes** string by using the **encode** method of the string class.

▶ Create a packed **bytes** string from all your data by using the **struct.pack** function. You'll need to use one or more data-format specifiers listed in Table 8.2, such as `'h'` for 16-bit integer. Any strings you include need to have been already encoded as described in step 2.

▶ Finally, write out the byte string to the file by using the **write** method of a file object.

The process of reading from a binary file using the **struct** package is similar.

▶ Open the file in binary read mode (`'wb'`).

▶ Read in a string of bytes. You must specify the exact number of bytes to read, so you need to know the size of the record ahead of time; you can determine that by running the **struct.calcsize** function on the data-format string based on characters from Table 8.2.

```
bss = f.read(struct.calcsize('h'))
```

▶ Unpack the **bytes** string into a tuple of values by using the **struct.unpack** function. Because the result is a tuple, you need to use indexing to access individual elements, even if there is only one. Here's an example:

```
tup = unpack('h', bss)
return tup[0]
```

▶ If, in step 3, you read in a **bytes** string intended to be assigned to an ordinary Python string, use the **decode** method of the **bytes** class to convert each such string you read.

Because these techniques deal with the low-level placement of bytes, there are some special considerations due to big endian versus little endian and padding. But first, the next few subsections deal with specific problems:

▶ Writing and reading one number at a time

▶ Writing and reading several numbers at a time

▶ Writing and reading a fixed-length string

▶ Writing and reading a variable-length string

▶ Writing and reading combinations of mixed data

8.11.1 Writing and Reading One Number at a Time

The issues in reading and writing a single packed number at a time—integers, in this example—are fairly simple, but in this process of reading, remember that a tuple is returned and it needs to be indexed, even if there is only one.

```
from struct import pack, unpack, calcsize

def write_num(fname, n):
    with open(fname, 'wb') as f:
        bss = pack('h', n)
        f.write(bss)

def read_num(fname):
    with open(fname, 'rb') as f:
        bss = f.read(calcsize('h'))
        t = struct.unpack('h', bss)
        return t[0]
```

With these definitions in place, you can read and write individual integers to files, assuming these integers fit into the short-integer (16-bit) format. Larger values may need a bigger data format.

Here's an example:

```
write_num('silly.dat', 125)
print(read_num('silly.dat'))   # Write the number 125.
```

8.11.2 Writing and Reading Several Numbers at a Time

This problem is similar to the one in the previous section; however, because it returns more than one number, the simplest solution is to interpret the return value of the **read** function as a tuple. For variety's sake, we use floating-point numbers this time—three of them.

```
from struct import pack, unpack, calcsize

def write_floats(fname, x, y, z):
    with open(fname, 'wb') as f:
        bss = pack('fff', x, y, z)
        f.write(bss)

def read_floats(fname):
    with open(fname, 'rb') as f:
        bss = f.read(calcsize('fff'))
        return unpack('fff', bss)
```

Note that `'fff'` can be replaced by `'3f'` in this example. The next example shows how you'd use these functions to read and write three floating-point numbers at a time.

```
write_floats('silly.dat', 1, 2, 3.14)
x, y, z = read_floats('silly.dat')
print(x, y, z, sep='    ')
```

The three values are printed—the last with a noticeable rounding error.

```
1.0    2.0    3.140000104904175
```

8.11.3 Writing and Reading a Fixed-Length String

Strings, which you might think should be simplest of all to handle, present special problems for binary storage. First, because you cannot assume that Python strings use single-byte format, it's necessary to encode or decode them to get **bytes** strings.

Second, because strings vary in length, using binary operations raises the question of just how many characters you should read or write! This is a nontrivial problem. But there are at least two solutions. One solution is to specify how many characters to read or write as part of a function call.

```
from struct import pack, unpack, calcsize

def write_fixed_str(fname, n, s):
    with open(fname, 'wb') as f:
        bss = pack(str(n) + 's', s.encode('utf-8'))
        f.write(bss)

def read_fixed_str(fname, n):
    with open(fname, 'rb') as f:
        bss = f.read(n)
        return bss.decode('utf-8')
```

This pair of functions must agree ahead of time on precisely how long the string is to be read or written. So they must be perfectly in sync.

When the `write_fixed_str` calls the **pack** function, that function automatically truncates or pads the string (with additional null bytes) so that it comes out to length n.

```
write_fixed_str('king.d', 13, "I'm Henry the VIII I am!")
print(read_fixed_str('king.d', 13))
```

The second line reads only 13 characters, as there are only 13 to read. It prints

```
I'm Henry the
```

8.11.4 Writing and Reading a Variable-Length String

This approach is more sophisticated than the one in the previous section, because the user of the functions can give any string as an argument, and the right number of bytes will be written or read.

```python
from struct import pack, unpack, calcsize

def write_var_str(fname, s):
    with open(fname, 'wb') as f:
        n = len(s)
        fmt = 'h' + str(n) + 's'
        bss = pack(fmt, n, s.encode('utf-8'))
        f.write(bss)

def read_var_str(fname):
    with open(fname, 'rb') as f:
        bss = f.read(calcsize('h'))
        n = unpack('h', bss)[0]
        bss = f.read(n)
        return bss.decode('utf-8')
```

The `write_var_str` function has to do some tricks. First, it creates a string format specifier of the form h*num*s. In the next example, that format specifier is `h24s`, meaning, "Write (and later read) an integer followed by a string with 24 characters."

The `read_var_str` function then reads in an integer—in this case, 24—and uses that integer to determine exactly how many bytes to read in. Finally, these bytes are decoded back into a standard Python text string.

Here's a relevant example:

```python
write_var_str('silly.dat', "I'm Henry the VIII I am!")
print(read_var_str('silly.dat'))
```

These statements print

```
I'm Henry the VIII I am!
```

8.11.5 Writing and Reading Strings and Numerics Together

Here are a pair of functions that read and write a record consisting of a nine-length string, a ten-length string, and a floating-point number.

```
from struct import pack, unpack, calcsize

def write_rec(fname, name, addr, rating):
    with open(fname, 'wb') as f:
        bname = name.encode('utf-8')
        baddr = addr.encode('utf-8')
        bss = pack('9s10sf', bname, baddr, rating)
        f.write(bss)

def read_rec(fname):
    with open(fname, 'rb') as f:
        bss = f.read(calcsize('9s10sf'))
        bname, baddr, rating = unpack(
          '9s10sf', bss)
        name = bname.decode('utf-8').rstrip('\x00')
        addr = baddr.decode('utf-8').rstrip('\x00')
        return name, addr, rating
```

Here's a sample usage:

```
write_rec('goofy.dat', 'Cleo', 'Main St.', 5.0)
print(read_rec('goofy.dat'))
```

These statements produce the following tuple, as expected:

```
('Cleo', 'A Str.', 5.0)
```

Note ▶ The **pack** function has the virtue of putting in internal padding as needed, thereby making sure that data types align correctly. For example, four-byte floating-point values need to start on an address that's a multiple of 4. In the preceding example, the **pack** function adds extra null bytes so that the floating-point value starts on a properly aligned address.

However, the limitation here is that even though using the **pack** function aligns everything within a single record, it does not necessarily set up correct writing and reading of the *next* record. If the last item written or read is a string of nonaligned size, then it may be necessary to pad each record with bytes. For example, consider the following record:

```
bss = pack('ff9s', 1.2, 3.14, 'I\'m Henry'.
encode('utf-8'))
```

Padding is a difficult issue, but depending on the system the code is running, occasionally you have to worry about it. The Python official specification says that a write operation will be compatible with the alignment of the last object written. Python will add extra bytes if needed.

So to align the end of a structure to the alignment requirement of a particular type (for example, floating point), you end the format string with the code for that type; but the last object can, if you want, have a repeat count of 0. In the following case, that means you need to write a "phantom" floating-point value to guarantee alignment with the next floating-point type to be written.

```
bss = pack('ff9s0f', 1.2, 3.14,
    'I\'m Henry'.encode('utf-8'))
```

◀ Note

8.11.6   Low-Level Details: Big Endian Versus Little Endian

Consider the problem of writing three integers and not only one.

```
import struct

with open('junk.dat', 'wb') as f:
    bstr = struct.pack('hhh', 1, 2, 100)
    datalen = f.write(bstr)
```

If you evaluate the variable **datalen**, which stores the number of bytes actually written, you'll find that it's equal to 6. You can also find this number with **calcsize**. That's because the numbers 1, 2, and 100 were each written out as 2-byte integers (format **h**). Within Python itself, such integers take up a good deal more space.

You can use similar code to read the values back from file later.

```
with open('junk.dat', 'rb') as f:
    bstr = f.read(struct.calcsize('hhh'))
    a, b, c = struct.unpack('hhh', bstr)
    print(a, b, c)
```

After running these statement blocks, you should get the following values for a, b, and c, reflecting the same values that were written out:

```
1 2 100
```

This next example uses a more interesting case: two integers followed by long integer. After this example, we'll discuss the complications involved.

```
with open('junk.dat', 'wb') as f:
    bstr = struct.pack('hhl', 1, 2, 100)
    datalen = f.write(bstr)

with open('junk.dat', 'rb') as f:
    bstr = f.read(struct.calcsize('hhl'))
    a, b, c = struct.unpack('hhq', bstr)
```

This example should work just as before (except that it uses the **hhl** format rather than **hhh**), but printing out the bytes string, bstr, reveals some important details:

```
b'\x01\x00\x02\x00\x00\x00\x00\x00d\x00\x00\x00\x00\x00
\x00\x00'
```

Here are some things to notice.

▶ If you look closely at the byte arrangement, both this example and the previous code (if you look at the **bytes** string) reveal the use of *little-endian* byte arrangement: Within an integer field, the least significant digits are placed first. This happens on my system, because it is a Macintosh using a Motorola processor. Each processor may use a different standard.

▶ Second, because the long integer (equal to 100, or hex value d) must start on a 32-bit border, 2 bytes of padding are placed between the second argument and the third. The note at the end of the previous section mentioned this issue.

One of the things that can go wrong is trying to read a data file when the processor used to write the data used big-endian byte arrangement when your system uses little-endian, and vice versa. Therefore, the **struct** functions enable you to exercise some control by specifying big or little endian at the beginning of the format string. Table 8.3 lists the low-level modes for handling binary data.

Table 8.3. Low-Level Read/Write Modes

SYMBOL	MEANING
<	Little endian
>	Big endian
@	Native to local machine

For example, to pack two long integers into a string of bytes, specifically using little-endian storage, use the following statement:

```
with open('junk.dat', 'wb') as f:
    bstr = struct.pack('<hhl', 1, 2, 100)
    datalen = f.write(bstr)
```

8.12 Using the Pickling Package

Exhausted yet? The pickling interface provides a much easier way to read and write data files.

Conceptually, a pickled data file should be thought of a sequence of Python objects, each existing in a kind of "black box," which is read from or written to by pickling. You can't go inside these objects as they exist on disk (or at least you can't do so easily), but you shouldn't need to. You just read and write them one at time.

Figure 8.3 provides a conceptual picture of such a data-file arrangement.

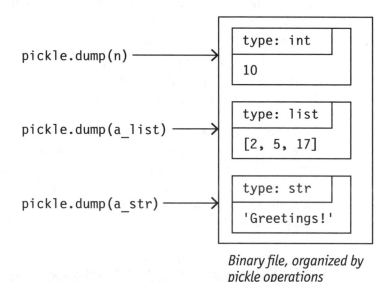

Binary file, organized by pickle operations

Figure 8.3. A pickled data file

The beauty of this protocol is that when you read items back into your program, you read them as full-fledged objects. To inquire the type of each object read, you can use the **type** function or simply pass the object to the **print** function.

Pickling is supported by the following two functions:

```
import pickle
pickle.dump(value, file_obj)     # Write object to file.
value = pickle.load(file_obj)    # Load object from file.
```

With this approach, all you need to know is that you are reading and writing Python objects, one at a time—although these may include collections, so they can be very large. It's not even necessary to know what types you're reading and writing ahead of time, because you can find that out through inspection.

For example, the following block of code writes three Python objects, which in this case happen to be a list, a string, and a floating-point value.

```
import pickle

with open('goo.dat', 'wb') as f:
    pickle.dump([1, 2, 3], f)
    pickle.dump('Hello!', f)
    pickle.dump(3.141592, f)
```

The procedure is simple and reliable, assuming the file is meant to be read by another Python application using the **pickle** package. For example, the following block of code reads these three objects from the file goo.dat and prints out both the string representation and the type of each object.

```
with open('goo.dat', 'rb') as f:
    a = pickle.load(f)
    b = pickle.load(f)
    c = pickle.load(f)
    print(type(a), a)
    print(type(b), b)
    print(type(c), c)
```

This example prints

```
<class 'list'> [1, 2, 3]
<class 'str'> Hello!
<class 'float'> 2.3
```

Pickling is easy to use in part because—in contrast to reading simple sequences of bytes—the effect is to load a Python object in all its glory. You can do many things with the object, including taking its type and, if it's a collection, its length.

```
if type(a)==list:
    print('The length of a is ', a)
```

The only real limitation to pickling is that when you open a file, you may not know how many objects have been written. One solution is to load as many objects as you can until the program raises an **EOFError** exception. Here's an example:

```
loaded = []
with open('goo.dat', 'rb') as f:
    while True:
        try:
            item = pickle.load(f)
        except EOFError:
            print('Loaded', len(loaded), 'items.')
            break
        print(type(item), item)
        loaded.append(item)
```

8.13 Using the "shelve" Package

The **shelve** package builds a filewide database on top of the **pickle** interface. The former contains the ability of the latter, so that you don't have to import both at the same time.

```
import shelve
```

The interface to this package is simple. All you need to do is to open a file through **shelve.open**, which provides a direct entrée into the shelving interface. The object returned can then be used as a virtual dictionary.

shelf_obj = **shelve.open(***db_name***)**

You can choose any name you wish for shelf_obj, which is only a variable, of course. The *db_name* is the same as the file name, minus its .db extension, which is automatically added to the name of the disk file or device.

When this function call is successfully executed, the database file will be created if it does not exist; but in any case it will be opened for both reading and writing operations.

Further operations are then easy. Just treat the object returned (stored in a variable we're representing by the placeholder shelf_obj) as you would any data dictionary (**dict** type). Here's an example, in which nums is being used as the dictionary name in this case:

```
import shelve
nums = shelve.open('numdb')
```

```
nums['pi'] = (3.14192, False)
nums['phi'] = (2.1828, False)
nums['perfect'] = (6, True)
nums.close()
```

Notice that the dictionary is referred to through the variable num in this case; but unlike other dictionaries, it's finally closed with a simple call to its **close** method, which empties the buffer and writes out any pending operations to disk.

This dictionary, which now resides on disk, can be reopened at any time. For example, a simple loop prints out all the existing keys.

```
nums = shelve.open('numdb')
for thing in nums:
    print(thing)
```

Given the data placed into this dictionary earlier, this loop would print the following keys:

```
pi
phi
perfect
```

You can also print individual values, of course.

```
print(nums['pi'])
```

This statement prints the value associated with the key, 'pi'.

```
3.14192
```

Finally, after you open the dictionary with the shelving interface, you must eventually close it, which forces any pending changes to be written out.

```
nums.close()
```

The following special rules apply to the shelving interface:

▶ Although the data dictionaries that result are **dicts** like any other, the keys must be strings. No other kinds of keys are supported.

▶ As usual, the associated values can be of any type, but they must be "pickleable."

▶ Remember that the **dict** name must be a simple name; the interface will automatically place a file on disk by appending a .db extension. However, do not use this extension yourself in the Python code.

The beauty of this interface is that for very large data sets, it's potentially far more fast and efficient than ordinarily picking, or almost any other access technique. The shelving interface will not, at least for large data sets, read in the entire dictionary; rather, it will look at an index to determine the location of a value, and then automatically seek to that location.

Note ▶ By default, when you use a shelf to access, say, `stuff['Brian']`, what you get is a copy, and not the original data. So, for example, if `my_item` is a list, the following does not cause changes to the file:

```
d[key].append(my_item)
```

However, the following statements do cause changes:

```
data = d[key]
data.append(my_item)
d[key] = data
```

◀ Note

Chapter 8   *Summary*

Python supports flexible, easy techniques for reading and writing to both text files and binary files. A binary file is a file that is not intended to express all data as printable characters but instead is used to store numeric values directly.

Binary files have no universally recognized format. Determining a format, and writing data out in that format, is an important issue in working with binary. With Python, several high-level options are available.

The **struct** package enables you to read and write Python values by translating them into fixed-size, regular data fields. The **pickle** package enables you to read and write fully realized Python objects to disk. Finally, the **shelve** interface lets you treat the disk file as one large data dictionary, in which the keys must be strings.

Python also supports interaction with the file systems through the **os** package, which includes the **os.path** subpackage. These packages provide functions for finding and removing files, as well as reading the directory system. From within IDLE, you can use **help(os)** and **help(os.path)** to learn about the capabilities.

Chapter 8	*Review Questions*

1 Summarize the differences between text and binary files.

2 What are some situations in which the use of text files would be the best solution? In what situations might you want to use binary files instead?

3 What are some of the problems in reading and writing a Python integer directly to disk using binary operations?

4 Name an advantage of using the **with** keyword instead of opening a file directly.

5 When you read a line of text, does Python include the trailing newline? When you write a line of text, does Python append a newline?

6 What file operations enable random-access operations?

7 When would you be most likely to use the **struct** package?

8 When would pickling be the best choice?

9 When would use of the **shelve** package be the best choice?

10 What is a special restriction when using the **shelve** package, as opposed to using other data dictionaries?

Chapter 8	*Suggested Problems*

1 Carry out the code refactoring to make the program simpler and more efficient, as described in a note at the end of 8.9.3, "Adding an Assignment Operator to RPN."

2 Write a program that returns a list of all those files in the current directory that have a .py extension.

3 Modify the RPN Interpreter example in Section 8.9.3 to recognize a wider array of errors. Try to recognize situations that represent a syntax error in terms of the RPN language.

4 Write a couple of programs designed to be used together: one program that writes records in a fixed-length binary format, and another that reads records in this same format. The format is a 20-character name field, a 30-character address field, and a 16-bit integer field for each of the following: age, salary, and performance rating (on a scale of 1 to 10). The "write" program should prompt the user for any number of such records until the user indicates that they want to quit. The "read" program should read all the records into a list.

5 Write the same read and write programs, but this time use the **pickle** interface.

9 Classes and Magic Methods

Python has class. In the world of programming languages, that means the ability to write user-defined types and give them abilities. A class is defined by what it does as much as what it contains. Most modern programming languages have this feature. Python adds a twist. It has something called *magic methods*, which are automatically called in response to certain circumstances.

Writing classes in Python is extremely simple at first. But it gets interesting quickly.

9.1 Classes and Objects: Basic Syntax

The basic syntax for writing a class in Python is shown here.

```
class class_name:
    statements
```

The `statements` consist of one or more statements, indented. You can't write zero statements, but you can use the **pass** keyword as a no-op; this is useful as a placeholder, when you want to define what the class does later.

For example, we could define a Car class this way:

```
class Car:
    pass
```

We could also define a Dog and a Cat class:

```
class Dog:
    pass

class Cat:
    pass
```

So what do you do with a class in Python? Simple. You can create any number of instances of that class, also called *instances*. The following statements create several instances of Car:

```
car1 = Car()
car2 = Car()
car3 = Car()
```

Or you can create instances of the Dog class:

```
my_dog = Dog()
yr_dog = Dog()
```

So far, none of these instances does anything. But that's about to change. The first thing we can do with a class is to create variables for the class as a whole. These become *class variables*, and they are shared by all its instances. For example, suppose Car was defined this way:

```
class Car:
    accel = 3.0
    mpg = 25
```

Now, printing any instance of Car will produce these values.

```
print('car1.accel = ', car1.accel)
print('car2.accel = ', car2.accel)
print('car1.mpg   = ', car1.mpg)
print('car2.mpg   = ', car2.mpg)
```

These statements print

```
car1.accel = 3.0
car2.accel = 3.0
car1.mpg   = 25
car2.mpg   = 25
```

But here's the twist: Any one of the instances of Car can be given its own value for the variable, accel. Doing this overrides the value of the class variable, which has the value 3.0. We can create an instance, my_car, and assign a value for accel.

```
my_car = Car()
yr_car = Car()
my_car.accel = 5.0
```

Figure 9.1 illustrates this relationship. In the my_car object, accel has become an instance variable; in yr_car, it's still a class variable.

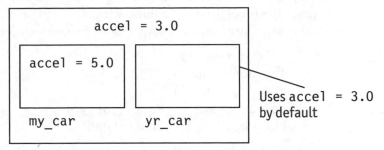

Car class

accel = 3.0

accel = 5.0

Uses accel = 3.0
by default

my_car   yr_car

Figure 9.1. Class variable versus instance variable

9.2 More About Instance Variables

Unlike other languages, Python has instance variables that are not created in the class—at least not directly. Instead, instance variables are added on an ad hoc basis or in the **__init__** method.

The general rule is that you create an instance variable in the same way you'd create any variable—by assigning it a value. With an instance variable, you need to use the dot (.) syntax.

```
object.var_name = value
```

For example, we can create a class named Dog, create an instance, and then give that instance several attributes—that is, instance variables.

```
class Dog:
    pass

my_dog = Dog()     # Create instance of Dog.
my_dog.name = 'Champ the Wonder Dog'
my_dog.breed = 'Great Dane'
my_dog.age = 5
```

Three data variables are now attached to the object named my_dog. They are name, breed, and age, and they can all be accessed as such.

```
print('Breed and age are {} and {}.', my_dog.breed,
    my_dog.age)
```

This statement prints

Breed and age are Great Dane and 5.

At this point, `name`, `breed`, and `age` are all attributes of the `my_dog` object only. If you create some other Dog objects, they will not necessarily have these same attributes (that is, instance variables). However, we can choose to attach these same attributes to another Dog object whenever we want.

```
yr_dog = Dog()
top_dog = Dog()
hot_dog = Dog()
hot_dog.name = 'Hotty Totty'
hot_dog.breed = 'Dachshund'
```

How do you ensure that every object of the same class has these attributes (instance variables)? The answer is that's what the `__init__` method is for!

9.3 The "__init__" and "__new__" Methods

For each class, the `__init__` method, if defined, is automatically invoked whenever an object of the class is created. You can use this method to make sure every instance of the class supports the same common set of variables . . . but each will have its own values.

```
class class_name:
    def __init__(self, args):
        statements
```

The word **self** is not a keyword but rather the name of the first argument, which is a reference to the individual object. This argument could be any legal name, but it's a universal convention to use **self**.

The *args* are arguments—separated by commas if there is more than one—passed to the object when it's first created. For example, we could revise the Dog class definition to include an `__init__` method.

```
class Dog:
    def __init__(self, name, breed, age):
        self.name = name
        self.breed = breed
        self.age = age
```

Now when an object of class Dog is created, it must be given three arguments, which are then passed to the `__init__` method. Here's an example:

```
top_dog = Dog('Handsome Dan', 'Bulldog', 10)
```

The statement creates a Dog object called `top_dog` and then invokes the `__init__` method for the class. The effect of the `__init__` method in this case is to assign instance variables as if the following statements were executed:

```
top_dog.name = 'Handsome Dan'
top_dog.breed = 'Bulldog'
top_dog.age = 10
```

Similarly, you can create another object called `good_dog`, which passes along different data to the superclass functions.

```
good_dog = Dog('WonderBoy', 'Collie', 11)
```

In general, `__init__` methods tend to have the pattern shown here, although they can do other initialization work if you want.

```
class class_name:
    def __init__(self, val1, val2, ...):
        self.instance_var1 = val1
        self.instanct_var2 = val2
        ...
```

Python actually uses the `__new__` method to create objects, but most of the time, you'll want to stick to writing and implementing the `__init__` method to perform initialization. There are two major exceptions.

▶ When you want to use some special technique for allocating memory. That's an advanced technique not covered in this book, but there are usually few people who need to use it.

▶ When you attempt to subclass an immutable or built-in class. This is a more common problem, and it's handled in the next chapter, in Section 10.12, "Money and Inheritance."

9.4 Classes and the Forward Reference Problem

Just as functions in Python have a forward reference issue, so do Python classes. The issue is that a class must be defined before it's instantiated. To *instantiate* a class means to use it to create an object.

Here's a situation that poses a problem in forward reference to a class.

```
class Marriage:
    def __init__(self):
        self.wife = Person('f')
        self.husband = Person('m')
```

```
a_marriage = Marriage()    # Instantiate the class.

class Person:
    def __init__(self, gender):
        self.gender = gender
```

This silly program fails, but not because it's silly. You should be able to see the problem: The first few lines are executed, causing the class Marriage to be defined and therefore come into existence as a class; but the sixth line then *instantiates* the class by trying to create an actual object called a_marriage.

That, in turn, shouldn't be a problem. But when the object comes into existence and its **__init__** method is called, that method tries to create a couple of objects called wife and husband, objects of the Person class. And that's the problem. The Person class has not yet been defined and cannot be used to create new objects.

The solution is clear: Just move the sixth line to the end of the file. In that way, both classes are defined before either is instantiated.

```
a_marriage = Marriage()
```

In general, forward reference to classes are not a problem if you follow a few rules.

- Make sure that all classes are defined before any of them are instantiated. That's the main rule.

- Show extreme caution about classes that instantiate each other or (God forbid) a class that creates an instance of itself. Although there's a trick that enables you to pull that off, it's an area in which you really ought not to venture. Fools rush in where wise men fear to tread.

- However, classes containing other classes (in one direction), or those containing references to instances of classes, are generally not a problem. Beware of mutual dependencies, however.

9.5 Methods Generally

Methods differ from ordinary functions in a couple of ways. First, methods are defined within a class definition; this is what makes them methods.

```
my_obj.a_method(12)
```

Second, every time a method is called through an instance, a hidden argument is passed: a reference to the object through which it was called (**self**).

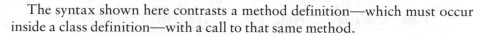

The syntax shown here contrasts a method definition—which must occur inside a class definition—with a call to that same method.

```
class class_name:
    def method_name(self, arg1, arg2, arg3...):
        statements

obj_name = class_name()
obj_name.method_name(arg1, arg2, arg3...)
```

Note that the definition of a method—but not the *call* to that method—includes the hidden first argument, **self**, so the definition has one more argument than the function call.

For example, consider the following class definition.

```
class Pretty:

    def __init__(self, prefix):
        self.prefix = prefix

    def print_me(self, a, b, c):
        print(self.prefix, a, sep='')
        print(self.prefix, b, sep='')
        print(self.prefix, c, sep='')
```

Having written this class, we can now test it by creating an instance and using it. Note how the calls to the method always have one fewer argument than the corresponding definitions, because the definitions explicitly include **self**, whereas calls to the methods do not.

```
printer = Pretty('-->')
printer.print_me(10, 20, 30)
```

This prints

```
-->10
-->20
-->30
```

Note, also, that within a method, the instance itself is always identified as **self**, and the instance variables are identified as **self**.*name*.

9.6 Public and Private Variables and Methods

One of the traditional goals of object oriented programming is *encapsulation*, which makes the internal contents of a class hidden to the outside world.

The philosophy of Python runs counter to that outlook. As a scripting language, Python tends to expose everything and let you try anything. There's less security and type checking than in other languages.

However, Python has a useful convention. Variable and method names beginning with an underscore (_) are intended to be private. Moreover, names beginning with a double underscore (__) are made inaccessible through a process called *name mangling*, assuming they are not "magic methods," as described later in this chapter.

A simple example serves to demonstrate how this works. Note that, in the following class definition, the variables x and y are not accessible from outside. However, within the class itself, all three variables (including __z) are accessible.

```
class Odd:
    def __init__(self):
        self.x = 10
        self.y = 20
        self.__z = 30

    def pr(self):
        print('__z = ', self.__z)
```

Given this class definition, the following statements are perfectly valid and do exactly what you'd expect.

```
o = Odd()
o.x      # 10
o.y      # 20
```

But the following expression causes an exception to be raised:

```
o.__z    # Error!
```

This last expression raises an error because Python replaces __z with a *mangled* name, generated from a combination of the class name and the variable name.

But __z is still accessible, without mangling, within method definitions of the same class, and that is why the pr method still works. Variable and method names are always accessible within the same class. But remember that in Python, such intraclass references need to be qualified with **self**.

9.7 Inheritance

Python provides support for inheritance, also known as "subclassing." Suppose you have a class, Mammal, that contains most of the methods you need to use in your program. However, you need to add or change a few of these methods. For example, you might want to create a Dog class whose instances can do anything a Mammal instance can do, plus more things.

The syntax for single inheritance with one base class is shown first.

```
class class_name(base_class):
    statements
```

The effect is to create a new class, *class_name*, which inherits all the class variables and methods belonging to *base_class*. The *statements* can add new variables and method definitions, as well as override existing definitions.

Every variable and method name in Python is *polymorphic*. Names are not resolved until run time. Consequently, you can call any method of any object, and it will be correctly resolved.

For example, the following class hierarchy involves a base class, Mammal, and two subclasses, Dog and Cat. The subclasses inherit the **__init__** and call_out methods from Mammal, but each implements its own version of the speak method.

```
class Mammal:
    def __init__(self, name, size):
        self.name = name
        self.size = size

    def speak(self):
        print('My name is', name)

    def call_out(self):
        self.speak()
        self.speak()
        self.speak()

class Dog(Mammal):
    def speak(self):
        print('ARF!!')

class Cat(Mammal):
    def speak(self):
        print('Purrrrrrr!!!!')
```

These definitions make possible the following statements:

```
my_cat = Cat('Precious', 17.5)
my_cat.call_out()
```

This last statement prints

```
Purrrrrrr!!!!
Purrrrrrr!!!!
Purrrrrrr!!!!
```

The Dog and Cat classes inherit the **__init__** method, unlike constructors in the C++ language. But this raises a question: What if the subclass needs to do additional initialization, even though we want to leverage the **__init__** definition from the base class as much as possible?

The solution is to write a new **__init__** method definition for the subclass, but make a call to the base-class version of **__init__** as follows. This results in calling all superclass initialization methods, even those inherited indirectly:

```
super().__init__
```

For example, the definition of Dog.__init__ initializes the breed variable itself and calls super().__init to do the rest of the initialization.

```
class Dog(Mammal):
    def speak(self):
        print('ARF!')
    def __init__(self, name, size, breed):
        super().__init__(name, size)
        self.breed = breed
```

9.8 Multiple Inheritance

Python's flexible syntax supports multiple inheritance. This allows you to create a class that inherits from two or more base classes.

```
class class_name(base_class1, base_class2, ...):
    statements
```

For example, in the following class definition, the Dog class inherits not only from the Mammal class but also from two others.

```
class Dog(Mammal, Pet, Carnivore):
    def speak(self):
        print('ARF!')
```

```
def __init__(self, name, size, breed):
    Mammal.__init__(self, name, size)
    self.breed = breed
```

The Dog class now inherits from not only the Mammal class but also the Pet and Carnivore classes. Therefore, each individual instance of Dog—that is, each Dog object—automatically contains attributes from the Pet and Carnivore classes, as well as Mammal.

Only the Mammal.__init__ method was called during initialization; however, other base classes could have been involved. For example, the family nickname could have been passed in and then initialized in Pet.__init__:

```
def __init__(self, name, size, nickname, breed):
    Mammal.__init__(self, name, size)
    Pet.__init__(self, nickname)
    self.breed = breed
```

When you use multiple inheritance, conflicts can arise. If you write a class that inherits from three different base classes, for example, the situation is not likely to cause problems as long as the base classes do not define the same methods or class variables. If they do use the same method or class-variable names as the other base classes, conflicts can arise.

9.9 Magic Methods, Summarized

In Python, a number of method names have a predefined meaning. All of these names use a double underscore prefix and suffix (they are referred to as *dunder* methods); so if you avoid using double underscores in your own method names, you don't have to worry about conflicting with these names.

Methods that use a predefined name are also called *magic methods*. They can be called like any other, but each is automatically invoked under certain conditions.

For example, the __**init**__ method is automatically called whenever an instance of the class is created. The usual response is to assign each of the arguments (other than **self**, of course) to an instance variable.

The general categories of these methods include the following.

▶ The __**init**__ and __**new**__ methods, which are automatically called to initialize and create an object. These were covered in Section 9.3.

▶ Object representation methods, including __**format**__, __**str**__, and __**repr**__. These are covered in Sections 9.10.1 and 9.10.2.

▶ Comparison methods, such as **__eq__** (test for equality), **__gt__** (greater than), **__lt__** (less than), and related methods. These are covered in Section 9.10.3.

▶ Binary operator methods, including **__add__**, **__sub__**, **__mult__**, division methods, and **__pow__**. These are covered in Section 9.10.4.

▶ Unary arithmetic operator methods, including **__pos__**, **__neg__**, **__abs__**, **__round__**, **__floor__**, **__ceil__**, and **__trunc__**. These are covered in Section 9.10.5.

▶ Bitwise operator methods **__and__**, **__or__**, **__lshift__**, and so on. These are almost never implemented by most Python programmers, because they would make sense only with the integer type (**int**), which already supports them. For that reason, they are not covered in this book.

▶ Reflection methods, including **__radd__**, **__rsub__**, **__rmult__**, and other names beginning with an **r**. It's necessary to implement these methods when you want to support operations between your class and another class that doesn't know about yours. These apply when your object is the operand on the right side. They are covered in Section 9.10.6.

▶ In-place assignment-operator methods, including **__iadd__**, **__isub__**, **__imult__**, and other names beginning with an **i**. These methods support assignment ops such as **+=**, taking advantage of it being an in-place operation and enabling it to be truly in place. But if you don't write such a method, you get **+=** "for free" as reassignment. Covered in Section 9.10.7.

▶ Conversion methods: **__int__**, **__float__**, **__complex__**, **__hex__**, **__orc__**, **__index__**, and **__bool__**. These are covered in Section 9.10.8.

▶ Container-class methods that enable you to create your own container. These methods include **__len__**, **__getitem__**, **__setitem__**, **__delitem__**, **__contains__**, **__iter__**, and **__next__**. These are covered in Section 9.10.9.

▶ Context and pickling (serialization) methods, including **__getstate__** and **__setstate__**. Normally, an object is "pickleable" as long as all of its components are. The methods in this category deal with special situations and are outside the scope of this book.

▶ The **__call__** method, which can be used to make the instances of a class directly callable as functions.

9.10 Magic Methods in Detail

The following subheadings detail the major kinds of magic methods that you're likely to find useful as an intermediate-to-advanced Python programmer. As mentioned, there are a few magic methods not covered here, because they are very rarely implemented by most Python programmers. See Python's official online documentation to get the full list and description of such methods.

9.10.1 String Representation in Python Classes

Several methods enable a class to represent itself, including **__format__**, **__str__**, and **__repr__**.

As Chapter 5 explained, the **format** function passes a format specifier to an object to be printed. The correct response is to return a string representation based on that specifier. For example, consider the following function call:

```
format(6, 'b')
```

Python evaluates this function call by calling the **__format__** method of the integer class, **int**, passing the specifier string, **'b'**. That method responds by returning a string containing the binary representation of the integer 6.

```
'110'
```

Here's the general flow of activity in string representation, summarized.

▶ The **format** function attempts to call the **__format__** method for an object, and it passes an optional format specifier. Implementing this method enables a class to return a formatted string representation. The default action is to call the **__str__** method.

▶ The **print** function calls an object's **__str__** method to print the object; that is, it calls the **__str__** method for that object's class. If **__str__** is not defined, the class's **__repr__** method is called by default.

▶ The **__repr__** method returns a string containing the canonical expression of an object as it's represented in Python code. This method often does the same thing as **__str__**, but not always. This method is called directly by IDLE, or when **r** or **!r** is used.

▶ Finally, the **__repr__** method of the **object** class—which is the ultimate base class—may be called as the final default action. This method prints a simple statement of the object's class.

Figure 9.2 illustrates this flow of control visually.

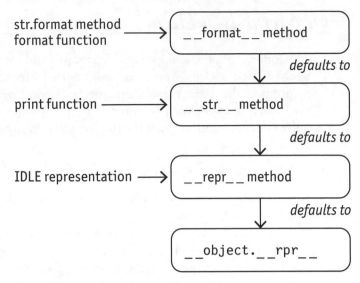

Figure 9.2. Flow of control in string representation

9.10.2 The Object Representation Methods

Table 9.1 lists the string representation magic methods, along with a description of each.

Table 9.1. Magic Methods Supporting Object Representation

METHOD SYNTAX	DESCRIPTION
__format__(self, *spec*)	Called when the object is given directly to the **format** function. The action of this method should be to return a formatted string. Few classes implement this method directly.
__str__(self)	This method should respond by returning a string that presents the object's data for the user. For example, if you created your own version of a Fraction class, you might print a value of three-fourths as 3/4.
	If this method is not implemented, the default action is to call the class's **__repr__** method.
__repr__(self)	This method is similar to the **__str__** method but has a slightly different purpose: It should return a string containing the canonical representation of the object as it would appear in Python code. If you implement this method but not **__str__**, then this method determines how strings are represented in both cases.

▼ *continued on next page*

Table 9.1. Magic Methods Supporting Object Representation (*continued*)

METHOD SYNTAX	DESCRIPTION
`__hash__(self)`	Called when the object is given as an argument to the **hash** function; it produces a hash code, enabling objects of this type to serve as keys in data dictionaries. This method should return an integer. Ideally, the integer should be as randomly picked as possible, so that even objects with similar values get a hash code that's not close. But if two values are equal, they must produce the same hash code.
`__bool__(self)`	Boolean conversion method. This method is called after any call to the **bool** function; it is also implicitly called whenever an object appears as a condition in a control structure such as **while** or **if**. Correct response is to return **True** or **False**; **False** should be returned only if the object is empty, is equal to **None**, or it contains a zero value.
	Remember that any object can be specified in any context that requires a condition. If the `__bool__` method is not implemented at all, the default behavior is to return **True**. So if you want to convert to **False** some of the time, you need to implement this method.
`__nonzero__(self)`	This is the Boolean conversion supported in Python 2.0. Python 3.0 requires the implementation of `__bool__` instead, if you want to support Boolean conversion.

The following example shows how a theoretical Point class could be written to support both the `__str__` and `__repr__` methods, as well as `__init__`. For the sake of illustration, the `__str__` and `__repr__` method return a string in a slightly different format.

```
class Point:
    big_prime_1 = 1200556037
    big_prime_2 = 2444555677

    def __init__(self, x = 0, y = 0):
        self.x = x
        self.y = y

    def __str__(self):
        s = str(self.x) + ', '
        s += str(self.y)
        return s
```

```
    def __repr__(self):
        s = 'Point(' + str(self.x) + ', '
        s += str(self.y) + ')'
        return s

    def __hash__(self):
        n = self.x * big_prime_1
        return (n + self.y) % big_prime_2

    def __bool__(self):
        return x and y
```

With this simple class definition in place, you can test the operation of the __**str**__ and __**repr**__ methods as follows.

```
>>> pt = Point(3, 4)
>>> pt
Point(3, 4)
>>> print(pt)
3, 4
```

Entering pt directly in IDLE causes the environment to print its canonical representation, which causes a call to the class's __**repr**__ method. But when pt is given as an argument to the **print** function, that function in turn calls the __**str**__ method to get a standard string representation of the object.

For the sake of illustration, the __**repr**__ method in this case returns a longer display string.

```
Point(3, 4)
```

9.10.3 Comparison Methods

The comparison methods enable objects of your class to be used in comparisons, including == and != (equal and not equal) and in inequalities, including >, <, >=, and <=. It's usually a good idea to implement the test for equality, at minimum, because otherwise the default behavior for == is to apply the **is** operator.

Comparison operators have some quirks we explain here that are documented in few places, in books or the Internet. The official spec contains much of this information but does not spell out all the consequences.

Here are some special features of the comparison operators in Python.

▶ To make objects of your class sortable with regard to other objects, define a less than (<) operation. For example, to put objects of your class into a collection and then sort it, you can implement __**lt**__ in relation to other objects of the same class. Doing so enables the **sort** method of a collection as well as **min** and **max**.

▶ But what about collections that contain both your objects and objects of other classes? This is doable. Comparisons do not have *reflection* operators—defining what happens if your object is on the right side of an operation—but they have something as good or better: symmetry.

▶ Instead of reflection operators, Python performs reflection by virtue of the rules of symmetry. If A > B, Python deduces that B < A. Therefore, if you implement both __**lt**__ and __**gt**__ for any combination of classes, you have in effect defined __**lt**__ for both directions.

▶ These rules also imply that you can often get the operations "for free," without having to implement all of them.

In Python 2.0, it was necessary to implement only one method, __**cmp**__, to support all the comparison operators. Python 3.0 does not support this feature.

Here's a simple class that provides the minimum code necessary to support all the comparison operators in Python 3.0, with regard to members of the same class. This class definition enables you to sort collections as long as they contain Dog objects only.

```
class Dog:
    def __init__(self, n):
        self.n = n

    def __eq__(self, other):
        '''Implementation of ==; provides != for free.'''
        return self.n == other.n

    def __lt__(self, other):
        '''Implementation of <; provides > for free.'''
        return self.n < other.n

    def __le__(self, other):
        ''' Implementation of <=; provides >= for free.'''
        return self.n <= other.n
```

After describing each of the comparison operators, we take another look at how symmetry works and how to make objects sortable with regard to other classes. Table 9.2 describes the comparison methods.

Table 9.2. Python Comparison Magic Methods

SYNTAX	DESCRIPTION
`__cmp__(self, other)`	Not used by Python 3.0 or higher. In 2.0, this method can be used to implement all the comparisons by returning either −1 (less than), 0 (equal), or 1 (greater than).
`__eq__(self, other)`	Test for equality. Called in response to the `==` operator, which tests to see whether contents are equal. The method should return either **True** or **False**.
	If this method is not implemented, Python tests "equality" by using the **is** operator.
`__ne__(self, other)`	Not equal. Called in response to the `!=` operator, which tests contents for being unequal. As with all the other methods listed here, the correct response is to return either **True** or **False**.
	If this method is not implemented, Python calls the test for equality and then reverses the logical meaning. Therefore, implementing the `__eq__` method is usually sufficient.
`__gt__(self, other)`	Greater-than test. This method is called in response to the `>` operator. Through the rules of symmetry, you can get a greater-than operation for free, as explained later, if you only need to compare to other objects of the same class.
`__lt__(self, other)`	Less-than test. This method is called in response to the `<` operator.
	To enable sorting in collections that contain objects of your class, this is the only comparison operator you need to implement. To enable sorting in collections containing objects of your class and other objects, you may need to implement `__gt__` as well.
`__ge__(self, other)`	Greater-than-or-equal-to test. This method is called in response to the `>=` operator being applied to objects of the class.
	This operator is not automatically supplied when you implement `__eq__` and `__gt__`. Instead, each comparison operator must be implemented separately, except that because of the rules of symmetry, you can get `__ge__` for free by implementing `__le__` (if you're only comparing to objects of the same class).
`__le__(self, other)`	Less-than-or-equal-to test. This method is called in response to the `<=` operator being applied to objects of the class.
	This operator is not automatically supplied when you implement `__eq__` and `__lt__`. Instead, each comparison operator must be implemented separately, except that because of the rules of symmetry, you can get `_le__` for free by implementing `__ge__` (if you're only comparing to objects of the same class).

Now let's look at how the rules of symmetry work in Python comparisons and how this enables us to create classes for which `<` is defined in both directions, thereby making the objects mutually sortable with any kind of object.

Python assumes the following rules apply to comparisons:

If A > B, then B < A.

If A < B, then B > A.

If A >= B, then B <= A.

If A <= B, then B >= A.

If A == B, then B == A; furthermore, we can conclude that A != B is not true.

Let's assume that you're interested in supporting comparisons only between your objects and other objects of the same class. In that case, you can write less code, because you can get half your comparison operators for free.

Now let's consider the more challenging issue: What if you want to make your objects mutually sortable with, say, numbers? The problem is that you have no access to source code for the **int**, **float**, **Decimal**, or **Fraction** class (among many other classes).

Assume your class is named Dog. For Dog objects to be mutually sortable with **int**, you need to support all of the following comparisons:

```
Dog < Dog
Dog < int
int < Dog
```

How do you implement this last comparison? Fortunately, there's a workaround. Implement greater than (**__gt__**) and you'll get int < Dog for free.

Here's an example of a Dog class that's mutually sortable with regard to numbers. Also, depending on how you initialize the instance variable, d, the Dog class also can be mutually sortable with regard to strings. By "mutually sortable," we mean that you can place these objects in the same list as other kinds of objects, and the entire list can be sorted; this is true for our Dog class, even if the list contains both numbers and dogs, or it contains both strings and dogs. An example at the end of this section demonstrates an example featuring dogs and integers.

Dog implements four methods:

```
class Dog:
    def __init__(self, d):
        self.d = d
```

```
    def __gt__(self, other):
        ''' Greater than (>). This method provides a
        less-than comparison through Rules of Symmetry.
        if a > b, then b < a.
        '''
        if type(other) == Dog:
            return self.d > other.d
        else:
            return self.d > other

    def __lt__(self, other):
        ''' Less than (<). This method must support
        comparisons to objects of the same class, as well
        as to numbers.
        '''
        if type(other) == Dog:
            return self.d < other.d
        else:
            return self.d < other

    # Defining __repr__ also gets us __str__.
    def __repr__(self):
        return "Dog(" + str(self.d) + ")"
```

Without the comments, this is a small class, although a good deal could be added to it, of course. This class definition enables code such as the following:

```
d1, d5, d10 = Dog(1), Dog(5), 10)
a_list = [50, d5, 100, d1, -20, d10, 3]
a_list.sort()
```

Printing a_list then produces

```
[-20, Dog(1), 3, Dog(5), Dog(10), 50, 100]
```

9.10.4 Arithmetic Operator Methods

Table 9.3 provides a summary of the magic methods that support an arithmetic operator or arithmetic function. These methods will most often be of interest when the class represents some kind of mathematical object, such as a point or a matrix; however, the addition sign (**+**) is supported by the string class (**str**) and other classes (such as lists) as a concatenation operator.

Table 9.3. Magic Methods for Arithmetic Operators

METHOD NAME	DESCRIPTION
__add__(self, *other*)	Addition. This method is invoked whenever an instance of the class is on the left side of an addition operation (**+**). The argument named *other* is a reference to the operand on the right.
__sub__(self, *other*)	Subtraction. This method is invoked whenever an instance of the class is on the left side of a subtraction operation (**-**). The argument named *other* is a reference to the operand on the right.
__mul__(self, *other*)	Multiplication. This method is invoked whenever an instance of the class is on the left side of a multiplication operation (*****). The argument named *other* is a reference to the operand on the right.
__floordiv__(self, *other*)	Floor division. This method is invoked whenever an instance of the class is on the left side of a floor division operation (**//**), which should round the result downward. The argument named *other* is a reference to the operand on the right. For example, in Python 3.0, the expression 7 // 2 produces 3 as the result.
__truediv__(self, *other*)	Ordinary division. This method is invoked whenever an instance of the class is on the left side of a division operation (**/**). In Python 3.0, if the operands are integers or floating point, this operation should produce a floating-point result not rounded down. The argument named *other* is a reference to the operand on the right. For example, in Python 3.0, the expression 7 / 2 produces 3.5 as its result.
__divmod__(self, *other*)	Division performed by the **divmod** function, which returns a tuple with two values: a quotient—rounded to the nearest integer—and a remainder. The argument named other is a reference to the argument on the right (the divisor). For example, a call to divmod(17, 2) returns the tuple (8, 1), because 8 is the ratio, rounded down, and 1 is the quotient.
__pow__(self, *other*)	Power function. This method is automatically invoked when the exponentiation operator (******) is used to raise some object to a specified exponent. For example, 2 ** 4 is 2 raised to the 4th power, or 16. The *other* argument is a reference to the argument passed to this function.

6

For example, **__add__** for a particular class is invoked when one of its objects is added to another object. This assumes, however, that the object is the left operand; if the object is the right operand, then its reflection method may be called—in this case, **__radd__**.

The following example utilizes the Fraction class from the **fractions** package. But if that package were not supported by Python, you could write such a class yourself.

```
import fractions

f = fractions.Fraction(1, 2)
print(f + 1)          # Calls Fraction.__add__
print(2 + f)          # Calls Fraction.__radd__
```

As mentioned earlier, the **__add__** method could be supported by any class that recognizes the addition operator (**+**), even if it's used for an operation such as string concatenation.

A hypothetical Point class can provide many good examples of how to implement these magic methods for arithmetic operators.

```
class Point:
    def __init__(self, x, y):
        self.x = x
        self.y = y

    def __add__(self, other):
        ''' Return a point containing self+other.'''
        newx = self.x + other.x
        newy = self.y + other.y
        return Point(newx, newy)

    def __sub__(self, other):
        ''' Return the distance between points.'''
        dx = self.x - other.x
        dy = self.y - other.y
        return (dx * dx + dy * dy) ** 0.5

    def __mul__(self, n):
        ''' Return point * a scalar number, n.'''
        newx = self.x * n
        newy = self.y * n
        return Point(newx, newy)
```

This sample class, which supports four magic methods (**__init__**, **__add__**, **__sub__**, and **__mul__**), illustrates some important points.

First, each of the arithmetic operator methods returns a value; that value, of course, can be assigned to a variable or used in any other kind of expression. Consider this example:

```
pt1 = Point(10, 15)
pt2 = Point(0, 5)
x = pt1 + pt2
```

The expression pt1 + pt2 results in the **__add__** method being called through the object pt1. In this method call, **self** is a reference to pt1 itself, and other becomes a reference to the object pt2. The result of the call is a new Point value, which is then passed to the variable x.

In this case, adding two points causes the corresponding coordinates to be added together; the resulting data is then returned as a new Point object.

The subtraction sign (-) is interpreted as a distance operator in this case. The method calculates the distance between two points and then returns it as a single floating-point value.

Finally, the multiplication sign (*) assumes that the left operand (the operand referred to by **self**) is a Point object, and the left operand is a scalar value, such as 1, 5, or 10. The action of the method is to multiply each value in the Point operand by the same integer, n. The result is then returned as a new Point object.

The syntax shown here is a reminder of how to create a new object of a given class.

Class(*args*)

This syntax creates a new instance of *Class*, initializing it with the specified *args*, which in turn are passed to the class's **__init__** method, if defined.

Note ▶ If there's any chance that an instance of the class might be combined in an operation with another type, and if that type does have code supporting the interaction, then a binary-operation method should return **NotImplemented** whenever it doesn't support the types; this gives the operand on the right side of the operation a chance to implement the operation. See Section 9.10.6 for more information.

◀| Note

9.10.5 Unary Arithmetic Methods

The methods in this category, similar to the ones listed in Section 9.9, tend to be implemented by classes that encapsulate some kind of number; however, they can also refer to other mathematical objects such as a point or matrix.

Table 9.4 lists the unary arithmetic methods.

Table 9.4. Magic Methods for Unary Arithmetic Operators

METHOD NAME	DESCRIPTION
`__pos__(self)`	Unary positive sign. This method is invoked when the plus sign (**+**) is applied to a single operand. It's rare that this operator ever does much besides return the object just as it is, because it is supported for the sake of completeness.
`__neg__(self)`	Unary negative sign. This method is invoked when the negative sign (**-**) is applied to a single operand.
`__abs__(self)`	Absolute value. This method is automatically invoked when the **abs** function is applied to an object of the class.
`__invert__(self)`	Bitwise inversion, which generates a result that contains 1 in every bit position in which the operand contains 0, and vice versa. This is called in response to the ~ operator. This is also called the *bitwise complement* or the one's complement.
`__bool__(self)`	Convert value to a Boolean. This conversion is invoked not only by **bool()**, but also by logical operators such as **not** and control structures that respond to a condition. The default action is to return **True** in response if this method is not defined.
`__round__(self, n)`	Precision-rounding function. This method is called by formatting functions that specify a limited precision and by the **round** function. The optional argument *n* specifies how many significant digits to round to. If omitted, the function should round to the nearest integer.
`__floor__(self)`	Round-down function. The effect should be to round those values down to the greatest integer that is not higher in value than the object. This method is called by the **math.floor** function, part of the **math** package.
`__ceil__(self)`	Round-upward function. The effect should be to round those values up to the lowest integer that is not lower in value than the object. This method is called by the **math.ceil** function, part of the **math** package.
`__trunc__(self)`	Round-downward method. This method is similar to `__floor__`, but instead of rounding up or down, it merely truncates the fractional portion of a floating-point value or values. For example, −3.5 is rounded up to −3.0, but 3.5 is rounded down to 3.0. This method is called by the **math.trunc** function, part of the **math** package.

Like the binary methods, these unary methods expect an implementation that creates a new object (that is, an instance) and returns it. This object should generally be of the same type as the object being operated on.

The Point class, introduced earlier, is a mathematical object that can be used to illustrate the use of some of these magic methods. To do that, we need to add the following method definition to the existing Point class definition:

```
def __neg__(self):
    newx = -self.x
    newy = -self.y
    return Point(newx, newy)
```

The following expression, for example, is not meant to change the internal value of my_point. Rather, it's intended to produce a new value that can be assigned or used.

```
-my_point
```

With this definition in place, we can now create Point class instances (Point objects) and apply arithmetic negation.

```
pt1 = Point(3, 4)
pt2 = -pt1
print(pt2.x, ', ', pt2.y, sep='')
```

This example prints

```
-3, -4
```

This result is, as you would hope, the arithmetic negation of a Point instance set equal to 3, 4. Its negation is a new instance of Point. The result is then assigned to pt2.

You can test a magic method by calling it directly. For example, suppose we add the following definition of the **__trunc__** method:

```
def __trunc__(self):
    newx = self.x.__trunc__()
    newy = self.y.__trunc__()

    return Point(newx, newy)
```

Given this definition, we can test the **__trunc__** method directly.

```
import math

pt1 = Point(5.5, -6.6)
pt2 = math.trunc(pt1)
print(pt2.x, ', ', pt2.y, sep='')
```

This example prints

```
5, -6
```

9.10.6 Reflection (Reverse-Order) Methods

The magic methods listed in this section are similar to the binary-operator methods presented earlier, with one critical difference: These methods are invoked when an object in question is the right (or rather, second) operand in an expression.

Note ▶ This discussion assumes the English-language standard of reading words left to right. This is how Python and other computer languages scan statements.

◀ Note

Suppose you have an expression adding two objects together, each of a different class:

```
fido = Dog()
precious = Cat()
print(fido + precious)
```

Python evaluates the expression `fido + precious` by first checking to see whether the Dog class implements an **__add__** method. There are several possibilities for what happens next.

▶ The left operand implements an **__add__** method and returns a value other than **NotImplemented**. Then no method of the right operand needs to be called.

▶ The left operand (or rather its class) does not implement an **__add__** method at all. In that case, Python checks to see whether the right operand implements an **__radd__** method.

▶ The left operand implements an **__add__** method, but that method decides it does not support interaction with an object like that on the right. Presumably, the **__add__** method has checked the type of the right operand and decided, "I don't support addition (**+**) with objects of this class." In that case, it should return **NotImplemented**. If so, Python checks to see whether the right operand implements an **__radd__** method.

Table 9.5 lists the reflection binary-operator methods.

Table 9.5. Magic Methods for Reflection Operations

METHOD NAME	DESCRIPTION
`__radd__(self, `*`other`*`)`	Right-side addition operator (**+**). This method is invoked in response to addition if the right operand defines this method, and if the left operand does not define `__`**add**`__` or else does define it but returns `NotImplemented`.
`__rsub__(self, `*`other`*`)`	Right-side subtraction operator (**-**). This method is invoked in response to subtraction if the right operand defines this method, and if the left operand does not define `__`**sub**`__` or else returns `NotImplemented`.
`__rmul__(self, `*`other`*`)`	Right-side multiplication operator (*****). This method is invoked in response to multiplication if the right operand defines this method, and if the left operand does not define `__`**mul**`__` or else returns `NotImplemented`.
`__rfloordiv__(self, `*`other`*`)`	Right-side floor division (**//**). This method is invoked in response to floor division if the right operand defines it, and if the left operand does not define `__`**floordiv**`__` or else returns `NotImplemented`. The method should return the result of the division, which may be a new object.
`__rtruediv__(self, `*`other`*`)`	Right-side division (**/**). This method is invoked in response to standard division (using a single forward slash) if the right operand defines this method but the left operand does not define `__`**div**`__` or else returns `NotImplemented`. The method should return the result of the division, which may be a new object.
`__rmod__(self, other)`	Right-side modulus division operator (**&**), also known as remainder division. This method implements modulus division if the right operand defines this method but the left operator does not define `__`**mod**`__` or else returns `NotImplemented`.
`__rdivmod__(self, `*`other`*`)`	Right-side of `divmod`. This method is invoked in response to a call to the `divmod` function if the second argument to the function defines this method but the first argument does not define `__`**divmod**`__` or else returns `NotImplemented`. The method should return a tuple in which the first element is a quotient and the second argument is a remainder.
`__rpow__(self, `*`other`*`)`	Right-side power operator (******). This method is invoked in response to exponentiation if the right operand defines this method, and if the left operand does not define `__`**pow**`__` or else returns `NotImplemented`. The method should return the result of the exponentiation, which may be a new object.

In most cases, the reverse-order methods are close echoes of their forward-order (left operand) versions. For example, it's easy to write reverse-order Point class methods by making small alterations to other magic methods.

However, in the case of this class, it isn't necessary to write most of these methods. For example, consider this code:

```
pt1 = Point(1, 2)
pt2 = Point(5, 10)
pt3 = pt1 + pt2
```

Assuming addition (**+**) is supported in this way—adding a Point instance to another Point instance—then **__add__** will be called through the left operand in this case (pt1); so therefore an **__radd__** would never be called through the right operand.

Symmetrical operations (a point added to a point) never invoke any of the right-side **r** magic methods.

Instead, the **r** methods are useful in asymmetrical situations—when an integer, for example, may be multiplied with a Point object. Suppose you want to support both of the following expressions:

```
pt3 = pt1 * 5
pt3 = 10 * pt1
```

The first of these two expressions results in invocation of the **__mul__** method, automatically called through the left operand, pt1.

The second statement is more problematic, because 10 is an integer, and the integer class (**int**) does not support multiplication with Point objects. Therefore, this statement requires that the Point class **__rmul__** method be implemented.

```
def __rmul__(self, n):
    ''' Return point * a scalar number, n '''
    newx = self.x * n
    newy = self.y * n
    return Point(newx, newy)
```

The body of this method definition is identical to the **__mul__** method definition. Although the Point object is now on the right side of the multiplication expression, it is still referred to through the **self** argument.

9.10.7 In-Place Operator Methods

Table 9.6 lists magic methods that provide support for combined assignment operations for any class, including **+=**, **-=**, and ***=**.

The **i** in these method names stands for "in place." If you implement these methods, you can make operators perform real in-place operations on objects of your class so that an actual data object in memory is modified.

If you support the operation involved (such as **__add__** used to implement addition) but not the corresponding **i** method, Python still supports the assignment op; this behavior is provided for free. But such operations are not in-place: Instead, they produce a new object, causing the variable to be reassigned to this new object.

For example, suppose you have an object and a second reference to it.

```
a = MyClass(10)
b = a
a += 1
print(a, b)   # Do a and b still have same value?
```

Here is the issue: If the operation a += 1 is an in-place operation, *then both a and b continue to refer to the same data*, which has been changed. But if a += 1 is not an in-place operation, the operation must assign new data to a, which breaks the association between a and b. In that case, a and b refer to different data after the operation.

The string class (**str**), being immutable, does not implement += as an in-place operation. Instead, it reassigns the string variable to reference a new object in memory.

Table 9.6. In-Place Operation Magic Methods

METHOD NAME	DESCRIPTION
__iadd__(self, *other*)	Combined addition-assignment operator method. This method is invoked in response to the += operator being applied to an object of the class—that object being on the left side of the operator. To successfully implement an in-place operation, this method should return **self**.
__isub__(self, *other*)	Combined subtraction-assignment operator method. This method is invoked in response to the -= operator being applied to an object of the class—that object being on the left side of the operator. To successfully implement an in-place operation, this method should return **self**.
__imul__(self, *other*)	Combined multiplication-assignment operator method. This method is invoked in response to the *= operator being applied to an object of the class—that object being on the left side of the operator. To successfully implement an in-place operation, this method should return **self**.
__idiv__(self, *other*)	Implements the /= operator. This method and the rest of the methods in this table follow similar guidelines to those above.
__igrounddiv__(self, *other*)	Implements the //= operator, which performs ground division (rounding down to nearest integer).
__imod__(self, *other*)	Implements the %=, which performs modular (remainder) division.
__ilshift__(self, *other*)	Implements the <<= operator, which performs bitwise left shift.
__irshift__(self, *other*))	Implements the >>= operator, which performs bitwise right shift.
__iand__(self, *other*)	Implements the &= operator, which performs binary AND.
__ior__(self, *other*)	Implements the |= operator, which performs bitwise OR.

▼ *continued on next page*

9

Table 9.6. In-Place Operation Magic Methods (*continued*)

METHOD NAME	DESCRIPTION
`__ixor__(self, other)`	Implements the `^=` operator, which performs bitwise exclusive-OR.
`__ipow__(self, other [, modulo])`	Implements the `**` operator, which calls the **pow** function. There is an optional third argument, *modulo*, which performs modular division after the exponentiation is performed.

When implementing these methods as true in-place operators (so that the data object in memory is modified), you should follow this procedure: First, modify the contents of the instance through which the method is called—that is, variables accessed through the **self** argument. Second, return a reference to the object by using

```
return self
```

For example, here's how the Point class might define the `__iadd__` and `__imul__` methods:

```
def __iadd__(self, other):
    self.x += other.x
    self.y += other.y
    return self

def __imul__(self, other):
    self.x *= other
    self.y *= other
    return self
```

9.10.8 Conversion Methods

A number of data conversion methods (see Table 9.7) are frequently useful to Python programmers.

For example, whenever an object is used in a context that requires a condition (such as an **if** statement or **while** loop), Python implicitly calls the **bool** conversion to get a **True** or **False** value. This conversion function in turn calls the `__bool__` method of the object's class. By writing such a method, you can determine how control structures interpret objects of your class when given as a condition.

The `__str__` method, of course, is important as a conversion for anything to be displayed as a string. However, `__str__` is covered in the previous section.

Table 9.7. Conversion Methods

METHOD	DESCRIPTION
`__int__(self)`	Called in response to the **int** conversion function. This method should return the integer equivalent of the object.
`__float__(self)`	Called in response to the **float** conversion function. This method should return the floating-point equivalent of the object.
`__complex__(self)`	Called in response to the **complex** conversion function. This method should return the complex-number equivalent of the object. For example, when `complex(1)` is executed, the value returned is `(1+0j)`.
`__hex__(self)`	Called in response to the **hex** conversion function, as well as by formatting functions. Used in Python 2.0 only.
`__oct__(self)`	Called in response to the **oct** conversion function, as well as by formatting functions. Used in Python 2.0 only.
`__index__(self)`	If the object is given as an index to a collection (such as tuple, string, or list), or a limit in a slicing operation, this method is called to return an actual index number, which must be an integer.
`__bool__(self)`	Described earlier, in Table 9.1. The method should return **True** or **False**, as appropriate. What most classes do is return **True** except in the case of zero values or empty containers.

The following class definition illustrates the use of the Point class with simple definitions for several of these methods.

```
class Point:
    def __init__(self, x = 0, y = 0):
        self.x = x
        self.y = y

    def __int__(self):
        return int(self.x) + int(self.y)

    def __float__(self):
        return float(self.x) + float(self.y)
```

The following IDLE session illustrates the use of these conversions. User input is shown in bold.

```
>>> p = Point(1, 2.5)
>>> int(p)
3
>>> float(p)
3.5
```

9.10.9 Collection Class Methods

Python enables you to create your own container classes. Most programmers, especially beginning to intermediate, rarely find this necessary. Python's built-in container classes (**list**, **dict**, **set**, and so on) are versatile, flexible, and powerful.

But you can, if you choose, implement your own containers using any storage mechanism you want. You could, for example, create dictionary classes that are implemented by an underlying binary tree rather than hash tables.

You can also create customized container classes that are built on some existing Python container class but add extra features. You can do that through either inheritance or containment, which are discussed in a practical example in Chapter 10, "Decimal, Money, and Other Classes."

Table 9.8 lists the magic methods you should support if building your own collection class, depending on how useful and robust you want those collections to be.

Table 9.8. Collection Class Magic Methods

SYNTAX	DESCRIPTION
`__len__(self)`	Returns an integer containing the number of elements in the collection.
`__getitem__(self, key)`	Returns an element from the collection, given a key to select it. This magic method responds to the use of indexing expressions, namely `obj[key]`. The *key* may well be an integer, in which case the method should perform an indexing operation. Or the key may be a non-integer, in the case of something like a data dictionary. In either case, the appropriate response is to return the selected element from the collection.
`__setitem__(self, key, value)`	The purpose of this magic method is similar to the `__getitem__` method, except that `__setitem__` sets the specified *value*—again, according to the *key*, which may be an index number if (for example) *key* is an integer. The element selected by the key should be replaced by the specified value.
	This is an example of modifying a value in place—that is, changing data in an existing object.
`__delitem__(self, key)`	This method deletes the specified item, using (once again) the key value to select that item.
`__iter__(self)`	Returns an iterator for the collection object; such an iterator is an object that implements the **next** method for the collection.
	The simplest way to implement the `__iter__` method, therefore, is to return **self** but then make sure that the class implements the `__next__` method directly.

Table 9.8. Collection Class Magic Methods (*continued*)

SYNTAX	DESCRIPTION
`__next__(self)`	This method may be implemented either by the class itself or by a helper class designed to work with the main class. In either case, this method should return the next element in an iteration, or else raise a **StopIteration** exception.
`__reversed__(self)`	This method, if implemented, should return an iteration of the collection that has values in reverse order.
`__contains__(self, item)`	This method should return **True** or **False**, depending on whether the specified item can be found in the collection.
`__missing__(self, key)`	This method is called if the collection is asked to access an element that does not exist. The method may return a value, such as **None**, or it may raise an exception, as appropriate.

The following code provides an example of a simple collection class. This is a dedicated Stack class. It does little more than implement some of the functions that a list already does; but the Stack class also implements peek, which returns the value of the "top" (or last) element without, however, popping it off the stack.

```python
class Stack:
    def __init__(self):
        self.mylist = []      # Containment used here!

    def append(self, v):
        self.mylist.append(v)

    def push(self, v):
        self.mylist.append(v)

    def pop(self):
        return self.mylist.pop()

    def peek(self):
        return self.mylist[-1]

    def __len__(self):
        return len(self.mylist)

    def __contains__(self, v):
        return self.mylist.__contains__(v)
```

```
        def __getitem__(self, k):
            return self.mylist[k]
```

Given this class definition, we can create a Stack object and then manipulate it as a collection. Here's an example:

```
st = Stack()
st.push(10)
st.push(20)
st.push(30)
st.push(40)
print('Size of stack is:', len(st))
print('First elem is:', st[0])
print('The top of the stack is:', st.peek())
print(st.pop())
print(st.pop())
print(st.pop())
print('Size of stack is:', len(st))
```

These statements result in the following output:

```
Size of stack is: 4
First elem is: 10
The top of the stack is: 40
40
30
20
Size of stack is: 1
```

If you're familiar with object oriented programming, you may note that the same results could have been achieved more easily in this case just by using inheritance. We could implement this dedicated Stack class by using the following:

```
class Stack(list):
    def push(self, v):
        self.append(v)

    def peek(self):
        return self[-1]
```

Given these few lines of code, this Stack class can carry out all the operations of the more elaborate class definition shown earlier.

This solution—*inheritance*—works only when you choose to build your collection class on top of an existing class, such as **list** or **dict**.

9.10.10 Implementing "__iter__" and "__next__"

The **__iter__** and **__next__** methods, along with the **next** function, require some elaboration. These methods enable objects of your class to produce a *generator* (or *iterator*), which in turn makes it usable in certain special contexts, such as a **for** loop. Let's start with some terminology.

▸ An *iterable* is an objected that can be iterated—or rather, stepped through—one element at a time. To be an iterable, an object must return an object in response to **__iter__**.

▸ An *iterator* is what a call to **__iter__** must return. An iterator is an object that can be used to step through a collection object.

▸ This iterator, which can be the same class or a separate class written just for this purpose, must respond to the **__next__** method—that is, it must implement this magic method, even if it does nothing else.

These abilities are important, because they enable instances of a class to be used with the Python **for** keyword. For example, suppose you have a four-dimensional Point object. If the iterator for such an object gets one of the four coordinates at a time, then the user of the class could use code like this:

```
my_point = Point()
for i in my_point:
    print(i)
```

This example would then print each of the four coordinates, one at a time.

As mentioned, a collection may be its own iterator; to do so, it returns **self** in response to the **__iter__** method, and it implements the **__next__** method itself.

Depending on the complexity of your container and the degree of flexibility you want, several approaches are possible to implement these methods.

▸ Passing a call to **__iter__** along to a collection object contained within the target. This is the simplest solution. It's essentially letting someone else handle the job.

▸ Implementing both **__iter__** and **__next__** in the collection class itself. The **__iter__** method returns **self** in this case, as well as initializing the iteration settings. However, such a solution makes it impossible to support more than one loop at a time.

▸ Responding to the **__iter__** method by creating a custom iterator object whose entire purpose is to support an iteration through the collection class. This is the most robust, and recommended, approach.

The next example illustrates the second approach, because it is, in most cases, relatively simple. To use this approach for the Stack class introduced earlier, add the following method definitions:

```
def __iter__(self):
    self.current = 0
    return self

def __next__(self):
    if self.current < len(self):
        self.current += 1
        return self.my_list[self.current - 1]
    else:
        raise StopIteration
```

An important coding technique here is to refer to the variable, `current`, as `self.current`. This causes the variable to be an instance variable and not a class or global variable.

When all the elements in a sequence or iteration have been stepped through by incrementing `self.current`, over and over the **__new__** method responds by raising the **StopIteration** exception. This has the effect of halting a **for** loop.

9.11   Supporting Multiple Argument Types

How do you write functions and methods that take more than one kind of argument? For example, suppose you want to write a Point class in such a way that a Point object can be multiplied either by a scalar number or by another Point object.

Python does not support overloading, but you can test the type of the argument at run time and, depending on that type, take a different set of actions. There are at least two ways to test the type of an object. One technique is to call the **type** function.

type(*object***)**

For example, you can test a data object or variable directly to see whether it has integer type.

```
n = 5
if type(n) == int:
    print('n is integer.')
```

A more reliable approach is to use the **isinstance** function. You can use one of two different versions.

```
isintance(object, class)
isintance(object, tuple_of_classes)
```

The first version determines the class of the object and then returns **True** if the object's class is either the same as the *class* argument or is derived from this argument—that is, the object must have a class identical to, or derived from, the second argument.

The second version of this syntax is the same, except that it enables you to include a tuple of (that is, an immutable list of) multiple classes.

Here's an example of the first syntax:

```
n = 5
if isinstance(n, int):
    print('n is an integer or derived from it.')
```

Here's an example of the second syntax. This technique enables you to test whether n contains any integer *or* floating-point number.

```
if isinstance(n, (int, float)):
    print('n is numeric.')
```

Remember that because of the use of **isinstance**, rather than **type**, *n* need not have **int** or **float** type; a type derived from **int** or **float** is sufficient. Such types are uncommon, but you could create one by subclassing.

So, for example, suppose you wanted to enable Point objects to support multiplication by both other Point objects and by numbers. You could do that by defining an **__mul__** method as follows:

```
def __mul__(self, other):
    if type(other) == Point:
        newx = self.x * other.x
        newy = self.y * other.y
        return Point(newx, newy)
    elif type(other) == int or type(other) == float:
        newx = self.x * other
        newy = self.y * other
        return Point(newx, newy)
    else:
        return NotImplemented
```

It's important to return **NotImplemented**, rather than raise an exception, if this class doesn't know how to handle an operation involving the class of *other*. By returning **NotImplemented**, you enable Python to inquire of the right operand whether its class supports an **__rmul__** method that would handle this situation.

This method could instead be defined by using the **isinstance** function to check on types rather than the **type** function.

```
def __mul__(self, other):
    if isinstance(other, Point):
        newx = self.x * other.x
        newy = self.y * other.y
        return Point(newx, newy)
    elif isinstance(other, (int, float)):
        newx = self.x * other
        newy = self.y * other
        return Point(newx, newy)
    else:
        return NotImplemented
```

In either case, support for multiplying by numbers is asymmetrical; such an operation may occur in an expression such as the following:

```
pt2 = 5.5 * pt1
```

The problem, of course, is that a magic method can't be added for integers or floating point, because we did not write those classes. Therefore, a Point class **__rmul__** method should be written.

```
def __rmul__(self, other):
    if isinstance(other, (int, float)):
        newx = self.x * other
        newy = self.y * other
        return Point(newx, newy)
    else:
        return NotImplemented
```

9.12 Setting and Getting Attributes Dynamically

A Python object can have many attributes; these include instance variables, methods, and properties. What all these attributes have in common is that they are *hard-coded*—that is, these names are fixed in the programming code.

But sometimes it's useful to set an attribute *dynamically*, setting the attribute name at run time in response to runtime conditions. This enables the user to suggest an attribute name, for example, or for the attribute name to be taken from a database or other application. Chapter 15, "Getting Financial Data off the Internet," uses this technique.

The **setattr** function has the syntax shown here.

```
setattr(object, name_str, value)
```

In this syntax, *object* is a reference to the object to be modified, *name_str* is a string containing the name of the attribute, and *value* is a data object or expression containing the value.

The **getattr** function has a complementary syntax.

```
getattr(object, name_str [, default_val])
```

Here's a simple example, entered in the IDLE environment. The attribute breed is added dynamically and set to 'Great Dane'.

```
>>> class Dog:
        pass

>>> d = Dog()
>>> setattr(d, 'breed', 'Great Dane')
>>> getattr(d, 'breed')
'Great Dane'
```

But actual examples will almost always pass a variable containing a string when using **getattr**. Here's an example:

```
>>> field = 'breed'
>>> getattr(d, field)
'Great Dane'
```

Chapter 9   *Summary*

Python provides a flexible and powerful means to do object oriented programming. The basic concept, that of a class, is essentially a user-defined type. But, as with other object oriented programming systems (OOPS!), such a type can include any number of method definitions. A method is a function defined in a class, usually called through an instance of that class.

```
my_dog = Dog('Bowser')
my_dog.speak()
```

Python methods have a required first argument that by convention is called **self**.

The **self** argument never explicitly appears in any method call; however, it must always appear in any method *definition* intended to be called through individual instances. The name **self** is a reference to the object itself.

Python is extremely polymorphic, due to the fact that variable and function names are never resolved until run time—that is, until a statement is executed. Therefore, any number of classes can define attributes of the same name, but the correct code for the particular object is always correctly accessed.

One of the most distinctive features of Python is that any class may avail itself of *magic methods*: method names that have a special meaning to Python and are automatically invoked under special circumstances. For example, the **__init__** method is invoked when an instance of the class is initialized. Magic method names are always characterized by having both leading and trailing double underscores (**__**). Therefore, if you avoid using such names yourself, there is no possibility of naming conflicts.

This chapter presented many of the magic methods supported in Python, including **__init__** and methods that support arithmetic and other operations.

Chapter 9   *Review Questions*

1 How would you describe the relationship of a class to its instances? For example, is it a one-to-one or a one-to-many relationship?

2 What kind of information is held only in an instance?

3 What information is held in a class?

4 What exactly is a method, and precisely how does it differ from a standard function?

5 Does Python support inheritance, and, if so, what is the syntax?

6 To what extent does Python support encapsulation (making instance or class variables private)?

7 What precisely is the difference between a class variable and an instance variable?

8 Within a class's method definitions, when does **self** need to be used, if at all?

9 What is the difference between the **__add__** and the **__radd__** methods?

10 When do you really need a reflection method? When do you not need it, even though you support the operation in question?

11 What is the **__iadd__** method called?

12 Is the **__init__** method inherited by subclasses? What do you do if you need to customize its behavior within a subclass?

Chapter 9   *Suggested Problems*

1 Write and test a three-dimensional Point class that supports addition and subtraction between two objects of this class, as well as multiplication by a scalar value (integers or floating point). In addition to an **__init__** method, you'll want to write magic methods, including **__str__**, **__repr__**, **__add__**, **__sub__**, **__mul__**, and **__rmult__**. The **__rmult__** method is necessary to support expression of the form n * point, where point is a Point object on the right side of the multiplication symbol.

2 Write and test a BankAcct class that contains at least the following state information: name, account number, amount, and interest rate. In addition to an **__init__** method, the class should support methods for adjusting the interest rate, for withdrawing and depositing (which can be combined in one method), for changing the interest rate, and for marking the passage of time—the last of which should automatically calculate interest for the number of days.

10 Decimal, Money, and Other Classes

In the movie *Superman III*, a computer genius figures out that if he can steal fractions of a penny in each transaction done by a bank, transferring that fraction to his own account, he can enrich himself. That's because a fraction of a penny multiplied by millions of transactions a day adds up to a fortune.

That's why bankers care about rounding errors. They're aware that fractions of a penny can add up. Precise amounts matter.

Early on, electronic computers were used for commercial purposes, making it important to record dollars and cents (or any currency) precisely, without errors. That's what this chapter is all about: utilizing ways of tracking data especially suited for financial purposes. This chapter will present the **Decimal** class and a Money class that we'll build up to.

We'll also look briefly at the **Fraction** and the built-in **complex** classes, although the latter is used mainly with advanced math and scientific applications.

10.1 Overview of Numeric Classes

Most of this book focuses on two kinds of numeric data: integer and floating point. These data types are sufficient for many applications. As you'll see, however, they are not perfect. Integers have the obvious drawback of not holding fractions, and floating-point data has rounding errors, as we'll show in this chapter.

This chapter introduces other data formats, including one that we'll develop ourselves, using the principles of Chapter 9, "Classes and Magic Methods."

▶ The **Decimal** class, which is a "fixed-point" data type that can hold decimal fractions, such as 0.02, precisely and without error.

▶ The **Money** class, which you can download or develop yourself. For the sake of illustration, this chapter takes the latter approach: developing this class ourselves.

327

▶ The **Fraction** class, which can store fractions such as one-third or one-seventh precisely and without any rounding errors, something that is not possible with the other classes.

▶ The **complex** class, which represents complex numbers from the world of higher math. Such numbers have both a "real" and an "imaginary" part.

If you're not familiar with the use of complex numbers from higher mathematics, don't worry. You can safely ignore these numbers unless you're doing the sort of work that requires it. If you're one of these people, you already know it.

None of these classes requires you to download anything from the Internet, and the **complex** class doesn't even require anything to be imported. It's a built-in class, just as **int**, **float**, and **str** are.

10.2   Limitations of Floating-Point Format

The problem with **float** values is that they're displayed in decimal format but internally stored in binary. A computer can store an amount such as 0.5 precisely, because that value maps directly to a binary fraction, but computers have problems with other fractions.

For example, if you could display a floating-point number in binary radix, the decimal amount 2.5 would look like this:

    10.1

But what about a decimal fraction such as 0.3? The problem is that 0.3 has to be stored as three-tenths—and tenths cannot be stored exactly in binary format, no matter how many digits of precision you have. This is because 1/10 is not a power of 2, unlike 1/2 or 1/4. Therefore, amounts have to be rounded in situations like this, producing small inaccuracies.

Here's an example in Python, easy to demonstrate from within IDLE:

    >>> 0.1 + 0.1 + 0.1
    0.30000000000000004

This result is mathematically wrong, and yet it indicates not a broken processor but the fact that every time floating-point operations deal with fractions like one-tenth, a tiny rounding error can crop up. Most programs just ignore these errors, because printing and formatting functions usually round after a certain number of digits, causing such errors to be hidden.

And usually that's fine. The assumption in programming is that tiny errors must be accepted when you work with floating point; it's just a price you pay.

In scientific and real-world applications, there's usually no infinite precision anyway. The sun, for example, is not *precisely* 93 million miles from Earth, just roughly.

Also, you can get rid of tiny errors like this by using the **round** function.

```
>>> round(1.0 + 1.0 + 1.0, 2)
0.3
```

But with financial applications, we'd like to do even better and not rely on constantly using the **round** function. Fractions matter, and even tiny errors are not acceptable, because they may accumulate over time. To a banker, $1.99 must be precisely $1.99.

Here are some more examples demonstrating rounding errors.

```
>>> 0.6 + 0.3 + 0.1          # Should produce 1.0
0.9999999999999999
>>> (0.6 + 0.3 + 0.1) / 2    # Should produce 0.5
0.4999999999999994
```

When you're dealing with business applications, particularly in the area of banking, it would be useful to be able to store a number like 44.31 precisely, with no errors of any kind.

Fortunately, Python provides a class that solves this problem: the **Decimal** class.

10.3 Introducing the Decimal Class

From within IDLE, execute the following **import** statement.

```
>>> from decimal import Decimal
```

We can now define any number of instances of the **Decimal** class, which—like the floating-point class, **float**—can hold fractional portions.

```
>>> my_dec = Decimal()
>>> print(my_dec)
0
```

As you can see, the default value of a **Decimal** instance is zero (0). But you can assign any decimal value you like, and it's stored precisely.

```
>>> d = Decimal('0.1')
>>> print(d + d + d)
0.3
```

This example does what you'd expect, but you should already see a twist to it. The **Decimal** variable, d, was initialized with a text string. It might seem much more natural to initialize it with a floating-point value. But look what happens if you do.

```
>>> d = Decimal(0.1)
>>> print(d)
0.1000000000000000055511512312578...
```

This result must seem strange. But there's a reason for it.

When 0.1 is used to initialize, a floating-point value (type **float**) is converted to **Decimal** format. As stated, **Decimal** can store 0.1 with absolute precision. But in this case, it first has to be converted from floating point; and the problem is, the floating-point value *already contains the rounding error within it*. This is eating the fruit of a poisoned tree.

How do we get around this problem? Initializing from a string is the best solution. Using "0.01" as the initializer says, "I want the decimal realization of what this string represents"—that is, the value without rounding errors.

Let's look at another example.

```
>>> d = Decimal('0.1')
>>> print(d + d + d)
0.3
```

This gives the right answer. Contrast it with the floating-point version.

```
>>> print(0.1 + 0.1 + 0.1)
0.30000000000000004
```

Here's another example. The following use of floating-point arithmetic shows an even more obvious error that the use of **Decimal** solves.

```
>>> print(0.1 + 0.1 + 0.1 - 0.3)
5.551115123125783e-17
>>> d1, d3 = Decimal('0.1'), Decimal('0.3')
>>> print(d1 + d1 + d1 - d3)
0.0
```

The **Decimal** class maintains precision. For example, if you perform arithmetic on instances of **Decimal** with two places of precision, including trailing zeros, those two places are maintained, as you can see here:

```
>>> d1, d3 = Decimal('0.10'), Decimal('0.30')
>>> d1 + d3
Decimal('0.40')
```

This behavior is useful in situations in which you're using **Decimal** objects to represent dollars and cents, and you want to preserve the two places of precision to the right of the decimal point. You could add a column of such numbers, and, as long as none of them had more than two digits of precision, the two places to the right would be maintained.

Here's another example:

```
>>> d1, d2 = Decimal('0.50'), Decimal('0.50')
>>> print(d1 + d2)
1.00
```

Note ▶ If you give an object to the **print** function, then, by default, it prints the standard string representation of the number. In the case of **Decimal** objects, this representation is a simple sequence of digits, with a decimal point as appropriate.

```
1.00
```

However, if you give a **Decimal** object as direct input in the IDLE environment, it prints the canonical representation, which includes the type name and quotation marks:

```
Decimal('1.00')
```

◀ Note

There are some other quirks of behavior of the **Decimal** class worth noting. If you multiply two of these objects together, the precision is not maintained but increased. Here is an example:

```
>>> d1, d3 = Decimal('0.020'), Decimal('0.030')
>>> print(d1 * d3)
0.000600
```

However, you can always adjust the precision of such an object by using the **round** function, which readjusts the number of digits to the right of the decimal point (getting rid of trailing zeros), as well as rounding figures up or down. Here's an example:

```
>>> print(round(d1 * d3, 4))
0.0006
>>> print(round(d1 * d3, 3))
0.001
```

10

Several rules apply to interacting with integer and floating-point values.

◗ You can multiply integers with **Decimal** objects freely, as well as add them.

◗ You can also initialize directly and precisely from an integer:

```
d = Decimal(5)
```

◗ Adding or multiplying a **Decimal** object by a floating-point value is an error. To perform such an operation, you convert the floating point to a **Decimal** object—for example, converting from a floating-point value and then rounding. Otherwise, arithmetic operations between the two types cause runtime errors.

So, for example, you can do the following, interacting with integers:

```
>>> d = Decimal(533)
>>> d += 2
>>> print(round(d, 2))

535.00
```

Performance Tip ▶ Creating **Decimal** objects takes about 30 times as long as creating floating-point objects, and arithmetic operations on floating-point are 60 times as fast as on **Decimal** objects. The moral is to use **Decimal** objects when you need them, but there are also good reasons for using floating-point values in most applications.

◀ Performance Tip

10.4 *Special Operations on Decimal Objects*

If you create a **Decimal** object and get help on it, the documentation reveals a large number of operations and methods.

```
>>> help(Decimal)
```

A great many of these are magic methods, and they exist to support all the basic arithmetic operations between two **Decimal** objects, or between a **Decimal** object and an integer. Other operations, such as logarithmic functions, are also supported.

Of the other methods, a great many are highly technical or are no-ops: They don't really do anything other than return the object as it currently is.

However, some of the methods are of interest to Python programmers generally. One of these is the **normalize** method. The action is to reduce the precision of the object to the minimum necessary, effectively getting rid of trailing zeros.

In the following example, **normalize** takes an object with precision of three places past the decimal point and returns an object with only one place of precision.

```
>>> d = Decimal('15.700')
>>> print(d)
15.700
>>> d2 = d.normalize()
>>> print(d2)
15.7
```

The **normalize** method will even get rid of the decimal point altogether if the fractional portion is zero.

```
>>> d = Decimal('6.00')
>>> print(d)
6.00
>>> d2 = d.normalize()
>>> print(d2)
6
```

However, when you change the precision of a **Decimal** value, you get an object having a different internal state, even though the values are considered equal when tested for equality (==). Assume the values of d and d2 in the previous example:

```
>>> d == d2
True
```

Decimal objects are immutable, just as integers, floating-point values, and strings are. However, the following code is legal, because it doesn't really change existing **Decimal** data; it just associates d with a new object. (Therefore, the **is** operator would reveal the objects to not be identical.) But remember, the original object is considered to be numerically equal to its normalized version.

```
>>> d2 = d              # Save old version of d in d2.
>>> d = d.normalize()   # Now d is normalized.
>>> d2 == d
True
>>> d2 is d
False
```

The **as_tuple** method gives major clues to the internal structure of such an object.

```
>>> d = Decimal('15.0')
>>> d.as_tuple()
DecimalTuple(sign=0, digits=(1, 5, 0), exponent=-1)
```

Here is what this suggests about the internal structure of the object.

▶ There is a sign bit (1 indicates negative; 0 indicates non-negative).

▶ The decimal digits (1, 5, 0) are stored individually.

▶ The precision is stored, as a negative exponent in this case, showing how many places to shift the decimal point to the right (or left if negative).

And in fact, you can use this same information, if you choose, to construct a **Decimal** object directly. Place a tuple inside parentheses, and then use the information to initialize an object:

```
>>> d = Decimal((0, (3, 1, 4), -2))
>>> print(d)
3.14
```

The general structure of such a tuple—a tuple that fully describes the state of a Decimal object—is shown here.

(sign_bit, (digit1, digit2, digit3...), exponent)

Another operation that is sometimes of practical use is the **getcontext** function, defined in the decimal package. Here's an example of use.

```
>>> decimal.getcontext()
Context(prec=28, rounding=ROUND_HALF_EVEN,
Emin=-999999, Emax=999999, capitals=1, clamp=0,
flags=[DivisionByZero, Inexact, FloatOperation,
Rounded], traps=[InvalidOperation, DivisionByZero,
Overflow])
```

This is a lot of information to wade through, but much of it's useful. First, prec=28 indicates that there's a maximum precision of 28 places. Second, the rounding technique, **ROUND_HALF_EVEN**, means that the final significant digit is rounded, if necessary, by checking whether the digit on its right is 5 or greater, in which case it's rounded up. The traps indicate what kinds of operations cause an exception to be raised.

10.5 A Decimal Class Application

We can use the **Decimal** class to add up a column of figures in which the precision is two places to right of the decimal point.

That's an appropriate way to add dollar and cents figures, so you can expect all amounts to be in the form 1.00 (one dollar), 1.50, 9.95, and so on. In such a situation, if we get fractions of a penny, we'll round them up or down to the nearest cent rather than just throwing all remainders away thoughtlessly.

Finally, the application will present the result in dollars-and-cents format—without, however, printing the currency symbols. (That's a feature we'll add in the next section.) When you're looking at the coding techniques, remember that a **Decimal** object is created most naturally and efficiently by initialization from a string.

```
money_amount = Decimal('1.99')
```

Here's the full application code. The action is to prompt the user for a number and—if the user did not enter an empty string—add the specified string of digits as a **Decimal** object. If the user presses Enter without typing input, the program breaks, stops, and prints the total.

```
from decimal import Decimal

total = Decimal('0.00')
while True:
    s = input('Enter amount in dollars and cents (#.##): ')
    if not s:
        break
    d = Decimal(s)
    d = round(d, 2)
    total += d

print('The sum of all these amounts is:', total)
```

The program could have used one of two different strategies in handling numbers with fractions smaller than 0.01. You could add all the smaller fractions together in the running total and do the rounding at the end. Instead, the approach here is to round amounts as each is entered.

Here's a sample session.

```
Enter amount in dollars and cents (#.##): 1
Enter amount in dollars and cents (#.##): 3.00
Enter amount in dollars and cents (#.##): 4.50
```

10

```
Enter amount in dollars and cents (#.##): 33.003
Enter amount in dollars and cents (#.##): 12.404
Enter amount in dollars and cents (#.##):
The sum of all these amounts is: 53.90
```

Because of how this application applies rounding—after each entry—the result is 53.90. But we could have done all the rounding at the end, which would in this case produce a slightly different result: 53.91.

10.6 Designing a Money Class

Money talks. So now we're going to create a Money class. You could download such a class. But it's instructive to create such a class yourself. In the process, we'll use a good many of the concepts from Chapter 9 in a practical example.

It might be useful to store decimal figures along with a *units* figure that represents the type of currency. We'll use three kinds, indicated by the value stored in an additional string field. The abbreviations in Table 10.1, by the way, are recognized internationally as standard names for these currencies.

Table 10.1. Abbreviations for Three Currencies

SYMBOL (to store in units, a str instance variable)	DESCRIPTION
'USD'	U.S. dollars
'EUR'	European dollars
'CAD'	Canadian dollars

Now there's a decision to make: Which of the following two approaches should we use?

▶ Containment. This approach views a Money object as a container for a **Decimal** object along with another object (the *units* field). The drawback is that for every operation you want the Money class to support, you need to write a separate magic method.

▶ Inheritance. This approach views a Money object as a specialized kind of **Decimal** object, in which the units field is added as an additional attribute.

Given this choice, inheritance is probably the better way to go; it's also more in keeping with the spirit of object orientation, which says that the relationship "A is a kind of B, only more specialized," is really an inheritance relationship.

Containment, on the other hand, is appropriate when the relationship is "A *has* a B." Containment works better in that case.

But there's a quirk in the Python language that makes inheritance difficult to use in this situation. A general guideline is that if you want to keep things simple, avoid inheriting from an immutable or built-in class. Unfortunately, that includes inheriting from **Decimal**.

Therefore, in this chapter we'll use object containment as a way of building a Money class around the **Decimal** class. Later, we'll show how to use inheritance to create a Money class, in Section 10.12, "Money and Inheritance."

Figure 10.1 shows the containment architecture. Each Money object contains two parts: a **Decimal** object , dec_amt, and a string called units.

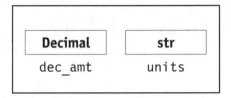

The Money Class

Figure 10.1. A Money class using containment

10.7 Writing the Basic Money Class (Containment)

Building a Money class around a **Decimal** object is easy to do in the beginning. Here's how we get started:

```
from decimal import Decimal

class Money():

    def __init__(self, v = '0', units = 'USD'):
        self.dec_amt = Decimal(v)
        self.units = units
```

With this simple class definition, you can create Money objects and display their attributes, although other operations and methods need to be added. The following example takes advantage of the default units being U.S. dollars.

```
>>> m1 = Money('0.10')
>>> print(m1.dec_amt, m1.units)
0.10 USD
```

10

But if this is all you can do, it's not impressive. The next thing to add is the ability to print Money objects in a meaningful and automatic way. Right now, if you print m1, it's not very useful.

```
>>> print(m1)
<__main__.Money object at 0x103cc6f60>
```

10.8 Displaying Money Objects ("__str__", "__repr__")

To determine how a Money object is printed, write a **__str__** method for the class. Here's a working version of the function, to be added to the class definition.

```
def __str__(self):
    s = str(self.dec_amt) + ' ' + self.units
    return s
```

And here's a sample session that takes advantage of this method.

```
>>> m1 = Money('5.01', 'CAD')
>>> print(m1)
5.01 CAD
```

As you can see, it's now easy to initialize and display Money objects, with the default type of units being USD, indicating the use of U.S. dollars.

But we also want to print a good canonical representation of the class. This requires a **__repr__** method definition, in addition to **__str__**.

```
def __repr__(self):
    s = ('Money(' + str(self.dec_amt) + ' ' +
        self.units + ')')
    return s
```

A class's **__repr__** function typically differs from a **__str__** function in that it identifies the class as well as showing its contents.

```
>>> m2 = Money('0.10')
>>> print(m2)
0.10 USD
>>> m2
Money(0.10 USD)
```

10.9 Other Monetary Operations

So far, all we can do with the Money class is create objects and print them. But to be useful, the class should support, at minimum, addition operations (**+**) between Money objects.

If we ignore the role of units for the moment, the __**add**__ function is easy to write. This version assumes that you only want to add Money objects to other objects of the same class.

```
def __add__(self, other):
    d = self.dec_amt + other.dec_amt
    return Money(str(d))
```

We can expand on this function definition by presupposing that whatever units are used by the left operand should be used by the result. Implementing that approach gives us a second version of the function definition. In the following code, the item to be added is shown in bold for the sake of illustration.

```
def __add__(self, other):
    d = self.dec_amt + other.dec_amt
    return Money(str(d), self.units)
```

Even more interesting, and useful, would be to convert the units in use on the right side to match those on the left after first multiplying by the currency-exchange rate. Although such numbers are changed on a daily basis, the program can be revised as needed to accommodate such changes. One way to do that would be to read in the currency-exchange rates from a file that is updated as needed.

To keep things simple for now, we're going to pick some exchange rates—the current ones as of this writing—and just assume that the program can be revised as needed. Because there are six possible conversions (from our three supported currencies), the best way to do that is with a dictionary. The key value is the result of concatenating two currency symbols. The value field shows what number the second currency must be multiplied by to produce the first.

```
exch_dict = {
    'USDCAD': Decimal('0.75'), 'USDEUR': Decimal('1.16'),
    'CADUSD': Decimal('1.33'), 'CADEUR': Decimal('1.54'),
    'EURUSD': Decimal('0.86'), 'EURCAD': Decimal('0.65')
}
```

So, for example, the value for the USDCAD key is 0.75, meaning that a Canadian-dollar figure is multiplied by 0.75 to get its equivalent in U.S. dollars. Now the final version of the function can apply the currency-exchange rate whenever two different currencies are added together.

The dictionary stores the exchange rates as Decimal objects, thereby making the subsequent arithmetic easier to perform.

```
def __add__(self, other):
    '''Money add function.
    Supports two Money objects added together; if
    the second has a different currency unit, then
    exchange rate must be applied before adding the
    two amounts together. Apply rounding of 2.
    '''
    if self.units != other.units:
        r = Money.exch_dict[self.units + other.units]
        m1 = self.dec_amt
        m2 = other.dec_amt * r
        m = Money(m1 + m2, self.units)
    else:
        m = Money(self.dec_amt + other.dec_amt,
                        self.units)
    m.dec_amt = round(m.dec_amt, 2)
    return m
```

Let's step through how this function works. As the comments (or rather, the doc string) point out, an exchange rate may be applied before the amounts are added together, assuming the units are not the same (such as U.S. dollars versus Canadian dollars). Although exchange rates are expressed as floating point in most locations, we store those rates here as **Decimal** objects, so that fewer conversions need to be done.

```
r = Money.exch_dict[self.units + other.units]
m1 = self.dec_amt
m2 = other.dec_amt * r
m = Money(m1 + m2, self.units)
```

In either case—whether an exchange rate is applied or whether it isn't—we also want a rounding factor of 2 to be applied, so that the money is always expressed with two digits of precision past the decimal point.

```
m.dec_amt = round(m.dec_amt, 2)
```

The new Money object, m, is finally returned by the **__add__** function.

With this function definition in place, along with the exch_dict, which can be made a class variable of Money, we can now add different currencies together—as long as they are one of the three currencies recognized by this program (although that list can be expanded as much as you want).

So, for example, we can add a U.S. dollar to a Canadian dollar and get a meaningful result.

```
>>> us_m = Money('1', 'USD')
>>> ca_m = Money('1', 'CAD')
>>> print(us_m + ca_m)
1.75 USD
```

Note ▶ This function definition works correctly, of course, as long as the three supported currencies are used. If units other than USD, CAD, or EUR are used, a **KeyError** exception results whenever mixed currencies are added.

◀ Note

Putting it all together, here's the complete Money class. It's not really complete, of course, because there are many operations we still could add, such as subtraction and multiplication by integers.

```
from decimal import Decimal

class Money():
    '''Money Class.
    Stores both a Decimal amount and currency units. When
    objects are added, exchange rate will be applied if
    the currency units differ.
    '''

    exch_dict = {
        'USDCAD': Decimal('0.75'), 'USDEUR': Decimal('1.16'),
        'CADUSD': Decimal('1.33'), 'CADEUR': Decimal('1.54'),
        'EURUSD': Decimal('0.86'), 'EURCAD': Decimal('0.65')
    }

    def __init__(self, v = '0', units = 'USD'):
        self.dec_amt = Decimal(v)
        self.units = units

    def __str__(self):
        s = str(self.dec_amt) + ' ' + self.units
        return s
```

10

```
def __repr__(self):
    s = ('Money(' + str(self.dec_amt) + ' ' +
        str(self.units) + ')')
    return s

def __add__(self, other):
    '''Money add function.
    Supports two Money objects added together; if
    the second has a different currency unit, then
    exchange rate (r) is applied before adding the
    two amounts together. Apply rounding of 2.
    '''

    if self.units != other.units:
        r = Money.exch_dict[self.units + other.units]
        m1 = self.dec_amt
        m2 = other.dec_amt * r
        m = Money(m1 + m2, self.units)
    else:
        m = Money(self.dec_amt + other.dec_amt,
                    self.units)
    m.dec_amt = round(m.dec_amt, 2)
    return m
```

That's the (for now) complete class definition—although, as mentioned, there are many operations you might want to add.

10.10   Demo: A Money Calculator

With the completed Money class definition in place, it's now possible to write a calculator application that can add up any number of money amounts in the three different currencies we currently support and give the answer in a common denomination.

Most of the code is easy to write, but user input must be broken down into numeric and units portions, something that does complicate the coding a little. Fortunately, much of the work is done by the **split** method of the **str** type.

```
from decimal import Decimal

# Place Money class definition here or import it.
```

```
def money_calc():
    '''Money addition calculator.
    Prompt for a series of Money objects until empty
    string is entered; then print results of the
    running total.
    '''
    n = 0
    while True:
        s = input('Enter money value: ')
        s = s.strip()
        if not s:
            break
        a_list = s.split()   # Split into amt, units.
        d = a_list[0]
        if len(a_list) > 1:
            m = Money(d, a_list[1])
        else:
            m = Money(d)
        if n == 0:
            amt = m
        else:
            amt += m
        n += 1
    print('Total is', amt)

money_calc()
```

The final line of this code, which executes the function, makes it into a complete program.

There's a subtlety to this function. It's desirable to let the first choice of currency (the units entered for the first line) determine the currency used for the final answer. This gives the user control of the results. Perhaps you want the results to be expressed in Canadian dollars or Euros, for example; you simply need to make sure the first entry uses those units.

The problem is, we're keeping a running total, and the usual way of keeping a running total is to start with an initial zero value. Here's an example:

```
amt = Money('0')
```

The problem here is that right now, USD is the default value for units; therefore, this initial choice, through the logic of the program, would predetermine that every result of this program is expressed in U.S. dollars.

10

What we'd like to do instead is to let the user determine the currency of the final results based on the first entry. But that means that we can't start with an initial zero value; it has to be set by the user.

Therefore, the variable n is used to record how many entries have been made. If and only if an item is the first entry, the variable amt is created for the first time.

```
if n == 0:
    amt = m
else:
    amt += m
n += 1
```

Note that addition assignment is supported, for Money as well as integers. This is a general feature of Python. If there's an __**add**__ function for the class, you get both **+** and **+=** operators supported for free, even though you didn't write an __**iadd**__ function. (However, as explained in Chapter 9, you can't take advantage of the fact that **+=** is an in-place operation.)

When the program runs, it prompts the user for a series of values, just as other adding machine applications in this book have done. When the user enters an empty string (by just pressing Enter), the function breaks the loop and then gives the total.

Here's a sample session.

```
Enter money value: 1.05
Enter money value: 2.00 CAD
Enter money value: 1.5   EUR
Enter money value: 1.00
Enter money value: 2.5 CAD
Enter money value:
Total is 7.16 USD
```

Notice how this session successfully added three different kinds of currencies. The final result is expressed in terms of U.S. dollars because the first entry, by default, was in U.S. dollars.

Here's a sample session that gives the result in Canadian dollars:

```
Enter money value: 1.50 CAD
Enter money value: 1.75 CAD
Enter money value: 2.00 USD
Enter money value: 1.00 USD
Enter money value:
Total is 7.24 CAD
```

Because the first Money object entered is in Canadian dollars, those units are used in the final result. However, you may notice that each and every time Canadian dollars are entered, the units, CAD, must be explicitly specified, because the default is always U.S. dollars.

In the next section, we're going to correct that U.S. bias, which should make our Canadian and European readers much happier!

10.11 Setting the Default Currency

To make our Money class friendlier to a wider group of people, we should enable users of the class to set default units other than U.S. dollars. An easy way to implement this feature is to tie it to a class variable and then let the user of the class change it as desired.

To do that, we first need to add a class variable to the Money class, a very easy change to make.

```
class Money():

    default_curr = 'USD'
```

Then we need to alter the __init__ function. This is trickier than it sounds, because although you can refer to class variables from within a method definition, you can't use such a reference in the argument list. So the following causes an error:

```
# This causes an ERROR!
def __init__(self, v='0', units=Money.default_curr):
```

It's frustrating that we can't do this. However, the following definition of the __init__ function works perfectly well, by replacing the default value (an empty string) with the value stored in default_curr.

```
def __init__(self, v='0', units=''):
    self.dec_amt = Decimal(v)
    if not units:
        self.units = Money.default_curr
    else:
        self.units = units
```

With the changes (shown in bold) made to the __init__ function, the class variable, default_curr, now becomes in effect the default value for units.

Finally, the `money_calc` function can easily be altered so that the units entered for the first item become the new default setting for the class. One line of code needs to be added, about three-quarters of the way through the loop.

```
if n == 0:             # If this is first entry...
    amt = m            # Create amt!
    Money.default_curr = m.units
```

With this change, the application now enables the user to specify a default different from U.S. dollars. All they have to do is specify the new default in the first money object they enter. For example, the user in the following sample session causes Canadian dollars (CAD) to be the default.

```
Enter money value: 1.0 CAD
Enter money value: 2.05
Enter money value: .95
Enter money value: 2
Enter money value:
Total is 6.00 CAD
```

In this case, it's easy to see that both the units used for the total, and the units used as the default currency, are Canadian dollars, and not U.S. dollars.

And in this next sample session, you can see that the default remains Canadian dollars, even if a different currency is entered in the middle of the series.

```
Enter money value: 2.0 CAD
Enter money value: -1
Enter money value: 10 USD
Enter money value: 5.01
Enter money value: -5.01
Enter money value:
Total is 14.30 CAD
```

You can see that all the Canadian amounts cancel out except for one Canadian dollar. A figure of 10 U.S. dollars was also entered. But the final result is printed in Canadian dollars—because the first figure was in CAD. So, although the sum contains 10 U.S. dollars, it's converted to the equivalent in CAD, plus the one Canadian dollar that was not canceled out, giving you 10 U.S. dollars in Canadian dollars (13.30), plus one Canadian dollar (1.00), for a grand total of 14.30.

You should note that changing the default units for the class is a little tricky; such a change affects all subsequent uses of the class as long as the program is running. (However, it does not affect future running of the program.) But if you show a little care, this shouldn't be a problem.

10.12 Money and Inheritance

What's the best way to get money? Inheritance, of course.

As we mentioned in Section 10.6, "Designing a Money Class," the more natural way to create a Money class based on an existing object type, **Decimal**, would be to use inheritance—that is, subclassing **Decimal**.

The problem is that the **Decimal** type is immutable. This creates a special challenge; that challenge is solved by a few lines of code, but how to write this code is not at all obvious. Not to worry, though. This section will give you that specialized knowledge.

Normally, inheritance would be easy to implement. Suppose that Money subclassed another class named Thingie, which is not immutable. In that case, you could use the following easy-to-write code:

```
class Money(Thingie):

    def __init__(self, v, units='USD'):
        super().__init__(v)
        self.units = units
```

What this approach says (and remember that this is the approach you'd use for most classes, but not **Decimal**) is "Call the superclass function to handle initialization of the first argument, but initialize the second argument, units, directly." Remember that units is the extra attribute that the Money class adds to the Thingie class.

But this approach fails with immutable classes such as **Decimal**. Instead, it's necessary to write a **__new__** method for the Money class. The allocation of the **Decimal** portion of the Money class is handled by **__new__**.

```
from decimal import Decimal

class Money(Decimal):

    def __new__(cls, v, units='USD'):
        return super(Money, cls).__new__(cls, v)

    def __init__(self, v, units='USD'):
        self.units = units

m = Money('0.11', 'USD')
print(m, m.units)
```

This small program prints the following:

```
0.11 USD
```

If you want to apply this coding technique to another situation involving an immutable superclass, here's what you need to remember: Use the **__new__** function to call the superclass version of **__new__**. The arguments should be the subclass name and **cls**, a reference to the class. Let this method initialize the portion of the class that originates in the superclass (in this case, v). Make sure to pass along the value returned by the superclass version of **__new__**.

```
def __new__(cls, v, units='USD'):
    return super(Money, cls).__new__(cls, v)
```

For other situations, we can generalize upon this pattern for any given class and superclass named MyClass and MySuperClass, and for superclass data, d:

```
class MyClass(MySuperClass):
    def __new__(cls, d, other_data):
        return super(MyClass, cls).__new__(cls, d)
```

Note ▶   We can further generalize this code as follows, in which d is data in the base class, and *other_data* is data in the subclass, which should be initialized in **__init__**.

```
class MyClass(MySuperClass):
    def __new__(cls, d, other_data):
        return super(MyClass, cls).__new__(cls, d)
```
◀ Note

Now, let's return to the Money example.

An **__init__** method still needs to be written if any additional attributes have been added by the subclass and need to be initialized. The **__init__** method should be used to initialize these other attributes.

```
def __init__(self, v, units='USD'):
    self.units = units
```

Even with these definitions in place, it's still necessary to print both the object itself (which inherits directly from **Decimal**) and the units, which is the attribute added by Money.

```
print(m, m.units)
```

But we can improve this situation by overriding the **__str__** method, to print a Money object in a more natural and direct way. Notice that the superclass version of this method is called to do much of the work.

```
def __str__(self):
    return super().__str__() + ' ' + self.units
```

This is a typical example of how you'd override the **__str__** method, regardless of whether you're subclassing an immutable class or a mutable class.

Note ▶ It may seem unreasonable that Python doesn't let you use the easy approach to subclassing another type, as shown earlier with the hypothetical superclass Thingie.

There are a number of reasons that's not feasible in Python. For one thing, if a superclass is immutable, that means its data can never be changed after it's created. Also, some built-in classes make use of the **__new__** function to initialize values, in addition to other actions, so that calling upon the superclass's **__init__** function is inadequate. The basic rule is this: If subclassing a built-in type the ordinary way doesn't work, you might need to subclass **__new__**.

◀ Note

10.13 The Fraction Class

The Decimal and Money classes can hold decimal figures, such as 0.53, with absolute precision. But these classes have their limitations, too.

What if you want to hold the value 1/3? The value cannot be represented in binary radix without rounding errors. But it's just as impossible to represent this amount in decimal radix! You would, mathematically speaking, need an infinite number of digits to store 1/3 (one-third) in either radix.

```
0.33333333333333333333333...
```

Fortunately, integers come to our rescue. Integers store numbers with absolute precision, and by creating objects with two parts—a numerator (top half) and a denominator (bottom half)—we can represent any number that's expressible as a ratio of two integers (see Figure 10.2).

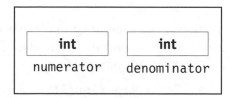

The Fraction Class

Figure 10.2. Structure of the Fraction class

Some issues arise, but these are all handled smoothly by the class. For example, 1/2, 2/4, and 100/200 are all mathematically equivalent. But thanks to internal methods, these are all reduced to the same internal representation *automagically*. Here's an example. First, we need to import the class.

```
from fractions import Fraction
```

Be sure to enter this statement exactly as shown. The word **fractions** is lowercase and plural; the word **Fraction** is uppercase and singular! Why the inconsistency, we're not sure.

In any case, after the class is imported, it can be used to deal with **Fraction** objects in a consistent, highly convenient way. Let's look again at the problem of dealing with 1/2, 2/4, and 100/200.

```
fr1 = Fraction(1, 2)
fr2 = Fraction(2, 4)
fr3 = Fraction(100/200)
print('The fractions are %s, %s, & %s.' % (fr1, fr2, fr3))
```

This example prints

```
The fractions are 1/2, 1/2, & 1/2.
```

All these **Fraction** objects are displayed as the same quantity, because they're automatically reduced to their simplest form.

```
>>> if fr1 == fr2 and fr2 == fr3:
        print('They are all equal!')
```

```
They are all equal!
```

Note ▶ By using one of the shortcuts pointed out in Chapter 4, you can replace the condition in this example by chaining the comparisons, producing a shorter version.

```
>>> if fr1 == fr2 == fr3:
        print('They are all equal!')
```
◀ Note

Fractions can be specified in other ways. For example, if only one integer is given during initialization, the class stores it as that integer divided by 1 (which is a ratio, of course). Here's an example:

```
>>> fr1 = Fraction(5)
>>> print(fr1)
5
```

Fractions can be converted from **Decimal** objects and floating-point values as well. Sometimes this works out fine, as here.

```
>>> fr1 = Fraction(0.5)
>>> print(fr1)
1/2
```

But sometimes it does not.

```
>>> fr2 = Fraction(0.01)
>>> print(fr2)
5764607523034235/576460752303423488
```

Wow, what happened here? The answer is that our old nemesis, the floating-point rounding error, has raised its ugly head again. The **Fraction** class did its best to accommodate that tiny little rounding error in the floating-point value 0.01, and consequently it came up with this ugly ratio.

There are a couple of solutions. One is to initialize directly from a string, as we did with **Decimal** objects.

```
>>> fr2 = Fraction('0.01')
>>> print(fr2)
1/100
```

That's better! Another option is to use the **limit_denominator** method. This method says that the denominator can only get so big. Given that limitation, the **Fraction** class generates the closest approximation it can . . . and that approximation usually turns out to be the number we wanted anyway.

```
>>> fr2 = Fraction(0.01).limit_denominator(1000)
>>> print(fr2)
1/100
```

Success!

But the real strength of the class is that it supports all the standard operations on all objects of type **Fraction**, and the results are guaranteed to be precisely correct. Here's an example:

```
>>> fr1 = Fraction(1, 2)
>>> fr2 = Fraction(1, 3)
>>> fr3 = Fraction(5, 12)
>>> print(fr1 + fr2 + fr3)
5/4
```

Therefore, 1/2, 1/3, and 5/12, when added together, produce 5/4. You can verify for yourself that this answer is correct.

Other arithmetic operations, such as multiplication, division, subtraction, and so on, are all supported and can be smoothly combined with integers.

```
>>> fr1 = Fraction(1, 100)
>>> print(fr1, 'times 50 =', fr1 * 50)
1/100 times 50 = 1/2
```

Considering that you can initialize a **Fraction** object from a string specifying a floating-point expression, such as `'0.1'`, can you initialize from a string such as `'1/7'`, which is what we'd really like to do?

Yes. This is especially convenient, and we'll use it in the upcoming application.

```
>>> fr1 = Fraction('1/7')
>>> print(fr1)
1/7
>>> fr1 += Fraction('3/4')
>>> print(fr1)
25/28
```

This conversion works only as long as there are no intervening spaces between the numerator, the forward slash (/), and the denominator. Few users are foolish enough to put in extra spaces. But if you're worried about the user doing that, you can always eliminate spaces in this way:

```
s = s.replace(' ', '')
```

Finally, you can always access the **numerator** and **denominator** members of a **Fraction** object. Remember, though, that these objects are simplified as soon as you enter them. Here's an example:

```
>>> fr1 = Fraction('100/300')
>>> print('numerator is', fr1.numerator)
numerator is 1
>>> print('denominator is', fr1.denominator)
denominator is 3
```

Now, let's create another adding machine application—this time for fractions. The fact that fractions can be entered as strings in the form `'x/y'` makes this application easy to write.

```
from fractions import Fraction

total = Fraction('0')

while True:
    s = input('Enter fraction (press ENTER to quit): ')
    s = s.replace(' ', '')  # Elim. spaces, just in case.
```

```
    if not s:
        break
    total += Fraction(s)

print('The total is %s.' % total)
```

Wow, this is a short program! One reason this is so easy to write is that users can enter fractions in the form they would usually use (such as `'1/3'` for one-third) without the need to bring in any extra code to lexically analyze this result. Yes, the Fraction class does it all for you!

However, the user cannot enter fractions in the form `'2 1/3'`. That particular amount would have to be entered as `'7/3'`.

Here's a sample session. Notice how smoothly the application handles both negative numbers and whole numbers, such as 2.

```
Enter fraction (press ENTER to quit): 2
Enter fraction (press ENTER to quit): 1
Enter fraction (press ENTER to quit): 1/2
Enter fraction (press ENTER to quit): 1/3
Enter fraction (press ENTER to quit): -3
Enter fraction (press ENTER to quit):
The total is 5/6.
```

Handling whole integers poses no problem, because an input such as 2 is translated into the fraction 2/1.

10.14 The Complex Class

Before ending this chapter, we'll look at one more built-in type in Python: the **complex** class. Like **int** and **float**, it's a fully built-in, immutable class; you don't even have to import anything.

Just what is a complex number? Fortunately, if you don't know what it is, you're almost certainly not a person who needs to know. The theory of complex numbers is understood by scientists and engineers working in advanced areas of math; other people might find the ideas interesting but almost never need to use them.

But, for what it's worth, a complex number—and you'll see this if you stick around—has two parts: a "real" part and an "imaginary" part. The imaginary part of a complex number is the answer to the age-old question, What is the square root of −1?

If you have some basic training in math, you may protest, "Negative numbers have no square roots! There is no number that, multiplied by itself, produces −1!" We empathize, but higher math presupposes such numbers.

10

If that's a problem, the only thing to be said is "Turn back now, or else abandon hope, all ye who enter." But professional mathematicians have worked out a series of techniques for dealing with such numbers.

Still with us? Okay. The first thing to be said about Python complex numbers is that you can write them as literal numbers. Here's an example:

```
z = 2.5 + 1.0j
```

At first glance, z looks like a real number that is the sum of 2.5 and 1.0 times a variable j. But it's not. It's a single object, in which the real portion is 2.5 and the imaginary portion is 1.0.

As with other classes we've looked at, the **complex** class produces objects that themselves are made up of smaller parts. Figure 10.3 displays the structure of a complex-number object.

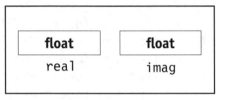

complex type

Figure 10.3. Structure of a Python complex number

Let's look at that assignment again.

```
z = 2.5 + 1.0j
```

If you understand complex numbers, you may object that the letter i (not j) should be used to represent the imaginary portion of a number. But j is used because the letter i is used by some engineers to represent electric current; also, i is a formatting character.

After this assignment, z is an object that has real and imaginary portions that can be accessed as **real** and **imag**, respectively.

```
print('Real part is %s and imaginary part is %s.'
      % (z.real, z.imag))
```

This prints

```
Real part is 2.5 and imaginary part is 1.0.
```

An alternative to writing a literal is to use an explicit **complex** conversion:

```
z = complex(5.7, 10)
```

If we then print the real and imaginary portions of z explicitly, as in the previous example, z is now described this way:

```
Real part is 5.7 and imaginary part is 10.0.
```

The ability to write complex numbers directly is a convenience. You can even exclude the "real" part, and if you do, the number still has type **complex**. So you can do things like this:

```
print(2j * 3j)
```

This statement produces the result of multiplying two complex numbers together (each of which has an imaginary portion in this case; the real portion exists but in each case is assumed to be 0). If you're familiar with the basic math of complex numbers, the result should not surprise you.

```
(-6+0j)
```

By the way, if you store this result in z and then examine z.real and z.imag, you'll find that each of these members is floating point, and not integer, despite the way the result is displayed in this case.

```
>>> print(type(z.imag))
<class 'float'>
```

The use of literal complex numbers, such as -6+0j, although convenient, creates some situations in which you need to be careful. Parentheses are not required, but errors can crop up if you omit them. For example, how do you think Python evaluates the following?

```
z = 0 + 2j * 0 + 3j
```

From the previous discussion, it might seem that Python would treat this statement as if written the following way:

```
z = (0 + 2j) * (0 + 3j)
```

This in turn would produce the complex number (-6+0j). But Python does not interpret the statement that way. How can it know that 0 is not just 0, a real number, instead of part of a complex number? Instead, the usual rules of precedence apply, and the statement is evaluated by performing multiplication first.

```
z = 0 + (2j * 0) + 3j
```

So now, printing z produces

```
3j
```

Note ▶   You might think that spacing changes things here, that entering $0 + 3j$ with internal spaces omitted, resulting in $0+3j$, changes the interpretation of the expression. It does not.

◀ Note

Even the expression $3j$ can be misleading if you're not careful. Any such expression is actually part of a complex number.

```
>>> z = 3j
>>> print(z.real)
0.0
```

You can, if you choose, have complex numbers with the imaginary portion currently set to zero. But the use of j ensures complex type.

```
>>> z = 2 + 0j
>>> print(z)
(2+0j)
>>> print(z.real, z.imag)
2.0 0.0
```

And here's another caveat: When you're writing code that includes complex numbers, it's a good idea to avoid making j a variable.

You can convert other numbers to **complex**, although the imaginary part will be assumed to be zero. But complex numbers cannot be converted to these other types (instead, you must assign from **.real** and **.imag** portions); they also cannot be compared to each other or to other numbers by using **>**, **<**, **>=**, or **<=**.

```
z = complex(3.5)    # This is valid; z.imag will be 0.
x = float(z)        # Not supported!
x = z.real          # But this is valid.
```

This should give you a good grounding in complex numbers in Python, although most of the discussion has been about input and output formats, along with the interpretation of literals.

Mathematically, complex numbers are not difficult to handle, given that floating-point math is already well supported. Addition is obvious, and multiplication follows these rules.

▶ Multiply the four parts together, using distribution to get four results.

▶ There will be a real portion (real times real).

▶ There will be two portions with one factor of j each. Add these together to get the new imaginary portion.

▶ There will be a j-squared portion (imaginary times imaginary). Convert j-squared to –1, which means reversing the sign of the –squared coefficient; then add that result back into the real portion.

That's how it's done! When you understand these simple rules, complex math is not such a mystery, after all.

Chapter 10 *Summary*

Most programming, or at least much of it, focuses on working with integers and floating-point numbers, but for certain areas of the data-processing industry, other data types may work better. Foremost among these is a **Decimal**, or fixed-point type, which can hold dollar-and-cents figures with more precision and accuracy than other data types can.

This chapter has shown that Python's support for alternative data formats is very strong. You can easily utilize the **Decimal**, **Fraction**, and **complex** classes in your own programs, without having to download anything off the Internet; the **complex** type doesn't even require importing.

You can also come up with your own classes, building on the existing ones. And, although you can download a Money class from the Internet, this chapter showed how to start creating your own Money class, using the techniques introduced in Chapter 9, "Classes and Magic Methods."

But not everything is as easy as it looks. Inheriting from an immutable class such as **Decimal** requires a particular coding technique shown in this chapter.

Chapter 10 *Review Questions*

1 Compare and contrast the advantages and disadvantages of the **float** and **Decimal** classes.

2 Consider two objects: Decimal('1.200') and Decimal('1.2'). In what sense are these the same object? Are these just two ways of representing the exact same value, or do they correspond to different internal states?

3 What happens if Decimal('1.200') and Decimal('1.2') are tested for equality?

4 Why is it usually better to initialize a **Decimal** object from a string than from a floating-point value?

5 How easy is it to combine **Decimal** objects with integers in an arithmetic expression?

6 How easy is it to combine **Decimal** objects and floating-point values?

7 Give an example of a quantity that can be represented with absolute precision by using the **Fraction** class but not the **Decimal** class.

8 Give an example of a quantity that can be represented exactly by either the **Decimal** or **Fraction** class but not by a floating-point value.

9 Consider two **Fraction** objects: Fraction(1, 2) and Fraction(5, 10). Do these two objects have the same internal state? Why or why not?

10 What is the relationship between the **Fraction** class and the integer type (**int**)? Containment or inheritance?

Chapter 10 *Suggested Problems*

1 Write a program that prompts the user for all needed information and then constructs a **Decimal** object by using a tuple. For example, the following tuple initializes an object to the value Decimal('12.10'):

    (0, (1, 2, 1, 0), -2)

2 Using the inheritance approach that was begun in Section 10.12, "Money and Inheritance," complete the class definition of Money so that addition, multiplication, and subtraction are all supported. Then write sample code to make sure that all these operations work.

3 Revise the Fraction-class calculator in Section 10.13 so that it accepts input in the form "N, D" as well as "N/D"—that is, the program should accept (and appropriately analyze) input such as "1, 7" as well as "1/7".

The Random and Math Packages

When one of the authors was little, he didn't like to spend a lot of time on arithmetic, because, he argued, someday everyone was going have computers to do all the arithmetic in the world. He was partly right. Arithmetic can still be useful, but the world is heavily computerized. Bar codes and cash registers do all you need, and you can always reach for your cell phone with its built-in calculator function.

But number crunching still matters. This chapter concerns not mundane arithmetic, but higher math functions, along with **random**, which is useful in game programs and simulations. For the most sophisticated 3-D games, you'll need to find even more advanced packages, but for simple games, **random** and **math** suffice.

The **random** and **math** packages require no downloading. All you have to do is import them using a simple syntax, and you're ready to go.

11.1 Overview of the Random Package

In many game programs and simulations, the ability to get random numbers, or rather, *pseudo-random numbers,* is essential.

A pseudo random number is taken from a sequence that behaves as if randomly chosen. This chapter uses a few commonsense notions to test this behavior.

Random numbers can be chosen from any of several *distributions.* The distribution determines the range into which the random number must fall—and also where the numbers appear most frequently.

For example, the **random.randint** function produces an integer value from a specified range, in which each integer has an equal probability of being chosen. You could have it simulate the roll of a fair six-sided die, for example, and expect each number to come up about one-sixth of the time.

To use this package, place the following statement at the beginning of a source file.

```
import random
```

359

11.2 A Tour of Random Functions

The **random** package consists of a number of functions, each supporting a different random distribution. Table 11.1 summarizes the more commonly used functions from the **random** package.

Table 11.1. Common Random Package Functions

SYNTAX	DESCRIPTION
normalvariate(_mean_, _dev_**)**	Produces a classic normal distribution, known as a _bell curve_. Height and width vary: It may be "taller" or "flatter." The argument _mean_ is the value around which the values center; the argument _dev_ is the standard deviation. Roughly two-thirds of the values tend to fall within one standard deviation. (So a bigger standard deviation creates a wider bell curve.)
randint(_a_, _b_**)**	Produces a random integer in the range _a_ to _b_, inclusive, in which each integer has the same probability of being selected; this is a uniform distribution. For example, _randint(1, 6)_ simulates the results of a perfectly fair six-sided die.
random()	Produces a random floating-point number in the range 0 to 1, excluding the high endpoint. The range is continuous but uniform in distribution, so that if you divide it into N subranges, values should fall into each of them with roughly 1/N probability.
sample(_population_, _k_**)**	Produces _k_ elements at random from a sample population. The population is a list, tuple, set, or compatible collection class. To use on dictionaries, you first convert to a list.
shuffle(_list_**)**	Randomly shuffles a list. This is one of the most useful of all the functions in the package. No value is returned, but the contents of the list are shuffled, so that any element may end up in any position. For example, if the numbers 0 through 51 are assigned to represent the cards in a 52-card deck, `shuffle(range(52))` produces a list representing a shuffled deck.
uniform(_a_, b**)**	Produces a random floating-point number in the range _a_ to _b_. The distribution is continuous and uniform.

11.3 Testing Random Behavior

A series of random numbers should exhibit certain behaviors.

▶ Rough conformance to expectation. If you perform a number of trials, in which values from 1 to N are equally likely, we should expect each value to come up roughly 1/N of the time.

▶ Variation. However, you should expect variation. If you run 100 trials with 10 uniform values, you should not expect each value to come up exactly 1/10th of the time. If that happens, the pattern is too regular and suspiciously nonrandom.

▶ Decreasing variation with large N. Yet as the number of trials increase, we should expect the ratio of expected hits to the number of actual hits to get closer and closer to 1.0. This is the so-called Law of Large Numbers.

These are easy qualities to test. By running tests with a different number of trials, you should be able to see the ratio of predicted hits to actual hits gets closer to 1.0. Here's a function designed to test these qualities.

```python
import random
def do_trials(n):
    hits = [0] * 10
    for i in range(n):
        a = random.randint(0, 9)
        hits[a] += 1
    for i in range(10):
        fss = '{}: {}\t {:.3}'
        print(fss.format(i, hits[i], hits[i]/(n/10)))
```

This function begins by creating a list with 10 elements. Each of these elements holds a count of hits: For example, `hits[0]` will store the number of times a 0 is generated, `hits[1]` will store the number of times a 1 is generated, `hits[2]` will store the number of times a 2 is generated, and so on.

The first loop generates n random numbers, in which each number is an integer in the range 0 to 9. The elements in the `hits` list are then updated as appropriate.

```python
    for i in range(n):
        a = random.randint(0, 9)
        hits[a] += 1
```

The key statement within this loop, of course, is the call to **random.randint**, which (in this case) produces an integer in the range 0 to 9, inclusive, with a uniform probability of getting any of the various values.

The second loop then prints a summary of the results, showing how many times each number 0 to 9 was generated and how that number matches against the predicted number of hits, which is n/10 in each case.

In the following session, the function is used to generate and record the results of 100 trials.

```
>>> do_trials(100)
0: 7     0.7
1: 13    1.3
2: 10    1.0
3: 4     0.4
4: 11    1.1
5: 10    1.0
6: 7     0.7
7: 11    1.1
8: 12    1.2
9: 15    1.5
```

This run of 100 trials shows that n equal to 100 isn't nearly enough to get convincingly uniform results. The ratio of actual hits to predicted hits goes from a low of 0.4 to a high of 1.5. But running1000 trials produces more even results.

```
>>> do_trials(1000)
0: 103    1.03
1: 91     0.91
2: 112    1.12
3: 102    1.02
4: 110    1.1
5: 101    1.01
6: 92     0.92
7: 96     0.96
8: 87     0.87
9: 106    1.06
```

Here the ratios of actual hits to expected hits (n/10) are much closer, on the whole, to 1.0. They get closer still if we increase the number of trials to 77,000.

```
>>> do_trials(77000)
0: 7812    1.01
1: 7700    1.0
```

```
2: 7686    0.998
3: 7840    1.02
4: 7762    1.01
5: 7693    0.999
6: 7470    0.97
7: 7685    0.998
8: 7616    0.989
9: 7736    1.0
```

Remember, the ratios of expected hits (one-tenth of all the trials) to actual hits (ranging from 7470 to 7840) comprise the third column.

Although this approach is not entirely scientific, it's sufficient to confirm the three qualities we expected to see in random-number behavior. Each of the 10 possible values (0 through 9) is produced roughly one-tenth of the time, variation is seen, and, as the number of trials increases, variation grows smaller as a percentage of the number of trials. And that's what we wanted!

11.4 A Random-Integer Game

One of the simplest games you can write with Python is the number guessing game, in which the user makes repeated guesses as to a number that the program selected in advance, in secret. During each round, the user makes a guess and the program responds by saying "Success" (the user wins), "Too high," or "Too low." A simple version of this game was introduced in Chapter 1.

The game is uninteresting unless the secret number chosen by the program is different each time; furthermore, this number should be as unpredictable as possible, which is the whole point of random numbers.

Here's the code for a simple version of the game. This version begins by picking a random number from 1 to 50, inclusive.

```python
import random
n = random.randint(1, 50)
while True:
    guess = int(input('Enter guess:'))
    if guess == n:
        print('Success! You win.')
        break
    elif guess < n:
        print('Too low.', end=' ')
    else:
        print('Too high.', end=' ')
```

Here's a sample session. Assume that the function call `random.randint(1, 50)` returns the value 31. The user doesn't learn that this value has been selected until the end of the game.

```
Enter guess: 25
Too low. Enter guess: 37
Too high. Enter guess: 30
Too low. Enter guess: 34
Too high. Enter guess: 32
Too high. Enter guess: 31
Success! You win.
```

This game can be improved in a couple of ways. First, it should ask users whether they want to play again after each game. Second, if users get bored during any given round of the game, they should be able to exit early. Here's the improved version.

```python
import random

def play_the_game():
    n = random.randint(1, 50)
    while True:
        guess = int(input('Enter guess (0 to exit): '))
        if guess == 0:
            print('Exiting game.')
            break
        elif guess == n:
            print('Success! You win.')
            break
        elif guess < n:
            print('Too low.', end=' ')
        else:
            print('Too high.', end=' ')

while True:
    play_the_game()
    ans = input('Want to play again? (Y or N): ')
    if not ans or ans[0] in 'Nn':
        break
```

11.5 *Creating a Deck Object*

The **shuffle** function is one of the most useful in the **random** package. This function, as you might guess, is especially useful for simulating a deck of cards, and you'd be right. But it's extensible to other situations as well.

The action of **shuffle** is to rearrange the order of a list so that any element can appear in any position. The number of elements does not change, nor do the number of duplicate items, if any. So, for example, suppose you shuffle the following list:

```
kings_list = ['John', 'James', 'Henry', 'Henry', 'George']
```

Next, we use **random.shuffle** to randomize the order.

```
random.shuffle(kings_list)
```

If you now print the list, you'll see that no matter how the shuffling went, there are still two Henrys, and one each of John, James, and George. The order, however, will almost certainly change.

The shuffling algorithm is a fairly universal one.

For I in range(0, N-2),

   J = randint(I, N-1)

   Swap list[I] with list[J]

The action of the **random.shuffle** function is to rearrange a list in place, replacing all the old values but not moving the list itself in memory.

One of the best ways to encapsulate the functions of a deck is to create a Deck class and use it to instantiate Deck objects. It should have the following properties.

▶ It will contain a list of numbers from 0 to N. With a 52-card deck, each of these numbers can be mapped to a card with a unique rank and suit.

▶ Upon initialization, the Deck object will shuffle itself.

▶ You can then ask the Deck object to deal a card from the "top" (the beginning of the list), one at a time, returning the card as a number from 0 to 51.

▶ When all the cards are dealt, the Deck object automatically reshuffles itself.

When complete, this will be a lovely example of object oriented programming. An instance of the Deck object will maintain its internal state. The following implementation enables you to create an auto-reshuffling deck of any size.

```
import random

class Deck():

    def __init__(self, size):
        self.card_list = [i for i in range(size)]
        random.shuffle(self.card_list)
        self.current_card = 0
        self.size = size

    def deal(self):
        if self.size - self.current_card < 1:
            random.shuffle(self.card_list)
            self.current_card = 0
            print('Reshuffling...!!!')
        self.current_card += 1
        return self.card_list[self.current_card - 1]
```

The value "dealt" by a deck, by the way, can be turned into a playing card with a unique combination of rank and suit.

```
ranks = ['2', '3', '4', '5', '6', '7', '8', '9',
         '10', 'J', 'Q', 'K', 'A']
suits = ['clubs', 'diamonds', 'hearts', 'spades' ]
my_deck = Deck(52)

# Deal twelve poker hands, so user can compare before
#  and after shuffling.

for i in range(12):
    for i in range(5):
        d = my_deck.deal()
        r = d % 13
        s = d // 13
        print(ranks[r], 'of', suits[s])
    print()
```

The Deck class has some limitations. When the deck is reshuffled, there will still be some cards in play—that is, cards still on the table. Those do not get shuffled back in. Instead, the shuffled deck is created from the discard pile only.

Cards in play remain on the table from the time they're dealt. Only when a new hand is dealt do the cards in play join the discard pile. This creates a relationship between the deck, the cards in play, and the discard pile, as shown in Figure 11.1.

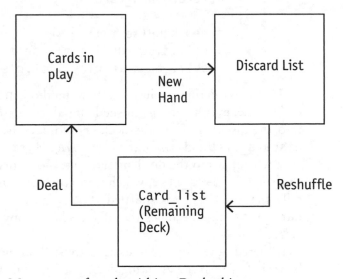

Figure 11.1. Movement of cards within a Deck object

At one time, this is how the game of blackjack (also known as twenty-one) was played in casinos. Occasionally it still is: one standard deck, dealt all the way down to the last card, and then reshuffled.

We can rewrite the Deck object as follows.

```python
import random

class Deck():

    def __init__(self, size):
        self.card_list = [i for i in range(size)]
        self.cards_in_play_list = []
        self.discards_list = []
        random.shuffle(self.card_list)


    def deal(self):
        if len(self.card_list) < 1:
            random.shuffle(self.discards_list)
            self.card_list = self.discards_list
```

```
                self.discards_list = []
                print('Reshuffling...!!!')
        new_card = self.card_list.pop()
        self.cards_in_play_list.append(new_card)
        return new_card

    def new_hand(self):
        self.discards_list += self.cards_in_play_list
        self.cards_in_play_list.clear()
```

This class definition has one new method, new_hand, which should be called whenever a hand is finished and all the cards currently in play are put into the discards. Then the deck should add the cards currently in play to discard_list and clear cards_in_play_list.

The changes to the deal method are more involved. Now, instead of just shuffling the card_list, which normally contains all the cards in the deck, only the discard pile is shuffled. The resulting list is then transposed with card_list; this becomes the new deck to draw from. Then discard list is cleared.

If there is a reshuffle while cards are still on the table, those cards will not be reshuffled, so the resulting deck size may not be the same. But then how do those cards in play ever get back into the deck? Simple. They will be added to the discards at the end of the current hand and then eventually reshuffled back into the deck.

Note ▶ You might want to make further changes to this class, based on changing rules of blackjack in Las Vegas casinos. For example, you might want to accommodate the six-deck "shoe" that most casinos use. That's actually just a matter of allocating the right deck size; it doesn't alter the code shown here. You also might want to revise some of the methods so that the dealer has a way to reshuffle early (for example, by writing a new method to do just that).

◀ Note

11.6 Adding Pictograms to the Deck

If you like, you can change the initialization of the Deck class so that it stores small pictures of standard playing cards rather than only storing numbers. If you do that, then you don't have to have a separate piece of code that translates the numbers 0 through 51 into the names of the playing cards. Instead, you can print the card symbols directly, as done in the following version.

```
def __init__(self, n_decks=1):
    self.card_list = [num + suit
        for suit in '\u2665\u2666\u2663\u2660'
        for num in 'A23456789TJQK'
        for deck in range(n_decks)]
    self.cards_in_play_list = []
    self.discards_list = []
    random.shuffle(self.card_list)
```

Note that this version of the program creates a deck that's a multiple of the standard 52-card deck. Creating "decks" that have multiple decks within them might be a good way of simulating a six-deck "shoe" played in Las Vegas.

Given this version of the **__init__** method, the Deck object now contains representations of cards that appear as follows, if you were to print them all.

```
A♥  2♥  3♥  4♥  5♥  6♥  7♥  8♥  9♥  T♥  J♥  Q♥  K♥
A♦  2♦  3♦  4♦  5♦  6♦  7♦  8♦  9♦  T♦  J♦  Q♦  K♦
A♣  2♣  3♣  4♣  5♣  6♣  7♣  8♣  9♣  T♣  J♣  Q♣  K♣
A♠  2♠  3♠  4♠  5♠  6♠  7♠  8♠  9♠  T♠  J♠  Q♠  K♠
```

Here's a complete version of the revised Deck class, along with a small program that prints a hand of five cards (as in Poker). This version assumes a six-deck shoe, although you can easily revise it to use only one deck.

```
# File deck_test.py
# ----------------------------------------

import random

class Deck():

    def __init__(self, n_decks=1):
        self.card_list = [num + suit
            for suit in '\u2665\u2666\u2663\u2660'
            for num in 'A23456789TJQK'
            for deck in range(n_decks)]
        self.cards_in_play_list = []
        self.discards_list = []
        random.shuffle(self.card_list)


    def deal(self):
        if len(self.card_list) < 1:
            random.shuffle(self.discards_list)
```

```
        self.card_list = self.discards_list
        self.discards_list = []
        print('Reshuffling...!!!')
    new_card = self.card_list.pop()
    self.cards_in_play_list.append(new_card)

    return new_card

def new_hand(self):
    self.discards_list += self.cards_in_play_list
    self.cards_in_play_list.clear()

dk = Deck(6)            # Use six-deck shoe.
for i in range(5):
    print(dk.deal(), end=' ')
```

And here's a sample session. You got two pair. Lucky!

9♥ 9♥ T♠ 4♦ T♣

11.7 Charting a Normal Distribution

In mathematics and statistics, the normal distribution is the classic bell curve. That it occurs so often in nature is not just a fluke. It's the shape that Pascal's Triangle converges to, as you go down into deeper levels. It's the shape predicted by the Binomial Theorem as it generates these numbers.

For example, the height of the average American man is roughly five feet, ten inches. If you take a random sampling of this population, you should find, on average, that the vast majority of men are within a few inches of this height. There will, of course, be some outliers who are particularly short or tall. However, as you get farther away from the average, these outliers become rarer.

The result is a bell curve. A large percentage of the population should surround the average (or *mean*), creating a bulge around that mean. Normal distributions are controlled by two main factors: the mean and the standard deviation.

The mean is the average value, the middle of the curve. The standard deviation, also called *sigma*, determines how narrow or wide the curve is. Over a long enough time, values should be produced in accord with the rules in Table 11.2.

Table 11.2. Effect of Standard Deviations

NUMBER OF STANDARD DEVIATIONS	PERCENT OF POPULATION (AS PREDICTED)
One	68 percent, on average, should fall within one standard deviation of the mean.
Two	95 percent, on average, should fall within two standard deviations of the mean.
Three	99.7 percent, on average, should fall within three standard deviations of the mean.

Here's how to read Table 11.2. As an example, suppose you have a normal distribution with a mean of 100 and a standard deviation of 20. You should expect, in the long run, about 68 percent of the numbers produced by the **normalvariate** function to fall within 80 and 120. You should expect 95 percent of the numbers produced to fall within 40 and 160.

Yet with all the probability distributions in the **random** package, they are just that: *probability* distributions. In the short run especially, nothing is certain. For a given trial, the probability a number will fall into the range 40 to 160, given the conditions outlined here, is 95 percent; there's a 5 percent change of falling outside the range.

But that's not saying that such occurrences *cannot happen*. Events with only a 5 percent probability can and do happen all the time. And events with probabilities of 1 in a million or less happen every day—every time someone wins the lottery!

Therefore, if you take only a few sample results, you may not see anything that looks like a bell-shaped curve. Fortunately, because of the Law of Large Numbers, demonstrated in Section 11.3, "Testing Random Behavior," if you take many sample values, you should see behavior that is fairly predictable.

The following program is designed to take advantage of the Law of Large Numbers by allowing for an arbitrarily large number of sample results, scaling down the numbers so that they can be easily graphed, and then printing the resulting graph.

```
import random

def pr_normal_chart(n):
    hits = [0] * 20
    for i in range(n):
        x = random.normalvariate(100, 30)
        j = int(x/10)
```

```
        if 0 <= j < 20:
            hits[j] += 1
    for i in hits:
        print('*' * int(i * 320 / n))
```

This function calls the **normalvariate** function any number of times; then it uses the results to make a simple character-based graph. The key line calls **random.normalvariate** with a mean of 100 and a standard deviation of 30:

```
    x = random.normalvariate(100, 30)
```

The standard deviation does not have to be 30, of course. You can experiment by modifying this number. A smaller deviation will make for a thinner, more pronounced graph; a larger deviation will make the curve look flatter.

The code then collects the results into twenty "buckets" by transforming the number x into an integer from 0 through 20 by the use of division and an **int** conversion. It will be rare that a random number falls outside this range, unless you increase the standard deviation.

The result, x, is divided so that it can index into the hits array. In each bucket, we accumulate the number of hits in the corresponding range.

```
    j = int(x/10)
    if 0 <= j < 20:
        hits[j] += 1
```

Each number of hits is then scaled down by multiplying by 320 and dividing by n. This enables the argument n to be as large as you choose while not increasing the overall number of asterisks (*) to be printed. Without scaling, you could not input a large value for n without overrunning the screen with asterisks.

```
    for i in hits:
        print('*' * int(i * 320 / n))
```

Why the use of these particular numbers—100, 30, and 320? We settled on these figures through trial and error, to achieve nice-looking results. You can experiment with using different numbers.

You can enter a relatively low number of trials—say, 500. Figure 11.2 shows typical results. The chart produced shows a graph that looks roughly like a bell curve but is clearly off; it's not nearly what the math would predict for large n.

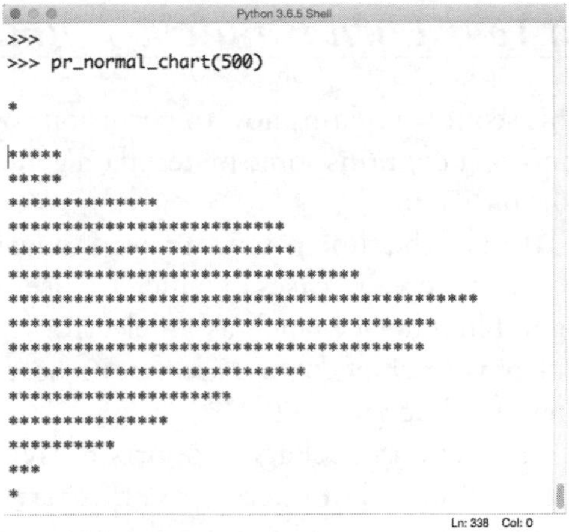

```
● ● ●                    Python 3.6.5 Shell
>>>
>>> pr_normal_chart(500)

*

*****
*****
**************
***************************
***************************
************************************
*****************************************************
******************************************
*******************************************
******************************
********************
**************
*********
***
*
                                              Ln: 338  Col: 0
```

Figure 11.2. Normal distribution after 500 trials

But this figure used only 500 trials, which is not that large a sample for statistical purposes; it should reveal the general pattern but deviate significantly in places, and it does.

In Figure 11.3, the number of trials is increased from 500 to 199,000. Because of the scaling written into the function, the overall number of asterisks to be printed does not significantly change. But now the shape conforms much more closely to a mathematically perfect bell curve.

```
● ● ●                    Python 3.6.5 Shell
>>> pr_normal_chart(199000)

*
****
*******
*************
**********************
******************************
*******************************************
*************************************************
************************************************
*************************************
***********************
*************
*******
****
*
                                              Ln: 55  Col: 4
```

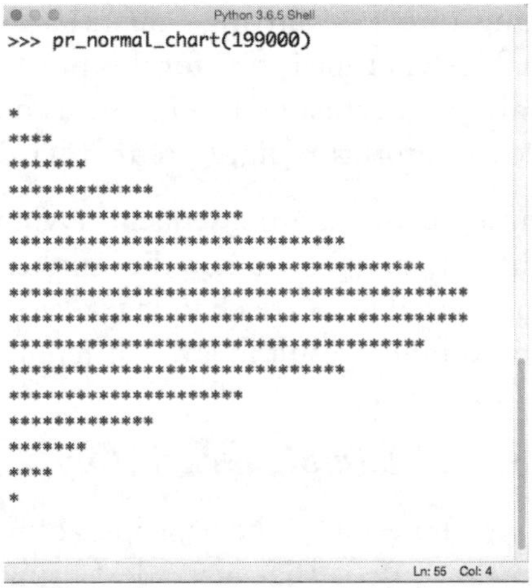

Figure 11.3. Normal distribution after 199,000 trials

With samples larger than 199,000 (200,000 or so), you should continue to get results that—at this rough level of granularity—look like a mathematically perfect bell curve.

11.8 *Writing Your Own Random-Number Generator*

This section explains how to write your own random-number generator if you choose. It contains some material on generators originally discussed in *Python Without Fear*.

Most of the time you won't need to write your own random-number generator, but there are cases in which it's useful. Maybe you're writing the code for a gambling device, such as an electronic slot machine or online Poker game. One of your chief concerns is that no user be able to crack the code and predict what will happen next.

The **random** package supports fairly high-quality random-number distribution. But without access to an external randomization device—such as a device that measures radioactive decay—one must use pseudo-random numbers, and these numbers, while useful, are not bulletproof. Any sequence can in theory be cracked.

Writing your own pseudo-random generator enables you to generate a sequence that no one has yet cracked.

11.8.1 *Principles of Generating Random Numbers*

Generally, a pseudo-random sequence can achieve sufficiently random behavior by doing two things.

▶ Picking a *seed* (a starting value) that is difficult or impossible for humans to guess. System time is fine for this purpose. Although the time is not random—it is always increasing in value—it is measured down to the microsecond, and the least significant digits are very hard for humans to predict.

▶ Using a pseudo-random sequence, which generates each number by applying a mathematical operation on the number before it. This involves complex transformations. These are chaotic transformations, in that even small differences in initial values result in large differences in results.

11.8.2 *A Sample Generator*

Chapter 4 presented the principles of writing a generator in Python. The most important rule is that instead of using a **return** statement, you substitute a **yield** statement. A **yield** gives a value in response to the **next** function—which may be called directly or in a **for** loop—and retains the internal state until it's called again.

This is all part of a larger process described in Section 4.10, "Generators." Although a function containing **yield** doesn't seem to return an object, it does: It returns a generator object, also called an *iterator*. The generator object is what actually yields values at run time.

So—and this is the strange part—the function describes what the generator does, but the generator itself is actually an object returned by the function! Admittedly, this is a little counterintuitive.

Here's a simple random-number generator, which produces floating-point values in the range 0 to roughly 4.2 billion, the size of a four-byte integer.

```
import time

def gen_rand():
    p1 = 1200556037
    p2 = 2444555677
    max_rand = 2 ** 32
    r = int(time.time() * 1000)
    while True:
        n = r
        n *= p2
        n %= p1
        n += r
        n *= p1
        n %= p2
        n %= max_rand
        r = n
        yield n
```

The result is a random-number generator that (and you can verify this yourself) seems to meet the obvious statistical tests for randomness quite well. It is still a relatively simple generator, however, and in no way is intended to provide the best possible performance. It does observe some basic principles of randomness.

With this generator function defined, you can test it with the following code:

```
>>> gen_obj = gen_rand()
>>> for i in range(10): print(next(gen_obj))

1351029180
211569410
1113542120
1108334866
```

```
538233735
1638146995
1551200046
1079946432
1682454573
851773945
```

11.9   Overview of the Math Package

The **math** package provides a series of functions useful in many scientific and mathematical applications.

Although most of the services of the **math** package are provided as functions, the package also includes two useful constants: **pi** and **e**. Depending on how you import the package, these constants are referred to as **math.pi** and **math.e**.

The **math** package is another package provided in any standard Python download. You never have to search for it or download it. Importing it is sufficient.

```
import math
```

You can also import symbols selectively, of course.

11.10   A Tour of Math Package Functions

The most commonly used functions in the **math** package fall into the major categories summarized in Table 11.3.

Table 11.3. Common Math Package Functions, by Category

CATEGORY	DESCRIPTION
Standard trigonometric functions	These include **sin**, **cos**, and **tan**, which are the sine, cosine, and tangent functions, respectively; each of these takes an angle as input and produces a ratio of one side of a right triangle to another.
Inverse trigonometric functions	These are functions closely related to the first category, but instead of taking an angle and returning a ratio of two sides of a right triangle, they take a ratio and return an angle. This category includes **asin**, **acos**, and **atan**.
Degree and radian conversion	The two functions, **degrees** and **radians**, convert from radians to degrees (in the first case), and from degrees to radians (in the second). These are frequently useful with trigonometric functions, which use radians, even though degrees are more familiar to most people.

Table 11.3. Common Math Package Functions, by Category (*continued*)

CATEGORY	DESCRIPTION
Hyperbolic functions	The hyperbolic-function category includes hyperbolic versions of the trigonometric and inverse-trigonometric functions. The names are formed by placing an "h" on the end of the name, giving **sinh**, **cosh**, and **tanh**.
Logarithmic functions	The **math** package provides a flexible set of logarithmic calculations, including support for a variety of bases. These functions are the inverse of exponentiation. They include **log2**, **log10**, and **log**, for finding logs of base 2, 10, and e, respectively. The last can also be used with any base you specify.
Conversion to integer	Several functions enable conversion of floating-point numbers to integer, including both **floor** (always rounding down) and **ceil** (always rounding up).
Miscellaneous	These include **pow** (power, or exponentiation) and square root, **sqrt**.

11.11 *Using Special Values (pi)*

The rules for naming a constant from a Python package—technically a data object—are the same as for functions. If you use **import math**, which is recommended, all references to objects from the package must be qualified. Here's an example:

```
import math
print('The value of pi is:', math.pi)
```

But if pi is imported directly, then it can be referred to without qualification.

```
from math import pi
print('The value of pi is:', pi)
```

Table 11.4 lists objects in the package; these are approximations, of course.

Table 11.4. Math Package Data Objects

DATA OBJECT	DESCRIPTION
pi	Mathematical value pi, the ratio of a circumference to a diameter in a perfect circle. Equal to 3.141592653589793.
e	Mathematical value e. Equal to 2.718281828459045.
tau	Python 3.0 only. This is a mathematical value equal to 2 multiplied by pi. Equal to 6.283185307179586.
inf	Infinity. Used with IEEE math only.
nan	Not a Number. Used with IEEE math only.

The last two data objects in Table 11.4 are provided for full support of all the states of a floating-point coprocessor. These values are rarely used in Python, however, because the language does not allow you to get infinity through division by zero; such an action raises an exception in Python.

The value **math.pi**, however, is widely used in math and science applications. Here's a simple one: Get the diameter of a circle and return its circumference.

```
from math import pi

def get_circ(d):
    circ = d * pi
    print('The circumference is', circ)
    return circ
```

One notable omission from this list of constants is the mathematical value phi, also known as the *golden ratio*. But this value is relatively easy to produce yourself: It's 1 plus the square root of 5, the result of which is then divided by 2.

```
import math
phi = (1 + math.sqrt(5))/ 2
```

Or, without the use of the **math** package, you could calculate it this way:

```
phi = (1 + 5 ** 0.5)/ 2
```

In either case, its closest approximation in Python is 1.618033988749895.

11.12 Trig Functions: Height of a Tree

Trigonometric functions have many practical uses. In this section, we'll demonstrate a simple one: calculating the height of a tree.

Consider the right triangle shown in Figure 11.4. The right angle (90 degrees) is fixed, but the other two angles can vary. We pick the angle closest to us. Depending on the measure of this angle, we can (through trigonometric functions) predict the ratio of the lengths of any two of the sides.

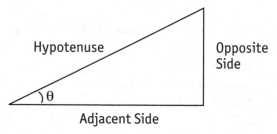

Figure 11.4. A right triangle

The three basic trig functions—sine, cosine, and tangent—are defined as follows. In Python, as in most other programming languages and libraries, these three functions are implemented as **sin**, **cos**, and **tan** functions, respectively.

$$sine(\theta) = opposite\ side\ <B>\ /\ hypotenuse\ <C>$$

$$cosine(\theta) = adjacent\ side\ <A>\ /\ hypotenuse\ <C>$$

$$tangent(\theta) = opposite\ side\ <B>\ /\ adjacent\ side\ <A>$$

So, for example, if the opposite side were one half the length of the adjacent side, then the tangent would be 0.5.

What has this got to do with the height of trees? Plenty. Consider the following scenario: A human observer is stationed 1,000 feet from the base of a tree. He doesn't know the height of the tree, but he's certain about the distance to the base, because this has been measured before. Using his trusty sextant, he measures the angle of the top of the tree above the horizon. This gives him an angle, θ.

Figure 11.5 illustrates this scenario.

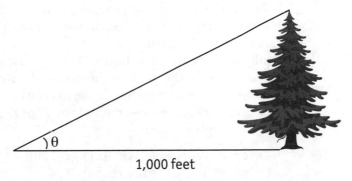

1,000 feet

Figure 11.5. Figuring the height of a tree

Now it takes only a little algebra to come up with the correct formula. Remember the formula for a tangent function.

$$tangent(\theta) = opposite\ side\ <B>\ /\ adjacent\ side\ <A>$$

Multiplying both sides by A and rearranging, we get the following rule of calculation.

$$opposite\ side\ <B> = tangent(\theta)\ *\ adjacent\ side\ <A>$$

So, to get the height of the tree, you find the tangent of the angle of elevation and then multiply by the distance to the base, which in this case is 1,000 feet. Now it's easy to write a program that calculates the height of a tree.

```
from math import tan, radians

def get_height(dist, angle):
    return tan(radians(angle)) * dist

def main():
    while True:
        d = float(input('Enter distance (0 to exit): '))
        if d == 0:
            print('Bye!')
            break
        a = float(input('Enter angle of elevation: '))
        print('Height of the tree is', get_height(d, a))

main()
```

The core of the program is the line that does the calculation:

```
return tan(radians(angle)) * dist
```

Although this is a simple program, it does have one subtlety, or gotcha. All the Python trig functions use radians. They do not use degrees unless the degrees are first converted.

A full circle is defined as having 360 degrees; it also is defined as having 2*pi radians. So if the user is going to use degrees—which most people use in real life—you need to apply the **math.radians** function to convert from degrees to radians (or else just multiply by 2*pi/360).

Here's a sample session:

```
Enter distance (0 to exit): 1000
Enter angle of elevation: 7.4
Height of the tree is 129.87732371691982
Enter distance (0 to exit): 800
Enter angle of elevation: 15
Height of the tree is 214.35935394489815
Enter distance (0 to exit): 0
Bye!
```

Note ▶ In this example, we used the variation on **import** statement syntax that imports specific functions. This is often a good approach if you are sure that there won't be conflicts with the particular names that were imported.

```
from math import tan, radians
```

◀ Note

11.13 Logarithms: Number Guessing Revisited

Other functions from the **math** package that are frequently useful are the logarithmic functions, listed in Table 11.5.

Table 11.5. Math Package Logarithm Functions

DATA OBJECT	DESCRIPTION
`log10(x)`	Logarithm base 10. (What exponent would 10 have to be raised to, to produce *x*?)
`log2(x)`	Logarithm base 2. (What exponent would 2 have to be raised to, to produce *x*?)
`log(x, base=e)`	Logarithm using specified *base*. The second argument is optional; by default, the function finds the "natural logarithm" using base e.

If the concept of logarithm is already familiar to you, proceed to Section 11.13.2 to see the practical use of a logarithm in a program. You can read Section 11.13.1 (next) to learn more about logarithms.

11.13.1 How Logarithms Work

A logarithm is the inverse of exponentiation. If you remember that definition, logarithms are less intimidating. For example, assume the following is true:

$$base ** exponent = amount$$

Then it follows that the following equation must also be true:

$$Logarithm\text{-}of\text{-}base\ (amount) = exponent$$

In other words, what a logarithm calculates is the exponent needed to achieve a certain amount. This is easier to understand with some examples. First of all, let's assume a base of 10. Notice in Table 11.6 how quickly the amounts increase as the exponent does.

Table 11.6. Exponent Function with Powers of 10

10 RAISED TO THIS EXPONENT	PRODUCES THIS RESULT
1	10
2	100
3	1000

▼ *continued on next page*

Table 11.6. Exponent Function with Powers of 10 (*continued*)

10 RAISED TO THIS EXPONENT	PRODUCES THIS RESULT
3.5	3162.277
4	10000
4.5	31622.777

Now, to understand logarithms using base 10, we only need to reverse the columns (see Table 11.7). You should notice from these tables how slowly the exponent increases as the amount does. Logarithmic growth is very slow—and is always overtaken by simple linear growth.

Table 11.7. Logarithms, Base 10

TAKING LOG-BASE 10 OF	PRODUCES THIS RESULT
10	1
100	2
1000	3
3162.277	3.5 (approx.)
10000	4
31622.777	4.5 (approx.)

Remember that some of the results in Table 11.7 are approximate. For example, if you take the base-10 logarithm of 31,622.777, you'll get a number very close to 4.5.

11.13.2 Applying a Logarithm to a Practical Problem

Now let's return to the number guessing game. If you play the game a few times, you should see there's an obvious strategy for getting the answer in less than N guesses, where N is the size of the range. The worst strategy would be to start with 1, then go one higher, guessing 2, and so on, until you've covered the whole range.

On average, that strategy would take N/2 guesses to succeed: 25 guesses if the range is 1 to 50. But with the right strategy, you should be able to do much better than that, raising the following question.

> **For a range of size N, what is the maximum number of steps that an ideal strategy would require to get the answer?**

What's the best strategy for N = 3? Obviously, you should guess the middle number, 2, and then guess either 1 or 3 for the next guess. This guarantees you need never take more than two guesses, even though there are three values. With more than three, we might need another guess. But two guesses are sufficient for N = 3.

The next "ceiling" should occur at N = 7, and you should see why. It's because you can guess the middle value, 4, and then—if this guess is not successful—limit yourself to the top three numbers (requiring two more guesses) or the bottom three numbers (also requiring two more guesses). Therefore, three guesses are enough for N = 7.

If you think about it, each step up, requiring an additional guess, can be obtained by doubling N at the last step and adding 1. For example, Figure 11.6 illustrates how the number of guesses needed increases from 1 to 2 to 3, as N increases from 1 to 3 to 7.

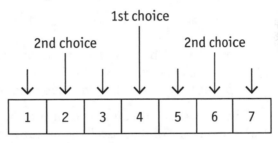

Figure 11.6. How three guesses are needed at N = 7

We can now determine the maximum number of guesses required at certain numbers. When N falls between these numbers, we round upward to the next step—because to get the maximum number of guesses needed, we must assume a worst-case scenario. Table 11.8 shows the progression.

Table 11.8. Maximum Number of Guesses Required by the Game

SIZE = N	N + 1	NUMBER OF GUESSES REQUIRED = LOG2(N+1)
1	2	1
3	4	2
7	8	3
15	16	4
31	32	5
63	64	6

The numbers in the leftmost column of Table 11.8 list ranges of numbers in the game; not all numbers are listed, but only those that "step up"—that is, require an additional guess. Each of these is an upper limit—so that for N = 15 or less, for example, up to four guesses are required. But for any range greater than 15, more guesses are required.

The numbers in the leftmost column are each 1 less than a power of 2. When added to 1, they correspond to a power of 2. Therefore, to get the numbers in the rightmost column—which contains the number of guesses needed—you must take logarithm base 2 of N+1.

The final step is to round upward to the nearest integer, because the number of steps taken must be an integer, and not floating point. The correct formula is

Maximum guesses needed = ceiling(log-base-2(N + 1))

Writing the program, with the aid of the **math** package, is now easy.

```
from math import log2, ceil

n = int(input('Enter size of range: '))
x = ceil(log2(n + 1))
print('Max. number of guesses needed is', x)
```

This program, in addition to using the **math.log2** function, also uses **math.ceil**, one of the miscellaneous functions. The **ceil** function takes any number and rounds it upward to the lowest integer greater than or equal to its input.

Now, if you run the program, you can answer the question we posed earlier. As usual, user input is shown in bold.

```
Enter size of range: 50
Max. number of guesses needed is 6.
```

So that's the answer. If you follow the ideal strategy—which is to make a guess in the middle of the available range—you should never need more than six guesses.

As for the strategy, you pick a number as close as you can to the midpoint of the available range. This range should always be what's left over after you use all the information you've gotten from previous guesses. For example, if you guess 25 and the computer says, "Too high," you should adjust the range to 1 to 24 instead of 1 to 50.

This strategy reflects a binary-search pattern, which should, on average, reduce the number of available choices by roughly 50 percent each time, until the result is found.

Chapter 11 *Summary*

This chapter explored how two of the most commonly used packages—**random** and **math**—can be used in practical ways in your programs. Both of these packages come preinstalled with the Python download.

The **random** package provides a variety of distributions. The most commonly used ones were explored in this chapter: **randint**, returning a random integer with uniform distribution across a given range; **shuffle**, which rearranges the contents of a list as if it were a deck of cards; and **normalvariate**.

The classic normal probability distribution tends to generate values close to the specified mean. Outlier values are always possible, but the farther a value is from the mean, the less frequently it's generated.

The chapter then showed how to use some of the most common functions from the **math** package, including **tan**, which calculates tangents, and the logarithmic functions. The Python implementation of logarithms includes **log10**, **log2**, and finally **log**, which calculates logarithms in any base.

Chapter 11 *Review Questions*

1 What exactly is a probability distribution? How can you predict the values at all, if they are supposed to be random?

2 What is the difference, if any, between true random numbers and pseudo-random numbers? Why are the latter considered "good enough"?

3 What are the two major factors that govern how a "normal" probability distribution behaves?

4 Give an example of a normal distribution in real life.

5 How would you expect a probability distribution to behave in the short run? How would you expect it to change as the number of trials increases?

6 What kind of object can be shuffled by using **random.shuffle**?

7 Name several general categories of functions in the **math** package.

8 How is exponentiation related to logarithms?

9 What are the three logarithmic functions supported by Python?

Chapter 11 *Suggested Problems*

1 Revise the number guessing game in Section 11.4, "A Random Integer Game," so that it lets the user specify a range of values at the beginning, rather than always using 1 to 50.

2 Write an application that determines the length of a hypotenuse of a right triangle, given two pieces of information: the nearest angle, measured in degrees, and the length of the adjacent side.

3 By taking advantage of the Deck object presented in Section 11.5, write a game program that deals a Poker hand of five cards. Then prompt the user to enter a series of numbers (for example: "1, 3, 5") that selects cards to be replaced during a draw phase. Then print the result of drawing the new cards.

The "numpy" (Numeric Python) Package

12

We now come to one of the best parts of Python: packages that perform sophisticated math operations on large amounts of data. The key package that enables many of these abilities is called **numpy**.

Some of these operations can be written with the core Python language, but many applications run much faster and compactly with help from the **numpy** package. Statistical analysis can be done with a simple, high-level commands in **numpy** rather than by writing complex functions, running as much as *a hundred times as fast.*

Whether you pronounce it "NUM-pee" or "num-PIE," the **numpy** package may well become your favorite.

12.1 Overview of the "array," "numpy," and "matplotlib" Packages

The next two chapters cover the usage of several packages: **array**, **numpy**, **numpy.random**, and the **matplotlib** packages.

12.1.1 The "array" Package

You might not want to use this package much, but it has some of the basic features of the **numpy** package. The **array** package does, however, enable you to interface with contiguous blocks of data created by other programs.

12.1.2 The "numpy" Package

The **numpy** package is the core of the technology discussed in this chapter. It builds on the concept of contiguous memory—introduced by the **array** package—but it does much more. The **numpy** package provides efficient handling of one-dimensional arrays (which are something like lists), batch processing (in which you operate on an array or large portions of that array at the same time), and high-level support for creating and maintaining multidimensional arrays.

12.1.3 The "numpy.random" Package

The **numpy.random** package is automatically downloaded as part of the **numpy** package. It provides much of the same functionality described in Chapter 11 but is optimized for use with **numpy** arrays.

12.1.4 The "matplotlib" Package

This package is really more than one, but they are downloaded together: **matplotlib** and **matplotlib.pyplot**. With the help of these packages, you'll be able to create a **numpy** array and then call on plot routines to beautifully plot the resulting graph for you.

Chapter 13, "Advanced Use of 'numpy'," covers the plotting library. This chapter deals with **numpy** basics.

12.2 Using the "array" Package

The generic **array** package doesn't do much, but it conceptually provides a foundation for how **numpy** works. This package supports one-dimensional arrays only. One advantage of this package is that it doesn't need to be downloaded.

```
import array
```

This package, along with all the other packages introduced in this chapter, deals with arrays in the strict C and C++ sense, instead of lists.

So what are these things called "arrays"?

Like a list, an *array* is an ordered collection in memory in which elements can be referred to by index number. But unlike lists, arrays are assumed to contain fixed-length data. Data is contiguous, meaning that all elements are placed next to each other in memory.

Figure 12.1. helps illustrate the difference. In a Python list, a number of references are involved, although you don't normally see these. (In C they would be pointers.)

A list object has a reference to the location of the actual list, which can be moved, but each object in this list is a reference to the actual data. This is what enables Python to mix different types of data in the same list.

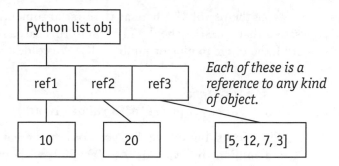

Figure 12.1. Storage of Python lists

As Figure 12.2 shows, an array is simpler in its design. The array object itself is just a reference to a location in memory. The actual data resides at that location.

Because the data is stored in this way, elements must have a fixed length. They also need to have the same type. You can't store a random Python integer (which may take up many bytes of memory, in theory), but you can have integers of fixed length.

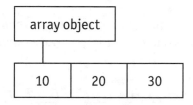

All of these items are next to each other in memory and have the same size.

Figure 12.2. Contiguous array storage

Arrays store data more compactly than lists do. However, indexing arrays turns out to be a bit slower than indexing Python lists, because Python list-indexing is heavily optimized behavior.

One of the advantages to using the **array** package is that if you interact with other processes or C-language libraries, they may require that you pass data in a contiguous block of memory, which is how the arrays in this chapter are stored.

To use the **array** package, import it and then create an array by calling **array.array** to allocate and initialize an array object. For example, here's how to get a simple array of the numbers 1, 2, 3:

```
import array
a = array.array('h', [1, 2, 3])
```

Note the use of 'h' here as the first argument. It takes a single-character string that specifies the data type—in this case, 16-bit (2-byte) integers (limiting the range to plus or minus 32K). We could create a larger array by using the **range** function.

```
import array
a = array.array('h', range(1000))
```

This works, but notice that you could not create an array of numbers from 1 to 1 million this way (or 0 to 999,999) without increasing the size of the data type from short integer ('u') to long integer ('l'), because otherwise you would exceed what can be stored in a 16-bit integer array.

```
import array
a = array.array('l', range(1_000_000))
```

Warning: Don't try printing this one, unless you're prepared to wait all day!

At this point, you might object that integers in Python are supposed to be "infinite" or, rather, that the limits on integers are astronomical. That's correct, but you give up this flexibility when you deal with fixed-length structures.

One of the limitations of the **array** package and its **array** type is that it supports one-dimensional arrays only.

12.3　Downloading and Importing "numpy"

To try out or use any of the code in the remainder of this chapter, you'll need to download **numpy** if you haven't already. If you're working in IDLE or writing a Python script and if you attempt to import **numpy**, Python will raise a **ModuleNotFoundError** exception if the **numpy** package is not present.

If that happens, you need to download it. The easiest way to do that is to use the **pip** utility, assuming that it's present.

One of the benefits of **pip** is that it goes out to the standard storage locations for publishing packages on the Internet, finds the requested software, and downloads it for you. So, assuming **pip** is present on your system, all you need to do is start a DOS box or Terminal application, and then type the following:

```
pip download numpy
```

If you're working with a Macintosh system and you have Python 3 installed, you may instead need to work with the command **pip3**.

```
pip3 download numpy
```

Note ▶ On a Macintosh system, problems may sometimes arise because Python 2.0 may be preloaded. You may download **numpy** as described in this section but find that it is not available for use with IDLE, possibly because the version numbers are not in sync. If that happens, start IDLE by typing **idle3** from within Terminal.

```
idle3
```

◀ Note

12.4 Introduction to "numpy": Sum 1 to 1 Million

From now on, we're going to assume you were able to download **numpy**. If not, try Googling for help on the Internet. The next step, of course, is to import **numpy**.

```
import numpy as np
```

Assuming there is no error, you may ask, Why the **as np** clause? Importing **numpy** in this way is not a requirement; it's a suggestion. But with this package, the name **numpy** can turn out to be part of some long statements, so the **as np** clause is a good idea. It enables you to refer to the package through a shorter name. For some programmers, the use of this particular short name has become a convention.

Note ▶ The data type created by the standard **numpy** routines is called **ndarray**. This stands for "N-dimensional array."

◀ Note

But why use **numpy** at all? To understand why, consider the problem of adding up a million numbers—specifically, 1 to 1,000,000.

If you're mathematically inclined, you may know there's an algebraic formula that enables you to do this in your head. But let's assume you don't know this formula. You can agree that the task is a good benchmark for the speed of a language. Here's how you'd sum up the numbers most efficiently using the core Python language:

```
a_list = list(range(1, 1_000_001))
print(sum(a_list))
```

That's not bad by the standard of most languages. Here is the **numpy**-based code to do the same thing. Notice how similar it looks.

```
import numpy as np

a = np.arange(1, 1_000_001)
print(sum(a))
```

In either case, the answer should be 500,000,500,000.

To measure the difference in these two approaches, we need to use performance benchmarks. The **time** package is very useful for getting timing information.

```
import numpy as np
from time import time

def benchmarks(n):
    t1 = time()

    a_list = list(range(1, n + 1))    # Old style!
    tot = sum(a_list)

    t2 = time()
    print('Time taken by Python is', t2 - t1)
    t1 = time()

    a = np.arange(1, n + 1)            # Numpy!
    tot = np.sum(a)

    t2 = time()
    print('Time taken by numpy is ', t2 - t1)
```

If this function is used to sum the first ten million numbers, here are the results, measured in seconds:

```
>>> benchmarks(10_000_000)
Time taken by Python is 1.2035150527954102
Time taken by numpy is   0.05511116981506348
```

Wow, that's a difference of almost 24 to 1. Not bad!

Performance Tip ▶ If you isolate the time of doing the actual addition—as opposed to creating the initial data set—the contrast is significantly greater still: about *60 times as fast.* Creating these more accurate benchmarks is left as an exercise at the end of the chapter.

◀ Performance Tip

12.5 Creating "numpy" Arrays

The previous section showed one way of creating a large **numpy** array.

```
a = np.arange(1, n + 1))
```

This statement generates a range beginning with 1, up to but not including the end point n + 1; then it uses this data to initialize a one-dimensional **numpy** array.

There are many ways to create and initialize a **numpy** array—so many, in fact, that it's beyond the scope of this chapter to explain every one of them. But this section serves as an introduction to the most common ways of creating **numpy** arrays, as summarized in Table 12.1.

Table 12.1. Common Array-Creation Functions in "numpy"

NUMPY FUNCTION	PRODUCES
`arange`	An array made up of integers in specified range, using syntax similar to Python **range** function.
`linspace`	Array of values evenly spaced within the specified range. This function handles floating-point values, so it can handle small, fractional gradations if desired. (Although technically it can accept integers, it's primarily intended for use with floating point.)
`empty`	An uninitialized array. Values are "random," but not statistically valid for random sampling.
`eyes`	An array with 1's on a diagonal; other cells are 0's.
`ones`	An array initialized to all 1's (either integer, floating point, or Boolean **True** values).
`zeros`	An array initialized to all 0 values (either integer, floating point, or Boolean **False** values).
`full`	An array filled with a specified value placed in every position of the array.
`copy`	An array copied, member by member, from another **numpy** array.
`fromfunction`	An array initialized by calling the same function on each element, taking its index or indexes as input.

The sections that follow provide details. Many of these functions enable you to specify a *dtype* argument, which determines the data type of each and every element in a **numpy** array. This feature lets you create arrays of different base types. A *dtype* specifier may be either (1) one of the symbols shown in Table 12.2 or (2) a string containing the name. In the former case, the symbol should usually be qualified:

```
import numpy as np
np.int8      # Used as a dtype
'int8'       # Also used as a dtype
```

Table 12.2. "dtype" Values Used in "numpy"

DTYPE VALUE	DESCRIPTION
bool	Boolean value; each element is **True** or **False**.
int	Standard integer size. Typically the same as **int32**.
int8	Signed 8-bit integer. Range is −128 to 127.
uint8	Unsigned 8-bit integer.
int16	Signed 8-bit integer. Range is plus or minus 32K.
uint16	Unsigned 32-bit integer.
int32	Signed 32-bit integer. Range is roughly plus or minus 2 billion.
uint32	Unsigned 32-bit integer.
int64	Signed 64-bit integer. Range is exponentially higher than that for **int32** but still finite.
uint64	Unsigned 64-bit integer.
float	Standard floating-point size.
float32	32-bit floating point.
float64	64-bit floating point.
complex	Complex-number data type. An input of 1.0 would be converted to 1.+0.j.
'i'	Standard-size integer.
'f'	Standard-size floating point.
'U*num*'	Unsigned character type. If *num* appears, you can use it to specify a fixed-length string type. For example, <U8 means storage of a string of up to eight characters in length.

The last line of Table 12.2 creates a fixed-length string type. Strings shorter than this length can be assigned to elements of this type. But strings that are longer are truncated. For an example, see Section 12.5.8, "The 'full' Function."

12.5.1 The "array" Function (Conversion to an Array)

The most straightforward way to create a **numpy** array is to use the **array** conversion on a Python data source, such as a list or tuple. This syntax supports several other arguments, including *subok* and *ndmin*. Look at online help for more information. This section focuses on the more commonly used arguments.

```
array(data, dtype=None, order='K')
```

The result is a **numpy** array of the specified type; if *dtype* is not specified or is set to **None**, the function infers a data type large enough to store every element. (This is a nontrivial issue with integers, because Python integers do not have fixed lengths.)

The *order* determines how higher-dimensional data is ordered; the default, **'K'**, means to preserve the storage of the source data, whatever it is. **'C'** means to use row-major order (which is what the C language uses), and **'F'** means to use column-major order (which is what FORTRAN uses).

As an example, you can initialize from a Python list to create a one-dimensional array of integers.

```
import numpy as np
a = np.array([1, 2, 3])
```

You can just as easily create a two-dimensional array, or higher, by using a multidimensional Python list (a list of lists):

```
a = np.array([[1, 2, 3], [10, 20, 30], [0, 0, -1]])
print(a)
```

Printing this array within IDLE produces

```
array([[  1,  2,  3],
       [ 10, 20, 30],
       [  0,  0, -1]])
```

numpy is designed to handle arrays with smooth, rectangular shapes. If you use higher-dimensional input that is "jagged," the array conversion must compensate by constructing as regular an array as well as it can.

So from within IDLE, you write this code:

```
>>> import numpy as np
>>> a = np.array([[1, 2, 3], [10, 20, 300]])
>>> a
array([[  1,   2,   3],
       [ 10,  20, 300]])
```

But here's what happens if the second row is made longer than the first:

```
>>> a = np.array([[1, 2, 3], [10, 20, 300, 4]])
>>> a
array([list([1, 2, 3]), list([10, 20, 300, 4])],
      dtype=object)
```

Now the array is forced into being a one-dimensional array of objects (each one being a list) rather than a true two-dimensional array.

12.5.2 The "arange" Function

The **arange** function creates an array of values from 1 to N, similar to the way the Python **range** function does. This function is limited to generating one-dimensional arrays.

```
arange([beg,] end [,step] [dtype=None])
```

The arguments to **arange** are nearly the same as the arguments to the Python built-in **range** function.

In addition, the *dtype* argument specifies the type of each element. The default argument value is **None**, which causes the function to infer the data type. It uses an integer large enough to accommodate all the values in the range, such as 'int32'.

```
import numpy as np
a = np.arange(1, 1000001)  # Create array a million long.
```

12.5.3 The "linspace" Function

The **linspace** function is similar to the **arange** function, but **linspace** handles floating-point as well as integer values; the steps between values can be of any size.

This function is especially useful in situations in which you want to provide a set of points or values along a line, in which those values are evenly spaced. As with the **arange** function, **linspace** is limited to producing a one-dimensional array.

The syntax shown here summarizes the most important arguments of this function. For a more complete description, see the **numpy** documentation.

```
linspace(beg, end, num=50, endpoint=True, dtype=None)
```

The values *beg* and *end* are self-explanatory, except that the *end* value is, by default, included in the range of values generated (in contrast to **arange**). If the *endpoint* argument is included and is set to **False**, then the *end* value is not included.

The *num* argument specifies how many values to generate. They will be as evenly spaced in the range as possible. If not specified, *num* is set to 50 by default.

The *dtype* argument specifies the data type of every element. If not specified or if given the value **None**, the **linspace** function infers the data type from the rest of the arguments; this usually results in using **float** values.

Suppose you want to create a **numpy** array with a range of values that occur every 0.25 units. The following statement produces such an array.

```
import numpy as np
a = np.linspace(0, 1.0, num=5)
```

Displaying this array in IDLE produces

```
array([0. , 0.25, 0.5 , 0.75, 1.  ])
```

Five elements (and not four) were required to get this result, because by default, the **linspace** function includes the endpoint as one of the values. Therefore, *num* was set to 5. Setting it to 6 gets the following results:

```
>>> a = np.linspace(0, 1.0, num=6)
>>> a
array([0., 0.2, 0.4, 0.6, 0.8, 1. ])
```

You can specify any number of elements, as long as the element is a positive integer. You can specify any data type listed in Table 12.2, although some are more difficult to accommodate. (The **bool** type produces unsatisfying results.) Here's an example:

```
>>> np.linspace(1, 5, num=5, dtype=np.int16)
array([1, 2, 3, 4, 5], dtype=int16)
```

In this case, integers worked out well. However, if you specify a range that would normally require floating-point values and use an integer type, the function has to convert many or all of the values to integer type by truncating them.

12.5.4 The "empty" Function

The **empty** function generates an uninitialized **numpy** array. If you want to produce an array in which the initial values are not initialized but rather are set later, and if you want to save time by not initializing twice, you may want to use the **empty** function. Be careful, however, because using uninitialized values is a risky practice. It's reasonable when you're trying to perform every last trick to increase execution speed—*and* if you're sure that the elements will be given meaningful values before being used.

Don't assume that because the values are uninitialized that they are useful random numbers for the purposes of simulations or games. These numbers have statistical anomalies that make them poor data for random sampling.

```
numpy.empty(shape, dtype='float', order='C')
```

The *shape* argument, the only required argument in this case, is either an integer or a tuple. In the former case, a one-dimensional array is created. A tuple specifies a higher-dimensional array. For example, (3, 3) specifies a two-dimensional, 3 × 3 array.

The *dtype* argument determines the data type of each element. By default, it is set to **'float'**. (See Table 12.2 for a list of *dtype* settings.)

The *order* argument determines whether the array is stored in row-major or column-major order. It takes the value **'C'** (row-major order, as in C) or **'F'** (column-major order, as in FORTRAN). C is the default.

The following example creates a 2 × 2 array made up of 16-bit signed integers.

```
import numpy as np
a = np.empty((2, 2), dtype='int16')
```

Displaying this array in IDLE (and thereby getting its canonical representation) produces

```
array([[0,  0],
       [0, -3]], dtype=int16)
```

Your results may vary, because the data in this case is uninitialized and therefore unpredictable.

Here's another example. Remember that although the numbers may look random, don't rely on this "randomness." It's better to consider such uninitialized values to be "garbage." This means don't use them.

```
a = np.empty((3, 2), dtype='float32')
```

Displaying this array in IDLE produces

```
array([[1.4012985e-45, 2.3509887e-38],
       [9.1835496e-41, 3.5873241e-43],
       [1.4012985e-45, 2.3509887e-38]], dtype=float32)
```

12.5.5 The "eye" Function

The **eye** function is similar to the **identity** function in **numpy**. Both create the same kind of array—specifically, an "identity" array, which places 1's in the positions [0,0], [1,1], [2,2], [3,3] and so on, while placing 0's everywhere else.

This function produces a two-dimensional array only.

```
numpy.eye(N, M=None, [k,] dtype='float', order='C')
```

The *N* and *M* arguments, respectively, specify the number of rows and columns. If *M* is not specified or is specified as **None**, then it's automatically set to the value of *N*.

The *k* argument, which is optional, can be used to move the diagonal. The default, 0, utilizes the main diagonal (see the upcoming example). Positive and negative integer values, respectively, move this diagonal up and down.

The *dtype* argument determines the data type of each element. By default, it is set to **'float'**. See Table 12.2 for a list of settings.

The *order* argument determines whether the array is stored in row-major or column-major order, and it takes the value **C** (row-major, as in the C language) or **F** (column-major, as in FORTRAN). C is the default.

Here's an example:

```
a = np.eye(4, dtype='int')
```

Displaying this array in IDLE produces

```
array([[1, 0, 0, 0],
       [0, 1, 0, 0],
       [0, 0, 1, 0],
       [0, 0, 0, 1]])
```

Or we can create a floating-point version, using the *dtype* default, **'float'**, and making it somewhat larger: 6 × 6 instead of 4 × 4.

```
a = np.eye(6)
```

The result looks like this when displayed in IDLE:

```
array([[1., 0., 0., 0., 0., 0.],
       [0., 1., 0., 0., 0., 0.],
       [0., 0., 1., 0., 0., 0.],
       [0., 0., 0., 1., 0., 0.],
       [0., 0., 0., 0., 1., 0.],
       [0., 0., 0., 0., 0., 1.]])
```

Arrays like this have a number of uses, but basically, they provide a way to do batch processing on large arrays when you want to do something special with coordinate pairs that match the identity relationship, R = C.

12.5.6 The "ones" Function

The **ones** function creates an array initialized to all 1 values. Depending on the data type of the array, each member will be initialized to either 1, an integer, 1.0, or the Boolean value **True**.

numpy.**ones(***shape*, *dtype*=**'float'**, *order*=**'C'***)*

These are the same arguments described for the **empty** function. Briefly, *shape* is either an integer (giving the length of a one-dimensional array) or a tuple describing N dimensions. The *dtype* is one of the values in Table 12.2. The *order* is either **'C'** (row-major order, as in the C language) or **'F'** (column-major order, as in FORTRAN).

Here's a simple example creating a 3 × 3 two-dimensional array using the default **float** type.

```
>>> import numpy as np
>>> a = np.ones((3,3))
>>> a
array([[1., 1., 1.],
       [1., 1., 1.],
       [1., 1., 1.]])
```

Here is another example, this time creating a 2 × 2 × 3 array of integers.

```
>>> a = np.ones((2, 2, 3), dtype=np.int16)
>>> a
array([[[1, 1, 1],
        [1, 1, 1]],

       [[1, 1, 1],
        [1, 1, 1]]], dtype=int16)
```

Finally, here's a one-dimensional array of Booleans. Notice that all the 1 values are realized as the Boolean value **True**.

```
>>> a = np.ones(6, dtype=np.bool)
>>> a
array([ True,  True,  True,  True,  True,  True])
```

This last kind of array—a Boolean array set to all-**True** values—will prove useful when running the Sieve of Eratosthenes benchmark to produce prime numbers.

12.5.7 The "zeros" Function

The **zeros** function creates an array initialized to all-0 values. Depending on the data type of the array, each member will be initialized to either 0, an integer, 0.0, or the Boolean value **False**.

```
zeros(shape, dtype='float', order='C')
```

These are the same common array-creation arguments described for the **empty** function. Briefly, *shape* is either an integer (giving the length of a one-dimensional array) or a tuple, describing N dimensions. The *dtype* is one of the values in Table 12.2. The *order* is either **'C'** (row-major order, as in the C language) or **'F'** (column-major order, as in FORTRAN).

Note ▶ The name of this function is tricky, because the English word "zeros" can also be spelled "zeroes." Remember to use the shorter spelling, **zeros**, only. Ah, English spelling—never mastered even by native English speakers!

◀ Note

Here is a simple example creating a 3 × 3 two-dimensional array using the default float type.

```
>>> import numpy as np
>>> a = np.zeros((3,3))
>>> a
array([[0., 0., 0.],
       [0., 0., 0.],
       [0., 0., 0.]])
```

Here's another example, this time creating a 2 × 2 × 3 array of integers.

```
>>> a = np.zeros((2, 2, 3), dtype=np.int16)
>>> a
array([[[0, 0, 0],
        [0, 0, 0]],

       [[0, 0, 0],
        [0, 0, 0]]], dtype=int16)
```

Finally, here's a one-dimensional array of Booleans. Notice that all the zero values are realized as the Boolean value **False**.

```
>>> a = np.zeros(5, dtype=np.bool)
>>> a
array([False, False, False, False, False])
```

12.5.8 The "full" Function

The **full** function creates a **numpy** array using the same arguments shown earlier for **empty**, **ones**, and **zeros**; however, **full** has one additional argument: a value to assign to each and every element.

numpy.**full**(*shape*, *fill_value*, *dtype*=**None**, *order*='**C**')

Briefly, *shape* is either an integer (giving the length of a one-dimensional array) or a tuple, describing N dimensions. The *dtype* is one of the values in Table 12.2. The *order* is either '**C**' (row-major order, as in the C language) or '**F**' (column-major order, as in FORTRAN).

If the *dtype* argument is either omitted or set to **None**, the function uses the data type of the *fill_value*, which is required for this function.

Here's a simple example creating a 2 × 2 array in which each element is set to 3.14.

```
>>> import numpy as np
>>> a = np.full((2, 2), 3.14)
>>> a
array([[3.14, 3.14],
       [3.14, 3.14]])
```

Here's another example; this one creates an array of eight integers, each set to 100.

```
>>> a = np.full(8, 100)
>>> a
array([100, 100, 100, 100, 100, 100, 100, 100])
```

This final example takes advantage of the fact that you can create a **numpy** array of strings—provided that all these strings observe a fixed maximum size.

```
>>> a = np.full(5,'ken')
>>> a
array(['ken', 'ken', 'ken', 'ken', 'ken'], dtype='<U3')
```

After the array is created in this way, with strings of size 3, each such string has, in effect, a maximum size. You can assign a longer string to any of these array elements, but it will be truncated.

```
a[0] = 'tommy'    # Legal, but only 'tom' is assigned.
```

12.5.9 The "copy" Function

The **numpy copy** function copies all the elements of an existing array. Because data is stored contiguously rather than through references, deep copying versus shallow copying is generally not an issue for **numpy** arrays.

An example should suffice. Suppose you already have an array, a_arr, and you want to make a full copy of it and call the copy b_arr.

```
import numpy as np

b_arr = np.copy(a_arr)
```

12.5.10 The "fromfunction" Function

The **numpy fromfunction** function (yes, that's a mouthful) is among the most powerful ways to create an array; we'll use it in the next section to create a multiplication table. The **fromfunction** enables you to create and initialize an array by calling another function that works *as if* it were transforming indexes into arguments.

> `numpy.fromfunction(`*func*`, `*shape*`, dtype='`**float**`')`

The *shape* is an integer or tuple of integers, just as with some of the other functions. The length of this tuple determines the rank of the array (the number of dimensions); it also determines how many arguments that the *func*—a callable—must accept.

There's a twist here in that *shape* must be a tuple and not a scalar, so you may have to use a tuple expression such as **(5,)** in order to create one-dimensional data sets.

Here's a simple example: We want to create a one-dimensional array corresponding to the first five natural numbers. You can do this with **arange**, but **fromfunction** provides another way. It requires us, however, to provide a callable.

```
import numpy as np

def simple(n):
    return n + 1

a = np.fromfunction(simple, (5,), dtype='int32')
```

The resulting array is displayed as follows in IDLE:

```
array([1, 2, 3, 4, 5], dtype=int32)
```

This might be better expressed with a lambda function. (See Chapter 3, "Advanced Capabilities of Lists," for more information on lambdas.)

```
a = np.fromfunction(lambda n:n+1, (5,), dtype='int32')
```

But higher-dimensional arrays are common. Here's an example that creates a two-dimensional array in which each element is equal to the total of its two indexes.

```
def add_it(r, c):
    return r + c

a = np.fromfunction(add_it, (3, 3), dtype='int32')
```

This code could also be written with a lambda.

```
a = np.fromfunction(lambda r,c:r+c, (3, 3), dtype='int')
```

In either case, if the resulting array is displayed in IDLE, it has the following representation:

```
array([[0, 1, 2],
       [1, 2, 3],
       [2, 3, 4]])
```

At the beginning of this section, we stated that **fromfunction** works *as if* the function were being called for each element, with the arguments being the index or indexes at that position.

What **fromfunction** actually does is create an array or arrays, in which one of the dimensions (or *axis*) is set to a series of whole numbers. For a one-dimensional array of size 6, this is the numbers 0 through 5.

```
[0 1 2 3 4 5]
```

This is an *identity* array in that each element is equal to its index.

For the two-dimensional 3 × 3 array used in the previous example, **fromfunction** creates two arrays: one for each of the two axes.

```
[[0 0 0],
 [1 1 1],
 [2 2 2]]

[[0 1 2],
 [0 1 2],
 [0 1 2]]
```

These are identity arrays along specific axes. In the first array, each element is equal to its row index; in the second array, each element is equal to its column index.

The implementation of **fromfunction** operates on the arrays. As a result, the *callable* argument (the other function being called) is executed only once! But it is executed on one or more arrays—one for each dimension—enabling batch processing.

If you use **fromfunction** the way it was designed to be used, this underlying implementation works. But if you do unorthodox things, strange results are possible. Consider the following code, which should produce a 3 × 3 array.

```
a = np.fromfunction(lambda r, c: 1, (3, 3), dtype='int')
```

12

You'd probably expect the result to be a 3 × 3 array in which each element is set to 1. Yet this function call (you can easily try it out) returns 1 as a scalar value!

12.6 Example: Creating a Multiplication Table

Suppose you want to create the classic multiplication table for numbers from 1 to 10. There is more than one way to do that with **numpy**. You could create an empty array, for example, and assign values to the elements.

With **numpy**, you could also do something similar. You could create an array initialized to all-zero values, for example, and then write a nested loop to assign R * C to each element—actually, it's (R+1)*(C+1).

By far the most efficient approach would be to use **fromfunction** to create an array that called a function to generate the values, without writing any loops at all. This is the **numpy** philosophy: As much as possible, let the package do all the work by using batch operations. You should be writing relatively few loops.

Here's the solution:

```
import numpy as np

def multy(r, c):
    return (r + 1) * (c+ 1)

a = np.fromfunction(multy, (10, 10), dtype=np.int16)
```

You could write this more compactly by using a lambda function. (Lambdas are explained in Chapter 3, "Advanced Capabilities of Lists.")

```
a = np.fromfunction(lambda r,c: (r+1) * (c+1),
    (10, 10), dtype=np.int16)
```

Printing the result, a, produces a nice-looking multiplication table.

```
>>> print(a)
[[  1   2   3   4   5   6   7   8   9  10]
 [  2   4   6   8  10  12  14  16  18  20]
 [  3   6   9  12  15  18  21  24  27  30]
 [  4   8  12  16  20  24  28  32  36  40]
 [  5  10  15  20  25  30  35  40  45  50]
 [  6  12  18  24  30  36  42  48  54  60]
 [  7  14  21  28  35  42  49  56  63  70]
 [  8  16  24  32  40  48  56  64  72  80]
 [  9  18  27  36  45  54  63  72  81  90]
 [ 10  20  30  40  50  60  70  80  90 100]]
```

You can improve the appearance by getting rid of the brackets in the display. That's relatively easy to do if we first convert to a string and then use the **str** class **replace** method.

```
s = str(a)
s = s.replace('[', '')
s = s.replace(']', '')
s = ' ' + s
```

As mentioned in Chapter 4, replacing a character with the empty string is a convenient way to purge all instances of a character. This example calls the **replace** method to get rid of both kinds of brackets. Finally, a space is inserted at the front of the string to make up for the loss of two open brackets.

Now, printing this string produces a pleasing display.

```
>>> print(s)
 1   2   3   4   5   6   7   8   9  10
 2   4   6   8  10  12  14  16  18  20
 3   6   9  12  15  18  21  24  27  30
 4   8  12  16  20  24  28  32  36  40
 5  10  15  20  25  30  35  40  45  50
 6  12  18  24  30  36  42  48  54  60
 7  14  21  28  35  42  49  56  63  70
 8  16  24  32  40  48  56  64  72  80
 9  18  27  36  45  54  63  72  81  90
10  20  30  40  50  60  70  80  90 100
```

12.7 Batch Operations on "numpy" Arrays

The real power and speed of a **numpy** array become clear when you start to do large-scale, or batch, operations on the array—either on the whole array or on selected pieces created by slicing. This lets you operate on selected rows and columns, or even intersections.

Once you've created a **numpy** array, you can do any number of arithmetic operations on it by combining it with a scalar value. Table 12.3 lists some of the things you can do. This is far from an exhaustive list. In this table, *A* is a **numpy** array, and *n* is a scalar value, such as a single integer or floating-point number.

Table 12.3. Some Scalar Operations on "numpy" Arrays

OPERATION	PRODUCES
A + n	Array with *n* added to each element of A.
A – n	Array with *n* subtracted from each element of A.
A * n	Array with *n* multiplied with each element of A.
n ** A	A number raised to the power of each element of A, producing another array with the results.
A ** n	Each element in A is raised to the power *n*.
A / n	Array with *n* dividing into each element of A.
A // n	Array with *n* dividing into each element of A but using ground division.

Each of these operations has an assignment operator associated with it, as do ordinary Python operations. For example, to double each member of a **numpy** array named my_array, use the following:

```
my_array *= 2   # Double each element of my_array
```

Another simple, and very powerful, version of **numpy** batch operations is to use arithmetic on two **numpy** arrays of the same shape—which implies that the number of dimensions match, as well as the size of each dimension. Table 12.4 shows some of these operations.

Table 12.4. Some Array-to-Array Operations

OPERATION	PRODUCES
A + B	Array generated by adding each element of A to the corresponding element of B.
A – B	Array generated by subtracting each element of B from the corresponding element of A.
A * B	Array generated by multiplying each element of A with the corresponding element of B.
A ** B	Array generated by raising each element in A to the exponent taken from the corresponding element in B.
A / B	Array generated by dividing each element of B into the corresponding element of A.
A // B	Array generated by dividing each element of B into the corresponding element of A, but using ground division.

For example, let's start with a simple 4 × 4 array.

```
import numpy as np

A = np.array([[0, 1, 2, 3], [4, 5, 6, 7],
              [8, 9, 10, 11], [12, 13, 14, 15]])
print(A)
```

Printing A gives a nice result.

```
[[ 0  1  2  3]
 [ 4  5  6  7]
 [ 8  9 10 11]
 [12 13 14 15]]
```

This is a familiar pattern. Is there a way to produce such an array without having to enter all the data directly? Yes, there are at least two! The simplest technique is to generate the numbers from 1 to 15 to form a simple array, and then use the **numpy reshape** function to rearrange it into a 4 × 4 array with the same elements.

```
A = np.arange(16).reshape((4,4))
```

The other way (which is slightly more verbose) is to use **fromfunction** to do the job. In either case, you can apply this pattern to much, much larger arrays, with a shape such as 200 × 100 or even 1,000 × 3,000.

In the case of creating a 4 × 4 array, the function call would be

```
A = np.fromfunction(lambda r, c: r*4 + c, (4, 4))
```

Suppose, also, that we have an array named B of matching shape and size.

```
B = np.eye(4, dtype='int16')
print(B)
```

These statements print the following:

```
[[ 1  0  0  0]
 [ 0  1  0  0]
 [ 0  0  1  0]
 [ 0  0  0  1]]
```

Now the fun begins. We can produce a new array, for example, by multiplying every element in A by 10. From within IDLE, here's what that looks like:

```
>>> C = A * 10
>>> print(C)
[[  0.  10.  20.  30.]
```

```
[ 40.  50.  60.  70.]
[ 80.  90. 100. 110.]
[120. 130. 140. 150.]]
```

To produce the array now referred to by the variable C, each and every element of A has been multiplied by 10. We might also produce an array that contains the squares of all the elements in A. We can do this by multiplying A by itself, which does a member-by-member multiplication of each element.

```
>>> C = A * A
>>> print(C)
[[  0.   1.   4.   9.]
 [ 16.  25.  36.  49.]
 [ 64.  81. 100. 121.]
 [144. 169. 196. 225.]]
```

Keep in mind there's no requirement that **numpy** arrays have a perfect square or perfect cubic shape—only that they're rectangular. You can always reshape an array. For example, the 4 × 4 array just shown can be reshaped into a 2 × 8 array.

```
>>> print(C.reshape((2,8)))

[[  1.   4.   9.  16.  25.  36.  49.  64.]
 [ 81. 100. 121. 144. 169. 196. 225. 256.]]
```

If we want to change A in place, that's entirely doable with an assignment operator, *=. Arrays are mutable.

```
>>> A *= A
```

Finally, let's assume that the square numbers are assigned to A itself using the statement just shown (A *= A). The next operation multiplies A by B. Because B is an eye (or identity) array, what do you think the result is?

```
>>> C = A * B
>>> print(C)
[[  0.   0.   0.   0.]
 [  0.  25.   0.   0.]
 [  0.   0. 100.   0.]
 [  0.   0.   0. 225.]]
```

Again, the result is a member-by-member multiplication.

12.8 Ordering a Slice of "numpy"

You can take slices of a one-dimensional **numpy** array just as you can with a Python list; the next section deals with higher-dimensional arrays.

Given a **numpy** array, you can print a slice of it, just as you can with a Python list. Here's an example:

```
>>> A = np.arange(1, 11)
>>> print(A)
[ 1  2  3  4  5  6  7  8  9 10]
>>> print(A[2:5])
[3 4 5]
```

One of the interesting things you can do with a **numpy** slice is to assign a scalar value to it. The result is to assign this same value to each position in the slice.

```
>>> A[2:5] = 0
>>> print(A)
[ 1  2  0  0  0  6  7  8  9 10]
```

And you can do more. You can operate on a slice of an array just as you can with a full array. If you use assignment, such operations happen in place. For example, you could add 100 to each of these three elements, rather than setting them to zero.

```
>>> A[2:5] += 100
>>> print(A)
[  1   2 103 104 105   6   7   8   9  10]
```

Remember that when you combine arrays together through standard operations, the size of the two arrays must match. This applies to slices as well. For example, the following is valid, because the shapes match.

```
A[2:5] *= [100, 200, 300]
```

The effect is to multiply the third, fourth, and fifth elements of A by 100, 200, and 300, respectively. That operation produces the following array (assuming we apply it to the original value of A):

```
[   1    2  300  800 1500    6    7    8    9   10]
```

Now, how can we use some of these features to solve practical problems? One of the classic benchmarks is the algorithm known as the Sieve of Eratosthenes, which is an efficient way of producing a large group of prime numbers.

Let's start with the numbers between 0 and 50, inclusive. The procedure (which we'll generalize later) is to eliminate all the numbers that are not prime and then print the ones left. First, here's the array we start with.

```
>>> A = np.arange(51)
>>> print(A)
[ 0  1  2  3  4  5  6  7  8  9 10 11 12 13 14 15 16
 17 18 19 20 21 22 23 24 25 26 27 28 29 30 31 32 33
 34 35 36 37 38 39 40 41 42 43 44 45 46 47 48 49 50]
```

We want to zero out all the numbers that are not prime.

▶ Zero out element A[1], because 1 is not a prime number.

▶ Zero out all multiples of 2, starting with 2 squared.

▶ Zero out all multiples of 3, starting with 3 squared.

▶ Repeat the procedure for 5 and 7.

The following code carries out the first two steps.

```
>>> A[1] = 0
>>> A[2 * 2::2] = 0
>>> print(A)
[ 0  0  2  3  0  5  0  7  0  9  0 11  0 13  0 15  0
 17  0 19  0 21  0 23  0 25  0 27  0 29  0 31  0 33
  0 35  0 37  0 39  0 41  0 43  0 45  0 47  0 49  0]
```

The meaning of A[2 * 2::2] is to take a slice beginning with the index number 2 squared, which is 4, then go to the end of the array (because the middle argument is blank), and then move through the array two elements at a time. Everything in this slice is set to 0.

Notice that each index position, in this particular example, corresponds to the value of a number from 0 to 50 in this case. So to zero out the number 8, for example, we set A[8] to zero. This keeps the programming simple.

The results show that A[1] has been zeroed out, as well as all the even numbers other than 2 itself. We can do the same thing for multiples of 3.

```
>>> A[3 * 3::3] = 0
[ 0  0  2  3  0  5  0  7  0  0  0 11  0 13  0  0  0
 17  0 19  0  0  0 23  0 25  0  0  0 29  0 31  0  0
  0 35  0 37  0  0  0 41  0 43  0  0  0 47  0 49  0]
```

After repeating the procedure for multiples of 5 and 7, we finally get an array in which all the values are either 0 or are prime numbers.

```
[ 0  0  2  3  0  5  0  7  0  0  0 11  0 13  0  0  0
 17  0 19  0  0  0 23  0  0  0  0  0 29  0 31  0  0
  0  0  0 37  0  0  0 41  0 43  0  0  0 47  0  0  0]
```

Now, how do we print all the nonzero values? You could write a loop, of course, that goes through the array and either prints a value if it is nonzero, or adds it to a list. Here's an example:

```
my_prime_list = [i for i in A if i > 0]
```

That's not bad, but **numpy** provides a way that's even more efficient and more compact! You can create a Boolean array just by specifying a condition.

```
A > 0
```

The Boolean array that gets produced, which we'll look at more closely in Section 12.10, can be applied to array A itself as a *mask*—just by using the indexing operation. The effect in this case is to produce a new array from A, satisfying the condition that the element is greater than 0.

We previously zeroed out all nonprime numbers in A; therefore, by taking the nonzero values remaining in A, we get only prime numbers as a result.

```
>>> P = A[A > 0]
>>> print(P)
[ 2  3  5  7 11 13 17 19 23 29 31 37 41 43 47]
```

So there you have it: all the primes not larger than 50.

12.9 Multidimensional Slicing

numpy arrays provide an even more powerful slicing ability: getting slices of any number of dimensions supported by the source array. We can start by seeing the effect of an (apparently) one-dimensional slice of a two-dimensional array. Let's start with a familiar 4 × 4 array.

```
>>> A = np.arange(1,17).reshape((4,4))
>>> print(A)
[[ 1  2  3  4]
 [ 5  6  7  8]
 [ 9 10 11 12]
 [13 14 15 16]]
```

What would happen if we took the two middle elements—1 and 2?

```
>>> print(A[1:3])
[[ 5  6  7  8]
 [ 9 10 11 12]]
```

The result, clearly, is to produce the middle two rows. Now, how can we get the middle two columns? Actually, that turns out to be almost as easy.

```
>>> A[:, 1:3]
array([[ 2,  3],
       [ 6,  7],
       [10, 11],
       [14, 15]])
```

Take another look at that array expression.

```
A[:, 1:3]
```

The colon before the comma says, "Select everything in this dimension"—in this case, the row dimension. The expression `1:3` selects all the columns beginning with index 1 (the second column) up to but not including index 3 (the fourth column). Therefore, the expression says, "Select all rows, with the intersection of columns 1 up to but not including column 3—that is, the second and third columns."

The general syntax for indexing and slicing an array of N dimensions is shown here.

```
array_name[ i1, i2, i3,... iN ]
```

In this syntax, each of the arguments *i1* through *iN* may be either a scalar value—which must be an index in range—or a slice. You can use at most N such arguments, where N is the number of dimensions (the rank) of the array. For each scalar used, the dimensionality of the result is reduced by one.

Therefore, slicing a two-dimensional array as `A[2, 1:4]` produces a one-dimensional array as a result. Slicing it as `A[2:3, 1:4]` would get the same elements but would be two-dimensional, even though it would have only one row that was not empty. (This issue matters, because most operations on arrays must match in size and number of dimensions.)

Any of the *i* values in this syntax may be omitted; in each such case, its value is assumed to be the colon (`:`), which says, "Select all the elements in this dimension." If there are fewer than N arguments, then the first M dimensions (where M is the number of arguments) get the values assigned, and the last N–M dimensions assume the colon as their default.

Table 12.5 lists a series of examples. In this table, A is a two-dimensional array and A3D is a three-dimensional array.

Table 12.5. Examples of "numpy" Indexing and Slicing

EXAMPLE	DESCRIPTION
`A[3]`	The entire fourth row, returned as a one-dimensional array.
`A[3,:]`	Same as above.
`A[3,]`	Same as above.
`A[:,2]`	The entire third column, returned as a one-dimensional array.
`A[::2,2]`	Get every other row from the third column.
`A[1:3,1:3]`	The intersection of the second and third columns with the second and third rows, returned as a two-dimensional array.
`A3D[2,2]`	The third row of the third plane (a plane being a level in the third dimension), returned as a one-dimensional array. Takes all columns in that row.
`A3D[2, 2, :]`	Same as above.
`A3D[:, 1:3, 2]`	A two-dimensional array containing the third column from the second and third rows, intersecting with all planes.
`A3D[::2, 1:3, 2]`	Same as above, but get every other plane (as opposed to every plane), starting with the first.
`A3D[0, 0, 1]`	A single element, taken from second column of the first row of the first plane.

Let's look at a more practical example. Suppose you're writing a computer simulation called the Game of Life, and you have the following grid, realized as a **numpy** array that we'll call G, for "grid." The 1's are in bold for clarity.

```
[[0 0 0 0 0 0]
 [0 0 1 0 0 0]
 [0 0 1 0 0 0]
 [0 0 1 0 0 0]
 [0 0 0 0 0 0]
 [0 0 0 0 0 0]]
```

A 1 represents a living cell; a 0 represents a dead cell. You'd like to get a count of all the neighbors around a specific cell, say, G[2, 2]. A fast way to do that is to get the two-dimensional slice that includes the columns before, after, and including 2, intersecting with the rows before, after, and including 2.

```
>>> print(G[1:4, 1:4])

[[0 1 0]
 [0 1 0]
 [0 1 0]]
```

Remember that the index numbers used are 1 and 4, and not 1 and 3, because the slice expressions always mean *up to but not including* the endpoint.

This gives us a nice cross-section of all the cells neighboring G[2,2], not including the cell itself. To get the neighbor count, therefore, it's only necessary to sum this cross-section and then subtract the value of the cell itself.

```
neighbor_count = np.sum(G[1:4, 1:4]) - G[2, 2]
```

The result is 2. In the Game of Life, that would indicate that the cell in the middle is "stable": In the next generation, it will experience neither a birth nor a death event.

12.10 *Boolean Arrays: Mask Out That "numpy"!*

We've already shown a use for Boolean arrays used as masks. Section 12.7, "Batch Operations on 'numpy' Arrays," used the following expression at the end:

```
A > 0
```

Assuming that A is a **numpy** array, this expression means "For each element of A, produce an element that is **True** if the element in A is greater than 0, and **False** if the element is not greater than 0." The resulting array will have the same shape as A.

For example, start with an array named B:

```
B = np.arange(1,10).reshape(3,3)
```

B, when printed, looks like this:

```
[[1 2 3]
 [4 5 6]
 [7 8 9]]
```

Now let's apply the condition B > 4.

```
B1 = B > 4
```

The result is to produce a Boolean array, B1, with the following contents:

```
[[False False False]
 [False  True  True]
 [ True  True  True]]
```

B1 has the shame shape as B, but each element is either **True** or **False** rather than being an integer. The general rule is as follows.

> Whenever a comparison operator (such as ==, <, or >) is applied to a **numpy** array, the result is a Boolean array of the same shape.

One way to use this array is to zero out all elements that don't meet the condition of being greater than 4, by multiplying the two arrays—B and (B>4)—together.

```
>>> print(B * (B > 4))

[[0 0 0]
 [0 5 6]
 [7 8 9]]
```

When working with Boolean arrays, you should note that the use of parentheses is often critical, because comparison operators have low precedence.

But an even better use of a Boolean array is to use it as a mask—in which case it selects in elements with a corresponding **True** value in the mask, and selects out elements with a corresponding **False** value.

Using a Boolean array as a mask produces a one-dimensional array, regardless of the shape of the array operands.

```
array_name[bool_array]     # Use bool_array as a mask.
```

For example, we could use a mask to get all elements greater than 7. The result is a one-dimensional array containing 8 and 9.

```
>>> print(B[B > 7])
[8 9]
```

Here's a more sophisticated use: Get all elements whose remainder, when divided by 3, is 1. There are three elements of B that meet this condition: 1, 4, and 7.

```
>>> print(B[B % 3 == 1])
[1 4 7]
```

A difficulty arises when you try to introduce complex conditions involving **and** and **or** keywords, even though these operations should work with Booleans. A good solution is to apply the bitwise operators (**&**, **|**) to the Boolean masks. The **&** symbol performs bitwise AND, whereas the **|** symbol performs bitwise OR.

You can also use multiplication (*****) and addition (**+**) to get the same results.

For example, to create a Boolean array in which the test for each element of B is "greater than 2 and less than 7," you could use the following:

```
B2 = (B > 2) & (B < 7)            # "AND" operation
```

Let's break this down semantically.

▶ B is a two-dimensional array of integers.

▶ B > 2 is a Boolean array of the same shape as B.

▶ B < 7 is another Boolean array, again of the same shape as B.

▶ The expression (B > 2) & (B < 7) uses binary AND (&) to achieve an "and" effect between these two Boolean arrays.

▶ The resulting Boolean array is assigned to the variable B2. This array will contain True and False values, in effect produced by Boolean operations on the two arrays which serve as operands.

You can then apply the mask to B itself to get a one-dimensional array of results in which each element is greater than 2 *and* less than 7.

```
>>> print(B[B2])
[3 4 5 6]
```

In this next example, bitwise OR is used to create a Boolean array from an "or" operation. That resulting Boolean array is then applied as a mask to B, and the final result selects all elements of B that are either equal to 1 or greater than 6.

```
>>> print(B[ (B == 1) | (B > 6)])      # "OR" operation
[1 7 8 9]
```

12.11 "numpy" and the Sieve of Eratosthenes

Let's return to the Sieve of Eratosthenes example and benchmark how **numpy** does compared to a standard Python list solution.

The goal of the algorithm is to produce all the prime numbers up to N, where N is any number you choose in advance. Here's the algorithm.

Create a one-dimensional Boolean array indexed from 0 to N.

Set all elements to True, except for the first two elements, which are set to False.

For I running from 2 to N:

    If array[I] is True,

        For J running from I*I to N, by steps of I:

            Set array[J] to False

The result of these steps is a Boolean array. For each index number higher than 2, corresponding to a **True** element, add that index number to results.

Here is an obvious way to implement this algorithm as a Python function:

```python
def sieve(n):
    b_list = [True] * (n + 1)
    for i in range(2, n+1):
        if b_list[i]:
            for j in range(i*i, n+1, i):
                b_list[j] = False
    primes = [i for i in range(2, n+1) if b_list[i]]
    return primes
```

Can we do better with **numpy**? Yes. We can improve performance by taking advantage of slicing and Boolean masking. In keeping with the general flavor of the algorithm, we use an array of Booleans, indexed from 2 to N–1.

```python
import numpy as np

def np_sieve(n):
    # Create B, setting all elements to True.
    B = np.ones(n + 1, dtype=np.bool)
    B[0:2] = False
    for i in range(2, n + 1):
        if B[i]:
            B[i*i: n+1: i] = False
    return np.arange(n + 1)[B]
```

So where does this implementation of the algorithm manage to do better? The function still has to loop through the array, one member at a time, looking for each element with the value **True.** This indicates that the index number is prime, because its corresponding element in the Boolean array has not been eliminated yet.

But the inner loop is replaced by a slice operation that sets every element in the slice to **False.** Assuming there are many elements, we can perform all these operations more efficiently with a batch operation rather than a loop.

```python
B[i*i: n+1: i]  = False
```

The other advanced technology used here is a Boolean mask to produce the final results: a **numpy** array from 0 to n, inclusive, which after the masking operation will contain only the prime numbers in that range.

```python
return np.arange(n + 1)[B]
```

Now, we'd like to know about the performance of this operation. By using the **time** package, you can perform benchmark tests designed to show which approach is faster. The following code adds lines that report the number of milliseconds taken. The added lines are in bold. The **return** statement is omitted, because you probably don't need to print all the primes up to 1 million, for example, if you're only interested in speed.

```
import numpy as np
import time

def np_sieve(n):
    t1 = time.time() * 1000
    B = np.ones(n + 1, dtype=np.bool)
    B[0:2] = False
    for i in range(2, n + 1):
        if B[i]:
            B[i*i: n+1: i] = False
    P = np.arange(n + 1)[B]
    t2 = time.time() * 1000
    print('np_sieve took', t2-t1, 'milliseconds.')
```

You can put in similar lines of timing code to benchmark the non-**numpy** version.

What the benchmarks show is that for relatively small numbers, the **numpy** version takes more time, and not less, than the other version. But for large N, especially greater than 1,000, np_sieve starts pulling ahead. Once N gets greater than 10,000 or so, the **numpy** version takes half the time the other version odes. That may not be the spectacular results we were looking for, but it's an increase in speed of 100 percent. Not bad.

Is this section playing fair? Yes. It's admittedly possible to implement the non-**numpy** version, sieve, by using more lists and more list comprehension. However, we've found that such attempts at code enhancement actually make the function run more slowly. Therefore, for large N, the **numpy** version remains the high-speed champ.

12.12 Getting "numpy" Stats (Standard Deviation)

One of the areas in which **numpy** excels is getting statistics on large data sets. Although you could get any of this information yourself by working with standard Python lists, this is where **numpy** arrays are many times faster.

Table 12.6 lists the statistical-analysis functions for **numpy** arrays. Each of these works by calling the corresponding method for the **ndarray** class; so you can use either the function or the method version.

These functions have a series of important arguments, which we'll cover later.

Table 12.6. Statistical Functions for "numpy" Arrays

FUNCTION	RETURNS
`min(A)`	The lowest element in the data set. Will return the element lowest along each dimension if the *axis* argument is specified; the same applies to each function listed here.
`max(A)`	The highest element.
`mean(A)`	The arithmetic mean, which is the sum of the elements divided by the number of elements. When applied to an individual axis (as you'll see in the next section), it will sum and divide along rows or columns as appropriate.
`median(A)`	The median element, which is the element in the group having an equal number of elements higher and lower.
`size(A)`	The number of elements.
`std(A)`	Standard deviation, a classic measure of variance.
`sum(A)`	The sum of all elements in the data set, or the sum of all elements in the specified subset.

Let's start by looking at how these functions apply to simple one-dimensional arrays. As the next section shows, you have more choices when applying them to higher-dimensional arrays.

The performance speeds of the statistical functions are impressive, as you'll see. First, let's generate an array to operate on. We can use a subpackage of **numpy** to generate random numbers—specifically, the **numpy.random** function, **rand**, which takes an array shape as input and generates an array of that shape. Each element is a random floating-point number between 0.0 and 1.0.

```
import numpy as np
import numpy.random as ran
A = ran.rand(10)
```

Printing A produces an array full of random floating-point values.

```
[0.49353738 0.88551261 0.69064065 0.93626092
 0.17818198 0.16637079 0.55144244 0.16262533
 0.36946706 0.61859074]
```

The **numpy** package can handle much bigger data sets and handle them efficiently, such as the following large array. But note: Don't print this unless you want Python to be busy for a long, long time!

```
A = ran.rand(100000)
```

This statement creates an array of 100,000 elements, each of which is a random floating-point value, and it does it in a fraction of a second. Even more astonishing is the speed with which **numpy** statistical functions process this array. The following IDLE session demonstrates how quickly you can get stats on this large data set.

```
>>> import numpy as np
>>> import numpy.random as ran
>>> A = ran.random(100000)
>>> np.mean(A)
0.49940282901121
>>> np.sum(A)
49940.282901121005
>>> np.median(A)
0.5005147698475437
>>> np.std(A)
0.2889516828729947
```

If you try this session yourself, you should experience the response times as instantaneous, even the standard deviation.

Most of these stats are straightforward in meaning. Because the probability distribution in this case is a uniform distribution from 0.0 to 1.0, you'd reasonably expect the mean to be close to 0.5, which it is: approximately 0.4994. The sum is exactly 100,000 times that, or about 49,940. The median is not the same as the mean, although you'd expect it to be close to the center of values, which it is: just over 0.50.

The standard deviation is what statisticians would predict for a uniform distribution like this: just under 0.29. So roughly 60 percent of the values fall within one standard deviation (plus or minus) of the mean.

Using **numpy** saves you from having to do this calculation yourself, but it's useful to review how standard deviation is calculated and what it means. Assume A and A2 represent arrays, and i refers to elements:

$A2 = (i - mean(A)) \wedge 2$, for all i in A.

$std(A) = sqrt(mean(A2))$

In plainer language, these equations mean the following:

▶ Figure out the average of the elements in array A. This is also called the mean.

▶ Subtract the mean from each element in A to create a new array full of "deviations."

▶ In this array of deviations, square each member, and call the resulting array A2.

▶ Find the average of all elements in A2, take the square root of the result, and voila! You have produced the standard deviation of the array you started with.

Although **numpy** provides the standard-deviation function for free, it's useful to see what it would take to produce the result through the standard batch operations. First, getting A2 would be easy enough: Subtracting the mean of A (a scalar) from A itself gives us an array filled with deviations. All these are then squared.

$$A2 = (A - mean(A)) ** 2$$

Having obtained this new array, we need only get the square root of the mean of the deviations.

$$result = (mean(A2)) ** 0.5$$

Or, in terms of Python code, it requires the **np** qualifier to call the **mean** function:

```
>>> A2 = (A - np.mean(A)) ** 2
>>> result = (np.mean(A2)) ** 0.5
>>> result
0.2889516828729947
>>> np.std(A)
0.2889516828729947
```

The results, as you can see, are precisely the same in both cases—calculating standard deviation "the hard way" and getting it from **np.std**—which is good evidence that the **numpy** routines are following the same algorithm.

It's instructive to run the standard deviation function on an even larger array—say, an array of 1 million random numbers—and the equivalent code in Python, using standard lists.

Now comes the interesting part: If you benchmark this technique with a list of 1 million elements in size, against a **numpy** version with an array containing the same data, the **numpy** version—getting the standard deviation directly—beats out the non-**numpy** version by a factor of more than 100 to 1!

Here's the full benchmark code:

```python
import numpy as np
import time
import numpy.random as ran

def get_std1(ls):
    t1 = time.time()
    m = sum(ls)/len(ls)
    ls2 = [(i - m) ** 2 for i in ls]
    sd = (sum(ls2)/len(ls2)) ** .5
    t2 = time.time()
    print('Python took', t2-t1)

def get_std2(A):
    t1 = time.time()
    A2 = (A - np.mean(A)) ** 2
    result = (np.mean(A2)) ** .5
    t2 = time.time()
    print('Numpy  took', t2-t1)

def get_std3(A):
    t1 = time.time()
    result = np.std(A)
    t2 = time.time()
    print('np.std took', t2-t1)

A = ran.rand(1000000)
get_std1(A)
get_std2(A)
get_std3(A)
```

Running all three gets the following results, expressed in parts of a second. Remember this is the time taken to get standard deviation *for 1 million elements.*

```
Python took 0.6885709762573242
Numpy  took 0.0189220905303955
np.std took 0.0059509277343750
```

You can see how enormous the gains in performance are, as we go from Python lists, to **numpy** arrays, to finally using **numpy** to get standard deviation directly, with a single function call.

The increase in speed from not using **numpy** at all, compared to using **np.std** (the **numpy** standard deviation function) is well over 100 to 1. Now that's greased lightning!

12.13   Getting Data on "numpy" Rows and Columns

Section 12.12, "Getting 'numpy' Stats (Standard Deviation)," assumed the simplest possible case: getting statistics on a floating-point array of one dimension. However, all those functions accept other arguments. You can look these up in online documentation or in IDLE, through the help command.

The most important argument, other than the array itself, is the *axis* argument, which is used with higher dimensions—that is, dimensions greater than one.

Let's start with another array of random numbers—this time, integers. To produce such an array, you can use the **randint** function of the **numpy.random** package. Here's an example:

```
import numpy as np
import numpy.random as ran
A = ran.randint(1, 20, (3, 4))
print(A)
```

Here's some sample output. Your results, of course, will vary.

```
[[ 4 13 11  8]
 [ 7 14 16  1]
 [ 4  1  5  9]]
```

The **numpy.random** package has its own **randint** function, just as the **random** package does. This is another reason that using namespace qualifiers is so important. In this case, using the **numpy random** package, the function takes *begin* and *end* arguments, as you'd expect, but it also takes an additional argument: a tuple giving the shape of the array.

Another thing to note is that with **ran.randint**, the *begin* and *end* arguments include numbers starting with the *begin* argument, up to but not including the *end* argument. So this example produces numbers up to 19.

Finally, the *shape* argument—which comes after the *begin* and *end* arguments—is (3, 3), which causes the random integers to be placed throughout a 3 × 3 array.

Here it is again. Your mileage will vary.

```
[[  4 13 11   8]
 [  7 14 16   1]
 [  4  1  5   9]]
```

As you learned in the previous section, the **numpy** statistical functions can be used to study this array as one large source of data. If **np.mean** is applied directly to the array, for example, it gets the mean of all 20 elements.

```
>>> np.mean(A)
7.75
```

Likewise, we can sum the data or get the standard deviation.

```
>>> np.sum(A)
93
>>> np.std(A)      # standard deviation
4.780603169754489
```

The fun part comes when we collect statistics along an axis: either the row or the column dimension. Such operations enable the treatment of a **numpy** array as if it were a spreadsheet, containing totals for each row and column. However, it's easy to get the axis confused. Table 12.7 should help clarify.

Table 12.7. Use of the "axis" Argument

SETTING	DESCRIPTION
axis = 0	Create a row collecting data for each column. Size of the resulting one-dimensional array is the number of columns.
axis = 1	Create a column collecting data for each row. Size of the resulting one-dimensional array is the number of rows.

For even higher dimensional arrays, the axis settings can run higher. The axis settings can even be tuples.

Although it may be confusing at first, the way to approach the word "axis" is to think of it like a Cartesian coordinate system, as the name suggests. Look at A again.

```
[[  4 13 11   8]
 [  7 14 16   1]
 [  4  1  5   9]]
```

The argument setting `axis=0` refers to the first axis, which means rows (because row-major order is assumed). Therefore, to sum along `axis=0` is to sum along the traditional X axis. Summing as it goes, the function sums each column in turn, starting with the lowest-numbered column and moving right. The result is

[15 28 32 18]

The argument setting `axis=1` refers to the second axis, which means columns. Therefore, to sum along `axis=1` is to sum along the traditional Y axis. In this case, the sums start with the lowest-numbered row and move downward. The result is

[36 38 19]

When summation is done along the X axis, the **numpy** package collects data on the *other* dimensions. So, although `axis=0` refers to rows, columns are being summed. Figure 12.3 illustrates how this works.

Figure 12.3. How "axis=0" and "axis=1" work

Let's take another example; this one is easier to see how its effects work. Let's start with an array in which each element is equal to its column number.

```
B = np.fromfunction(lambda r,c: c, (4, 5),
    dtype=np.int32)
```

Printing this array produces

```
[[0 1 2 3 4]
 [0 1 2 3 4]
 [0 1 2 3 4]
 [0 1 2 3 4]]
```

Summing along axis 0 (producing column totals) should give us a multiple of 4 each time. Summing along axis 1 (producing row totals) should give us 10 each time.

And, in fact, that's what we get.

```
>>> np.sum(B, axis = 0)     # row, totaling cols.
array([ 0, 4, 8, 12, 16])
>>> np.sum(B, axis = 1)     # col, totaling rows.
array([10, 10, 10, 10])
```

This is admittedly confusing because `axis=0`, which should refer to rows, actually sums all the dimensions except rows (in this case, columns). And `axis=1` actually sums all the dimensions except columns (in this case, rows).

Can we use this data to produce something like a spreadsheet? What we'd like to do is to total all the rows, for example, and then concatenate the results onto the array, using the results as an additional column.

Let's start by, once again, getting both the starting array and the row-by-two totals.

```
B = np.fromfunction(lambda r,c:c, (4, 5), dtype=np.int32)

B_rows = np.sum(B, axis = 1)
```

Now, can we "glue on" the one-dimensional `B_rows` to the two-dimensional array, B?

Yes, the solution is to use the **c_** operator, as follows:

```
B1 = np.c_[B, B_rows]
```

The array B1 is similar to B, the array we started with, but B1 has an additional column, this one made up of the totals of each row. When printed, it's displayed as

```
[[ 0  1  2  3  4 10]
 [ 0  1  2  3  4 10]
 [ 0  1  2  3  4 10]
 [ 0  1  2  3  4 10]]
```

This is part of a "spreadsheet" display, with the last column representing sums of rows. With a few more lines of code, we can produce a more complete spreadsheet, in which the bottom row contains sums of the columns.

To do this, we get the sums of all the columns of B1. The setting `axis=0` moves along the X axis, getting totals as it moves; therefore, it creates a row containing column totals.

```
B_cols = np.sum(B1, axis = 0)
```

The following statement then glues on the row, along the bottom of B1.

```
B2 = np.r_[B1, [B_cols]]
```

Printing B2 prints the following results:

```
[[ 0  1  2  3  4 10]
 [ 0  1  2  3  4 10]
 [ 0  1  2  3  4 10]
 [ 0  1  2  3  4 10]
 [ 0  4  8 12 16 40]]
```

So there we have it: transformation of an ordinary array into a spreadsheet display that includes totals of all rows and columns along the bottom and the right.

The whole procedure can be placed in a function that will operate on any two-dimensional array.

```
def spreadsheet(A):
    AC = np.sum(A, axis = 1)
    A2 = np.c_[A, AC]
    AR = np.sum(A2, axis = 0)
    return np.r_[A2, [AR] ]
```

For example, suppose you have the following array:

```
>>> arr = np.arange(15).reshape(3, 5)
>>> print(arr)
[[ 0  1  2  3  4]
 [ 5  6  7  8  9]
 [10 11 12 13 14]]
```

Here's what happens if you use the spreadsheet function and print the results:

```
>>> print(spreadsheet(arr))
[[  0   1   2   3   4  10]
 [  5   6   7   8   9  35]
 [ 10  11  12  13  14  60]
 [ 15  18  21  24  27 105]]
```

The spreadsheet function can be altered to print summary statistics for other operations, such as mean, median, standard deviation (**std**), and so on.

Chapter 12 *Summary*

The **numpy** package supports manipulation and statistical analysis of large data sets, with abilities that go far beyond those of standard Python arrays. But this chapter, long though it is, has only begun to explore those abilities.

One simple test of performance speed is to add up a large set of numbers. In the test of adding up all the numbers from 1 to 1 million, the **numpy** version of the program beats the ordinary version by a factor of 10 to 1. But when the benchmark is run on the manipulation of data and not on array creation, the contrast is much greater still.

The **numpy** package provides many ways to create a standard **numpy** array, called an **ndarray**, or an "N-dimensional array." The type is distinguished by the ease with which you can create arrays of more than one dimension.

This **numpy** type has built-in support for statistical analysis, including addition, mean, median, and standard deviation. You can perform these operations on rows, columns, and slices.

Much of the power of the **numpy ndarray** type stems from the ability to take slices of these arrays, either one-dimensional or higher-dimensional, and then perform sophisticated batch operations on them—that is, doing many calculations at once. The slicing ability extends smoothly to any number of dimensions.

This **numpy** type has built-in support for statistical analysis, including addition, mean, median, and standard deviation. You can perform these operations on rows, columns, and slices.

In the next chapter, Chapter 13, we'll explore more advanced capabilities that are built on top of **numpy** standard types (**ndarray**), particularly the ability to plot mathematical equations.

Chapter 12 *Review Questions*

1 What are the advantages, if any, of the built-in **array** package?

2 What are some limitations of the **array** package?

3 State some major differences between the **array** package and **numpy**.

4 Describe the differences between the **empty**, **ones**, and **zeros** functions.

5 What is the role of the callable argument in the **fromfunction** function used to create new arrays?

6 What happens when a **numpy** array is combined with a single-value operand (a scalar, such as an **int** or a floating-point value) through addition, as in the expression A + n?

7 Can combined operation-assign operators (such as **+=** or ***=**) be used in array-to-scalar operation? What is the effect?

8 Can fixed-length strings be included in a **numpy** array? What happens when a string of longer length is assigned to such an array?

9 What happens when two **numpy** arrays are combined through an operation such as addition (**+**) or multiplication (*****)? What requirements must be met to combine two **numpy** arrays?

10 How do you use a Boolean array as a mask for another array?

11 What are three distinct ways, using both standard Python and its packages, to get the standard deviation of a large set of data? Rank the three of them according to execution speed.

12 What is the dimensionality of an array produced by a Boolean mask?

Chapter 12 *Suggested Problems*

1 Revise the benchmarks used in Section 12.4, "Introduction to 'numpy': Sum 1 to 1 Million," so that they measure the creation and summation of the data sets separately—that is, report the relative speeds of Python list creation versus **numpy** array creation, and then report the speeds of adding the numbers together.

2 Use the **numpy.random** package to generate an array of 1,000 ×1,000 random floating-point numbers. Measure the speed of creating this array. Measure the mean and standard deviation of the numbers in this array.

3 Generate an array of random integers between 0 and 99, inclusive. Then, using Boolean arrays, mask out all integers except those meeting any of the following three conditions: N == 1, N is a multiple of 3, or N > 75. Print the results.

4 Generate a 10 × 10 array full of 1's. Then zero out the middle 8 × 8 portion, leaving only the outer regions of the array set to 1. That would include the four corners and the edges. Print the results. (Hint: There is more than one way to do this, but slicing is particularly efficient.)

5 Perform a similar operation for a 5 × 5 × 5 "cube," leaving all visible portions set to 1, while the inner 3 × 3 × 3 cube is zeroed out. Then print the five horizontal planes constituting this cube.

13 Advanced Uses of "numpy"

Your introduction to the world of **numpy** has just begun. One of the most interesting things you can do is plot charts, building on top of **numpy** data types and functions. You'll need to download and import the **matplotlib** package as well as **numpy**.

There are many things you can set, such as color, range, extent, and other factors, but getting started is simple. After covering the plotting capabilities, this chapter examines other advanced uses of the **numpy** package:

▶ Financial applications

▶ Linear algebra: dot products and outer products

▶ Operations on fixed-length records of all kinds

▶ Reading and writing large amounts of data

13.1 Advanced Math Operations with "numpy"

Before you start plotting curves, you'll need to know about the mathematical functions operating on the standard **numpy ndarray** type.

Table 13.1 lists the most common of the functions. These are extremely useful in plotting graphs. Most of them take an array as argument and return an array of the same shape.

Table 13.1. High-Level "numpy" Math Operations

OPERATION	DESCRIPTION
numpy.**cos**(A)	Return the cosine of each element in A, as explained in Chapter 11, "The Random and Math Packages." The input to this function is assumed to be in radians and not degrees. That's assumed for the other trig functions as well.

▼ continued on next page

Table 13.1. High-Level "numpy" Math Operations (*continued*)

OPERATION	DESCRIPTION
numpy.**sin**(*A*)	Return the sine of each element in A. As with **cos**, the results are returned in an array of matching shape.
numpy.**tan**(*A*)	Return the tangent of each element.
numpy.**exp**(*A*)	Return e raised to the power of each element in A.
numpy.**power**(*X*, *Y*)	Raise each element in X by its corresponding value in Y. These two arrays must have the same shape, or one or both must be scalar.
numpy.**radians**(*A* | *x*)	Convert degrees to radians; the argument may be an array of the same shape or may be scalar.
numpy.**abs**(*A*)	Take the absolute value of each element in A.
numpy.**log**(*A*)	Take the natural logarithm of each element in A.
numpy.**log10**(*A*)	Take the logarithm base 10 of each element in A.
numpy.**log2**(*A*)	Take the logarithm base 2 of each element in A.
numpy.**sqrt**(*A*)	Take the square root of each element in A.
numpy.**arccos**(*A*)	Inverse cosine function.
numpy.**arcsin**(*A*)	Inverse sine function.
numpy.**arctan**(*A*)	Inverse tangent function.
numpy.**hcos**(*A*)	Hyperbolic cosine.
numpy.**hsin**(*A*)	Hyperbolic sine.
numpy.**htan**(*A*)	Hyperbolic tangent.
numpy.**append**(*A*, *B*)	Create a new array by appending the contents of array B onto the end of array A.
numpy.**pi**	Get the value of pi.
numpy.**e**	Get the value of e.

These functions have additional arguments. A common argument is the *out* argument, which names an output array in which to place the results. Such an array must match the source array in size and shape. Here's an example:

```
import numpy as np
A = np.linspace(0, np.pi, 10)
B = np.empty(10)
np.sin(A, out=B)
```

This last line puts the results into B. The following statement would have the same effect, except that every time you call it, you allocate a new array. In some cases, it's more efficient to use an existing array to store the results.

```
import numpy as np
A = np.linspace(0, np.pi, 10)
B = np.sin(A)
```

To see all the arguments available to be called for each of these functions, use the **np.info** command.

numpy.**info**(*numpy.function_name*)

For example, the following commands, given from within IDLE, provide manageable chunks of information on specific **numpy** functions:

```
import numpy as np
np.info(np.sin)
np.info(np.cos)
np.info(np.power)
```

Most of the functions listed here are designed to operate on a single **numpy** array. A few functions have variations. The **numpy power** function takes at least two arguments: X and Y. Either or both can be an array; but if they are both arrays, they must have the same shape. The effect of the function is to raise each X value to a power specified by the corresponding element of Y.

For example, the following statements raise each of the elements in array A to the power of 2 (that is, to square each element).

```
>>> import numpy as np
>>> A = np.arange(6)
>>> print(A)
[0 1 2 3 4 5]
>>> print(np.power(A, 2))
[ 0  1  4  9 16 25]
```

Other functions are often used in conjunction with the **numpy linspace** function, which in turn is heavily used in plotting equations, as you'll see in Section 13.3, "Plotting Lines with 'numpy' and 'matplotlib.'"

For example, the following statements combine the **sin** function with the constant, **pi**, to get a series of 10 values that reflects the value of the sine function as its inputs increase from 0 to pi and then decrease back to 0.

```
>>> A = np.linspace(0, np.pi, 10)
>>> B = np.sin(A, dtype='float16')
>>> print(B)
[0.000e+00 3.420e-01 6.431e-01 8.657e-01 9.849e-01
 9.849e-01 8.662e-01 6.431e-01 3.416e-01 9.675e-04]
```

In this example, the data type **float16** was chosen so as to make the numbers easier to print. But a still better way to do that is to use some of the formatting techniques from Chapter 5. Now the results are easier to interpret.

```
>>> B = np.sin(A)
>>> print(' '.join(format(x, '5.3f') for x in B))
0.000 0.342 0.643 0.866 0.985 0.985 0.866 0.643 0.342
0.000
```

This small data sample demonstrates the behavior of the sine function. The sine of 0 is 0, but as the inputs increase toward pi/2, the results approach 1.0; then they approach 0 again as the inputs increase toward pi.

13.2 Downloading "matplotlib"

We can use all this data to plot graphs in Python with the help of **numpy** and another package: **matplotlib**, which has to be downloaded and imported.

The first step in downloading a package is to bring up the DOS Box (Windows) or Terminal application (Macintosh).

As explained in Chapter 12, every Python download should come with the **pip** utility or with **pip3**. Use the **install** command of the **pip** utility. Assuming you're connected to the Internet, the following command directs the utility to download the **matplotlib** software.

```
pip install matplotlib
```

If you use **pip** at the command line and it is not recognized, try using **pip3** (which is the name of the utility when Python 3 is installed on a Macintosh system).

```
pip3 install matplotlib
```

Note ▶ If neither the **pip** nor **pip3** command worked, check how you spelled **matplotlib**. The spelling is tricky. To see the range of commands possible, type

```
pip help
```

◀ Note

13.3 Plotting Lines with "numpy" and "matplotlib"

Now you're ready to have some fun. After **matplotlib** is downloaded, import it.

```
import numpy as np
import matplotlib.pyplot as plt
```

You don't have to give **matplotlib.pyplot** the short name **plt**, but **plt** is widely used and recognized. The full name, **matplotlib.pyplot**, is cumbersome, and most programmers use **plt** by convention.

Two of the major functions used for plotting include **plt.plot** and **plt.show**. The syntax shown here is a simplified view; we'll show more of it later.

```
plt.plot( [X,] Y [,format_str] )
plt.show()
```

In this syntax, square brackets are not intended literally but indicate optional items.

The simplest calls to **plot** usually involve two one-dimensional array arguments: X and Y. Where X is omitted, it's assumed to be the array [0, 1, 2... N-1], where N is the length of Y. But most often, you'll want to include both X and Y arguments.

The action is to take pairs of points from X and Y, in which X and Y are the same length, and to plot them on a graph. Each value in X is matched to the corresponding value in Y to get an (x, y) point. All the points are then plotted and connected.

Here's a simple example, using the **np.linspace** and **np.sin** functions.

```
import numpy as np
import matplotlib.pyplot as plt

A = np.linspace(0, 2 * np.pi)
plt.plot(A, np.sin(A))
plt.show()
```

If you've downloaded both **numpy** and **matplotlib**, and if you enter this code as shown, your computer should display the window shown in Figure 13.1. The window remains visible until you close it.

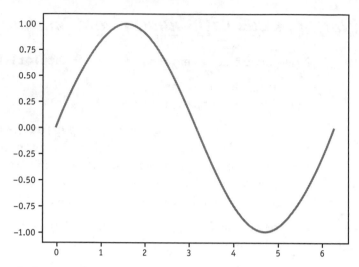

Figure 13.1. A sine graph

This is simple code, but let's step through each part of it. The first thing the example does is import the needed packages.

```
import numpy as np
import matplotlib.pyplot as plt
```

Next, the example calls the **numpy linspace** function. This function, remember, generates a set of values, including the two specified endpoints, to get a total of N evenly spaced values. By default, N is 50.

```
A = np.linspace(0, 2 * np.pi)
```

Therefore, array A contains floating-point numbers beginning with 0, ending in 2 * pi, and 48 other values evenly spaced between these two values.

The call to the **plot** function specifies two arrays: A, which contains 50 values along the X axis, and a second array, which contains the sine of each element in A.

```
plt.plot(A, np.sin(A))
```

The function looks at each element in A and matches it with a corresponding value in the second array, to get 50 (x, y) pairs. Finally, the **show** function tells the software to display the resulting graph onscreen.

We can, of course, just as easily graph the cosine function instead, by deleting the call to **np.sin** and replacing it with **np.cos**.

```
import numpy as np
import matplotlib.pyplot as plt

A = np.linspace(0, 2 * np.pi)
plt.plot(A, np.cos(A))
plt.show()
```

In this version, each value in A is matched with its cosine value to create an (x, y) pair. Figure 13.2 shows the resulting graph.

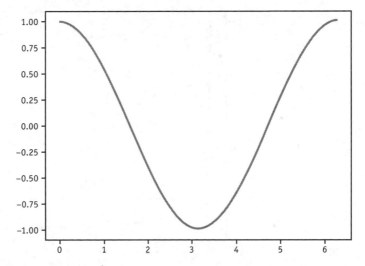

Figure 13.2. A cosine graph

But you aren't limited to trigonometric functions. The flexibility of **numpy** arrays—particularly how they can be operated on as a unit—makes the plotting power of **matplotlib** both simple and versatile.

For example, what if you wanted to plot a graph of the *reciprocal* function—that is, 1/N? If N is 5, its reciprocal is 1/5, and vice versa.

We start by creating a range of values for X. This is why the **np.linspace** function is so useful; it creates a source of values (as many as you want) from the desired domain. Often these values will be monotonically increasing along the X axis.

Starting with the value 0 would be a problem, because then 1/N would cause division by 0. Instead, let's start with the value 0.1 and run to values as high as 10. By default, 50 values are generated.

```
A = np.linspace(0.1, 10)
```

Now it's easy to plot and show the results by using A and 1/A to provide values for the (x, y) pairs. Each value in A gets matched with its reciprocal.

```
plt.plot(A, 1/A)
plt.show()
```

Figure 13.3 shows the results.

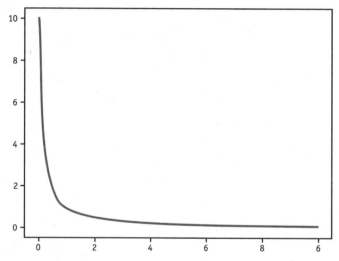

Figure 13.3. Plotting the reciprocal function

The function creates points by combining values from A and 1/A. So, for example, the first (x, y) pair is

```
(0.1, 10.0)
```

The second point is formed in the same way, combining the next value in A with its reciprocal in the second set. Here are some points that could be plotted.

```
(0.1, 10.0), (0.2, 5.0), (0.3, 3.3)...
```

A less interesting, but illustrative, example is to plot a handful of points and connect them. Let's specify five such values:

```
(0, 1)
(1, 2)
```

```
(2, 4)
(3, 5)
(4, 3)
```

The plot for this graph would be created by the following statement:

```
plt.plot([0, 1, 2, 3, 4], [1, 2, 4, 5, 3])
```

If the X argument is omitted, the default is [0, 1, 2, ... N–1], where N is the length of the Y array. Therefore, this example could be written as

```
plt.plot([1, 2, 4, 5, 3])
```

In either case, calling the **show** function puts the graph on screen, as illustrated by Figure 13.4.

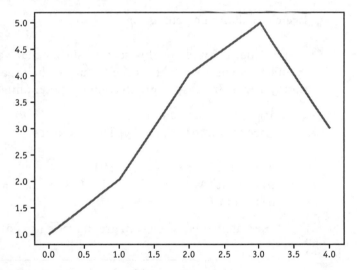

Figure 13.4. A primitive graph of five points

Note that you don't necessarily have to use ascending values. You can use any points to create arbitrary lines. Here's an example:

```
plt.plot([3, 4, 1, 5, 2, 3], [4, 1, 3, 3, 1, 4])
```

The points to be plotted would be

```
(3, 4), (4, 1), (1, 3), (5, 3), (2, 1), (3, 4)
```

Those points, in turn, form a pentagram (more or less), as shown in Figure 13.5. All the points are plotted, and then line segments are drawn between one point and the next.

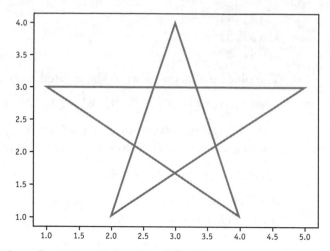

Figure 13.5. Plot of a pentagram

The final example in this section shows that you can graph formulas as complex as you like. This is the beauty of being able to operate directly on **numpy** arrays. It's easy to graph complex polynomials. Here's an example:

```
import numpy as np
import matplotlib.pyplot as plt

A = np.linspace(-15, 20)
plt.plot(A, A ** 3 - (15 * A ** 2) + 25)
plt.show()
```

These statements, when run, graph a polynomial as shown in Figure 13.6.

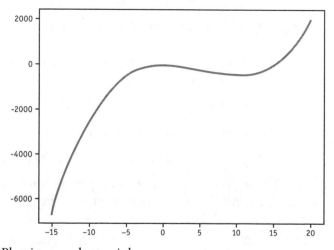

Figure 13.6. Plotting a polynomial

13.4 Plotting More Than One Line

What if you'd like to show more complex graphs, such as a graph that contains both a sine function and a cosine function so you can compare them? This is easy. You can, for example, make two calls to the **plot** function before showing the results.

```
import numpy as np
import matplotlib.pyplot as plt

A = np.linspace(0, 2 * np.pi)
plt.plot(A, np.sin(A))
plt.plot(A, np.cos(A))
plt.show()
```

Alternatively, two **plot** statements could have been combined into one by placing four arguments in a single statement.

```
plt.plot(A, np.sin(A), A, np.cos(A))
```

In either case, Python responds by displaying the graph shown in Figure 13.7.

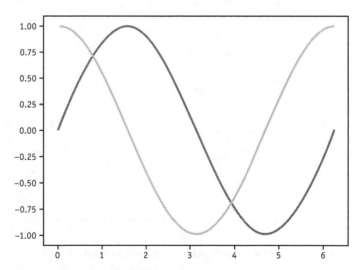

Figure 13.7. Sine and cosine plotted together

The **matplotlib** package automatically plots curves of two different colors: orange and blue. These show up nicely on a computer screen, but in a black-and-white printout, you may not be able to see the difference.

Fortunately, the plotting software provides other ways of differentiating curves through the formatting arguments, which we look at next.

The more complete syntax for the **plot** function is shown here.

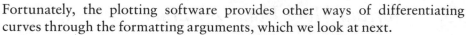

plt.plot(*X1, Y1,* **[***fmt1,***]** *X2, Y2,* **[***fmt2,***]** ... **)**

What this syntax indicates is that you can include any number of X, Y pairs of arrays. From each such pair, a set of (x, y) points is created by combining pairs of corresponding elements. You can then add optional format arguments.

The *fmt* arguments are useful for differentiating lines by giving them contrasting colors and styles. For example, the following **plot** statement causes the plot for the cosine function to consist of small circles.

```
plt.plot(A, np.sin(A), A, np.cos(A), 'o')
plt.show()
```

The sine curve has no format specifier, so it takes on a default appearance. The resulting graph differentiates between the two curves nicely, as you see in Figure 13.8. By default, different colors are assigned to the two lines.

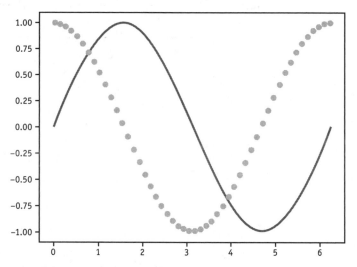

Figure 13.8. Sine and cosine differentiated

This formatting creates a dramatic contrast. But we can create even more of a contrast by specifying a style for the sine curve. The ^ format symbol specifies that the curve will be made up of tiny triangles.

While we're at it, let's bring in another plotting function, **title**. This simple function is used to specify a title for the graph before calling the **show** function. The **xlabel** and **ylabel** functions specify labels for the axes.

```
plt.plot(A, np.sin(A), '^', A, np.cos(A), 'o')
plt.title('Sine and Cosine')
plt.xlabel('X Axis')
plt.ylabel('Y Axis')
plt.show()
```

Figure 13.9 shows the resulting graph, complete with title and axis labels.

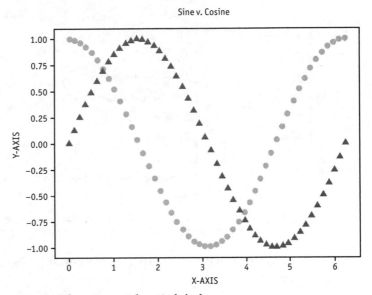

Figure 13.9. Sine and cosine with axis labels

If you get help on the **plt.plot** function, it provides you a reference to all the formatting characters. These characters can be combined in strings such as 'og', meaning "Use small green circles for this line."

The characters used to specify colors are listed in Table 13.2.

Table 13.2. Color Characters in Plot Format Strings

CHARACTER	COLOR
b	Blue
g	Green
r	Red
c	Cyan
m	Magenta
y	Yellow
k	Black
w	White

The characters that specify shapes are shown in Table 13.3.

Table 13.3. Shape Characters in Plotting Format Strings

CHARACTER	SHAPE
.	Points
,	Pixels
o	Circles
v	Down arrow
^	Up arrow
<	Left-pointing arrow
>	Right-pointing arrow
s	Squares
p	Pentagons
*	Stars
h, H	Hexagons (small and large, respectively)
+	Plus signs
d, D	Diamonds (light and heavy, respectively)

Remember that you can specify any combination of color and shape. Here's an example:

```
'b^'        # Use blue triangles.
```

Note ▶ Yet another technique for differentiating between lines is to use labels, along with a legend, to show how the information corresponds to lines of particular color and/or style. This technique is explained in Chapter 15, "Getting Financial Data off the Internet." ◀ Note

13.5 Plotting Compound Interest

Imagine the following scenario. You're going to be given a trust fund in which you have your choice of plans. Plan A would add two dollars every year. But you can't touch the money until you cash out. At that point, you get all the money, and the fund terminates. The two dollars is the only source of increase.

Alternatively, under plan B, the same conditions apply, except that instead of two dollars being added to the fund every year, plan B starts with one dollar and then it increases by 10 percent a year.

It would seem the choice is easy. One fund increases by two dollars a year, while the other increases—at least in the beginning—by only 10 cents. Obviously, plan A is better, isn't it? It's 20 times as good!

But plan A grows at a constant rate, while plan B compounds. Every good mathematician, as well as accountant, should know the following.

✱ **Exponential growth (such as compound interest), however slow, must eventually overtake linear growth, however fast.**

This is an amazing fact, especially when you consider that it implies that compound growth of .001% on a single dollar must eventually overtake a steady income of a million a year! This is quite true, by the way, but it would take lifetimes for the compounding fund to overtake the million-dollar fund.

This dynamic is easy to show with a graph. Start by creating a **numpy** array, A, representing values along an axis of time. Set it to measure the passing of 60 years.

```
A = np.linspace(0, 60, 60)
```

Then we plot a linear-growth function of $2 a year versus a compound-growth function using 10 percent a year—which is mathematically equivalent of raising the number 1.1 to a power, N, where N is the number of years.

```
2 * A       # Formula for increase of $2 a year
1.1 ** A    # Formula for growth of 10% a year
```

We'll use a format string to specify that the first curve is made of little circles, for the sake of contrast ("o").

```
plt.plot(A, 2 * A, 'o', A, 1.1 ** A)
```

Alternatively, the two curves could be created by separate statements—with additional spaces inserted here for clarity's sake.

```
plt.plot(A,  2 * A,  'o')  # +$2 a year (with circles)
plt.plot(A,  1.1 ** A)     # Compound 10% a year
```

Next, let's specify some useful labels and finally show the graph.

```
plt.title('Compounded Interest v. Linear')
plt.xlabel('Years')
plt.ylabel('Value of Funds')
plt.show()
```

Figure 13.10 displays the results. For the first 30 years, the linear fund ($2 a year) outpaces the compound fund. However, between years 30 and 50, the accelerating growth of plan B becomes noticeable. Plan B finally equals and surpasses the linear fund shortly before year 50.

Compounded Interest v. Linear

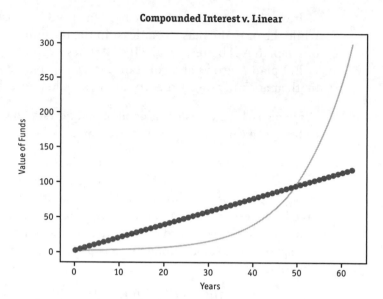

Figure 13.10. Compound growth plotted against linear

So if you have 50 years to wait, plan B is the better choice. Eventually, plan B greatly outperforms plan A if you can wait long enough. The compound growth will reach thousands, even millions, of dollars long before the other plan does.

Note ▶ The labels along the X axis start in year 0 and run to year 60. Section 13.12, "Adjusting Axes with 'xticks' and 'yticks'," shows how these years could be relabeled—for example, by starting in the year 2020 and running to the year 2080—without changing any of the underlying data or calculations.

◀ Note

13.6 Creating Histograms with "matplotlib"

Histograms provide an alternative way of looking at data. Instead of presenting individual data points and connecting them, a *histogram* shows how frequently the results fall into subranges.

The data is collected into buckets, or *bins*, each bin representing a range. We did that manually for some of the problems in Chapter 11, "The Random and Math Packages," but the **numpy** and **matlibplot** packages do this work automatically.

Let's start with a simple example. Suppose you have a list containing the IQ of each person on your software development team. You'd like to see which scores tend to be the most common.

```
IQ_list = [91, 110, 105, 107, 135, 127,  92, 111, 105,
      106, 130, 145, 145, 128, 109, 108,  98, 129, 100,
      108, 114, 119,  99, 137, 142, 145, 112, 113 ]
```

It's easy to convert this Python list into a **numpy** array. First, however, we'll make sure we've imported the necessary packages.

```
import numpy as np
import matplotlib.pyplot as plt

IQ_A = np.array(IQ_list)
```

Graphing this data as a histogram is the easiest step of all, because it requires only one argument. The **hist** function produces this chart. Then, as usual, the **show** function must be called to actually put the results onscreen.

```
plt.hist(IQ_A)
plt.show()
```

Wow, that was easy! There are some additional arguments, but they're optional.

One of the main reasons for providing the **show** function, by the way, is so that the graph can be tweaked in various ways before being displayed onscreen. The following example creates the histogram, gives it a title, and finally shows it.

```
plt.hist(IQ_A)
plt.title('IQ Distribution of Development Team.')
plt.show()
```

Figure 13.11 displays the resulting graph.

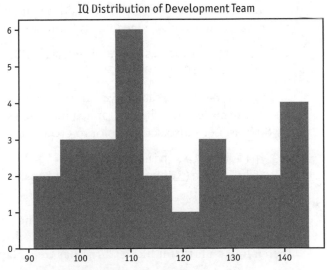

Figure 13.11. IQ scores shown in a histogram

This graph reveals a good deal of information. It shows that the frequency of IQ scores increases until 110, at which point it drops off. There's a bulge again around 140.

A more complete syntax is shown here.

```
plt.hist(A [, bins=10] [, keyword_args] )
```

The first argument, *A*, refers to a **numpy** array and is the only required argument.

The *bins* argument determines the number of subranges, or bins. The default setting is 10, which means that the function determines the difference between the highest and lowest values and divides by 10 to get the size of each subrange. But you can specify settings other than 10.

```
plt.hist(A, bins=50)    # Place results into 50 bins.
```

Other keyword arguments accepted by this function include **color**, which takes a string containing one of the characters shown in Table 13.2; **align**, which takes one of the values 'left', 'right', or 'mid'; and **cumulative**, which is a Boolean that indicates cumulative results are to be graphed. For more information, use help.

```
>>> help(plt.hist)
```

Another use of histograms is to graph a normal distribution curve. We showed how to do this in Chapter 11, but the approach here gives even better results.

We start by using the **numpy** randomization package to generate 200,000 data points in a normal distribution. This distribution has a mean of 0.0 and a standard deviation of 1.0. But by adding and multiplying, we can convert to an array of values with a mean of 100 and a standard deviation of 10.

```
A = np.random.standard_normal(200000)
A = A * 10 + 100
```

In graphing these results, we can rely on the default setting of 10 bins, but results are more satisfying if graphed into even smaller subranges. So we specify 80 bins. Let's also set the color to green while we're at it.

```
plt.hist(A, bins=80, color='g')
plt.title('Normal Distribution in 80 Bins')
plt.show()
```

The result is an appealing-looking normal-distribution graph, shown in Figure 13.12. If you can see it in green (as it is displayed on a computer screen), then it looks a little bit like a Christmas tree. Happy holidays!

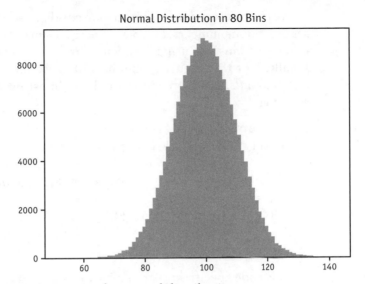

Figure 13.12. Histogram of a normal distribution

You might wonder: Can you present this data as a completely smooth line rather than as a series of bars?

You can. **numpy** provides a **histogram** function that enables you to generate frequency numbers for a series of subranges (bins). The general syntax, shown here, displays the two most important arguments.

```
plt.histogram(A [, bins=10] [, keyword_args] )
```

The action of the function is to produce a new array; this array contains the result of the histogram. Each element in this new array is a frequency number corresponding to one of the bins. By default, the number of bins is 10. So for the resulting array:

▶ The first element contains the number of values from A that occur in the first bin (the first subrange).

▶ The second element contains the number of values from A that occur in the second bin (the second subrange).

▶ And so on.

The value returned is actually a tuple. The first element of this tuple contains the frequency numbers we want to plot. The second element contains the exact edges of the bin. So, to get the data we need, use the following syntax:

```
plt.histogram(A, bins)[0]
```

We can now generate a smooth normal-distribution curve. Generate a large set of random numbers, and place the results in 50 bins. (You can pick another number of bins, but using between 50 and 100 tends to produce good results.) Finally, plot the frequency numbers of those bins. This example employs *2 million trials*, but there still should be almost no noticeable delay, which is amazing.

```
import numpy as np
import matplotlib.pyplot as plt

A = np.random.standard_normal(2000000)
A = A * 10 + 100
B = np.histogram(A, 50)[0]
plt.plot(B)
plt.show()
```

This code specifies no argument for the "X-axis" array; instead, it's handled by default. The plotting software uses 0, 1, 2 . . . N–1 for the X coordinates, where N is the length of the B array, which contains the result of the **histogram** function.

Figure 13.13 shows the results produced by this example.

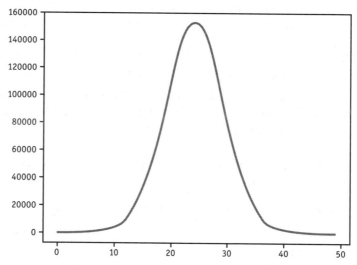

Figure 13.13. Smooth drawing of a normal distribution curve

The resulting figure is a smooth, pleasing curve. The X axis, however, may not be what you expect. The numbers along the X axis show the bin numbers.

13

The range consists of the lowest random number generated to the highest; this range is then divided into 50 parts. The Y axis shows the frequency of hits in each bin.

But instead of placing the bin numbers along the X axis, it's more useful to display values from the distribution itself. The simplest *correct* way to do that is to use "X-axis" values that represent the median points of each bin. The next example does that by using the second array returned by **np.histogram**. That array contains the edges of the bins—that is, the lowest value of the sub-range represented by each bin.

That may sound complicated, but it's only a matter of adding a couple of lines of code. In this case, X represents the edges of the bins—and then X is modified to contain the median point of those bins. In this way, the frequencies get plotted against values in the distribution (centered at 100) rather than bin numbers.

```
import numpy as np
import matplotlib.pyplot as plt

A = np.random.standard_normal(2000000)
A = A * 10 + 100
B, X = np.histogram(A, 50)
X = (X[1:]+X[:-1])/2   # Use bin centers rather than edges.
plt.plot(X, B)         # Plot against values rather than
plt.show()             #   bin numbers.
```

The X values are calculated by getting the median value of each subrange—by taking the bottom and top edges (which are one off in position) and averaging them. The expression X[1:] shifts one position, because it starts with the second element. The expression X[:-1] excludes the last element to make the lengths equal.

```
X = (X[1:]+X[:-1])/2   # Use bin centers rather than edges
```

If you look at the revised plot of the histogram (Figure 13.14), you can see it plots values centered at 100 with a standard deviation of 10. A standard deviation of 10 means that roughly 95 percent of the area of the curve should fall within two deviations (80 to 120), and more than 99 percent of the area should fall within three standard deviations (70 to 130).

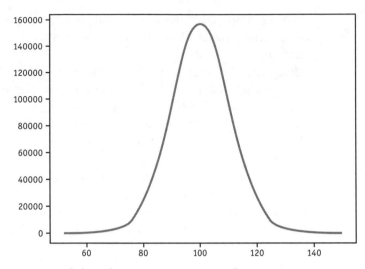

Figure 13.14. Normal distribution curve centered at 100

The **histogram** function has other uses. For example, you can use it to replace some of the code in Chapter 11, demonstrating the Law of Large Numbers. The example in that section collected data in a series of bins. The **histogram** function does the same thing as the code in that section but does it many times as fast.

Performance Tip ▶ You should observe through this chapter and Chapter 12 that many **numpy** functions echo actions that can be performed in Chapter 11, "The Random and Math Packages," by importing **random** and **math**. But the **numpy** versions, especially with large data sets (such as the 2,000,000 random numbers generated for the most recent examples) will be many times as fast.

So when you have a choice, prefer to use **numpy**, including its **random** sub-package, for large numeric operations.

◀ Performance Tip

Some of the other arguments are occasionally useful. To learn about all of them, you can get help from within IDLE.

```
>>> np.info(np.histogram)
```

13.7 Circles and the Aspect Ratio

Sometimes you'll want to adjust the relative size of the X and Y axes; this is especially true when you draw a geometric shape. In this section, we'll show how to draw a circle. Usually, you don't want it to look like an ellipse, so we'll adjust the aspect ratio between X and Y to be equal before showing the graph.

There's more than one way to draw a circle; the other way is left as an exercise for the end of the chapter. In this section, we'll use an approach utilizing trig functions. Imagine a little bug traveling around the outside of a circle, starting at 0 degrees at the coordinate (1,0), as shown in Figure 13.15. The bug continues until it's made a complete trip.

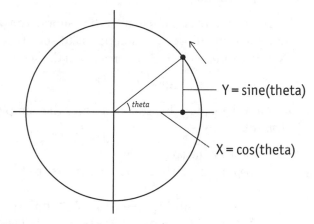

Figure 13.15. "Bug on a circle" about 42 degrees

Each point on the circle corresponds to an angle, which we call *theta*. For example, the point on the circle that is 90 degrees counterclockwise from the starting point has a value of 90 degrees—or rather, the equivalent in radians (pi / 2). Figure 13.15 shows the bug having traveled about 42 degrees (roughly equal to 0.733 radians).

At each point on the circle, the X coordinate of the bug's position is given by

```
cosine(theta)
```

Likewise, the Y coordinate of the bug's position is given by

```
sine(theta)
```

By tracking the bug's journey, we get a set of points corresponding to a trip around the circle. Each point on this journey corresponds to the following (x, y) coordinates:

```
(cosine(theta), sine(theta))
```

Therefore, to graph a complete circle, we get a set of points corresponding to many angles on this imaginary trip, from 0 to 2 * pi (equal to 360 degrees). Then we graph the resulting (x, y) pairs. And we'll get 1,000 data points to get a nice, smooth curve.

```
import numpy as np
import matplotlib.pyplot as plt

theta = np.linspace(0, 2 * np.pi, 1000)
plt.plot(np.cos(theta), np.sin(theta))
plt.show()
```

If you run these statements, they should draw a circle, but the result looks more like an ellipse. The solution is to specify a **plt.axis** setting that forces X and Y units to be equally spaced on the screen.

```
plt.axis('equal')
```

Now, let's plug this statement into the complete application, including the **import** statements.

```
import numpy as np
import matplotlib.pyplot as plt

theta = np.linspace(0, 2 * np.pi, 1000)
plt.plot(np.cos(theta), np.sin(theta))
plt.axis('equal')
plt.show()
```

Now the code produces the perfect circle onscreen, as shown in Figure 13.16.

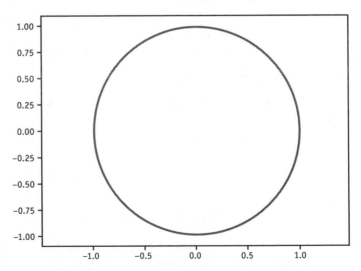

Figure 13.16. A perfect circle

13.8 Creating Pie Charts

The versatility of the **numpy** and **matplotlib** packages extends even to pie charts. This is an effective way of illustrating the relative size of several pieces of data.

The syntax for the **plt.pie** function is shown here. As with other plotting functions, there are other arguments, but only the most important are shown here.

plt.pie(*array_data*, *labels=***None**, *colors=***None***)*

The first argument, *array_data*, is a collection containing a relative size for each category. The *labels* argument is a collection of strings that label the corresponding groups referred to in the first argument. The *colors* argument is a collection of strings specifying color, using the values listed earlier in Table 13.2. And all the collections must have the same length.

This is a simple function to use once you see an example. Suppose you have data on the off-hours activities of your development team, and you want to see a chart. Table 13.4 summarizes the data to be charted in this example.

Table 13.4. Weekly Activity of Development Team

ACTIVITY	HOURS PER WEEK (AVERAGE)	COLOR
Poker	3.7	black ('k')
Chess	2.5	green ('g')
Comic books	1.9	red ('r')
Exercise	0.5	cyan ('c')

It's an easy matter to place each column of data into its own list. Each list has exactly four members in this case.

```
A_data   = [3.7, 2.5, 1.9, 0.5]
A_labels = ['Poker', 'Chess', 'Comic Books', 'Exercise']
A_colors = ['k', 'g', 'r', 'c']
```

Now we plug these figures in to a pie-chart plot, add a title, and display. The aspect ratio of the pie chart can be fixed using a **plt.axis('equal')** statement, just as we did for the circle; otherwise, the pie will appear as an ellipse rather than a circle.

```
import numpy as np
import matplotlib.pyplot as plt
```

```
plt.pie(A_data, labels=A_labels, colors=A_colors)
plt.title('Relative Hobbies of Dev. Team')
plt.axis('equal')
plt.show()
```

Figure 13.17 shows the resulting pie chart.

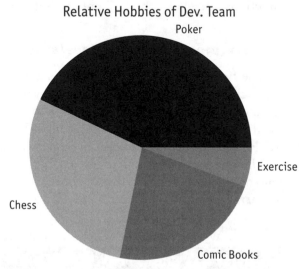

Figure 13.17. A pie chart

13.9 Doing Linear Algebra with "numpy"

Before wrapping up these two chapters on the **numpy** package, we'll take a look at one of the most useful areas, at least to a mathematician or engineer: linear algebra, which often involves vectors (arrays) and matrixes (multidimensional arrays).

It isn't necessary to use separate "vector" or "matrix" collection types with **numpy**. You don't even need to download or import new subpackages. You just apply the appropriate functions.

13.9.1 The Dot Product

As these last two chapters have shown, you can multiply arrays with scalars, and arrays with arrays. The requirement in the second case is that two arrays multiplied together must have the same shape. We can summarize this relationship as follows:

```
(A, B) * (A, B) => (A, B)
```

You can multiply an array of shape A, B to another array of shape A, B and get a third array of the same shape. But with **numpy**, you can also multiply arrays together by using the dot-product function, **dot**, but it has slightly more complex rules.

numpy.**dot**(*A, B, out*=**None**)

A and B are two arrays to be combined to form a dot product; the *out* argument, if specified, is an array of the correct shape in which to store the results. The "correct shape" depends on the size of A and B, as explained here.

The dot product of two one-dimensional arrays is simple. The two arrays must have the same length. The action is to multiply each element in A to its corresponding element in B, and then sum those products, producing a single scalar value.

```
D. P. = A[0]*B[0] + A[1]*B[1] + ... + A[N-1] * B[N-1]
```

Here's an example:

```
>>> import numpy as np
>>> A = np.ones(5)
>>> B = np.arange(5)
>>> print(A, B)
[1. 1. 1. 1. 1.] [0 1 2 3 4]
>>> np.dot(A, A)
5.0
>>> np.dot(A, B)
10.0
>>> np.dot(B, B)
30
```

You should be able to see that the dot product of B with B is equal to 30, because that product is equal to the sum of the squares of its members:

```
D. P. = 0*0 + 1*1 + 2*2 + 3*3 + 4*4
      = 0 + 1 + 4 + 9 + 16
      = 30
```

We can generalize this:

```
D. P.(A, A) = sum(A * A)
```

The dot product between a couple of two-dimensional arrays is more complex. As with ordinary multiplication between arrays, the shapes must be compatible. However, they need only match in one of their dimensions.

Here is the general pattern that describes how a dot product works with two-dimensional arrays:

```
(A, B) * (B, C) => (A, C)
```

Consider the following 2 × 3 array, combined with a 3 × 2 array, whose dot product is a 2 × 2 array.

```
A = np.arange(6).reshape(2,3)
B = np.arange(6).reshape(3,2)
C = np.dot(A, B)
print(A, B, sep='\n\n')
print('\nDot product:\n', C)

[[0 1 2]
 [3 4 5]]

[[0 1]
 [2 3]
 [4 5]]

Dot product:
 [[10 13]
 [28 40]]
```

Here's the procedure.

▶ Multiply each item in the first row of A by each corresponding item in the first column of B. Get the sum (10). This becomes C[0,0].

▶ Multiply each item in the first row of A by each corresponding item in the second column of B. Get the sum (13). This becomes C[0,1].

▶ Multiply each item in the second row of A by each corresponding item in the first column of B. Get the sum (28). This becomes C[1,0].

▶ Multiply each item in the second row of A by each corresponding item in the second column of B. Get the sum (40). This becomes C[1,1].

You can also take the dot product of a one-dimensional array combined with a two-dimensional array. The result is that the array shapes are evaluated as if they had the following shapes:

```
(1, X) * (X, Y) => (1, Y)
```

For example, you could take the dot product of [10, 15, 30] and the following array, which we'll call B:

```
[[0 1]
 [2 3]
 [4 5]]
```

This next statement shows the dot product between a one-dimensional array and the two-dimensional array, B. The resulting dot product has a shape of (1, 2):

```
>>> print(np.dot([10, 15, 30], B))
[150, 205]
```

Can we come up with intuitive, real-world examples that show the usefulness of a dot product? They abound in certain kinds of math and physics, such as three-dimensional geometry. But there are simpler applications. Let's say you own a pet shop that sells three kinds of exotic birds. Table 13.5 shows the prices.

Table 13.5. Prices for Birds in Pet Shop

PARROTS	MACAWS	PEACOCKS
$10	$15	$30

Let's further suppose that you have tracked sales figures for two months, as shown in Table 13.6.

Table 13.6. Monthly Sales Figures for Birds

BIRDS	OCTOBER SALES	NOVEMBER SALES
Parrots	0	1
Macaws	2	3
Peacocks	4	5

What you'd like to do is get the total bird sales for these two months. Although it's not difficult to pick out the data, it's easier to take the dot product and let the function **np.dot** do all the math for you.

Figure 13.18 shows how to obtain the first element in the result: 150. Multiply each of the sales figures by the corresponding sales figure for the first month.

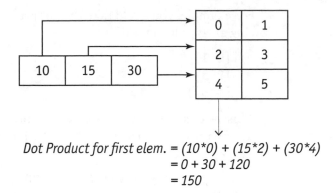

Dot Product for first elem. = (10*0) + (15*2) + (30*4)
= 0 + 30 + 120
= 150

Figure 13.18. How a dot product is calculated, part I

Following this procedure, you get 0 + 30 + 120, totaling 150.

You can obtain the other figure, 205, in the same way (see Figure 13.19). Multiply each of the prices by the corresponding sales figure in the second month, and then total. Following that procedure, you get 10 + 45 + 150, totaling 205.

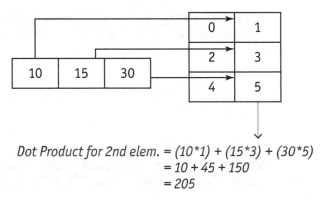

Dot Product for 2nd elem. = (10*1) + (15*3) + (30*5)
= 10 + 45 + 150
= 205

Figure 13.19. How a dot product is calculated, part II

The full dot product is therefore

```
[150, 205]
```

In this case, the dot product gives the total sales figures for all birds, in each of the two months tracked (October and November).

13.9.2 The Outer-Product Function

Another way of multiplying arrays is to use the **outer** function to calculate the *outer product*. This is most often used between two one-dimensional arrays to produce a two-dimensional array. If this function is used on higher-dimensional arrays, the input in each of those arrays is flattened into one dimension.

> numpy.outer(A, B, out=None)

The action of the function is to calculate the outer product of arrays A and B and return it. The **out** argument, if included, specifies a destination array in which to place the results. It must already exist and be of the proper size.

To obtain the outer product, multiply each element of A by each element of B, in turn, to produce a two-dimensional array. In terms of shape, here's how we'd express the relationship:

```
(A) * (B) => (A, B)
```

Simply put, the outer product contains every combination of A * B, so that if C is the result, then C[x, y] contains A[x] multiplied by B[y].

Here's a relatively simple example:

```
>>> import numpy as np
>>> A = np.array([0, 1, 2])
>>> B = np.array([100, 200, 300, 400])
>>> print(np.outer(A, B))
  [[  0   0   0   0]
   [100 200 300 400]
   [200 400 600 800]]
```

In this example, the first element of A is multiplied by each element of B to produce the first row of the result; that's why every number in that row is 0, because 0 multiplied by any value is 0. The second element of A (which is 1) is multiplied by each element of B to produce the second row, and so on for the third row.

One obvious use for the outer product is a problem we solved in Chapter 11, "The Random and Math Packages": how to create a multiplication table. The **numpy** package supports an even simpler solution, and one that is faster in any case.

```
>>> A = np.arange(1,10)
>>> print(np.outer(A, A))
```

Wow, that's pretty simple code! The result is

```
[[ 1  2  3  4  5  6  7  8  9]
 [ 2  4  6  8 10 12 14 16 18]
 [ 3  6  9 12 15 18 21 24 27]
 [ 4  8 12 16 20 24 28 32 36]
```

```
[ 5 10 15 20 25 30 35 40 45]
[ 6 12 18 24 30 36 42 48 54]
[ 7 14 21 28 35 42 49 56 63]
[ 8 16 24 32 40 48 56 64 72]
[ 9 18 27 36 45 54 63 72 81]]
```

As in Chapter 11, we can use some string operations to clean up the result, eliminating the square brackets.

```
s = str(np.outer(A, A))
s = s.replace('[', '')
s = s.replace(']', '')
print(' ' + s)
```

We can, if we choose, combine these four statements into two, more compact, statements.

```
s = str(np.outer(A, A))
print(' ' + s.replace('[', '').replace(']', ''))
```

Finally, this produces

```
1  2  3  4  5  6  7  8  9
2  4  6  8 10 12 14 16 18
3  6  9 12 15 18 21 24 27
4  8 12 16 20 24 28 32 36
5 10 15 20 25 30 35 40 45
6 12 18 24 30 36 42 48 54
7 14 21 28 35 42 49 56 63
8 16 24 32 40 48 56 64 72
9 18 27 36 45 54 63 72 81
```

13.9.3 Other Linear Algebra Functions

In addition to dot product and outer product, **numpy** provides other linear-algebra functions. Remember, they require no separate "matrix" type. The standard **numpy** array type, **ndarray**, can be used with any of these functions.

But the list of the functions related to linear algebra is a long one and requires an entire book of its own. For more explanation, see the official online documentation at

https://docs.scipy.org/doc/numpy/reference/routines.linalg.html

Table 13.7 summarizes some of the more common linear and higher-math functions supported by numpy.

Table 13.7. Common Linear-Algebra Functions

SYNTAX	DESCRIPTION
np.**dot**(A, B [,*out*])	Compute the dot product between *A* and *B*.
np.**vdot**(A, B)	Compute the vector dot product.
np.**outer**(A, B [,*out*])	Compute the outer product formed by multiplying each element in *A* by each element in *B*. Flatten *A* and *B* into one-dimensional inputs as needed.
np.**inner**(A, B [,*out*])	Compute the inner product of *A* and *B*.
np.**tensordot**(A, B [,*out*])	Compute the tensor dot product of *A* and *B*.
np.**kron**(A, B)	Compute the Kronecker product of *A* and *B*.
np.**linalg.det**(A)	Compute the linear-algebra determinant of *A*.

13.10 Three-Dimensional Plotting

The subject of three-dimensional plotting is advanced, and to fully present the subject here would take a long book by itself! However, by looking at the plotting of the surface of a sphere, you can get an idea how **numpy** functions you've already seen help you create three-dimensional surfaces.

The following example requires the importing of packages you're already familiar with, but it also includes the **mpl_toolkits** package. Fortunately, if you've downloaded the other packages, this package has been downloaded for you, so all you have to do is import it.

```
from mpl_toolkits.mplot3d import Axes3D
import matplotlib.pyplot as plt
import numpy as np

fig = plt.figure()
ax = fig.add_subplot(111, projection='3d')

# Make data
ua = np.linspace(0, 2 * np.pi, 100)
va = np.linspace(0, np.pi, 100)
X = 10 * np.outer(np.cos(ua), np.sin(va))
Y = 10 * np.outer(np.sin(ua), np.sin(va))
Z = 10 * np.outer(np.ones(np.size(ua)), np.cos(va))

# Plot the surface
ax.plot_surface(X, Y, Z, color='w')
plt.show()
```

Most of the calculation here involves getting the sine and cosine of angles as they run from 0 to 2 * np.pi and then multiplying the results by taking outer products. Finally, a set of three-dimensional points are described by the three arrays X, Y, and Z, and the software graphs the surface of the sphere from that. Figure 13.20 shows the resulting graph.

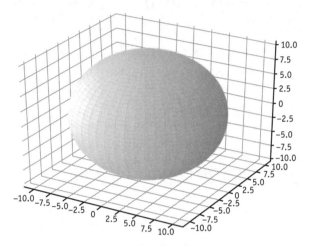

Figure 13.20. Three-dimensional projection of a sphere

13.11 "numpy" Financial Applications

The **numpy** package's powerful range of functions extends to the area of finance. For example, given data about interest rates and payment schedules, you can use the **pmt** function to determine your monthly payment for a house or car.

numpy.**pmt**(*rate*, *nper*, *pv* [, *fv*] [, *when*])

The *rate* is the interest rate expressed as a floating-point number rather than a percentage. For example, a rate of 0.065 would amount to an interest rate of 6.5 percent. Because this is the rate for each individual payment period, you'd need to divide by 12 to get the monthly interest rate from the yearly rate.

The *nper* argument is the total number of payment periods. You need to multiply the number of years by 12 if the payments are to be monthly rather than yearly.

The *pv* argument is the present value. This is the amount of money being borrowed.

The optional arguments include *fv*, the expected future value (which assumes that this money would be paid back at the end). Another optional argument is *when*, which can optionally take the value 1 or 0 to indicate whether a payment is due at the beginning or end of the payment period, respectively.

Assume the following data:

▶ The interest rate is 6.5 percent. Divide by 12 to get monthly interest.

▶ The loan is for 20 years. Multiply by 12 to get the number of monthly payments.

▶ The amount borrowed is $250,000.

Given this data, we can easily use the **numpy pmt** function to determine the monthly payment that will be required.

```
>>> import numpy as np
>>> np.pmt(0.065 / 12, 20 * 12, 250000)
-1863.93283878775
```

Therefore, the monthly payment, rounded to the nearest cent, is $1,863.93. This amount is expressed as a negative number, because it represents the net cash flow.

We can write a function enabling the user to tweak the interest rate, years, and amount to determine the monthly payment, as follows.

```
import numpy as np
def monthly_payment():
    '''Calculate monthly payment, after
    getting input data and calling np.pmt.'''

    # Calculate monthly rate.
    s = 'Enter rate as a yearly percentage fig.: '
    rate = (float(input(s)) / 100) / 12

    # Calculate no. of periods
    nyears = int(input('Enter number of years: '))
    nper = nyears * 12

    # Get loan amount.
    pv = float(input('Enter amount of loan: '))

    # Print results
    payment= -1 * np.pmt(rate, nper, pv)
    print('The monthly payment is: $%.2f' % payment)
```

Here's a sample session:

```
>>> monthly_payment()
Enter rate as a yearly percentage fig.: 5.0
Enter number of years: 30
Enter amount of loan: 155000
The monthly payment is: $832.07
```

Therefore, given an annual interest rate of 5 percent on a 30-year loan of $155,000, the monthly payment is $832.07.

The **numpy** functions also calculate which portion of the monthly payment goes to paying down the principal versus paying the interest. Those two amounts, which together equal the monthly payment, are determined by the functions shown here.

$numpy$.**ppmt**($rate$, per, $nper$, pv [, fv] [, $when$])
$numpy$.**ipmt**($rate$, per, $nper$, pv [, fv] [, $when$])

The additional argument here is per, which specifies which payment period we're currently in, in which the payment periods run from 0 to $nper$–1. The $nper$ argument still specifies the total number of these payment periods.

We can combine one of these functions, **ppmt**, with the calculation of the total payment, to plot a graph showing what percentage of the total monthly payment, over time, is applied to principal as opposed to interest.

```
import numpy as np
import matplotlib.pyplot as plt

# Set up basic parameters
rate = 0.05 / 12      # Assume 5% a year.
nper = 30 * 12        # Assume 30 years on loan.
pv = 155000           # $155,000 is amount of loan.

# Generate total payment
Total = -1 * np.pmt(rate, nper, pv)

# Plot each month's payment (A) as a ratio of Total
A = np.linspace(0, nper)
B = -1 * np.ppmt(rate, A, nper, pv) / Total
plt.plot(A, B)

# Set labels of axes, and display
plt.xlabel('Months')
plt.ylabel('Percentage Applied to Principal')
plt.show()
```

Figure 13.21 shows the results. In the beginning of the loan's lifetime, only a small portion is applied to the principal; the rest goes to interest. But as the loan matures, the percentage of the monthly payment applied to principal approaches 100 percent.

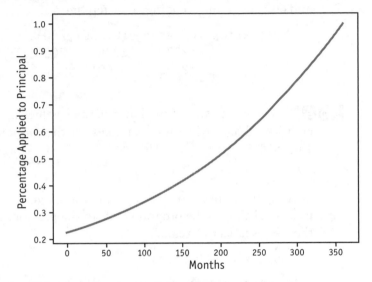

Figure 13.21. Plot of payments applied to principal

13.12 Adjusting Axes with "xticks" and "yticks"

Figure 13.21 in the previous section was a good first attempt at a financial plot, but it lacks a couple of features.

First, the Y axis has ticks that run from 0.2 to 1.0. It would be more illustrative if the axis ran the full distance from 0 to 1. It would be more useful still to see the axis ticks labeled with percentages, as in "0%" to "100%".

Second, the X axis has ticks corresponding to months but it would be more useful for them to mark off years. It might be even better to use labels for those years so that they start with year 2020 and go forward to 2050. We're assuming the loan starts being serviced in the year 2020.

The **xticks** and **yticks** functions solve these problems. Both functions take two arguments. The first specifies a series of data points to be ticked off. The second argument specifics a series of labels to use at each point. (If there are more labels than ticks, the excess labels are ignored.)

For the Y axis, we want to specify ticks every 0.2 units but start at 0.0 rather than 0.2, and then label those units as percentage figures. Remember that the inputs of the **arange** function give beginning, ending, and step figures.

```
plt.yticks(np.arange(0.0, 1.1, 0.2),
           ('0', '20%', '40%','60%', '80%', '100%'))
```

For the X axis, we want to tick off every 60 months (five years) rather than the default, which is every 50 months. Here the inputs to **arange** are 0, 361, and 60 as beginning, ending, and step figures.

```
plt.xticks(np.arange(0, 361, 60),
           ('2020', '2025', '2030', '2035', '2040',
            '2045', '2050') )
```

Note ▶ The **np.arange** function generates values *up to but not including* the endpoint. That's why these examples use the endpoints 1.1 and 361 instead of 1.0 and 360.

◀ **Note**

All that you need to do now is add these two statements (**plt.yticks** and **plt.xtticks**) to the program code in the previous section. Let's also change the X-axis label to "Years."

```
plt.xlabel('Years')
```

Now Figure 13.22 produces a nice-looking result.

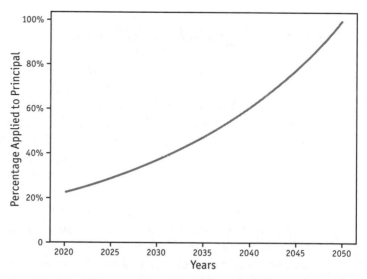

Figure 13.22. Plot of payments with "xticks" and "yticks" adjustments

This is an interesting function to graph, because it increases a little slowly at first but then accelerates later.

13.13 "numpy" Mixed-Data Records

You can store other data in a **numpy** array—even store text strings—just as you can in a Python list. There is a difference, however, in that **numpy** arrays can store strings only as a part of fixed-length structures.

When you work with arrays of strings, **numpy** imposes a fixed length if you don't, based on the longest string. Here's an example:

```
>>> Words = np.array(('To', 'be', 'orNotToBe'))
>>> Words
array(['To', 'be', 'orNotToBe'], dtype='<U9')
```

What this example tells us is that Words has been created as an array with three members, each a string in which the type is U9. Therefore, each element is exactly large enough to hold Python strings, each of which can hold at most nine characters.

You can always assign a string value that's shorter than nine characters. But if you attempt to assign a longer string, it's truncated to nine characters in this case.

```
>>> Words[0] = 'My uncle is Caesar.'
>>> Words[0]
'My uncle '
```

However, you can optionally specify a longer maximum length for strings, such as 20.

```
>>> Words = np.array(('To', 'be', 'orNotToBe'),
            dtype = 'U20')
```

In this example, the length of `'orNotToBe'` would determine the maximum string length by default, but instead the length was specifically determined by `'U20'`. Now you can assign a longer string to an element without its being truncated.

```
>>> Words[0] = 'My uncle is Caesar.'
>>> Words[0]
'My uncle is Caesar.'
```

Before we leave the topic of strings, note that **U***n* denotes a Unicode string, which accepts standard Python strings. **S***n* denotes **bytes** strings.

Very often, when handling large amounts of information, you'll want to store records that combine numeric and string data. To do that with **numpy** arrays, you'll need to create structured arrays, storing a combination of data types. The *dtype* field enables you to create such structures by using a *name* to identify each field.

```
dtype = [(name1, format1), (name2, format2) ...)]
```

Each of the name and format specifiers is a Python string, and each is useful, as you'll see. Here's an example:

```
>>> X = np.array([(12, 33, 'Red'),
                  (0, 1, 'Blue'),
                  (27, 103, 'Yellow'),
                  (-1, -2, 'Blue') ],
      dtype = [('a', 'i4'), ('b', 'i4'), ('color', 'U10')])
>>> print(X)
[(12,  33, 'Red') ( 0,   1, 'Blue') (27, 103, 'Yellow')
 (-1,  -2, 'Blue')]
```

Notice how the *dtype* argument is used to describe the fields:

```
dtype = [('a', 'i4'), ('b', 'i4'), ('color', 'U10')]
```

Now, how do you access and manipulate the information in this array? One way to get at parts of this data is to index it twice. For example, the following statement accesses the first field within the first element.

```
>>> X[0][0]
12
```

But it's more useful to get all the numeric data associated with one of the named fields, which (remember) are named 'a', 'b', and 'color' in this case. Here's how you'd get all the integers associated with the first field, 'a':

```
>>> print(X['a'])
[12  0  27  -1]
```

After the next series of statements, variable A refers to a **numpy** array containing all the integers collected from the field named 'a'. After this data has been collected into a one-dimensional array, we can take the sum, mean, and standard deviation, among other things.

```
>>> A = X['a']
>>> np.sum(A)
38
>>> len(A)
4
```

```
>>> np.mean(A)
9.5
>>> np.std(A)
11.324751652906125
```

We can do the same things for B, the array formed by taking the second integer field from each element in X.

```
>>> B = X['b']
>>> print(B)
[ 33   1  103  -2]
```

Finally, we can collect all the values in the 'color' field and get a list of strings:

```
>>> C = X['color']
>>> print(C)
['Red' 'Blue' 'Yellow' 'Blue']
```

Any of these columns, by the way, can be changed as a group. For example, to zero out the entire 'b' column, use the following statement, which alters the contents of X.

```
>>> X['b'] = 0
```

13.14 Reading and Writing "numpy" Data from Files

One of the main ways you get data is by reading it from a file, either binary or text. This section shows how to read a text file directly into a **numpy** array.

For simplicity's sake, let's assume that the data you want to read is stored in a series of records, one to a line, with fields separated by commas. This is a common way to store data. For this section, we'll look a file of 10 records, although you can, of course, have thousands or even millions of such records.

Let's suppose that the name of the file is team_data.txt, and it contains records on your development team:

- IQ, as an integer

- Height, as a floating-point number

- Age, an integer

- Last performance rating (from 0.0 to 4.0), as floating point

- College or university, a Unicode string

Here are the contents. Such a file is often called a comma-separated value (CSV) file.

```
101, 70.5, 21, 2.3, Harvard
110, 69.5, 22, 3.1, MIT
130, 76.0, 21, 3.5, Cal Tech
120, 72.5, 29, 3.7, Yale
120, 73.2, 33, 2.9, Harvard
105, 68.0, 35, 3.0, U. of Wash.
107, 74.0, 44, 2.7, Tacoma Comm. College
140, 67.0, 30, 3.1, Oregon State
100, 72.5, 31, 2.0, UCLA
```

Remember, this data set could be thousands of records long, but we're using 10 records for the sake of illustration.

The first thing we need to do is create a list of tuples to represent the structure of each record. The name of each column is included, so that we can refer to it later.

```
dt=[('IQ', 'i2'), ('Height', 'f4'), ('Age', 'i2'),
    ('Rating', 'f4'), ('College', 'U30')]
```

Any of these fields can be a different size. For example, if you needed integers larger than 2 bytes in size, you could use 4-byte integers ('i4'). And if you wanted to store more precise floating-point numbers, you could use 'f8'. But the cost of having such fields is to cause the array to have a bigger footprint in memory.

Let's stick with the settings we've used. The following syntax shows how to read a text file into a **numpy** array. There are other arguments, which you can look up online. Some of those enable you to skip specified rows or columns.

array = **np.loadtxt(**_fname_, _dtype_=**<class 'float'>**,
    delimiter**)**

This function is easy to use. It doesn't require that you open the file ahead of time. Instead, it automatically opens the file for reading in text mode. If the file can't be opened, an **IOError** exception is raised.

The *fname* argument is a string containing the name of the file to open; it can be a complete path name. The *dtype* argument is an array describing the data format, such as the dt list created earlier. The delimiter, in these examples, is a comma.

The following statement loads the text file shown at the beginning of this section.

```
team_a = np.loadtxt('team_data.txt', dt, delimiter=',')
```

After this statement is executed, the variable `team_a` now contains the following, which you'll see if you print it.

```
array([(101, 70.5, 21, 2.3, ' Harvard'),
       (110, 69.5, 22, 3.1, ' MIT'),
       (130, 76. , 21, 3.5, ' Cal Tech'),
       (120, 72.5, 29, 3.7, ' Yale'),
       (120, 73.2, 33, 2.9, ' Harvard'),
       (105, 68. , 35, 3. , ' U. of Wash.'),
       (107, 74. , 44, 2.7, ' Tacoma Comm. College'),
       (140, 67. , 30, 3.1, ' Oregon State'),
       (100, 72.5, 31, 2. , ' UCLA')],
    dtype=[('IQ', 'i2'), ('Height', 'f4'),
           ('Age', 'i2'), ('Rating', 'f4'),
           ('College', 'U30')])
```

There's at least one quirk in this example. The strings all have a leading space. That's because the delimiter was only a comma. There are several ways to solve this problem. The simplest way is probably to make the delimiter into a combination comma and space (', ').

```
team_a = np.loadtxt('team_data.txt', dt, delimiter=', ')
```

You can now isolate columns as you choose and manipulate them or analyze the data, as we demonstrated in the previous section.

```
iq_a    = team_a['IQ']
ht_a    = team_a['Height']
age_a   = team_a['Age']
rat_a   = team_a['Rating']
```

Here's a printout of the `iq_a` array, containing all the elements taken from the IQ field of each row:

```
[101 110 130 120 120 105 107 140 100]
```

You can analyze this data by using the **numpy** statistical functions.

```
print('Mean IQ of the dev. team is %.2f.' %
  np.mean(iq_a))
print('Std. dev. of team\'s IQ is %.2f.' % np.std(iq_a))
```

These statements, when executed, print the following:

```
Mean IQ of the dev. team is 114.78.
Std. dev. of team's IQ is 12.95.
```

One of the interesting things you can do with multiple columns is find the Pearson correlation coefficient. This measures the relationship of two arrays of equal length. A positive correlation means that the more you get of A, the more you get of B. A perfect correlation (1.0) would mean a perfect linear relationship, in which a 10 percent increase in one quantity is always accompanied by a 10 percent increase in the other.

Conversely, –1.0 is a perfect negative correlation: the more you have of one, the less you get of the other.

What is the correlation between height and IQ on the development team? You can determine that through the following calculation:

```
>>> np.corrcoef(iq_a, ht_a)[0, 1]
-0.023465749537744517
```

This result suggests there's a negative correlation between IQ and height on this development team, but it's a tiny one. If the most important thing is to have an IQ, the shorter guys have an advantage, but very slightly. The correlation is close to 0.0, showing that the two sets of data—IQ and height—are only mildly related.

Note that the return value of the **np.corrcoef** function is actually a 2 × 2 array. To convert this to a single figure, use the index [0,1] or [1,0].

You can optionally manipulate an array before writing it back out. For example, suppose you want to change the performance rating system so that instead of running from 0.0 to 5.0, it runs from 0.0 to 10.0. You can do that by multiplying the whole column by 2.

```
team_a['Rating'] *= 2
```

You can also append new rows of data at any time by using the **np.append** function. Here's an example:

```
new_a = np.array((100, 70, 18, 5.5, 'C.C.C.'), dtype=dt)
team_a = np.append(team_a, new_a)
```

Finally, you can write an array back out to a text file by using the **savetxt** function, which has a number of arguments.

np.savetxt(*fname*, *array*, *fmt*='%.18e', *newline*='\n',
        header='', *footer*='')

The text file is opened automatically, assuming that *fname* is a legal target. The format string, *fmt*, is not a *dtype* array like that shown earlier. Instead, it's a format string that uses percent signs to specify fields as shown in Chapter 5, "Formatting Text Precisely." Here's an example using the data array, team_a, developed in this section.

```
fmt_str = '%i, %.1f, %i, %.1f, %s'
np.savetxt('team_data.txt', team_a, fmt=fmt_str)
```

Chapter 13 *Summary*

The range of what you can do with the **numpy** package is amazing. These last two chapters have been devoted to that topic, and we have yet to exhaust it.

This chapter gave an introduction to plotting two-dimensional graphs. The basic idea is that you use the **plot** function of the **matplotlib** package and pass two numeric arrays of equal length. The plotting software combines each element in the first array with its corresponding element in the second array, and from these combinations gets a sequence of (x, y) pairs. These pairs are plotted as points, with the **plot** function drawing lines to connect them as smoothly as possible.

But that's only the beginning. Using other functions, you can create pie charts, histograms, and other figures. And although the math of geometrical surfaces in three dimensions is more complex, the basic principles for plotting apply to creating three-dimensional shapes as well.

This chapter also showed how financial projections and linear-algebra operations are supported by the **numpy** package, including the ability to graph functions. Finally, the chapter ended by showing how to store fixed-length records in **numpy** arrays, as well as reading and writing them to text files.

Chapter 15, "Getting Financial Data off the Internet," will show how to get financial information from the web, download it, and graph it.

Chapter 13 *Review Questions*

1 What are your options, if any, for increasing the contrast between different figures that occupy the same graph?

2 After reading this chapter, can you state what the advantage of compound interest is compared to a higher rate of interest that does not compound?

3 What exactly is a histogram? Name one way of producing such a graph with **numpy**.

4 How do you adjust the aspect ratios between the X and Y axes, if needed?

5 Summarize the differences in array multiplication between two arrays, as it is used in these three forms: dot product, outer product, and standard multiplication of two **numpy** arrays.

6 Which **numpy** function could you use to calculate your monthly mortgage payment before you purchase a house?

7 Can **numpy** arrays store string data? If so, state at least one limitation that is imposed on this data.

Chapter 13 *Suggested Problems*

1 Plot function curves for the following functions:

$$Y = X\text{-}squared$$

$$Y = X\text{-}cubed$$

$$Y = log\text{-}base\text{-}2(X)$$

2 Plot a perfect circle like the one shown in Section 13.7, "Circles and the Aspect Ratio," but instead of using a polar coordinate approach, use a more Cartesian approach that maps an X value directly to one or two Y values. Specifically, take advantage of the formula

$$X\text{-}squared + Y\text{-}squared = Radius\text{-}squared$$

To graph the unit circle, therefore, use the following, solving for Y:

$$X\text{-}squared + Y\ squared = 1$$

Using this approach, however, only produces a semicircle. (Why?) Graph two curves, as needed, to draw a complete circle.

3 Print a chart for the first 20 periods of a 10-year mortgage, showing how much of an interest payment goes to principal and how much goes to interest. Graph two lines.

Multiple Modules and the RPN Example

If you program in Python for any length of time, you'll reach a point where you want to place your code in more than one source file—that is, a *module*. There are many advantages to using multiple modules in a single project. For example, multiple developers can work on different modules in tandem, even though they're part of the same project. Think of trying to create something as complex as Microsoft Windows without modular development!

Python modules are easy to work with, for the most part, but there are some gotchas that can crop up and bite you, like a snake. But not to worry. We'll safely steer you around those gotchas.

This chapter also completes the Reverse Polish Notation example this book has been developing in Chapters 3, 6, 7, and 8. This application will interpret an RPN language powerful enough to support loops and decision making.

14.1 Overview of Modules in Python

In Python, modules are objects just as other things are, and each has its own attributes. This has important consequences.

Every Python script has at least one module. This is true even when you're working within IDLE; in that case, the module is named **__main__**, which you can verify by printing the built-in identifier, **__name__**.

```
>>> print(__name__)
__main__
```

In this chapter, we'll assume you're working with at least one Python source file, which will be the main module. This file, when run, is renamed **__main__** regardless of the file's actual name.

You can use the **import** statement to import as many other source files as you want, bringing them into the project using the same syntax as you would

477

with a package. The program is always started by running the main module. After opening the main module (from within IDLE), open the Run menu and choose Run Module.

There are some general guidelines for importing, which, if you follow, should minimize your chances of getting into trouble.

▶ Import another source file by using an **import** statement, just as you would with packages, without, however, using the .py extension.

▶ You can import functions as well as module-level variables (that is, variables not local to a function). You should refer to imported variables through their qualified names. For example, if e is defined in a module my_math.py, then, from the main module, refer to it as my_math.e.

▶ Note this exception: If you are never, ever going to change the value of a variable, it's safe to refer to it directly. For example, if pi is a constant, you can refer to it simply as pi in another module.

▶ Avoid mutual importation. If mod_a.py imports mod_b.py, then mod_b.py shouldn't import mod_a.py. Furthermore, any circular "loop" of importation should be avoided. If A imports B and if B imports C, then C should not import A.

There are exceptions to rule 4. It's possible to make circular importation work, as you'll see, but the simplest way to avoid trouble is to just say no.

14.2 Simple Two-Module Example

Let's start with a program you'd like to split into two modules, in which the main module resides in run_me.py.

The file can be composed as an IDLE script that you then save. The **import** statement allows this module to call a function defined in another file.

```
# File run_me.py ------------------------------

import printstuff            # Import printstuff.py.

printstuff.print_this('thing') # Call imported func.
```

This program imports the file printstuff.py but refers to the module in code as printstuff—without the .py extension. (Sorry if we've gotten repetitive.) Here's the listing for printstuff.py, which should be placed in your working directory along with run_me.py.

```
# File printstuff.py --------------------------

def print_this(str1):
    print('Print this %s.' % str1)
```

Now run the run_me.py file directly. You don't need to do anything else to get the other module to be part of the project, assuming it's in the same directory.

The action of the **import** statement is to run the contents of printstuff.py, which contains one function definition. The action of the **def** statement is to create the function as a callable object.

Note ▶ Remember that in an **import** statement, the .py file extension is always implied, and it would be a mistake to include it. The rest of the name must obey the standard rules for forming file names.

◀ Note

Because the function, print_this, is imported from another module with a simple version of **import**, the function must be referred to with the module-name qualifier, printstuff.

```
printstuff.print_this('thing')
```

Before continuing, let's review all the steps, one at a time.

▶ From within IDLE, choose the New File command from the File menu. IDLE responds by providing a plain-text, editable window. Enter the following. (Comments don't need to be entered, but the rest should be entered exactly as shown.)

```
# File run_me.py   --------------------------

import printstuff             # Import printstuff.py

printstuff.print_this('thing')  # Call the func
```

▶ Save this file as run_me.py.

▶ Open a new file again. Enter the following:

```
# File printstuff.py --------------------------

def print_this(str1):
    print('Print this %s.' % str1)
```

▶ Save this file as printstuff.py.

▶ Open the Windows menu, and choose run_me.py. (This switches focus back to the first file, or rather, module.)

▶ Run this file by choosing the Run Module command from the Run menu.

The program prints the following:

```
Print this thing.
```

The imported file could have contained module-level code—that is, code not part of a function definition. The module-level code is run directly. So this particular program could have been written this way:

```
# File run_me.py -----------------------------

import printstuff    # Import printstuff.py file,
                     #   and run the code there.


#--------------------------------------------------
# File printstuff.py

print('Print this thing.')
```

With this version of the program, printstuff.py contains module-level code, which is simply executed. The result of the program is to, again, print the following:

```
Print this thing.
```

This practice—running module-level code from anywhere but the main module—is not a standard practice, but it is supported. In general, though, it should be avoided.

Another thing that an imported module can do is to provide module-level variable assignments, which cause the creation of the named variables.

```
# File run_me.py -----------------------------

import printstuff     # Import printstuff.py file.

# The next statement then uses imported variables.

print('%s and %s' % (printstuff.x, printstuff.y))


# File printstuff.py -------------------------

x, y = 100, 200
```

Now, running the file run_me.py prints the following:

```
100 and 200
```

The variables x and y are imported from this other module, named printstuff, and therefore these variables are available to the main module as printstuff.x and printstuff.y.

Modules have an issue with global versus local access, just as functions do. For example, suppose you have the following code:

```
#File run_me.py -----------------------------

from foo_vars import z, print_z_val
import foo_vars

z = 100
print_z_val()

#File foo_vars.py ---------------------------

z = 0
def print_z_val():
    print('Value of z is', z)
```

If you run this program, it says that the value of z is still 0, which makes it look like the change to z in the main module (run_me.py) was ignored. What really happened is that the statement z = 100 created a version of z local to the main module. The problem is corrected as soon as z = 100 in run_me.py is changed to

```
foo_vars.z = 100
```

This statement causes run_me.py to use the version of z defined in foo_vars.py and nowhere else; therefore, the assignment of 100 to z now affects foo_vars.z.

Here's another complete example involving exactly two source files: a main program module and another module, poly.py.

```
# File do_areas.py ---------------------------------

import poly            # Import the file poly.py

def main():
    r = float(input('Enter radius:'))
    print('Area of circle is', poly.get_circle_area(r))
```

```
        x = float(input('Enter side:'))
        print('Area of square is', poly.get_square_area(x))

    main()


    # File poly.py ----------------------------------

    def get_circle_area(radius):
        pi = 3.141593
        return 3.141592 * radius * radius

    def get_square_area(side):
        return side * side

    def get_triangle_area(height, width):
        return height * width * 0.5
```

The main module is do_areas.py. The file poly.py is in the same directory. After you start do_areas.py, the first thing the program does is to import the file poly.py:

```
    import poly          # Import the file poly.py
```

When Python reads and executes this statement, it suspends execution of the main module (do_areas.py) and executes the file poly.py. It finds that file after automatically adding a .py extension to poly.

Trying to import the file name *with* an extension would cause an error, because Python would try to interpret poly.py as a hierarchical package name.

The effect of executing the code in poly.py is to create the three functions as callable objects, thanks to the three **def** statements. The **import** statement also makes the three function names visible to the main module—but only when used with the poly prefix as shown here:

```
    poly.get_circle_area(radius)
    poly.get_square_area(side)
    poly.get_triangle_area(height, width)
```

14.3 Variations on the "import" Statement

When you import your own modules, the **import** statement obeys the same rules shown earlier in this book. The simplest use enables a source file to have access to the module-level symbols defined in this other module; however, the names must be qualified with the module name.

    import *module_name*

So, if a function is created in the named module, you can call a function defined there, but only if you use the proper qualifier:

    module_name.function_name(*args*)

This also applies to variables.

    module_name.var

But if you list specific symbolic names by using the **from** syntax, those symbols are available directly.

    from *module_name* **import** *sym1, sym2, sym3...*

For example, in the example at the end of the previous section, the function names `get_circle_area` and `get_square_area` can be made directly available by using the **from/import** syntax. Here is the result.

```
# File do_areas.py ----------------------------------

from poly import get_circle_area, get_square_area

def main():
    r = float(input('Enter radius:'))
    print('Area of circle is', get_circle_area(r))

    x = float(input('Enter side:'))
    print('Area of square is', get_square_area(x))

main()


# File poly.py ----------------------------------

def get_circle_area(radius):
    pi = 3.141593
    return 3.141592 * radius * radius

def get_square_area(side):
    return side * side
```

```
def get_triangle_area(height, width):
    return height * width * 0.5
```

Given the way two of the functions are imported, they can be referred to without qualification—that is, without the dot (.) syntax. Moreover, they must be referred to without qualification if this is the only **import** statement.

```
from poly import get_circle_area, get_square_area
```

This statement, as it is, provides no access to the symbolic name get_triangle_area, because that function name was not imported in this case.

You can also choose to import all the symbols in the module, subject to limitations described in the next section. This syntax uses the asterisk (*) to mean "Import all symbols from the named module."

```
from poly import *
```

As a result of this statement, the source file poly.py is run, and all its module-level symbols become visible to the current source file without qualification. (This assumes that the source file poly.py is available in the current directory.)

Note ▶ The first time a source file is imported within a given project, Python executes the code in that file. Remember that executing a **def** statement causes Python to create a function at run time as a callable object. Unlike C or C++, Python does not create a function during a "compilation" phase. Instead, creation of functions is dynamic and can happen at any time during running of the program.

That's why it's necessary for Python to run the code in the named module; or rather, it runs all the module-level code, which ideally should perform variable assignments or function definitions (or both). After a module is executed in this way, it's not executed again, no matter how many times it's imported.

The functions that are created, of course, can be called any number of times. But the initial action of a **def** statement is only to create the function as a callable object, and not yet to call it. That distinction is important.

◀ Note

14.4 Using the "__all__" Symbol

The previous section pointed out that you can use the asterisk (*) to bring all the module-level code of the desired module into the program name space. For example, suppose you have the following application, combining a main program (run_me.py) with a module (module2.py).

```
# File run_me.py -----------------------------

from module2 import *

pr_nice('x', x)
pr_nice('y', y)


# File module2.py -----------------------------

x = 1000
y = 500
z = 5

def pr_nice(s, n):
    print('The value of %s is %i.' % (s, n))
    print('And z is %i.' % z)
```

When run, the program run_me.py prints

```
The value of x is 1000.
And z is 5!
The value of y is 500.
And z is 5!
```

As this example demonstrates, the **import** * syntax causes all module-level symbols defined in module2.py to be accessible from this module.

But do all the symbols in module2.py really need to be visible in run_me.py? In this case, they don't. The module-level variable z is used in the function definition for pr_nice, but it need not be visible to the main module.

When you use the version of **import** that uses the asterisk (*), Python allows you to control access through the use of the __all__ symbol in the module itself. Here's how it works.

▶ If the module does not assign a value to the special symbol __**all**__, then the importer of the module sees all the module-level (that is, global) symbols, exactly as you'd expect.

▶ If the module does assign a value to __**all**__, then only the listed symbols are visible to the importer of the module.

The syntax for __**all**__ is shown here.

```
__all__ = [sym_str1, sym_str2, sym_str3...]
```

This syntax implies that all the symbolic names listed for this statement are placed in strings, and generally, this means names in quotation marks. (See the upcoming example.)

Consider the previous example. The names x, y, and z are all visible to the importing module, run_me.py, as is the function name, pr_nice. But z didn't need to be visible as an import, because it's visible internally *within* the module named module2. Therefore, the module could have been written this way:

```
# File module2.py -----------------------------

__all__ = ['x', 'y', 'pr_nice']

x = 1000
y = 500
z = 10

def pr_nice(s, n):
    print('The value of %s is %i.' % (s, n))
    print('And z is %i.' % z)
```

The new statement to be added is highlighted in bold. You'll find that if you add this line and rerun run_me.py, the results are unchanged.

But if this new line of code doesn't change the results, why use it? The answer is that it helps limit proliferation of symbols when you're importing modules with the * syntax. Some large packages have thousands of module-level symbols. Using __all__ controls the proliferation of symbolic names, which you don't want to get out of hand. Otherwise, name conflicts can be a danger.

If the importer is not using the **import** * syntax to import symbols, the __all__ assignment has no effect.

Look again at the case in which z is not included in the list:

```
__all__ = ['x', 'y', 'pr_nice']
```

Yet even in this case, the variable z can still be referred to by the main module, in other ways. Here's an example:

```
# File listing for run_me.py ---------------------

from module2 import *   # Import x, y, pr_nice
from module2 import z   # Import z

print('z is %i, for heaven's sake!' % z)
```

This version of the code prints the following:

```
z is 10, for heaven's sake!
```

This example works, because in this case, z is imported on its own, in a separate statement.

14.5 Public and Private Module Variables

The previous section raised an issue: Can you make a module-level symbol "private" to a module?

Note ▶ The effect described in this section—of making names with a leading underscore (_) more difficult to import—is separate from the name mangling that takes place when you're attempting to access a private attribute (signified by leading double underscores) from outside a class.

See Section 9.6, "Public and Private Variables," for more information on name mangling.

◀ Note

Other computer languages tend to have ways of privatizing a symbolic name. In Python, that feature is deemphasized, because the philosophy of Python is to make it easy to create something and just run it. However, names beginning with an underscore have special properties in Python.

_name

When a name beginning with an underscore is created in a Python module, it's not accessible to another module that imports it using the **import *** syntax.

```
from mod_a import *
```

For example, the following program causes errors if run_me.py is run, because it assumes that _a and __b are accessible, but they're not.

```
# File run_me.py -----------------------------

from mod_a import *          # This will fail.

print(_a)
print(__b)


# File mod_a.py -------------------------------

_a, __b = 10, 100
```

The references to both _a and __b fail. This single-underscore rule applies to double underscores, too, of course. Changing the way you import the symbols makes the program run successfully, as in the following example.

```
# File run_me.py -----------------------------

from mod_a import _a, __b     # This now works.

print(_a)
print(__b)


# File a_mod.py ------------------------------

_a, __b = 10, 100
```

The difference between the two examples is that the second one uses the **import** keyword to recognize _a and __b specifically, rather than relying on the asterisk (*) syntax.

14.6 The Main Module and "__main__"

Earlier, we claimed that modules are objects and that they have attributes just as other objects do. Here's a simple program that creates some attributes and displays them. Note in particular what's printed as the module name.

```
# File run_me.py ------------------------------------
import mod_a

x = 1
y = 2

print('My name is %s.\n' %s __name__)

print(dir())
```

The output of the program is

```
My name is __main__.

['__annotations__', '__builtins__', '__doc__',
'__file__', '__loader__', '__name__', '__package__',
'__spec__', 'mod_a', 'x', 'y']
```

Why does the program say that its name is __**main**__?

The answer is that in any Python program—whether a single-module or a more complex one—the main module's name is changed from its file name to the special name __**main.**

This program imports a module named mod_a. Suppose mod_a has only one statement:

```
# File mod_a.py ----------------------------------

print('My name is %s.\n' % __name__)
```

When this module is imported and run, it prints the following:

```
My name is mod_a.
```

So this module's name was not changed from mod_a, which is the name obtained by taking its file name without the .py extension. A module's name is not changed unless it has become the main module—that is, the first module to be run.

There are some important consequences of these rules. First, when a module attempts to import the main module, it potentially creates two copies of every symbol in the main module, because now (in this example) there exists both __**main**__ and mod_a.

The name __**main**__ can be useful. Sometimes, you may want to test all the functions in a module, even though it's not normally the main module. In that case, you might run it stand-alone, in which case it would become the main module.

For this reason, the following code is common in professional Python. It directs Python to run a module-level statement only if the file is actually serving as the main module.

```
# File start_me_up.py ----------------------------

def call_me_first():
    print('Hi, there, Python!')

if __name__ == '__main__':
    call_me_first()
```

You can run a module as the main module, remember, by launching the Run Module command from the Run menu, while this file is being viewed in IDLE.

The point is this: If a module is going to be run stand-alone (usually as a test of whether that particular module's functions work), it needs to have module-level code that will call the functions. That's the point of testing **__name__** to see whether it is equal to **__main__**.

To put all this another way, this use of **__main__** is an extremely useful testing tool. It enables you to test differently modules individually. Then, when the overall program is run, modules will no longer be run independently but only as called by the main program, as usual.

14.7 Gotcha! Problems with Mutual Importing

Is it possible to have two modules that import each other, with each referring to symbols defined in the other module? You can do that, but when you do, problems can potentially arise, so be careful.

First, there are problems with importing the main module—the module that's the starting point for running the program. As mentioned in the previous section, when a module becomes the main module, its name is changed to **__main__**; but if it's imported by its file name, you create two copies of the module!

Could you create two modules (mod_a and mod_b) that import each other? We might picture this as shown in Figure 14.1.

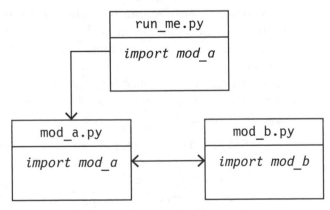

Figure 14.1. A potential architecture (unreliable)

This approach looks good, and sometimes it works. However, if it creates mutual dependencies between the two modules, it can fail. Here is one such example:

```
# File run_me.py -----------------------------------
import mod_a
mod_a.funcA(5)
```

```
# File mod_a.py ------------------------------------
import mod_b

def funcA(n):
    if n > 0:
        mod_b.funcB(n - 1)
```

```
# File mod_b.py ------------------------------------
import mod_a

def funcB(n):
    print(n)
    mod_a.funcA(n)
```

This program works, or at least it does until it gets more complex. All the main module does is import the two modules (mod_a and mod_b) and then run one of the functions. Although the functions are mutually dependent—each calls the other—there is an appropriate exit condition, and so the program runs fine, producing the following result:

```
4
3
2
1
0
```

Wonderful! Except that this code is easy to break. Suppose you add an innocent-looking statement to mod_a.py, producing the following (with a new statement shown in bold):

```
# File mod_a.py ------------------------------------
import mod_b

mod_b.funcB(3)

def funcA(n):
    if n > 0:
        mod_b.funcB(n - 1)
```

If you save the change to mod_a.py and rerun the program, starting with run_me.py, the program fails. The error message states that mod_a "has no attribute funcA."

What happened? When `mod_a.py` is imported, the first thing it does is to import `mod_b`. That should make it possible to call a function in `mod_b`, namely `funcB`. But when `funcB` is called, `mod_a` has not yet finished being run; therefore, `funcA` has not yet been created as a callable object.

Consequently, `funcB` is successfully called, but it attempts to call `funcA` before the latter exists. This explains the strange error message.

One way to avoid such problems is to carefully avoid calling *any* function until every function in the project has been defined, something we advised in Chapter 1, "Review of the Fundamentals," to solve the forward reference problem. An even safer approach is to only use importing that's unidirectional.

So how do you design a project that has unidirectional importing, while still making sure that every module that needs access to a function or variable gets that access? One solution is to put all common objects needed by the project into a module as far down in the hierarchy as possible (see Figure 14.2). This runs counter to the way many C or C++ programmers design their projects, but it's "the Python Way."

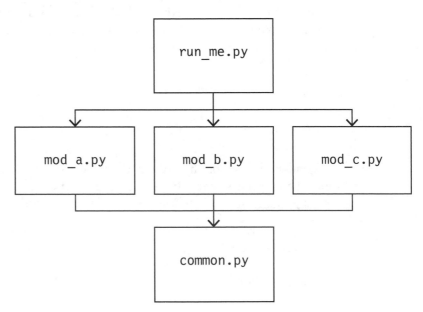

Figure 14.2. Unidirectional design of module importing

Another solution, which we'll demonstrate next in Section 14.8, is to pass along references to objects during function calls rather than import them.

14.8 RPN Example: Breaking into Two Modules

In the remainder of this chapter, we'll focus on the Reverse Polish Notation (RPN) language interpreter as shown in Chapter 8, "Text and Binary Files." That version of the program was able to read and execute RPN scripts stored in text files. It supported an assignment operator (=) that enabled the user to create variables.

The next step is to break the program into two modules. It would make sense, initially, to move the file-handling function to a separate module. The file I/O function, open_rpn_file, gets a file name from the user, opens the file, reads all the lines of text from the file into a list of strings, and returns this list.

In the next section, we'll add more file I/O statements to that module. For now, let's just use it to contain the function open_rpn_file, which we'll place in a Python source file named rpn_io.py.

Here's the resulting program from Chapter 8, but now reorganized into two files.

```
#File rpn.py --------------------------------------

import re
import operator
from rpn_io import *

# Provide a symbol table; values of variables will be
#    stored here.

sym_tab = { }

stack = []        # Stack to hold the values.

# Scanner: Add items to recognize variable names, which
#    are stored in the symbol table, and to perform
#    assignments, which enter values into the sym. table.

scanner = re.Scanner([
    (r"[ \t\n]", lambda s, t: None),
    (r"-?(\d*)?\.\d+", lambda s, t:
        stack.append(float(t))),
    (r"-?\d+", lambda s, t: stack.append(int(t))),
    (r"[a-zA-Z_][a-zA-Z_0-9]*", lambda s, t:
        stack.append(t)),
```

14

```python
        (r"[+]", lambda s, t: bin_op(operator.add)),
        (r"[-]", lambda s, t: bin_op(operator.sub)),
        (r"[*]", lambda s, t: bin_op(operator.mul)),
        (r"[/]", lambda s, t: bin_op(operator.truediv)),
        (r"[\^]", lambda s, t: bin_op(operator.pow)),
        (r"[=]", lambda s, t: assign_op()),
    ])


def assign_op():
    '''Assignment Operator function: Pop off a name
    and a value, and make a symbol-table entry.
    '''
    op2, op1 = stack.pop(), stack.pop()
    if type(op2) == str:    # Source may be another var!
        op2 = sym_tab[op2]
    sym_tab[op1] = op2


def bin_op(action):
    '''Binary Operation evaluator: If an operand is
    a variable name, look it up in the symbol table
    and replace with the corresponding value, before
    being evaluated.
    '''
    op2, op1 = stack.pop(), stack.pop()
    if type(op1) == str:
        op1 = sym_tab[op1]
    if type(op2) == str:
        op2 = sym_tab[op2]
    stack.append(action(op1, op2))


def main():
    a_list = open_rpn_file()
    if not a_list:
        print('Bye!')
        return

    for a_line in a_list:
        a_line = a_line.strip()
```

```
            if a_line:
                tokens, unknown = scanner.scan(a_line)
                if unknown:
                    print('Unrecognized input:', unknown)
        print(str(stack[-1]))

main()


#File rpn_io.py
#------------------------------------------

def open_rpn_file():
    '''Open-source-file function. Open a named
    file and read lines into a list, which is
    returned.
    '''
    while True:
        try:
            fname = input('Enter RPN source: ')
            if not fname:
                return None
            f = open(fname, 'r')
            break
        except:
            print('File not found. Re-enter.')
    a_list = f.readlines()
    return a_list
```

This version of the program is functionally identical to the one in Chapter 8, which reads RPN scripts from a file and uses a symbol table, `sym_tab`, to store variable names created as a result of assignments (=).

For example, this program should be able to read a text file, such as one containing the following RPN script, run it as a program, and print the result.

```
a_var 3 =
b_var 5 =
a_var b_var * 1 +
```

If you try entering this into a text file (let's call it `rpn_junk.txt`), run the program, and enter `rpn_junk.txt` as the file name when prompted, you should get the correct result, 16.

Note ▶ If you create the RPN source file within IDLE, don't be surprised if IDLE adds a .py extension.

◀ Note

Notice the **import** statement that was added to the main module:

```
from rpn_io import *
```

Because the `rpn_io` module contains only one function, the possibility of name conflicts is low. But you could import more selectively if you chose.

```
from rpn_io import open_rpn_file
```

14.9 RPN Example: Adding I/O Directives

The next step is to add high-level input and output directives to the RPN scripting language so that the user can input initial values for the program as well as print results.

Let's use a program design that adds four directives, described in Table 14.1.

Table 14.1. I/O Directives for the RPN Language

DIRECTIVE, WITH SYNTAX	DESCRIPTION
INPUT *var_name*	Get a value from the user, translate it into a numeric value, and store it in the symbol table as *var_name*.
PRINTS *quoted_string*	Print the specified string.
PRINTLN [*quoted_string*]	Print the specified string, if any, followed by a newline.
PRINTVAR *var_name*	Look up the value of *var_name* in the symbol table, and print it.

For the sake of illustration, and because it makes for a better overall design, we'll place the code to implement these four directives into the `rpn_io` file rather than the main module. This raises an issue. Two of the directives (INPUT and PRINTVAR) need access to the symbol table (`sym_tab`) created in the main module. How does this table get shared with the `rpn_io` module? As we showed in Section 14.6, having the two modules import each other is risky, because it can create interdependencies that cause the program to fail.

The simplest, safest solution is to pass along a reference to `sym_tab`, the dictionary that serves as the symbol table.

Just how, you may ask, do you pass a reference? Python always does this when passing arguments. It's a vital performance feature. If a function got a complete copy of a symbol table, that would slow down the program; moreover, it would deny the called function the ability to change data in the original copy of the table.

Changing data does work in this scenario, because we take advantage of dictionaries being mutable and therefore changeable at run time. You can have a function make changes to parts of the dictionary, sym_tab, and those changes will be effective. For example, the following statement adds a variable and its value to the table, even though sym_tab is passed as a reference.

```
sym_tab[var_name] = val
```

Here is the new version of main, in the file rpn.py, with the lines to be added appearing in bold:

```
def main():
    a_list = open_rpn_file()
    if not a_list:
        print('Bye!')
        return

    for a_line in a_list:
        a_line = a_line.strip()
        if a_line.startswith('PRINTS'):
            do_prints(a_line[7:])
        elif a_line.startswith('PRINTLN'):
            do_println(a_line[8:])
        elif a_line.startswith('PRINTVAR'):
            do_printvar(a_line[9:], sym_tab)
        elif a_line.startswith('INPUT'):
            do_input(a_line[6:], sym_tab)
        elif a_line:
            tokens, unknown = scanner.scan(a_line)
            if unknown:
                print('Unrecognized input:', unknown)
```

Most of these new (or altered) lines of code look for the presence of one of the directive names—PRINTS, PRINTLN, PRINTVAR, or INPUT—at the beginning of a line that's been read in from the target RPN code file. The **startswith** method of the string class provides an efficient way to check for these directives. When one of them is found, the program calls the appropriate function to handle it, passing the remainder of the line of RPN code.

Two of these functions (PRINTVAR and INPUT) also take a reference to the symbol table.

Here are the functions to be added to the file rpn_io.py. These functions carry out the four directives looked for by the main function.

```python
def do_prints(s):
    ''' Carry out PRINTS directive by printing a
    string.
    '''
    a_str = get_str(s)
    print(a_str, end='')

def do_println(s):
    ''' Carry out PRINTLN directive: print the
    optional string argument, if specified, and then
    print a newline, unconditionally.
    '''
    if s:
        do_prints(s)
    print()

def get_str(s):
    ''' Helper function for do_prints.
    '''
    a = s.find("'")
    b = s.rfind("'")
    if a == -1 or b == -1:
        return ''
    return s[a+1:b]

def do_printvar(s, sym_tab):
    ''' Carry out PRINTVAR directive; look up the
    variable name contained in the string s, and
    then look this name up in the symbol table.
    '''
    wrd = s.split()[0]
    print(sym_tab[wrd], end=' ')

def do_input(s, sym_tab):
    ''' Carry out INPUT directive; get value input
    from the end user, then enter this value in the
    symbol table, for name contained in string s.
    '''
    wrd = input()
    sym_tab[s] = float(wrd)
```

The functions used in this program are instructive because of their use of the argument `sym_tab`. The last two functions (`do_printvar` and `do_input`) get a reference to the symbol table as their second argument.

The reference, `sym_tab`, is not a copy of the symbol table created in the main module but rather is a direct reference to the original table itself. Because data dictionaries (such as the symbol table) are mutable, the `do_input` function is able to modify the table itself, and not just a copy.

Given support for these four directives, the RPN interpreter can now evaluate scripts that are close to being real programs. For example, the following script prompts for the sides of a right triangle, calculates the hypotenuse, and prints the results.

```
PRINTS 'Enter side 1: '
INPUT side1
PRINTS 'Enter side 2: '
INPUT side2
total side1 side1 * side2 side2 * + =
hyp total 0.5 ^ =
PRINTS 'Hypotenuse equals '
PRINTVAR hyp
```

Suppose that you write and save this RPN, placing it in a file called `rpn_hyp.txt`. Here is a sample session resulting from running the main module, rpn.py:

```
Enter RPN source: rpn_hyp.txt
Enter side 1: 30
Enter side 2: 40
Hypotenuse equals 50.0
```

The first line shown, "Enter RPN source," is printed by the Python program itself. The second, third, and fourth lines are actually printed by the RPN script—or rather, they are printed during the evaluation of that RPN script.

14.10 Further Changes to the RPN Example

There are still more things we can do to make this RPN interpreter a better program. One of the biggest problems is that the error reporting is still poor. For example, suppose the RPN script writer begins writing his script as follows:

```
PRINTS 'Enter side 1: '
INPUT side 1
```

Oops! In the second line, he entered an extra space when attempting to write `side1`. Given how the program `rpn.txt` is currently written, the symbolic name `side` will be entered into the symbol table and the 1 will be ignored, but later, when the script attempts to look up `side1` in the symbol table, that symbol will not be found.

With more sophisticated error handling, the interpreter might pinpoint the problem in line 2 (or rather, line 1 if we are using zero-based index numbers), pointing out that you can't give two arguments to the INPUT directive.

But at minimum, our Python program should catch the exception that arises and then print a polite message, along with a line number indicating where the error was discovered. To do this, we'll need to keep track of line numbers.

The beauty of this solution is that once line-number tracking is added, it's easy to add a control structure, *jump if not zero*, as you'll see in Section 14.10.2. Adding that one feature will greatly expand the capabilities of the RPN scripting language.

14.10.1 *Adding Line-Number Checking*

To add line-number checking to the RPN interpreter, we need to declare a new variable, `pc`, which needs to be module-level (not local) in the module `rpn.py`. Because it's global, it needs to be declared as **global** in any function that uses it and assigns it a new value.

Note ▶ Carefully observe the use of the **global** statement in the code here. The failure to use this keyword when needed can create some nasty bugs.

◀ Note

The first thing we need to do is add the program counter, `pc`, to the list of global variables at the beginning of the main module. After importing the necessary packages, as well as `rpn_io.py`, the source code begins with

```
sym_tab = { }    # Symbol table (for variables)
stack = []       # Stack to hold the values.
pc = -1          # Program Counter
```

The third line, which is here placed in bold, is the one that needs to be added.

In addition, a few lines need to be added to the main function. These are placed in bold in the following listing.

```
def main():
    global pc
    a_list = open_rpn_file()
    if not a_list:
        print('Bye!')
```

```
                return
        pc = -1
        while True:
            pc += 1
            if pc >= len(a_list):
                break
            a_line = a_list[pc]
            try:
                a_line = a_line.strip()
                if a_line.startswith('PRINTS'):
                    do_prints(a_line[7:])
                elif a_line.startswith('PRINTLN'):
                    do_println(a_line[8:])
                elif a_line.startswith('PRINTVAR'):
                    do_printvar(a_line[9:], sym_tab)
                elif a_line.startswith('INPUT'):
                    do_input(a_line[6:], sym_tab)
                elif a_line:
                    tokens, unknown = scanner.scan(a_line)
                    if unknown:
                        print('Unrecognized input:', unknown)
                        break
            except KeyError as e:
                print('Unrecognized symbol', e.args[0],
                        'found in line', pc)
                print(a_list[pc])
                break
```

Let's walk through what each of these additions does. First of all, the **global** statement is needed. Without it, Python would assume that the use of pc in the function was a reference to a local variable. Why? It's because assignments create variables—remember that there are no variable declarations in Python! Therefore, Python would have to guess what kind of variable was being created and, by default, variables are local.

The **global** statement tells Python not to interpret pc as a local variable, even if it's the target of an assignment. Python looks for a global (module-level) version of pc and finds it.

Next, pc is set to −1, in case it needs to be set to the initial position. The action of the program is to increment pc as each line is read, and we want it to be 0 after the first line is read.

```
        pc = -1
```

The next few lines increment pc as mentioned. Should the value then be so high as to be out of range for the list of strings, the program exits; this means we're done!

```
while True:
    pc += 1
    if pc >= len(a_list):
        break
```

Finally, code is added to the very end of the main function to catch the **KeyError** exception and report a useful error message if this exception is raised. Then the program terminates.

```
except KeyError as e:
    print('Unrecognized symbol', e.args[0],
            'found in line', pc)
    print(a_list[pc])
    break
```

With these changes made, errors in writing variable names trigger more intelligent error reporting. For example, if the variable side1 was never properly created (let's say that the user had entered side11 or side 1 earlier on), the interpreter now prints a useful message:

```
Unrecognized symbol side1 found in line 4
total side1 side1 * side2 side2 * + =
```

This message, should it happen, ought to tell you there is a problem with the creation of side1 or side2.

14.10.2 Adding Jump-If-Not-Zero

Now that the RPN interpreter has a working program counter (pc) in place, it becomes an easy matter to add a control structure to the RPN language: *jump if not zero*. With the addition of this one statement, you can give RPN programs the ability to loop and make decisions, thereby greatly increasing the usability of this language.

We could design the jump-if-not-zero feature as a directive, but it's more in keeping with the spirit of the language to make it an RPN expression.

    conditional_expr   line_num   ?

If the *conditional_expr* is any value other than zero, the program counter, pc, is set to the value of *line_num*. Otherwise, do nothing.

Could it possibly be that simple? Yes, it is! The only complication is that we need to permit *conditional_expr* to be a variable name, and also (although the use of this will likely be uncommon) permit *line_num* to be a variable.

So far, there are no line labels, so this isn't a perfect solution. (The implementation of line labels is left as an exercise at the end of the chapter.) The RPN writer will have to count lines, using zero-based indexing, to decide where to jump to.

Here's an example of what the user will be able to write.

```
PRINTS 'Enter number of fibos to print: '
INPUT n
f1 0 =
f2 1 =
temp f2 =
f2 f1 f2 + =
f1 temp =
PRINTVAR f2
n n 1 - =
n 4 ?
```

Do you see what this does? We'll return to that question later.

But look at the last line (n 4 ?). To understand what this does, remember that our program counter is designed to be zero-based. It didn't have to be, but that simplified some of the programming. Because the program counter is zero based, the last line—assuming n is not zero—causes a jump back to the fifth line (temp f2 =). This forms a loop that continues until n is zero.

As we promised, the jump-if-not-zero operator, ?, is easy to implement. Just add one line to the Scanner code and one short function. Here is the revised Scanner code, with the new line to be entered in bold.

```
scanner = re.Scanner([
    (r"[ \t\n]", lambda s, t: None),
    (r"-?(\d*)?\.\d+", lambda s, t:
        stack.append(float(t))),
    (r"-?\d+", lambda s, t: stack.append(int(t))),
    (r"[a-zA-Z_][a-zA-Z_0-9]*", lambda s, t:
        stack.append(t)),
    (r"[+]", lambda s, t: bin_op(operator.add)),
    (r"[-]", lambda s, t: bin_op(operator.sub)),
    (r"[*]", lambda s, t: bin_op(operator.mul)),
    (r"[/]", lambda s, t: bin_op(operator.truediv)),
    (r"[\^]", lambda s, t: bin_op(operator.pow)),
```

```
        (r"[=]", lambda s, t: assign_op()),
        (r"[?]", lambda s, t: jnz_op())
    ])
```

The new function, jnz_op, pops two items off the stack, looks them up in the symbol table if necessary, and carries out the operation itself, which is simple.

```
def jnz_op():
    global pc
    op2, op1 = stack.pop(), stack.pop()
    if type(op1) == str:
        op1 = sym_tab[op1]
    if type(op2) == str:
        op2 = sym_tab[op2]
    if op1:
        pc = int(op2) - 1
```

Note the importance of the **global** statement. To prevent pc from being interpreted as local, the **global** statement is necessary.

```
    global pc
```

The core of the function is the following two lines, which alter the program counter if op1 is nonzero (true).

```
    if op1:
        pc = int(op2) - 1
```

Let's view a sample session. Suppose that the script shown near the beginning of this section (we'll call it mystery.txt) is given to the RPN Interpreter.

```
Enter RPN source: mystery.txt
Enter how many fibos to print: 10
1 2 3 5 8 13 21 34 55 89
```

This program clearly prints out the first 10 Fibonacci numbers, aside from the first one. We've successfully interpreted an RPN script that's capable of doing something a different number of times, depending on user input.

14.10.3 Greater-Than (>) and Get-Random-Number (!)

Before leaving the topic of the RPN interpreter altogether, let's add two more features, which will aid in the creation of game programs. By adding a greater-than operator (>) and a get-random-number operator (!), we'll enable the writing of the number guessing game as an RPN script.

The greater-than operator will be like most RPN operations. It will pop two operands off the stack and then push a result on top of the stack.

```
op1   op2   >
```

The two operands are compared. If op1 is greater than op2, then the value 1 is pushed onto the stack; otherwise, the value 0 is pushed.

It turns out that the work required to implement this function comes down to only one line! We don't have to include an extra function to evaluate the greater-than operation, because it's already handled by **operator.gt**, a function imported from the **operator** package. Only one line needs to be added.

```
scanner = re.Scanner([
    (r"[ \t\n]", lambda s, t: None),
    (r"-?(\d*)?\.\d+", lambda s, t:
        stack.append(float(t))),
    (r"-?\d+", lambda s, t: stack.append(int(t))),
    (r"[a-zA-Z_][a-zA-Z_0-9]*", lambda s, t:
        stack.append(t)),
    (r"[+]", lambda s, t: bin_op(operator.add)),
    (r"[-]", lambda s, t: bin_op(operator.sub)),
    (r"[*]", lambda s, t: bin_op(operator.mul)),
    (r"[/]", lambda s, t: bin_op(operator.truediv)),
    (r"[>]", lambda s, t: bin_op(operator.gt)),
    (r"[\^]", lambda s, t: bin_op(operator.pow)),
    (r"[=]", lambda s, t: assign_op()),
    (r"[?]", lambda s, t: jnz_op())
])
```

That's it! It may occur to you that adding new operators, as long as they are standard arithmetic or comparison operators, is so trivial, we should add them all.

That would be correct, except that if you're depending on single punctuation marks to represent different operations, you'll soon run out of symbols on the keyboard. The problem is potentially solvable by making "LE", for example, stand for "less than or equal to," but if you use that approach, you need to rethink how the scanner analyzes tokens.

Armed with this one additional operator, it's now possible to make the Fibonacci script more reliable. Just look at the revised script.

```
PRINTS 'Enter number of fibos to print: '
INPUT n
f1 0 =
f2 1 =
```

```
temp f2 =
f2 f1 f2 + =
f1 temp =
PRINTVAR f2
n n 1 - =
n 0 > 4 ?
```

The last line now says the following: If n is greater than 0, then jump to (zero-based) line 4. This improves the script, because if the user enters a negative number, the RPN program doesn't go into an infinite loop.

Finally—although this is not necessary for most scripts—let's add an operation that gets a random integer in a specified range.

op1   op2   !

The action of this RPN expression is to call **random.randint**, passing op1 and op2 as the *begin* and *end* arguments, respectively. The random integer produced in this range is then pushed on the stack.

Adding support for this expression is also easy. However, it involves importing another package. The code will be easy to write if we can refer to it directly. Therefore, let's import it this way:

```
from random import randint
```

Now we need only add a line to add support for randomization. Again, here is the revised scanner, with the line to be added in bold.

```
scanner = re.Scanner([
    (r"[ \t\n]", lambda s, t: None),
    (r"-?(\d*)?\.\d+", lambda s, t:
        stack.append(float(t))),
    (r"-?\d+", lambda s, t: stack.append(int(t))),
    (r"[a-zA-Z_][a-zA-Z_0-9]*", lambda s, t:
        stack.append(t)),
    (r"[+]", lambda s, t: bin_op(operator.add)),
    (r"[-]", lambda s, t: bin_op(operator.sub)),
    (r"[*]", lambda s, t: bin_op(operator.mul)),
    (r"[/]", lambda s, t: bin_op(operator.truediv)),
    (r"[>]", lambda s, t: bin_op(operator.gt)),
    (r"[!]", lambda s, t: bin_op(randint)),
    (r"[\^]", lambda s, t: bin_op(operator.pow)),
    (r"[=]", lambda s, t: assign_op()),
    (r"[?]", lambda s, t: jnz_op())
])
```

With all these additions to the RPN interpreter, it's now possible to write some interesting scripts. Here's the RPN version of the number guessing game.

Admittedly, it has a major limitation: no line labels! For clarity, then, we show the script here with line numbers (the targets of jumps) shown in bold—as well as with leading 0's, which, though not required, are not invalid either:

```
n 1 50 ! =
PRINTS 'Enter your guess: '
INPUT ans
ans n > 07 ?
n ans > 09 ?
PRINTS 'Congrats! You got it! '
1 011 ?
PRINTS 'Too high! Try again. '
1 01 ?
PRINTS 'Too low! Try again. '
1 01 ?
PRINTS 'Play again? (1 = yes, 0 = no): '
INPUT ans
ans 00 ?
```

This script is probably still difficult to follow, so it might help you to think of it with virtual line numbers placed in for the sake of illustration. These line numbers are imaginary; you can't actually put them in the file at this point! However, you might want to write them down on a piece of paper as you're programming.

```
00: n 1 50 ! =
01: PRINTS 'Enter your guess: '
02: INPUT ans
03: ans n > 07 ?
04: n ans > 09 ?
05: PRINTS 'Congrats! You got it! '
06: 1 011 ?
07: PRINTS 'Too high! Try again. '
08: 1 01 ?
09: PRINTS 'Too low! Try again. '
10: 1 01 ?
11: PRINTS 'Play again? (1 = yes, 0 = no): '
12: INPUT ans
13: ans 00 ?
```

This script takes advantage of a coding trick. If the jump-if-not-zero operation is given a constant, nonzero value, it amounts to an unconditional jump.

14

Therefore, the following statement on lines 08 and 10 unconditionally jumps to the second line (numbered 01):

```
1 01 ?
```

Now you should be able to follow the flow of the script and see what it does. Here's a sample session, assuming the script is stored in the file `rpn_game.txt`.

```
Enter RPN source: rpn_game.txt
Enter your guess: 25
Too low! Try again. Enter your guess: 33
Too low! Try again. Enter your guess: 42
Too high! Try again. Enter your guess: 39
Too low! Try again. Enter your guess: 41
Congrats! You got it! Play again? (1 = yes, 0 = no): 0
```

14.11   RPN: Putting It All Together

There's still more that can be done to improve the RPN application, but what we've developed in this chapter is a strong start. It has variables as well as control structures and even has the ability to generate random numbers.

Before leaving the subject, let's review the structure of the program. The main module, `rpn.py`, imports several packages and one module, `rpn_io.py`.

There's a circular relationship here, in that the main module creates a symbol table that the other module needs access to. But this is easily facilitated by having some of the function calls pass `sym_tab`. The functions thereby get a reference to `sym_tab`, which they can then use to manipulate the table (see Figure 14.3).

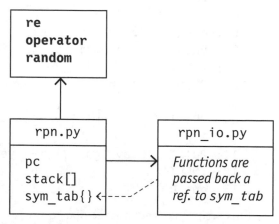

Figure 14.3. Final structure of the PRN project

Here's the final listing of the main module, rpn.py. Most of the work of the module is done by the scanner object. The use of the Scanner class was explained in Chapter 7, "Regular Expressions, Part II."

```python
#File rpn.py ---------------------------------------

import re
import operator
from random import randint
from rpn_io import *

sym_tab = { }    # Symbol table (for variables)
stack = []       # Stack to hold the values.
pc = -1          # Program Counter

# Scanner: Add items to recognize variable names, which
#   are stored in the symbol table, and to perform
#   assignments, which enter values into the sym. table.

scanner = re.Scanner([
    (r"[ \t\n]", lambda s, t: None),
    (r"-?(\d*)?\.\d+", lambda s, t:
        stack.append(float(t))),
    (r"-?\d+", lambda s, t: stack.append(int(t))),
    (r"[a-zA-Z_][a-zA-Z_0-9]*", lambda s, t:
        stack.append(t)),
    (r"[+]", lambda s, t: bin_op(operator.add)),
    (r"[-]", lambda s, t: bin_op(operator.sub)),
    (r"[*]", lambda s, t: bin_op(operator.mul)),
    (r"[/]", lambda s, t: bin_op(operator.truediv)),
    (r"[>]", lambda s, t: bin_op(operator.gt)),
    (r"[!]", lambda s, t: bin_op(randint)),
    (r"[\^]", lambda s, t: bin_op(operator.pow)),
    (r"[=]", lambda s, t: assign_op()),
    (r"[?]", lambda s, t: jnz_op())
])

def jnz_op():
    ''' Jump on Not Zero operation.
    After evaluating the operands, test the first op;
    if not zero, set Program Counter to op2 - 1.
    '''
```

```
            global pc
            op2, op1 = stack.pop(), stack.pop()
            if type(op1) == str:
                op1 = sym_tab[op1]
            if type(op2) == str:
                op2 = sym_tab[op2]
            if op1:
                pc = int(op2) - 1     # Convert op to int format.

        def assign_op():
            '''Assignment Operator function.
            Pop off a name and a value, and make a symbol-table
            entry.
            '''
            op2, op1 = stack.pop(), stack.pop()
            if type(op2) == str:     # Source may be another var!
                op2 = sym_tab[op2]
            sym_tab[op1] = op2



        def bin_op(action):
            '''Binary Operation function.
            If an operand is a variable name, look it up in
            the symbol table and replace with the corresponding
            value, before being evaluated.
            '''
            op2, op1 = stack.pop(), stack.pop()
            if type(op1) == str:
                op1 = sym_tab[op1]
            if type(op2) == str:
                op2 = sym_tab[op2]
            stack.append(action(op1, op2))

        def main():
            '''Main function.
            This is the function that drives the
            program. After opening the file and getting operations
            into a_list, process strings in a_list one at a time.
            '''
            global pc
            dir('__main__')
            a_list = open_rpn_file()
```

```
        if not a_list:
            print('Bye!')
            return
        pc = -1
        while True:
            pc += 1
            if pc >= len(a_list):
                break
            a_line = a_list[pc]
            try:
                a_line = a_line.strip()
                if a_line.startswith('PRINTS'):
                    do_prints(a_line[7:])
                elif a_line.startswith('PRINTLN'):
                    do_println(a_line[8:])
                elif a_line.startswith('PRINTVAR'):
                    do_printvar(a_line[9:], sym_tab)
                elif a_line.startswith('INPUT'):
                    do_input(a_line[6:], sym_tab)
                elif a_line:
                    tokens, unknown = scanner.scan(a_line)
                    if unknown:
                        print('Unrecognized input:', unknown)
                        break
            except KeyError as e:
                print('Unrecognized symbol', e.args[0],
                      'found in line', pc)
                print(a_list[pc])
                break

    main()
```

When this source file is run, it starts the main function, which controls the overall operation of the program. First, it calls the open_rpn_file function, located in the file rpn_io.py.

Because this file is not large and there are relatively few functions, the **import** * syntax is used here to make all symbolic names in rpn_io.py directly available.

```
#File rpn_io.py
-------------------------------------------

def open_rpn_file():
    '''Open-source-file function.
    Open a named file and read lines into a list,
    which is then returned.
    '''
    while True:
        try:
            fname = input('Enter RPN source: ')
            if not fname:
                return None
            f = open(fname, 'r')
            break
        except:
            print('File not found. Re-enter.')
    a_list = f.readlines()
    return a_list

def do_prints(s):
    '''Print string function.
    Print string argument s, without adding a newline.
    '''
    a_str = get_str(s)
    print(a_str, end='')

def do_println(s=''):
    '''Print Line function.
    Print an (optional) string and then add a newline.
    '''
    if s:
        do_prints(s)
    print()

def get_str(s):
    '''Get String helper function.
    Get the quoted portion of a string by getting text
    from the first quote mark to the last quote mark. If
    these aren't present, return an empty string.
    '''
```

```
        a = s.find("'")
        b = s.rfind("'")
        if a == -1 or b == -1:
            return ''
        return s[a+1:b]

    def do_printvar(s, sym_tab):
        '''Print Variable function.
        Print named variable after looking it up in
        sym_tab, which was passed from main module.
        '''
        wrd = s.split()[0]
        print(sym_tab[wrd], end=' ')

    def do_input(s, sym_tab):
        '''Get Input function.
        Get input from the end user and place it in
        the named variable, using a reference to the
        symbol table (sym_tab) passed in as a reference.
        '''
        wrd = input()
        if '.' in wrd:
            sym_tab[s] = float(wrd)
        else:
            sym_tab[s] = int(wrd)
```

14

Chapter 14   *Summary*

In this chapter, we explored various ways of using the **import** statement in
Python, to create multiple-module projects that can involve any number of
source files.

Using multiple modules in Python does not work in quite the way it works
in other languages. In particular, importing in Python is safer of it's *unidirectional*, meaning that A.py can import B.py, but if so, B should not import A.
You can get away with A and B importing each other, but only if you know
what you're doing and are careful not to create mutual dependencies.

Likewise, you should show some care in importing module-level variables
from another module. These are best referred to by their qualified names, as
in mod_a.x and mod_a.y. Otherwise, any assignment to such a variable, outside the module in which it is created, will cause the creation of a new variable
that is "local" to the module in which it appears.

Finally, this chapter completed the programming code for the RPN interpreter application that has been developed throughout this book. This chapter
added the question mark (**?**) as a jump-if-not-zero operation, a comparison
(**>**), and the exclamation mark (**!**) as a random-number generator. Adding
these operations greatly expanded the extent of what a script written in RPN
can do.

But those additions are far from final. There are many other important features you might want to support, such as line labels and better error checking.
These are left as exercises at the end of the chapter.

Chapter 14   *Review Questions*

1 Is it valid to use more than one **import** statement to import the same module
more than once? What would be the purpose? Can you think of a scenario in
which it would be useful?

2 What are some attributes of a module? (Name at least one.)

3 The use of circular importing—such as two modules importing each other—
can create dependencies and hidden bugs. How might you design a program
to avoid mutual importing?

4 What is the purpose of **__all__** in Python?

5 In what situation is it useful to refer to the **__name__** attribute or the string
'__main__'?

6 In working with the RPN interpreter application—which interprets an RPN
script, line by line—what are some purposes of adding a program counter?

7 In designing a simple programming language such as RPN, what are the minimum expressions or statements (or both) that you'd need to make the language primitive but complete—that is, able to make it theoretically possible to
carry out any computerized task?

Chapter 14   *Suggested Problems*

1 Currently, some data is shared between the two modules, rpn.py and rpn_
io.py. Can you revise the application so that common data is placed in a
third module, common.py?

2 Given the way the RPN interpreter program is written, it should be easy to
add operations, especially if they correspond to one of the operations defined

in the operator package. As a miniproject, add the following: test-for-less-than and test-for-equality. Your biggest challenge may be to find enough punctuation characters to represent all the different operators. However, if you alter the regular expressions used in scanning, you can come up with two-character operators, such as **==** to represent test-for-equality.

3 It would be nice for the RPN script writer to be able to add comments to her script. You should be able to implement this feature with the following rule: In each line of an RPN script, ignore all text beginning with a hashtag (#), forward to the end of the line.

4 The greater-than test (**>**) is a Boolean operator, producing either True or False (1 or 0). Can the writer of an RPN script produce the same effect as other logical operators without actually being provided with less than (**<**), AND, or OR operators? If you think about it, multiplication (*) replaces AND beautifully. Does addition (**+**) replace OR as well? For the most part, it does; however, the result is sometimes 2 rather than 1 or 0. Can you then create a logical NOT operator that takes an input of 0 and produces 1, but takes any positive number and produces 0? What we're really asking here is, Can you think of a couple of arithmetic operations that, when put together, do the same thing as logical OR?

5 The biggest piece still missing from the RPN script language is support for line labels. These are not exceptionally difficult to add, but they are not trivial, either. Any line that begins with *label*: should be interpreted as labeling a line of code. To smoothly implement this feature, you should do a couple of passes. The first pass should set up a "code table," excluding blank lines and compiling a second symbol table that stores labels along with each label's value; that value should be an index into the code table. For example, 0 would indicate the first line.

6 The error checking in this application can be further improved. For example, can you add error checking that reports a syntax error if there are too many operators? (Hint: What would be the state of the stack in that case?)

14

Getting Financial Data off the Internet

The last is often best, and we've saved the best for last. One of the most impressive things you can do with Python is download financial information and chart it, in a large variety of ways.

This chapter puts together many features used in earlier chapters, showing them off to practical use. You'll see how to go out and grab information off the Internet, get the desired information on the stock market, and use that data to produce colorful charts showing what your favorite stocks are doing.

It's going to be a fun ride.

15.1 Plan of This Chapter

Three modules make up the stock-market application for this chapter, as shown in Table 15.1. The files are available at **/brianoverland.com/books** in downloadable form, along with other files, including the RPN interpreter application.

Table 15.1. Modules Used in This Chapter

MODULE	DESCRIPTION
stock_demo	This module prints a menu and prompts the user to choose a command as well as select a stock.
stock_load	Downloads a data frame from the Internet.
stock_plot	Takes the information downloaded and plots it. This chapter develops four versions of this module, culminating in stock_plot_v4.

15.2 Introducing the Pandas Package

Say hello to the **pandas** package. Like **numpy**, it provides sophisticated storage. But **pandas** also comes with a built-in data reader that gets information from the Internet.

Before you can run any of the code in this chapter, you'll need to install **pandas** and **pandas_datareader**. From the DOS Box (Windows) or Terminal application (Mac), type the following, one at a time. Each command takes a few seconds to complete.

```
pip install pandas
pip install pandas_datareader
```

If you're running on a Macintosh, remember, you'll likely need to use **pip3** if **pip** doesn't work:

```
pip3 install pandas
pip3 install pandas_datareader
```

We also assume, because it will become important in this chapter, that you've installed both the **numpy** and **matplotlib** packages, as described in Chapters 12 and 13. But if not, you should download them now.

```
pip install numpy
pip install matplotlib
```

Or, in the Macintosh environment, use these commands:

```
pip3 install numpy
pip3 install matplotlib
```

Note carefully the exact spelling of **matplotlib**, which has a "mat" but no "math."

The **pandas** package creates a *data frame*, which is like a rudimentary table or database used for storing large amounts of information. Data frames have their own binary format. For that reason, they have to be translated into a **numpy** format before they can be plotted. Here's the statement that does that:

```
column = np.array(column, dtype='float')
```

The most interesting part of **pandas**, for now, is the data reader, which must be installed as shown earlier. This data reader helps download information.

15.3 "stock_load": A Simple Data Reader

Now, let's use a simple **pandas**-based application to read useful information. You can, if you choose, enter the following program into a text editor yourself and save it as `stock_load.py`. Entering the comments (including the doc strings), as usual, is not required if you just want to get this to run.

```
'''File stock_load.py ----------------------------

Does the work of loading a stock, given its ticker symbol.
Depends on files: None


'''
# pip install pandas_datareader
import pandas_datareader.data as web

def load_stock(ticker_str):
    ''' Load stock function.
    Given a string, ticker_str, load information
    for the indicated stock, such as 'MSFT,' into a Pandas
    data frame (df) and return it.
    '''
    df = web.DataReader(ticker_str, 'yahoo')
    df = df.reset_index()
    return df

# Get a data frame (stock_df) and print it out.
if __name__ == '__main__':
    stock_df = load_stock('MSFT')  # 'msft' also Ok.
    print(stock_df)
    print(stock_df.columns)
```

Assuming you can enter this program (or copy it from **brianoverland.com/books**) and run it, congratulations. You've just downloaded information on Microsoft stock (MSFT) for the past 10 years.

This is far too much information to display in a small space, so **pandas** displays only some of the information, using ellipses (. . .) to show that there was more information than could have been shown, as a practical matter. Here's some sample output:

	Date	High	...	Volume	Adj Close
0	2010-01-04	31.100000	...	38409100.0	24.720928
1	2010-01-05	31.100000	...	49749600.0	24.728914

2	2010-01-06	31.080000	...	58182400.0	24.577150
3	2010-01-07	30.700001	...	50559700.0	24.321552
4	2010-01-08	30.879999	...	51197400.0	24.489288
5	2010-01-11	30.760000	...	68754700.0	24.177786

The program prints more information than this; the output shown here gives only the first 10 lines printed.

After printing all the data on Microsoft stock for 10 years, the program then prints the structure of the data frame itself—specifically, a list of columns.

```
Index(['Date', 'High', 'Low', 'Open', 'Close', 'Volume',
'Adj Close'], dtype='object')
```

Let's examine what this application does. It starts with a statement that imports the **pandas** data-reader package so that it can be referred to by a short name, **web**.

```
import pandas_datareader.data as web
```

Most of the work of this module is done by one function, load_stock, which has the following definition:

```
def load_stock(ticker_str):
    ''' Load stock function.
    Given a short string, ticker_str, load information
    for the indicated stock, such as 'MSFT,' into a Pandas
    data frame (df) and return it.
    '''
    df = web.DataReader(ticker_str, 'yahoo')
    df = df.reset_index()
    return df
```

If you've read Chapter 14, you may recall that testing the attribute __**name**__ serves a special purpose: It tells the app that if the current module is being run directly (thus making it the main module), then execute the lines that follow.

```
# Get a data frame (stock_df) and print it out.
if __name__ == '__main__':
    stock_df = load_stock('MSFT')  # 'msft' also Ok.
    print(stock_df)
    print(stock_df.columns)
```

The `load_stock` function is called, passing the Microsoft stock ticker name (MSFT). Most of the work of this function is done by the third line of code.

```
df = web.DataReader(ticker_str, 'yahoo')
```

This is almost too easy.

For a server name, the program uses yahoo. We believe this server will continue to be reliable in the foreseeable future, but, if necessary, you can search the Internet for another financial-data server.

The next step is to call the **reset_index** method. This method updates the index information for the columns. It's not obvious that you need to use this, but it turns out to be necessary. None of the code in this chapter works without it.

```
df = df.reset_index()
```

Finally, the data fame is returned to the module-level code. That code prints both the data frame itself and a summary of the columns in the data frame; we'll return to that summary later.

15.4 Producing a Simple Stock Chart

The next step in creating a stock-market application is to plot the data—although this section will do it in a minimal way, not putting up legends, titles, or other information at first.

Here are the contents of version 1 of the second module, `stock_plot`.

```
'''File stock_plot_v1.py --------------------------

Does the minimum to plot the closing price
of two fixed stocks. Depends on file stock_load.py
'''
import numpy as np
import matplotlib.pyplot as plt
from stock_load import load_stock

def do_plot(stock_df):
    ''' Do Plot function.
    Use stock_df, a stock data frame read from the web.
    '''
    column = stock_df.Close          # Extract price.
```

```
        column = np.array(column, dtype='float')
        plt.plot(stock_df.Date, column)      # Plot it.
        plt.show()                           # Show the plot.

# Run two test cases.
if __name__ == '__main__':
    stock_df = load_stock('MSFT')
    do_plot(stock_df)
    stock_df = load_stock('AAPL')
    do_plot(stock_df)
```

This module builds on the functionality of the first module, stock_load.py, by taking the data produced by the load_stock function; getting the data it needs from the data frame; converting it to **numpy** format; and plotting the graph.

Before we do anything else, the correct packages or modules (or both) need to be imported. The **numpy** and **matplotlib** packages need to be imported as we did in Chapters 12 and 13. But we also need to import load_stock from the module developed in the previous section, stock_load.

```
import numpy as np
import matplotlib.pyplot as plt
from stock_load import load_stock
```

After the data frame is read from the Internet, the do_plot function does most of the work. This function is passed a **pandas** data frame called stock_df.

```
def do_plot(stock_df):
    ''' Do Plot function.
    Use stock_df, a stock data frame read from the web.
    '''
    column = stock_df.Close               # Extract price.
    column = np.array(column, dtype='float')
    plt.plot(stock_df.Date, column)       # Plot it.
    plt.show()                            # Show the plot.
```

This function extracts the stock price, which, for this application, we access as the closing price—that being one of the columns in the data frame.

```
        column = stock_df.Close                  # Extract price.
```

Then the information is converted to a **numpy** array. The information is essentially the same, except now it's in **numpy** format. This conversion is necessary to ensure that the **matplotlib** routines successfully plot the graph.

```
column = np.array(column, dtype='float')
```

Finally, the price information is plotted against the information in the Date column.

```
plt.plot(stock_df.Date, column)      # Plot it.
```

The plot is then shown. This application displays two graphs in a row: one for Microsoft and another for Apple. Figure 15.1 shows the graph for Microsoft stock.

Figure 15.1. Microsoft stock prices

15.5 Adding a Title and Legend

Adding a title and a legend to a graph is not difficult. Part of this task—adding a title to a graph—was shown earlier, in Chapter 13. To display a title for a graph, you simply call the **title** function before the **plt.show** function is called.

> **plt.title(***title_str***)**

The argument ***title_str*** contains text to be placed at the top of the graph when it's shown.

Displaying a legend is a two-part operation:

▶ First, when you call the **plt.plot** method to plot a specific line, pass a named argument called **label**. In this argument, pass the text to be printed for the corresponding line.

▶ Before you call the **plt.show** function, call **plt.legend** (no arguments).

We show how this is done by making changes to the do_plot function and then showing the results. First, here's the new version of do_plot, with new and altered lines in bold.

```
def do_plot(stock_df):
    ''' Do Plot function.
    Use stock_df, a stock data frame read from web.
    '''
    column = stock_df.Close            # Extract price.
    column = np.array(column, dtype='float')
    plt.plot(stock_df.Date, column, label = 'closing price')
    plt.legend()
    plt.title('MSFT Stock Price')
    plt.show()                         # Show the plot.
```

Because this information is specific to Microsoft, let's not graph the Apple price information yet. In Section 15.8, we'll show how to graph the two stock prices side by side.

If you make the changes shown and then rerun the application, a graphical display is printed, as shown in Figure 15.2.

Figure 15.2. Microsoft stock with title and legend

15.6 Writing a "makeplot" Function (Refactoring)

While developing the application code for this chapter, we discovered that certain statements were repeated over and over again.

To be a professional programmer—or even a good amateur one—you should look for ways to reduce such code: to put the repetitive, boring parts of the program into a common function that you can call as often as you need. With the plotting software in this chapter, most of the work can be placed into a common function called makeplot, which is flexible enough to be used multiple ways.

This process is called *refactoring* the code.

In this section, we'll factor out a function called makeplot. The code that calls it will not do most of the plotting, as you'll see in the latter half of this section. Instead, the code will call makeplot and pass the following arguments:

▶ stock_df, the data frame originally produced by load_stock, and then passed along to the particular "do plot" function

◗ `field`, the name of the column (or *attribute*) you wish to graph

◗ `my_str`, the name to be placed in the legend, which describes what the particular line in the chart corresponds to, such as "MSFT" in Figure 15.3

This section, and the ones that follow, show how the `do-plot` functions call `makeplot` and pass along the needed information.

Here's the definition of `makeplot` itself. There are some things it doesn't do, such as call **plt.plot** or set the title, for good reasons, as you'll see. But it does everything else.

```
def makeplot(stock_df, field, my_str):
    column = getattr(stock_df, field)
    column = np.array(column, dtype='float')
    plt.plot(stock_df.Date, column, label=my_str)
    plt.legend()
```

Let's review each of these statements. The first statement inside the definition causes the specified column to be selected from the data frame, using a named attribute accessed by the built-in **getattr** function. The attribute, such as `Close`, needs to be passed in as a string by the caller.

The second statement inside the definition converts information stored in a **pandas** data frame into **numpy** format. The third statement does the actual plotting, using `my_str`, a string used for the legend, which is added to the plot.

But `makeplot` does not call **plt.show**, because that function should not be called until all the other plots have been put in the desired graph.

With `makeplot` defined, the rest of the code becomes shorter. For example, with `makeplot` available, the `do_plot` function in the last section can be revised as

```
def do_plot(stock_df, name_str):
    makeplot(stock_df, 'Close', 'closing price')
    plt.title(name_str + ' Stock Price')
    plt.show()
```

After calling `makeplot`, all this function has to do is to put up a title—which we have left as a flexible action—and then call **plt.show**. The second argument to `makeplot` selects the column to be accessed, and the third argument (`'closing price'`) is a string to be placed in the legend.

15.7 Graphing Two Stocks Together

When you look at Figure 15.2, you might say, "What happened to the graph for the Apple Computer stock price? I want to see that!"

We can put Apple back; in fact, we can do better. We can show both stock prices in the same graph, using the legend to clarify which line refers to which company.

However, this requires significant changes to the structure of this module. We have to change more than one function so that there's a function call that handles two stocks. Let's begin with the module-level code, which now passes two stock data frames instead of one.

```
# Run test if this is main module.
if __name__ == '__main__':
    stock1_df = load_stock('MSFT')
    stock2_df = load_stock('AAPL')
    do_duo_plot(stock1_df, stock2_df)
```

For each stock, a separate call is made to load_stock so that we don't have to alter the first module, stock_load.py. Both data frames are then handed to the do_duo_plot so that the two stocks are plotted together, along with a legend that includes both labels.

```
def do_duo_plot(stock1_df, stock2_df):
    '''Revised Do Plot function.
    Take two stock data frames this time.
    Graph both.
    '''
    makeplot(stock1_df, 'Close', 'MSFT')
    makeplot(stock2_df, 'Close', 'AAPL')

    plt.title('MSFT vs. AAPL')
    plt.show()
```

This function is short, because it makes two calls to the makeplot function—a function we wrote in the previous section—to do the repetitive, boring stuff. To review, here is the makeplot definition again:

```
def makeplot(stock_df, field, my_str):
    column = getattr(stock_df, field)
    column = np.array(column, dtype='float')
    plt.plot(stock_df.Date, column, label=my_str)
    plt.legend()
```

Note how the built-in **getattr** function is used to take a string and access the column to be displayed. This function was introduced in Section 9.12, "Setting and Getting Attributes Dynamically." Here this technique is a major coding convenience.

Figure 15.3 displays the result of the do_duo_plot function.

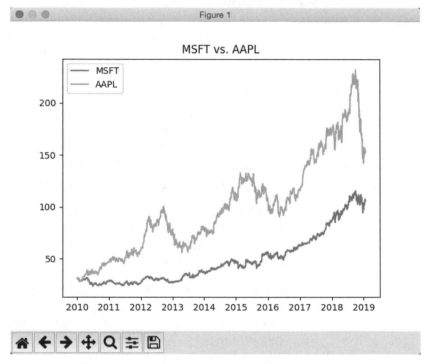

Figure 15.3. Graphing two stocks: MSFT versus AAPL

If you look closely at the code, you should see a flaw. "MSFT" and "AAPL" are *hard-coded*. That's fine when Microsoft and Apple are the two stocks you want to track. But what if you want to look at others—say, "IBM" and "DIS" (Walt Disney Co.)?

A good design goal is to create flexible functions; you should avoid hard-coding them so that you don't have to revise the code very much to accommodate new values.

Therefore, for this listing of the latest version of the stock_plot module—which we'll call version 2—we've revised the code so that the do_duo_plot function prints the appropriate labels and title, depending on the stocks passed to it.

```
'''File stock_plot_v2.py
---------------------------------

Plots a graph showing two different stocks.
Depends on stock_load.py
'''
import numpy as np
import matplotlib.pyplot as plt
from stock_load import load_stock

def do_duo_plot(stock1_df, stock2_df, name1, name2):
    ''' Do plot of two stocks.
    Arguments are data frames, which, in the symbol column,
    contain the ticker string.
    '''
    makeplot(stock1_df, 'Close', name1)
    makeplot(stock2_df, 'Close', name2)
    plt.title(name1 + ' vs. ' + name2)
    plt.show()

# Make a plot: do the boring, repetitive stuff.
def makeplot(stock_df, field, my_str):
    column = getattr(stock_df, field)
    column = np.array(column, dtype='float')
    plt.plot(stock_df.Date, column, label=my_str)
    plt.legend()

# Run test if this is main module.
if __name__ == '__main__':
    stock1_df = load_stock('MSFT')
    stock2_df = load_stock('AAPL')
    do_duo_plot(stock1_df, stock2_df, 'MSFT', 'AAPL')
```

Now we can control the two stocks that are chosen by changing relatively little code. For example, here's how you'd plot IBM versus Disney.

```
stock1_df = load_stock('IBM')
stock2_df = load_stock('DIS')
do_duo_plot(stock1_df, stock2_df, 'IBM', 'Disney')
```

Figure 15.4 displays the resulting graph, showing IBM versus the "Mouse House" (Disney).

There is a caveat to charting stocks this way: Without the help of color printing or color displays, it may not be easy to differentiate between the lines. Hopefully, even in this book (the printed version) the differences between the lines should show up in contrasting shading. But if this isn't satisfactory, one approach you might experiment with is using different styles for the two lines, as described in Chapter 13.

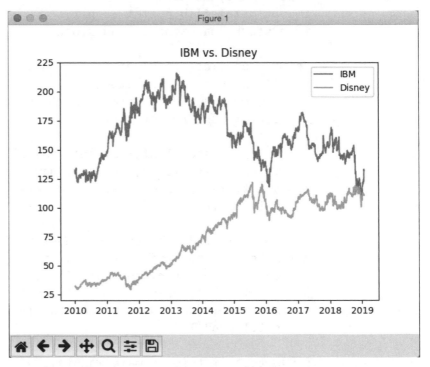

Figure 15.4. Graph of IBM versus Disney stock prices

Hmm . . . past performance, as brokers like to say, is no guarantee of future results. But if it were, our money would be on the Mouse.

15.8 Variations: Graphing Other Data

Let's go back and revisit the information available to us in the stock-market data frames. Section 15.3 printed the index for these frames.

```
Index(['Date', 'High', 'Low', 'Open', 'Close', 'Volume',
'Adj Close'], dtype='object')
```

So the data frame provides seven columns of data, as shown in Table 15.2.

Table 15.2. Column Names in a "pandas" Stock Data Frame

COLUMN NAME	DESCRIPTION
Date	The date corresponding to a given row (which has data for one day's stock report).
High	Highest price recorded for the day.
Low	Lowest price recorded for the day.
Open	Opening price of the stock on that day—that is, the price when trading opened that morning.
Close	Closing price for the day—that is, at the end of one day's trading.
Volume	Number of shares sold on the day in question. For major securities like Microsoft, this can run into the tens of millions.
Adj Close	Adjusted closing price.

Armed with this information, you can experiment by graphing different columns against the `Date` column, which holds the dates corresponding to each row. For example, we might, as an exercise, want to plot both the daily highs and the daily lows for a given stock.

The following code listing—we'll call this version 3—produces a combined high/low graph for a stock. New and altered lines, as usual, are shown in bold.

```
'''File stock_plot_v3.py
---------------------------------

Plots daily highs and lows for a stock.
Depends on stock_load.py
'''
import numpy as np
import matplotlib.pyplot as plt
from stock_load import load_stock

def do_highlow_plot(stock_df, name_str):
    ''' Do plot of daily highs and lows.
    Use high_price and low_price columns for one stock,
    which are passed through a stock data frame (stock_df).
    '''
    makeplot(stock_df, 'High', 'daily highs')
    makeplot(stock_df, 'Low', 'daily lows')
    plt.title('High/Low Prices for ' + name_str)
    plt.show()
```

```
# Make a plot: do the boring, repetitive stuff.
def makeplot(stock_df, field, my_str):
    column = getattr(stock_df, field)
    column = np.array(column, dtype='float')
    plt.plot(stock_df.Date, column, label=my_str)
    plt.legend()

# Run test if this is main module.
if __name__ == '__main__':
    stock_df = load_stock('MSFT')
    do_highlow_plot(stock_df, 'MSFT')
```

Figure 15.5 shows the resulting graph, charting both the daily high and the daily low stock prices.

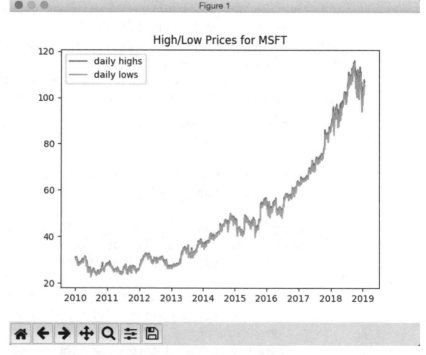

Figure 15.5. Graphing highs and lows of Microsoft stock

What else can we do with the data? Another useful piece of information is volume: the number of shares sold on any given day. Here's another plotting function, with new lines in bold.

```
def do_volume_plot(stock_df, name_str):
    ''' Plot the daily volume of a stock passed in as a
    data frame (stock_df).
    '''
    makeplot(stock_df, 'Volume', 'volume')
    plt.title('Volume for ' + name_str)
    plt.show()
```

When this function is run and is passed the data frame for MSFT, it produces the graph shown in Figure 15.6.

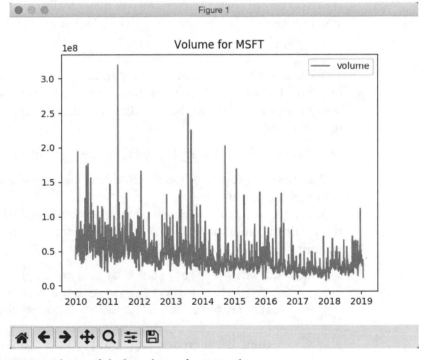

Figure 15.6. Chart of daily volume for a stock

The numbers on the left represent not millions of shares, but *tens* of millions. Because those numbers are too large to print without taking up large amounts of screen real estate, the number 1e8 is printed at the top of the graph. Consequently, figures on the left should be interpreted as multiplies of 10 million, which is equal to 1e8 (10 to the eighth power).

15.9 Limiting the Time Period

One thing we haven't controlled until now is the time period covered by the chart. What if you wanted to see the data for the stock in the past three months rather than 10 years?

Each day marks an active trading day: This includes Monday through Friday but not holidays. That's why there are roughly 240 "days" in a calendar year, and not 365. By the same logic, a month is roughly 20 days, and three months is roughly 60 days.

That being noted, the technique for restricting the duration of a data frame is to use our old friend, slicing. As you may recall from Chapter 3, the expression that gets the last N items of a string, list, or array is

```
[-N:]
```

We can apply this operation to a **pandas** data frame as well. The effect is to get the most recent N rows of data, ignoring everything else. Therefore, to restrict the data frame to the past three months (60 days), you use the following statement:

```
stock_df = stock_df[-60:].reset_index()
```

The **reset_index** method is also called, because it's necessary to keep the data accurate in this case.

When this statement is plugged in to the previous example, we'll get the last three calendar months (60 days) of volume data on a given stock rather than an entire year.

```
def do_volume_plot(stock_df, name_str):
    ''' Plot the daily volume of a stock passed in as a
    data frame(stock_df). GRAPH LAST 60 DAYS OF DATA ONLY.
    '''
    stock_df = stock_df[-60:].reset_index()
    makeplot(stock_df, 'Volume', 'volume')
    plt.title('Volume for ' + name_str)
    plt.show()
```

Now, when the application is run, you'll see only three months of data (Figure 15.7).

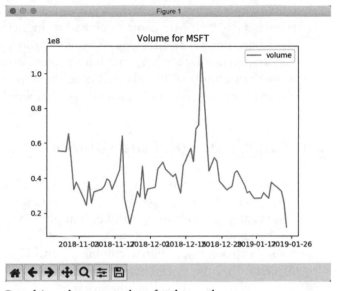

Figure 15.7. Graphing three months of volume data

The problem with this graph, as you can see, is that it gives X-axis labels in months/years/date rather than only month/year, with the result that the date and time information is crowded together.

But there's an easy solution. Use the mouse to grab the side of the chart's frame and then widen it. As you do so, room is made along the X axis so that you can see the date and time figures nicely, as shown in Figure 15.8.

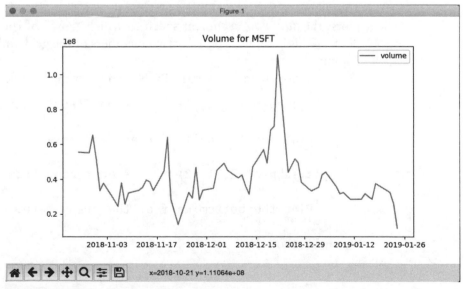

Figure 15.8. Widening a graph

With this graph, there's even more you can do. Within this time period, there is a day that Microsoft stock had its highest volume of sales. By moving the mouse pointer to the apex of the line, you can see that this high volume occurred in late December, and that the number of shares traded that day was more than 110,000,000: a hundred and ten million shares, worth more than eleven billion dollars. As Bill would say, that would buy a lot of cheeseburgers.

15.10 Split Charts: Subplot the Volume

Stock sales volume is more interesting when you can see it in combination with price. If a sharp rise or drop is combined with small volume, then the price change is likely to be a fluke: It might represent too few traders showing up that day.

But a strong price change combined with high volume is more substantial. It means that the price change was caused by the actions of many sellers or buyers, determined to chase the stock.

Therefore, what we'd really like to see is a *split plot*, a plot that lets us view price and volume next to each other. It turns out that the plotting package provides an easy way to do that. There is primarily one new method call you need to learn.

```
plt.subplot(nrows, ncols, cur_row)
```

This method call says that the plotting commands, up to the next call to **plt.subplot**, apply only to the indicated subplot. The *nrows* and *ncols* arguments specify the number of virtual "rows" and "columns" of separate plots; the *cur_row* argument specifies which "row" of the grid to work on next. In this case, we have only two members of the grid and only one virtual column.

Here's the general plan of the Python code for this double plot:

```
plt.subplot(2, 1, 1)       # Do first "row."

# Plot the top half of the graph here.

plt.subplot(2, 1, 2)       # Do second "row."

# Plot the bottom half of the graph here.

plt.show()
```

So subplotting isn't hard after all. We just need to plug what we already know in to this general scheme. Here is the code that does this.

```
def do_split_plot(stock_df, name_str):
    ''' Do Plot function, with subplotting.
    Use stock_df, a stock data frame read from web.
    '''
    plt.subplot(2, 1, 1)               # Plot top half.
    makeplot(stock_df, 'Close', 'price')
    plt.title(name_str + ' Price/Volume')
    plt.subplot(2, 1, 2)               # Plot bottom half.
    makeplot(stock_df, 'Volume', 'volume')
    plt.show()
```

This code has a twist. Only the top half should have a title; a title of the bottom half would be squeezed together with the X axis in the top half. Therefore, only one title is shown.

But otherwise, this example uses familiar-looking code. Figure 15.9 uses GOOGL (Google) as the selected stock.

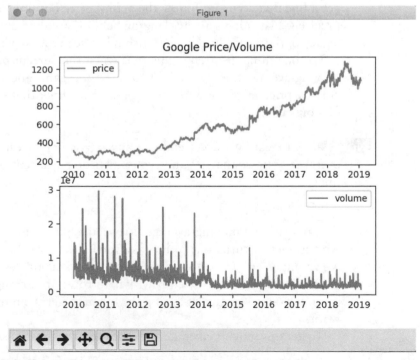

Figure 15.9. Subplot of GOOGL (Google), with volume

15.11 Adding a Moving-Average Line

One of the most useful additions you can make to a stock-market report is a moving-average line. Here's how a 180-day (six-month) moving-average line works.

▶ Start with a date having at least 180 preceding data points. You can start earlier if you want, in which case you should use as many preceding dates as are available.

▶ Average the closing price of all 180 dates preceding this one. This becomes the first point in the moving-average line.

▶ Repeat steps 1 and 2 for the next day: You now get a price that is the average of the 180 prices preceding the second day.

▶ Keep repeating these steps so that you produce a line charting average prices, each data point in this line averaging the prices of the 180 previous days.

As a result of following these steps—if you follow them faithfully—you'll get a line that seems to follow the actual price but (mostly) does not match it precisely. Instead, it's always lagging behind, weighed down, as it were, by the legacy of the past. But the relationship between the two lines is fascinating.

For one thing, it often seems that when the current price breaks above its moving-average line, it's poised for a strong gain; and conversely, when the current price falls below the moving-average line, that's often the beginning of a big fall.

Note ▶ A caveat: We don't endorse any particular investment strategy. However, many stock analysts and economists do pay attention to moving-average lines.

◀ Note

Calculating a moving-average line seems like an ideal job for a computer. And in fact, it turns out to be easy for Python, working with the packages we've imported. The **pandas rolling** function enables you to get a set of *n* previous rows for any given row, where rows are arranged chronologically. Then it's only a matter of taking the mean to get the moving-average line we want.

To get this moving-average line, use the function call shown here.

```
data_set = selected_column.rolling(n, min_periods=m).mean()
```

The *selected_column* is Open, Close, or whatever column we're using. The value *n* tells how many past days to use in the averaging. The *min_period* (which you can omit if you want) states how many previous data points need to be available for any given date, to be part of the moving average.

The reason this statement works is that for each day, the **rolling** function accesses the *n* previous rows. Taking the mean of this data gives us the moving average we were looking for. Essentially, **rolling** accesses 180 rows of data to produce a two-dimensional matrix; then the **mean** method collapses these rows into a single column, this one containing averages.

So, for example, here's a call that averages the previous 180 days, for each day:

```
moving_avg = column.rolling(180, min_periods=1).mean()
```

To make the rest of the code easy to write, let's first modify the makeplot function so that it accommodates an optional argument to create a moving-average line. The call to **rolling** has to be made while column is still a **pandas** column, and not a **numpy** column.

```
# Make a plot: do the boring, repetitive stuff.
def makeplot(stock_df, field, my_str, avg=0):
    column = getattr(stock_df, field)
    if avg:            # Only work if avg is not 0!
        column = column.rolling(avg, min_periods=1).mean()
    column = np.array(column, dtype='float')
    plt.plot(stock_df.Date, column, label=my_str)
    plt.legend()
```

Notice that this gives makeplot an additional argument, avg, but that argument, in effect, is optional; it has a default value of 0.

Now let's graph both a stock and its 180-day moving average, corresponding roughly to six months. New and altered lines, as usual, are in bold.

```
def do_movingavg_plot(stock_df, name_str):
    ''' Do Moving-Average Plot function.
    Plot price along with 180-day moving average line.
    '''
    makeplot(stock_df,'Close', 'closing price')
    makeplot(stock_df,'Close', '180 day average', 180)
    plt.title(name_str + ' Stock Price')
    plt.show()
```

Figure 15.10 shows the resulting graph—assuming AAPL (Apple) is the selected stock—containing the stock price as well as the 180-day moving-average line for those prices. The smoother line is the moving average.

Figure 15.10. Graph of stock price with 180-day moving average

Wow, it works!

And it's clear how to tweak this example. The following statement replaces 180 with 360, thereby doubling the period of averaging so that for any given day, the previous 360 days' prices are averaged in to produce the moving-average line rather than 180.

```
makeplot(stock_df,'Close', '360 day average', 360)
```

15.12 Giving Choices to the User

To have a usable application, you need to offer users choices and let them decide what data to chart. There are tens of thousands of possible graphs that might be displayed on any given day.

The most important choice is the stock to display information on. This is easy; it's simply a matter of prompting the user for a stock-ticker symbol, such as IBM, DIS, MSFT, or GOOGL.

The application can then print a simple graph of closing prices for the past decade, or it can print any of several types of graphs chosen from a menu. You can also put in a "quit" command.

A reasonable design for a starting application might be to offer the following menu:

```
0. Quit
1. Print simple closing-price graph.
2. Print highs and lows.
3. Print price/volume subplots.
4. Print price with 180-day moving average.
```

In order to support these operations, the stock _plot module needs to have several functions, each carrying out a different operation. This is a matter of copying and pasting code from previous sections.

The following listing shows the final version of the stock_plot module.

```python
# file stock_plot_v4.py -------------------------------

import numpy as np
import matplotlib.pyplot as plt
from stock_load import load_stock

def do_simple_plot(stock_df, name_str):
    ''' Do Plot function.
    Plot a simple graph of closing price.
    '''
    makeplot(stock_df,'Close', 'closing price')
    plt.title(name_str + ' Stock Price')
    plt.show()

def do_highlow_plot(stock_df, name_str):
    ''' Do High/Low Plot function.
    Plot both highs and lows for stock, then show.
    '''
    makeplot(stock_df, 'High', 'daily highs')
    makeplot(stock_df, 'Low', 'daily lows')
    plt.title('High/Low Graph for ' + name_str)
    plt.show()

def do_volume_subplot(stock_df, name_str):
    ''' Do Volume Subplot function.
    Plot closing price and volume subplots.
    '''
    plt.subplot(2, 1, 1)               # Plot top half.
    makeplot(stock_df, 'Close', 'price')
    plt.title(name_str + ' Price/Volume')
```

```
        plt.subplot(2, 1, 2)              # Plot bottom half.
        makeplot(stock_df, 'Volume', 'volume')
        plt.show()


    def do_movingavg_plot(stock_df, name_str):
        ''' Do Moving-Average Plot function.
        Plot price along with 180-day moving average line.
        '''
        makeplot(stock_df,'Close', 'closing price')
        makeplot(stock_df,'Close', '180 day average', 180)
        plt.title(name_str + ' Stock Price')
        plt.show()

    # Do the boring, repetitive stuff.
    def makeplot(stock_df, field, my_str, avg=0):
        column = getattr(stock_df, field)
        if avg:                          # Only plot avg if not 0!
            column = column.rolling(avg, min_periods=1).mean()
        column = np.array(column, dtype='float')
        plt.plot(stock_df.Date, column, label=my_str)
        plt.legend()

    if __name__ == '__main__':
        name_str = 'GOOGL'
        stock_df = load_stock(name_str)
        do_movingavg_plot(stock_df, name_str)
        do_simple_plot(stock_df, name_str)
        do_volume_subplot(stock_df, name_str)
        do_highlow_plot(stock_df, name_str)
```

Now it remains to write a module that prompts the user for selections and then calls the appropriate functions. That module will prompt for a stock-ticker symbol and then—if the stock in question was found—ask for a menu selection.

We could have started with a version that does not attempt to catch exceptions (runtime errors), but in view of all the things that can go wrong(a bad connection, typing an invalid stock-ticker symbol) this application turns out to be much more useful with the error checking (that is, the exception-handling code) added. Error checking is a good thing for many types of applications, but in this case, it's essential.

The following application handles errors by reprompting the user until successful or until the user enters an empty string, in which case the application terminates gracefully. As in Chapter 8, reprompting happens as needed, because of the combination of exception handling and the **while** loop. The loop never exits until the function returns; a side effect of exception handling is to jump down to the **except** statement and then (as a consequence) start at the top of the loop again.

```python
# file stock_demo.py -----------------------------

from stock_plot_v4 import *

menu_str = ('Menu choices:\n' +
'0. Exit\n' +
'1. Simple Plot of Prices\n' +
'2. Plot of Daily High/Low Prices\n' +
'3. Plot of Price with Volume Subplot\n' +
'4. Price plus Moving Average\n')

prompt_msg = 'Enter stock symbol (ENTER to exit): '
def main():
    while True:
        # Prompt and re-prompt user until a valid stock
        # symbol is entered OR user exits.
        try:
            s = input(prompt_msg)
            s = s.strip()
            if not s:            # On empty string, exit.
                return
            stock_df = load_stock(s)
            n = int(input(menu_str + 'Input choice: '))

            if n < 0 or n > 4:
                n = 0
            if n == 0:
                return

            fn = [do_simple_plot, do_highlow_plot,
                do_volume_subplot, do_movingavg_plot][n-1]
            fn(stock_df, s)
```

```
        except:
            print('Couldn\'t find stock. Re-try.')

    main()
```

One of the techniques employed here is the use of an open parentheses to enable line continuation, helping create the multiline string, **menu_str**.

Another technique is to index into a list of function names (callables) and then call the appropriate command. There are other ways to achieve the same effect—the obvious one being to use a series of **if/elif** statements—but the technique used here is compact and efficient.

An interesting aspect of this module is that it calls the `load_stock` function, even though that function is not defined in either this module or the module it imports directly, `stock_plot_v4.py`. But that module imports `stock_load.py`. Consequently, `stock_demo` imports `stock_load` indirectly.

There are many improvements that might still be made, but these are left for the suggested problems at the end of the chapter.

Chapter 15   *Summary*

We've come a long way in this book. In Chapter 1, our Python programs showcased a few statements that printed some values. Then, still in the first chapter, we used Python to print sophisticated sequences such as Fibonacci numbers. But in this chapter and the ones leading up to it, we added Python objects such as lists, matrixes, and sophisticated data frames.

The ability to grab information off the Internet, load it into data frames and arrays, and finally plot it is amazing. Graphical programming is among the most difficult challenges you can master, but thanks to its packages, Python reduces the problem to only a few lines of code. Even three-dimensional graphics were touched on in Chapter 13.

So if we ask the question "Python, what is it good for?," the answer is "Anything, as long as someone wrote a package for it!"

There are some other things to be said for the language. The most common things you'd want to do in most programs—get user input and then break up input into words, phrases, and numbers—are extremely well supported in Python. And the regular-expression package takes these abilities to a higher level.

Python's built-in abilities with lists, strings, dictionaries, and sets are so strong that one of the biggest challenges is just learning about all the options you have. You can go for a long time without realizing that collections are self-sorting or that you can get the sum of a list without writing a loop. It can take a while to learn every Python shortcut. We've written this book, in part, to cut down your time in learning to master this rich language.

There's also the occasional danger in Python, the treacherous bends in the river you may encounter while gliding downstream on a Python safari. We've tried to address most of those in this book as well, so when you finally meet the Python face to face, you'll find not a snake in the grass but a new friend and companion.

Chapter 15 *Review Questions*

1 Is there any difference between a **numpy** array and a **pandas** data frame? If there is, how do you convert between the two?

2 What things can go wrong when a user enters a stock-ticker symbol, and how should you respond?

3 Name some of the plotting methods used to create a stock-market chart.

4 In a stock-market chart, why is it important to print a legend? (Note: We're not talking about Hercules, King Arthur, or Batman.)

5 How do you restrict the duration of a **pandas** data frame so that it covers less than a year's time?

6 What is a 180-day moving average?

7 Did the final example in this chapter use "indirect" importing? If so, how, exactly?

Chapter 15 *Suggested Problems*

1 A desirable feature of our stock demo program would be to enable the user to specify the period of the moving-average line. That period has been set to 180 working days (equivalent to six months), but the program should provide adjustment of this time period as one option. You can, if you want, start out with a default of 180 days. But the user should be able to adjust this.

2 It would also be desirable to retain the stock-market selection until it is changed. If the user enters a blank string at the beginning, that should indicate a desire to exit the program. But subsequently, entering a blank line in response to the stock-market ticker prompt should cause the program to continue using the stock already selected.

3 Yet another desirable feature would be to enable the user to enter any number of stock-market ticker symbols (assuming they are all valid) and then graph all the stocks referred to. (Hint: To implement this feature, you might create a list of such symbols and pass it to one or more **for** loops that would get a data frame for each stock and then pass all that data to a function that plotted each and every stock, before showing the entire graph.)

 # Python Operator Precedence Table

Operators in Python expression are evaluated in the order shown in Table A.1 for Python 3.0.

Table A.1. Python Operators by Precedence

OPERATOR	DESCRIPTION
func(*args*)	Function call
collection[*begin* : *end* : *step*]	Slicing
collection[*index*]	Indexing
object.attribute	Property or member access
num ** *num*	Exponentiation
~*int*	Bitwise NOT
+*num*, −*num*	Plus/minus sign
*, /, %, //	Multiplication, division, remainder division, integer division (when operation is between two numbers); also multiplication of lists and strings: *list* * *n*
+, −	Addition and subtraction (when operation is between two numbers); also *str* + *str* produces string (or list) concatenation
int << *n*, *int* >> *n*	Left and right bit shifts
int & *int*	Bitwise AND
int ^ *int*	Bitwise XOR
int	*int*	Bitwise OR
in, not in, is, is not, <, <=, >, >=, !=, ==	Comparisons; each produces Boolean value (true/false)
not *val*[a]	Boolean NOT
val and *val*[a]	Boolean AND
val or *val*[a]	Boolean OR

a. The *val* may be almost any kind of value; Python will apply the operation bool() to convert before applying to conditionals—within, say, if or while. See notes that follow.

Other notes:

1 Where operators are at the same level of precedence, they are evaluated left to right.

2 Parentheses override precedence rules.

3 The special symbol = (not to be confused with ==, which is test for equality) is part of assignment-statement syntax and is not an operator.

4 With combined assignment-operator symbols (+=, *=, /=, etc.), the entire expression on the right is evaluated and then the assignment is carried out, regardless of precedence. For example, if x starts out as 12, then the statement x /= 3 + 9 sets x to 1, but the statement x = x / 3 + 9 sets x to 13.

5 Assignment-operator symbols include +=, –=, *=, /=, //=, **=, <<=, >>=, &=, ^=, |=. In each case, x op= y is equivalent to x = x op y; but note 4 applies.

6 As mentioned in Chapter 4, the Boolean operators apply short-circuit logic. If the first operand is true, the operator **and** returns the second operand. If the first operand is false, the operator **or** returns the second operand. Otherwise, the first operand is returned without evaluating the second operand.

7 To determine whether a value behaves as true or false, Python applies a Boolean conversion, **bool()**. For numeric values, zero is "false." For collections, an empty string or collection is "false." For most types, **None** is "false." In all other cases, the value behaves as if "true." (Comparisons, such as n > 1, always return **True** or **False**, which are fixed values.)

   By combining the last two rules, you should be able to see why Python responds as follows:

```
>>>print(None and 100)
None
>>>print(None or 100)
100
>>>print(not(''))
True
```

8 &, –, ^, and | have specialized uses with set objects, as intersection, difference, symmetric difference, and union, respectively.

Built-In Python Functions

In this appendix, square brackets in the syntax displays are not intended literally but indicate optional items.

The argument type *iterable* appears many times in this appendix. An *iterable* may be a collection, such as a string, list, or tuple, or any object whose class implements an **__iter__** method. Generators and ranges are also iterables.

Some of the functions (such as **min** and **max**) require a sequence or group of arguments to be *sortable*. To be sortable, a less-than operator (**<**) must be successfully applied to every combination of objects in the sequence.

Table B.1. Most Commonly Used Built-In Functions

TO DO THE FOLLOWING TASK:	CALL THESE FUNCTION(S):
Convert between ASCII and character format	**ch**, **ord**
Convert to **binary**, **oct**, **hex** string display	Call function of the same name.
Convert to **bool**, **bytes**, **complex**, **float**, **int**, **str**, **set**, or **list** data-object type.	Call function of the same name.
Divide, with modular division	**divmod**
Format an object to be printed	**format**
Generate a sequence of integers	**range**
Get absolute value	**abs**
Get input string from end user	**input**
Get length of a collection	**len**
Get type of object	**type**, **isinstance**
Get maximum from two or more values	**max**
Get minimum from two or more values	**min**
Merge two or more sequences	**map**, **zip**

▼ *continued on next page*

Table B.1. Most Commonly Used Built-in Functions. (*continued*)

TO DO THE FOLLOWING TASK:	CALL THESE FUNCTION(S):
Open a disk file for reading or writing	**open**
Print or display a series of values	**print**
Produce a sorted or reversed version of a collection	**sorted**, **reversed**
Round a fractional amount	**round**
Sum the elements of a collection	**sum**

abs(*x*)

Returns the absolute value of the numeric argument *x*. The result is non-negative; so negative arguments are multiplied by –1. In the case of a **complex** argument, the function returns the length of the real or imaginary vector as a non-negative, real-number result. The function uses the Pythagorean Theorem to find this value. For example:

```
>>> c = 3+4j
>>> abs(c)
5.0
```

In fact, this combination of features—using **abs** on a **complex** number—is a convenient shortcut for invoking the Pythagorean Theorem!

all(*iterable*)

Returns **True** if all the elements generated by *iterable* are "true"—that is, they produce **True** after a **bool** conversion is applied. In general, non-zero values and non-empty collections evaluate as true. For example:

```
>>> all([1, 2, 4])
True
>>> all([1, 2, 0])
False
```

any(*iterable*)

Returns **True** if at least one of the elements in *iterable* is "true," after a **bool** conversion is applied to each item. Remember that non-zero values and non-empty collections evaluate as "true." For example:

```
>>> any([0, 2, 0])
True
>>> any([0, 0, 0])
False
```

ascii(*obj*)

Produces an ASCII-only representation of the object, *obj*, returning it as a string. If non-ASCII characters are found in the output string, they are translated into escape sequences.

bin(*n*)

Binary-radix conversion. Returns a string containing a binary-radix representation of integer *n*, including the **0b** prefix. Inputs other than integer will cause Python to raise a **TypeError** exception.

For example:

```
>>> bin(7)
'0b111'
```

bool(*obj*)

Boolean conversion. This is an important conversion because it's implicitly called as needed by **if** and **while** statements, as well as by the **filter** function.

This function returns either **True** or **False**, depending on the value of *obj*. Each class can determine how to evaluate this function by implementing a **__bool__** method; but otherwise, the default behavior is to return **True**. Python classes tend to observe the following general guidelines. An object usually converts to **True** if it contains any of the following:

▶ A non-zero numeric value. (For complex numbers, this is any value other than 0+0j.)

▶ Non-empty collections, including lists and strings that are not empty.

Objects that usually convert to **False** include

▶ Any numeric value equal to zero

▶ A zero-length collection or sequence, or a zero-length string

▶ The special value **None**

For example:

```
>>> class Blah():
        pass
```

```
>>> b = Blah()
>>> b.egg = 0
>>> bool(b)
True
>>> bool(b.egg)
False
```

In this case, the object b automatically converted to **True**, because no **__bool__** method was defined for the class, but **b.egg** is equal to 0 and therefore **False**.

bytes(*source, encoding*)

Byte-string conversion function. Converts a source, typically a string, into a **bytes** string, in which each element has a byte value between 0 and 255, inclusive, and is stored in a single byte. In Python 3.0, it's typical for Python strings to use Unicode or UTF-8 representation, so that regular strings may occupy more than one byte per character. Therefore, ordinary strings need to be converted to produce **bytes** strings, if they need to contain one byte per character.

For example:

```
>>> bs = bytes('Hi there!', encoding='utf-8')
>>> bs
b'Hi there!'
```

callable(*obj*)

Returns **True** if the object *obj* can be called as a function. A true value indicates one or more of the following: *obj* is the name of a function, is created by a function definition, or is an instance of a class that implements **__call__**.

chr(*n*)

Returns the one-character string in which that character has Unicode value *n*. The lower part of this range includes ASCII characters. This is the inverse of the **ord** function. The domain of this function is 0x10FFFF. Values of *n* outside that domain cause a **ValueError** to be raised.

For example:

```
>>> chr(97)
'a'
```

compile(*cmd_str, filename, mode_str, flags*=0, *dont_inherit*=False, *optimize*=–1)

The **compile** function takes a string containing an expression, statement, or block of code (depending on *mode*) and returns a code object, which can then be executed by calling the **eval** or **exec** function. The *mode_str* string contains **'exec'**, **'single'**, or **'eval'**, to compile a module, single statement, or expression, respectively.

Because it enables execution of arbitrary strings of Python code, giving outsiders access through **exec** creates major security holes. In general, avoid it unless you have very good reason to use it. But here's a simple demonstration:

```
>>> command_str = '''
pi = 3.141592
print('pi/2 = ', pi/2)
'''
>>> cmd = compile(command_str, 'my_mod', 'exec')
>>> exec(cmd)
pi/2 = 1.570796
```

For more information, search online help. Remember that few people should use this function. If you execute an arbitrary user-input string, you're handling over control of everything in your program and the system.

complex(*real*=0, *imag*=0)

Complex-number conversion. Both *real* and *imag* arguments are optional, and each has a default value of 0. Given numeric input (as opposed to string input, which is explained in the next entry), the function responds by doing the following:

▶ Multiply the *imag* argument by 1j—that is, by the imaginary number, *i*.

▶ Add that to the *real* argument.

▶ Ensure that the result is a complex number, by adding or subtracting 0j if needed. (This usually follows from the first two rules.)

These simple rules encompass everything the conversion does. For example, a zero-value complex number is returned by default:

```
>>> complex()
0j
```

You can also provide an argument to the real portion only, creating a value that includes 0j to indicate its status as a complex rather than a real number.

```
>>> complex(5.5)
(5.5+0j)
```

The most common way to use this conversion is to use a real number or integer for each argument.

```
>>> complex(3, -2.1)
(3-2.1j)
```

You can also specify a complex argument for the first argument only, and the conversion will simply return the number as is.

```
>>> complex(10-3.5j)
(10-3.5j)
```

A quirk of this function is that you can specify a complex number for both arguments! The rules outlined earlier still apply. In the following example, the *imag* argument is 5j. This is multiplied by 1j, as usual, and the result is 5j * 1j = –5. That value is then added to the *real* argument, 1, to produce –4.

```
>>> complex(1, 5j)
(-4+0j)
```

complex(*complex_str*)

The complex-number conversion accepts a lone string argument of the form 'a+bj'—but it must have no internal spaces, and no second argument is allowed. Optional parentheses are accepted around a+bj. For example:

```
>>> complex('10.2+5j')
(10.2+5j)
>>> complex('(10.2+5j)')
(10.2+5j)
```

This function accepts strings that are valid complex numbers even if such numbers have only a real or only an imaginary portion. 0j will always be present in the result even if there is no non-zero imaginary portion. For example:

```
>>> complex('2')
(2+0j)
>>> complex('3j')
3j
```

Another quirk of this function is that *complex_str* is the only context in which you can use j in place of 1j; usually a number must be combined with j to distinguish it from any variable named j.

```
>>> complex('1+j')
(1+1j)
```

Note ▶ It's possible to produce values that use -0j instead of the usual +0j. For example, complex(1, -1j) produces (2-0j) even though complex(2, 0) produces (2+0j). The two results can be compared successfully with == but not with **is**. This phenomenon arises from floating-point representation including a sign bit; 0.0 and -0.0 are distinct objects, even though numerically equal.

◀ Note

See also the previous entry on **complex**.

delattr(*obj, name_str*)

Delete-attribute function. Removes an attribute from object *obj*, in which *name_str* is a string containing the name of the attribute. For example:

```
my_dog.breed = 'St Bernard'
...
a_str = 'breed'
delattr(my_dog, a_str)
```

After this statement is executed, the object my_dog no longer has a 'breed' attribute.

An **AttrbuteError** exception is raised if the *obj* does not already have the named attribute before the deletion. *See also* the **hasattr** and **setattr** functions.

dir([*obj*])

Directory function. Returns a list of attributes for the optional argument *obj*. If this object is a class, it shows all the attributes of the class. If the object is not a class, it gets the object's class and shows all that class's attributes.

If this argument is omitted, **dir** returns a list of attributes for the current context—either the current function or module. For example:

```
dir()      # Get attributes of the module.
```

Or, from within a function definition:

```
def demo():
    i = 1
    j = 2
    print(dir())
```

The call to demo prints the following:

```
['i', 'j']
```

The innocent-looking print(dir(i)), would print a rather long list, because i is an integer, and the integer class (**int**) has a fairly long list of attributes. Such a call has the same output as

```
print(dir(int))
```

divmod(*a, b*)

Divides *a* by *b* and then returns a tuple containing a/b, rounded downward to the nearest integer, along with the result, a % b, the remainder. This function is typically used with integers. For example:

```
quot, rem = divmod(203, 10)  # Result is 20, remainder 3
```

Either or both of the arguments *a* and *b* may be **float** values; but in that case, both of the return values will be in floating-point format. The quotient will have no fractional portion, but the remainder may. For example:

```
>>> divmod(10.6, 0.5)
(21.0, 0.09999999999999964)
```

The resulting tuple in this case should be (21.0, 0.1), but there is a small rounding error, as can happen with floating-point values. You can use the **round** function to help correct it.

enumerate(*iterable, start=0*)

Enumeration. Takes an *iterable* as input and returns a sequence of tuples, each having the form

> *number, item*

Here, *number* is an integer in a sequence beginning with *start* (0 by default) and increasing by 1 in each position; and *item* is an item produced by the *iterable*.

For example, if you want to take a list of strings and print each along with a sequential number, you could use the following loop:

```
beat_list = ['John', 'Paul', 'George', 'Ringo']
for n, item in enumerate(beat_list, 1):
    print('%s. %s' % (n, item))
```

This prints

```
1. John
2. Paul
3. George
4. Ringo
```

The value produced by the **enumerate** function, by the way, is an "enumerate" object, which can be used in a **for** statement, and can also, like other iterables, be turned into a list or tuple if desired. In this example, which starts with 1, the enumeration object produces tuples in this sequence:

(1, *item0*), (2, *item1*), (3, *item2*)...

If you want to print this iterable, you need to convert it to a list, or else use a **for** loop to step through it, as was done here.

eval(*expr_str* [, *globals* [, *locals*]])

Evaluates the Python expression contained in *expr_str*. Although this can be a way to write more compact code, it's potentially dangerous if you evaluate arbitrary input strings input by the user, unless the app is for your own use only.

The following example evaluates a Python expression and returns the result.

```
>>> a = 100
>>> eval('3 * a + 55')
355
```

The string must contain an expression and not a statement. Therefore, assignment statements cannot be used. However, expressions can contain function calls, and function calls, in turn, can execute statements.

One way to reduce the dangers of **eval** is to prevent access to symbols. The *globals* argument, by default, gives the setting for local symbols as well. Setting this argument to an empty dictionary prevents access to symbols. (But note that built-in functions are always accessible.)

```
>>> eval('3 * 100 + 55', {}) # This is fine.
355
>>> eval('3 * a + 55', {})    # ERROR; 'a' not defined
```

One way to bulletproof your code is to create a dictionary containing the symbols you want to be accessible; then give that dictionary as the *globals* argument:

```
>>> from math import *
>>> a = 25
>>> dict_1 = {'tan': tan, 'radians': radians, 'a': a }
>>> eval('1000 * tan(radians(a))', dict_1)
176.326980708465
```

The effect is to create a dictionary that restricts the **eval** statement to recognize only two functions (**tan** and **radians**) and one variable (a).

The *locals* argument isn't used much, but you can use it to restrict access to local symbols only. In that case, it won't usually permit access to functions.

```
eval('a * a + 100', {}, locals())
```

Note ▶   Although you can use the arguments to try to make **eval** safer, you can never fully bulletproof this usage if your application should happen to take an arbitrary string from the user and evaluate it. There are ways hackers can take advantage of such code to bring down a system. So again, take care.

◀ Note

exec(*object* [, *global* [, *locals*]])

See the **compile** and **eval** functions. The **compile** and **exec** functions are used by only the most advanced programmers. You should usually avoid this function because of the large security risks it can create.

Except for the few people who need it, this function is a classic case of overkill. Proceed at your own risk.

filter(*function, iterable*)

Generates a filtered sequence of values. Each item in the *iterable* is passed to *function* in turn. This, argument, *function*, should take one argument and return **True** or **False**.

If **True** is returned for a given element, the element gets included in the sequence generated by **filter**. Otherwise, the item is omitted.

In this next example, only negative numbers get included in the results. Other values get filtered out.

```
def is_neg(x):
    return x < 0

my_list = [10, -1, 20, -3, -2.5, 30]
print(list(filter(is_neg, my_list)))
```

The result produced by **filter** is a kind of iterable. You can convert it to a list if desired and print it; so the last of the lines just shown prints the following:

```
[-1, -3, -2.5]
```

The *function* argument may optionally be **None**. In that case, the items included in the result are those that evaluate to **True** when the **bool** conversion is applied. (Generally, any non-zero value or non-empty collection evaluates as true.)

float([x])

Floating-point conversion. If the optional argument *x* is specified, the result of converting the value to floating point is returned. Types that may be successfully converted to floating point include numeric types (such as integers) and strings containing a valid representation of a floating-point number.

Strings can include numeric representations such as `'4.105'`, `'-23E01'`, and `'10.5e-5'`. Positive and negative infinity can also be represented as `'Infinity'`, `'-Infinity'`, `'inf'`, and `'-inf'`.

```
n = 1
yyy = float(n)            # Assign 1.0 to yyy.
amt = float('-23E01')     # Assign -23E01 to amt.
```

If no argument is specified, the value 0.0 is returned. Note that the square brackets, in this case, indicate that the argument, *x*, is optional.

```
amt = float()             # Assign 0.0 to amt.
```

format(*obj,* [*format_spec*])

Format-string function, using the extended syntax for formatting described in Chapter 5, "Formatting Text Precisely." If the optional *format_spec* argument is specified, that argument is interpreted as a *spec* formatting code, as described in Chapter 5. Otherwise, the object is translated into its standard __**str**__ representation. In either case, a string is returned.

For example:

```
>>> format(1000000, ',')
'1,000,000'
```

The **format** method of the string class (**str**) calls this function once for each embedded print field. The result is to call the object's __**format**__ method if it's defined, or (by default) its __**str**__ method.

frozenset([*iterable*])

Returns a **frozenset** object, which is an immutable version of the **set** type. Note the use of parentheses in the following example, indicating that the argument is a tuple.

```
>>> frozenset((1, 2, 2, 3, 3, 4, 1))
frozenset({1, 2, 3, 4})
```

If the *iterable* argument is omitted, this function returns an empty **frozenset**.

getattr(*obj, name_str* [,*default*])

Get-attribute function. Returns the value of the named attribute for the object, *obj*; this value may have any type. The *name_str* argument is a string containing the attribute. If the attribute does not exist, the default value is returned; but if the named attribute does not exist and there's no default value, an **AttributeError** exception is raised.

The following example assumes that a Dog class exists.

```
>>> d = Dog()
>>> d.breed = 'Bulldog'
>>> attr_name = 'breed'
>>> getattr(d, attr_name)
'Bulldog'
```

See also **delattr**, **hasattr**, and **setattr**.

globals()

Returns a data dictionary, giving the names and values of global variables for the module that's currently executing.

hasattr(*obj, name_str*)

Returns **True** if the object, *obj*, has the attribute specified in *name_str*. The following example assumes that my_dog is an instance of a class, such as Dog:

```
>>> my_dog.breed = 'Husky'
>>> nm = 'breed'
>>> hasattr(my_dog, nm)
True
```

hash(*obj*)

Returns a hash value for the specified object, *obj*. This hash value is used by data dictionaries; as long as such a value is provided, the object, *obj*, can be used as a key. Classes whose objects do not support this function are not "hashable" and therefore cannot be used as dictionary keys.

This function is implemented by calling the **__hash__** method of the object's class. See Chapter 9 for more information.

Very rarely is there any reason to call **hash** or **__hash__** directly, except for testing purposes. The most important thing to remember is that if you write a class and want it to serve as a type that can be used as a key, then be sure to implement the **__hash__** magic method.

help([*obj*])

Prints help documentation for the specified object's class. This is used often within IDLE. If no object is specified, then an introductory page for the help system for Python is printed.

hex(*n*)

Hexadecimal conversion. Returns a string containing a hexadecimal-radix (base 16) representation of integer *n*, including the prefix, **0x**. Inputs other than integer cause Python to raise a **TypeError** exception.

For example:

```
>>> hex(23)
'0x17'
```

id(*obj*)

Returns a unique identifier for the object, obj. If two variables (obj1 and obj2) have the same identifier, then the expression obj1 is obj2 returns **True**—meaning that they refer to the same object in memory. (Note: Do not confuse this with test for equality, ==, which is a less restrictive condition.)

input([*prompt_str*])

Input function. Returns a string input by the user after waiting for the user to input zero or more characters and press Enter. The *prompt_str*, if specified, prints a string for prompting the user, such as "Enter name here: ". No extra space is automatically printed after this prompt string, so you may want to provide it yourself. For example:

```
my_name = input('Enter your name, please: ')
my_age = int(input('Enter your age, please: '))
```

int(*x, base*=10)

Integer conversion function. This function takes a numeric value or a string containing a valid integer representation and then returns an actual integer value. The *base* argument, if included, determines how to interpret the string of digits given as the argument; by default, decimal radix (base 10) is assumed, but another radix, such as 2 (binary), 8 (octal), or 16 (hexadecimal) may also be used. For example:

```
>>> int('1000', 16)
4096
```

For the first argument, you can specify an object of another numeric type, such as **float**. The **int** conversion truncates the fractional portion. For example:

```
>>> int(3.99), int(-3.99)
(3, -3)
```

To round to the nearest integer (or any significant digit) using a different rounding scheme, see the **round** function.

int()

The **int** conversion function for an empty argument list. This version of **int**, with no argument specified, returns the integer value 0.

See also the earlier entry for **int**.

isinstance(*obj, class*)

Returns **True** if object *obj* is an instance of the specified *class* or any type derived from that class. It's often recommended that you use this function instead of the **type** function. (The second argument can also be a tuple of types. In that case, this function returns **True** if the object is an instance of any of the specified classes.)

issubclass(*class1, class2*)

Returns **True** if *class1* is a subclass of *class2* or if the two arguments are the same class. A **TypeError** exception is raised if *class1* is not a class. As with **isinstance**, the second argument can also be a tuple of types.

For example:

```
>>> class Floopy(int):
        pass

>>> f = Floopy()
>>> issubclass(Floopy, int)
True
>>> issubclass(int, Floopy)
False
>>> issubclass(int, int)
True
>>> issubclass(f, int)   # TypeError: f is not a class
```

iter(*obj*)

Iteration function. This function call assumes that *obj* is an iterable—an object that returns an iterator. This includes standard collections and sequences, as well as generators.

If the argument is not an iterable, then calling **iter(obj)** causes a **TypeError** exception to be raised. If *obj* is an iterable, the call to **iter** should return an iterator object. Such an object does the actual stepping through a sequence of values by responding to **next**.

A few examples should clarify. First of all, you can't legally call **iter(obj)** if the object is not an iterable. For example:

```
>>> gen = iter(5)        # This raises a TypeError
```

However, the call is valid if the target object is a list, even if (as in this case) it is a short list containing only a single member.

```
>>> gen = iter([5])
```

It's more common, of course, to use **iter** on a longer list containing at least two members. The object returned—called an iterator or generator object—can then be used with **next** to access a stream of values, one at a time. For example:

```
>>> gen = iter([1, 2, 3])
>>> next(gen)
1
```

```
>>> next(gen)
2
>>> next(gen)
3
>>> next(gen)          # StopIteration exception raised.
```

The **iter** function has the effect of calling the **__iter__** magic method in the iterable object's class (such as a collection or generator), and the **next** function has the effect of calling the **__next__** method of an iterator object's class. Remember that it's a two-step process.

▶ Calling **iter** on an iterable, such as a collection, sequence, or range, returns an iterator object (such as gen in the previous example). Sometimes this happens implicitly; a **for** loop will do this for you automatically.

▶ Calling **next** on the iterator object gets you the next value yielded by the iteration. A **for** loop also does this automatically.

len(*sequence*)

Returns the number of elements currently stored in the *sequence*, which is usually a collection but may also be a sequence generated by the **range** function. In the case of a string, this gives the number of characters in the string.

```
>>> len('Hello')
5
```

This function is usually implemented by calling the **__len__** method for the object's class.

Note that although the sequence generated by the **range** function supports this function, there is no guarantee that other generators do.

list([*iterable*])

List conversion function. Takes an argument, which must be some kind of iterable, and returns a list. If a generator object is involved, the source of values must be finite in number.

If *iterable* is a string, the function returns a list in which each element is a one-character string.

```
>>> print(list('cat'))
['c', 'a', 't']
```

The square brackets in the syntax indicate that *iterable* is optional. If *iterable* is not specified, this function returns an empty list, [].

```
>>> new_list = list()      # Init new_list to empty list.
>>> new_list
[]
```

locals()

Returns a dictionary containing information on values in the local symbol table. This dictionary should not be altered directly. For example:

```
>>> def foobar():
        a = 2
        b = 3
        c = 1
        print(locals())

>>> foobar()
{'a':2, 'b':3, 'c':1}
```

map(*function, iterable1* [, *iterable2...*])

Takes a series of *iterables* and then returns another iterable, which may be used in a **for** statement, for example, or may be converted into a list by calling the **list** conversion.

The *function* argument is a callable that must take a number of arguments equal to the number of *iterables* provided in the other arguments to this function.

For each argument position in the *iterables*, the function is called and takes one element from each argument; the result is then placed in the resulting sequence generated by the **map** function. The resulting iterable will stop as soon as any of the arguments is exhausted.

For example:

```
>>> def multy(a, b, c):
        return a * b * c

>>> m = map(multy, [1, 20], [1, 20], [1, 50])
>>> print(list(m))
[1, 20000]
```

The result in this case is [1, 20000] because 1 * 1 * 1 produces 1, and 20 * 20 * 50 produces 20000.

The **map** function can be used with as few as one *iterable* argument; however, in such cases, list comprehension usually offers a better solution.

max(*arg1* [, *arg2*]...)

Returns the maximum value from a series of one or more arguments (brackets here are not intended literally). See the other entry for **max** for more information on how this function works.

```
>>> max(1, 3.0, -100, 5.25)
5.25
```

max(*iterable*)

Returns the maximum element from a finite *iterable* (which may be a collection, sequence, or generator object). In Python 3.0, all the elements must be sortable with regard to all the other elements, or else this function raises a **TypeError** exception.

Sorting is enabled by support for the less-than operator (**<**) for the objects involved; this means that the appropriate **__lt__** magic method must be defined for every combination of element.

But note that all built-in numeric types, except for **complex**, are sortable with regard to each other.

For example:

```
>>> from fractions import Fraction
>>> a_list = [1, Fraction('5/2'), 2.1]
>>> max(a_list)
Fraction(5, 2)
```

See also the previous listing for **max**.

min(*arg1* [, *arg2*]...)

Returns the minimum value from a series of one or more arguments (brackets here are not intended literally). See the other entry for **min** for more information on how this function works.

```
>>> min(1, 3.0, -100, 5.25)
-100
```

min(*iterable*)

Returns the minimum element from a finite *iterable* (which may be a collection, sequence, or generator object). In Python 3.0, all the elements must be sortable with regard to all the other elements, or else this function raises a **TypeError** exception.

Sorting is enabled by support for the less-than operator (**<**) for the objects involved; this means that the appropriate **__lt__** magic method must be defined for every combination of element.

But note that all built-in numeric types, except for **complex**, are sortable with regard to each other.

For example:

```
>>> from fractions import Fraction
>>> a_list = [1, Fraction('5/2'), 2.1]
>>> min(a_list)
1
```

See also the previous listing for **min**.

oct(*n*)

Returns a string containing the integer *n* in octal representation, including the octal prefix (**0o**). Inputs other than integer cause Python to raise a **TypeError** exception.

For example:

```
>>> oct(9)
'0o11'
```

open(*file_name_str, mode*='rt')

Attempts to open the file named by the first argument, which may include a complete path name or a name local to the current directory. If the file open is successful, a file object is returned. If not, an exception is raised, such as **FileNotFoundError**.

The *mode* is a string that should not contain more than two or three characters. Up to one character may be **'t'** or **'b'**, indicating whether the file is accessed as text or binary. The default is text (**'t'**).

The other character or characters determine whether the file-access mode is read, write, or read/write. The default is read mode (**'r'**). Table B.2 shows the read/write modes that may be combined with **'t'** (the default) or **'b'**, representing text and binary mode, respectively.

Table B.2. File Read/Write Modes

READ/WRITE FILE MODES	DESCRIPTION
r	Read mode. The file must already exist.
w	Write mode. The file will be replaced in its entirety.
a	Append mode. File pointer is set to end of file, but existing contents are not erased.
w+	Read/write mode. Truncates the file to zero bytes upon opening.
r+	Read/write mode. Performs no truncation upon opening.
x	Open for exclusive creation (write mode). Exception is raised if the file already exists.

Here's a simple example, opening a file in binary write mode ('wb'):

```
f = open('mydata.dat', 'wb')
```

This function has a number of other optional arguments that are occasionally used in specialized situations, not covered in this appendix. These other arguments include *buffering*, which by default is set to –1; and *encoding*, *errors*, and *newline*, each of which is set to **None** by default.

Note ▶ A file, once open, can be closed by calling the **close** method of the **file** class, which includes many other I/O methods. A file may also be closed automatically by using the **with** keyword, as explained in Appendix E.

◀ Note

ord(*char_str*)

Ordinal value function. Returns the number that is the ASCII or Unicode character code for the character contained in *char_str*. This argument is assumed to be a string containing exactly one character. If it is not a string or if it contains more than one character, a **TypeError** exception is raised.

The **ord** function is the inverse of the **chr** function.

```
>>> chr(ord('a'))
'a'
```

pow(*x, y* [, *z*])

Power function. Returns the same value that x ** y does—that is, it raises the numeric value *x* to the power of *y*. If *z* is specified, the function returns x ** y % z (divide the result by z and then return the remainder). For example:

```
>>> pow(2, 4)
16
>>> pow(2, 4, 10)
6
>>> pow(1.1, 100)
13780.61233982238
```

This last figure represents one dollar compounded at 10 percent annually for 100 years. The result is more than $13,000. (All good things come to those who wait!)

print(*objects, sep='', end='\n', file=*sys.stdout)

General-purpose **print** function. Default action is to get the string representation (**str**) of each of the objects and print them. By default, the **print** function prints an empty space between each of the objects' arguments; however, the **sep** argument may be used to specify another separator, including (if desired) an empty string, which would result in no separator at all.

Another named argument is **end**, which by default is a newline character; this determines what character, if any, is automatically printed at the end of all the output produced by this call to the **print** function. This is another argument that's often set to an empty string, giving the function caller more control over how often the output advances to the next line.

Finally, the default destination for the output is standard output (**sys.stdout**).

Here's an example using a customized separator: a semicolon followed by a space.

```
s1 = 'eenie'
s2 = 'meenie'
s3 = 'Moe'
print(s1, s2, s3, sep='; ')
```

This prints

```
eenie; meenie; Moe
```

This function is implemented by calling the **__str__** function for each of the objects to be printed.

range(*n*)

Returns a sequence of integers, starting with 0 up to but not including *n*. Therefore, `range(n)` produces 0, 1, 2, . . . *n-1*. You can use this sequence directly in a **for** statement; but if you want the sequence to have the full status of a list (so that you can print or index it), you need to apply a list conversion.

```
>>> list(range(5))
[0, 1, 2, 3, 4]
```

The expression **range(len(***collection***))** returns a sequence of integers corresponding to all the valid, non-negative indexes for the collection.

Remember that the value *n* is itself not included in the sequence. Instead, **range** generates integers from 0 up to but not including *n*.

range(*start, stop* [*, step*])

Returns a sequence of integers, just as in the other version of **range**. However, the *start* argument specifies an integer to begin the sequence on; *stop* is the number to end on; and the range extends up to, but not including, the *stop* argument. The *step* argument, if included, determines how much to increment each time.

If the *step* value is negative, the range goes in the reverse direction. It begins with the *start* value and then goes down to, but not including, the *stop* value. For example:

```
>>> list(range(1, 7, 2))
[1, 3, 5]
>>> list(range(5, 1, -1))
[5, 4, 3, 2]
```

See also the previous entry for **range**, which shows you can have as few as one argument.

repr(*obj*)

Produces a string representation of *obj*, similar to the action of the **str** conversion function; however, whereas **str** gives a standard string representation, **repr** gives the canonical representation of the object as it appears in code. Therefore, whereas `str(a_string)` prints a string as it is, without any surrounding quotation marks, `repr(a_string)` prints it with the quotes, because that's how it would appear in Python code.

For example:

```
>>> my_str = "Hi, I'm Brian!"
>>> print(repr(my_str))
"Hi, I'm Brian!"
```

The last two lines are equivalent to the following, because IDLE uses **repr** to display the value of an object rather than passing the object to **print**.

```
>>> my_str
"Hi, I'm Brian!"
```

This function is implemented by calling the **__repr__** function of the object's class.

reversed(*iterable*)

Produces a reverse generator over the elements in the source—that is, it iterates over items in the reverse of the order they have in *iterable*. You can use this generator in a **for** loop, the most typical use. Another thing you can do is to convert it to a list by using the **list** conversion function. For example:

```
>>> print(list(reversed([1, 2, 3])))
[3, 2, 1]
```

Technically, you can get the reverse generator of a string and attempt to display meaningful results. This is difficult to do, however, and requires the use of lists and the **join** function. Otherwise, look at what happens:

```
>>> str(reversed('Wow, Bob, wow!'))
'<reversed object at 0x11124bc88>'
```

The problem is that the **reversed** function, operating on a string, produces a generator object and not a string. But there are alternatives. The easiest solution is to use slicing directly on the string. For example:

```
>>> 'Wow, Bob, wow!'[::-1]
'!wow ,boB ,woW'
```

round(*x* [,*ndigits*])

Rounds a numeric value *x*, using *ndigits* to indicate at which position to do the rounding: Specifically, *ndigits* is an integer indicating how many positions to the right of the decimal point to perform the rounding. Negative numbers indicate a position to the left of the decimal point.

An *ndigits* value of 0 causes rounding to be done to the nearest unit (that is, to the nearest integer). An *ndigits* value of 1 rounds to the nearest tenth, and a value of –1 rounds to the nearest multiple of 10.

If *ndigits* is not specified, the function rounds to the nearest unit and returns the result as an integer rather than floating point. (The square brackets in the syntax indicate that this argument is optional.)

For example:

```
>>> round(12.555, 1)
12.6
>>> round(12.555, 2)
12.56
>>> round(12.555, 0)
13.0
>>> round(12.555)
13
>>> round(12.555, -1)
10.0
```

By default, the rounding mechanism rounds up or down, depending on the value of the digit to the right of the least significant digit in the result. If the digit is 5 or higher, then round upward; if 4 or lower, round downward. This behavior works for both positive and negative numbers, so "rounding upward" produces a value farther from 0. For example:

```
>>> round(-55.55)
-56
```

set([*iterable*])

Conversion function for Python sets. If the *iterable* argument is omitted, the result is empty. This is the standard way of representing an empty set in Python, because {} represents an empty dictionary rather than an empty set.

```
empty_set = set()
```

If the *iterable* is not empty, then the resulting set contains all the elements in the argument, but duplicates are dropped and order is not significant. For example:

```
>>> my_list = [11, 11, 3, 5, 3, 3, 3]
>>> my_set = set(my_list)
>>> my_set
{3, 11, 5}
```

setattr(*obj, name_str, value*)

Attribute-setting function. Although most setting of attributes is done directly, this function enables you to set an attribute to be determined later, at run time, rather than hard-coded. In this way, an attribute name can be determined at run time. The attribute might be provided by the user, or it might be determined by some attribute in a database with which the program interacts.

For example, the breed of a Dog object might be set this way:

```
d = Dog()
d.breed = 'Dane'
```

But if the attribute is not known ahead of time, the following statements do the same thing, setting the breed attribute to 'Dane' in this case.

```
attr_str = 'breed'
...
setattr(d, attr_str, 'Dane')  # set d.breed = 'Dane'
```

sorted(iterable [, *key*] [, *reverse*])

Produces a list that contains all the elements of an *iterable* but in sorted order. All the elements in the argument must be the same data type, or a compatible data type, in which order can be determined by applying the less-than (<) operator between any two elements. If such comparisons are not supported, a **TypeError** exception is raised.

Here's a simple example:

```
>>> sorted([5, 0, 10, 7])
[0, 5, 7, 10]
```

This function always produces a list, whereas the **reversed** function produces an iterable. The key argument is a function returning a *key* to sort by, and *reverse* indicates high-to-low order if **True**. Each must be a keyword argument if used.

str(*obj=''*)

Returns a string representation of the object, *obj*. If *obj* is not specified, this function returns an empty string.

This conversion is implemented by calling the __**str**__ method for the object's class. If the class has no __**str**__ method defined, then, by default, its __**repr**__ method is called. In many cases, the two methods display the same results; however, the difference is that the __**repr**__ method contains the representation of the object as it appears in code—string objects, for example, are returned with quotation marks.

Aside from its role in printing, this string conversion has other uses. For example, you might use this conversion if you want to count the number of 0's in a number.

```
>>> n = 10100140
>>> s = str(n)
>>> s.count('0')
4
```

str(*obj*=b'' [, *encoding*='utf-8'])

This version of **str** converts a **bytes** string (which is guaranteed to be made up of individual bytes) to a standard Python string, which may use two or more bytes to store a character. For example:

```
bs = b'Hello!' # Guaranteed to hold exactly six bytes
s = str(bs, encoding='utf-8')
print(s)        # Print a normal string, ? bytes per char.
```

See also the previous entry for **str**.

sum(*iterable* [, *start*])

Produces the sum of the elements in *iterable*. All the elements must be numeric; or they must at least support the __**add**__ method for objects of that type with each other and with integers. It will not concatenate strings.

This is a super convenient function for use with numeric lists, tuples, and sets. For example, here's a simple function that gets the average value of a numeric collection:

```
def get_avg(a_list):
    return sum(a_list)/len(a_list)
```

Here's an example that executes this function:

```
>>> get_avg([1, 2, 3, 4, 10])
4.0
```

The **sum** function can be used on other kinds of iterables, such as generators, as long as they produce a finite sequence. For example:

```
>>> def gen_count(n):
    i = 1
    while i <= n:
        yield i
        i += 1

>>> sum(gen_count(100))
```

Built-In Python Functions

```
5050
```

The effect of sum(gen_count(n)), in this case, is to add up all the numbers from 1 to n.

super(*type*)

Returns the superclass of the specified type. This is useful when you're inheriting from a class and you wish to call the superclass version of a particular method, such as __init__.

tuple([*iterable*])

Tuple conversion: returns an immutable sequence by taking the values from the *iterable*, which must be finite in size. The square brackets indicate that *iterable* is an optional argument; if omitted, the tuple returned is empty.

type(*obj*)

Returns the type of *obj*, which can be compared to other types at run time, using either test for equality (==) or **is**. For example:

```
>>> i = 5
>>> type(i) is int
True
>>> type(i) == int
True
```

The **type** function is often useful in Python in determining what the type of an argument is; it enables you to respond in different ways to different types of arguments. However, use of **isinstance** is usually recommended over the use of **type**, because **isinstance** takes subclasses into account.

zip(**iterables*)

Returns a sequence of tuples from a series of arguments. For each position, the tuple in the result is (i1, i2, i3... iN), where N is the number of arguments to this function and *i* is a value produced by the corresponding *iterable* argument. When the shortest of these arguments is exhausted, the function stops producing tuples.

That's a mouthful, but an example should help clarify. The following example demonstrates how **zip** can be used to create one list from the sum of two other lists: each element in *a* is added to the corresponding element in *b*.

```
a = [1, 2, 3]
b = [10, 20, 30]
c = [i[0] + i[1] for i in zip(a, b)]
```

Printing the results gives us

```
[11, 22, 33]
```

The expression zip(a, b), were you to convert it to a list and print it, produces a list of tuples, as shown:

```
>>> a_list = list(zip(a, b))
>>> a_list
[(1, 10), (2, 20), (3, 30)]
```

Compare the first three lines of the previous example with the following lines, which are more complicated and harder to maintain. This is a longer way of producing the same result.

```
a = [1, 2, 3]
b = [10, 20, 30]
c = []
for i in range(min(len(a), len(b))):
    c.append(a[i] + b[i])
```

Set Methods

This appendix lists the methods of the **set** type. It does not cover functions that also may be used with this type, such as **len**. For those, see Appendix B.

Table C.1. Most Commonly Used Set Methods.

TO DO THE FOLLOWING TASK:	CALL THESE METHOD(S):
Add element to a set	`add`
Clear all contents of a set	`clear`
Copy all contents of another set	`copy`
Delete an item from a set	`discard`, `pop`, `remove`
Determine if set is a subset or superset of another	`issubset`, `issuperset`
Perform set difference (set subtraction)	`difference`, `symmetric_difference`
Perform intersection	`intersection`
Perform union	`union`

Note: To determine if an element is a member of a particular set, use the **in** keyword.

set_obj.add(*obj*)

Adds an object, *obj*, to an existing set. The statement has no effect if *obj* is aslready a member of the set. Returns **None** in either case. For example:

```
a_set = {1, 2, 3}
a_set.add(4)        # Adds 4 to the set.
```

The set a_set is now equal to {1, 2, 3, 4}.

set_obj.clear()

Clears all the elements from an existing set. Takes no arguments and returns the value **None**.

```
a_set.clear()
```

set_obj.copy()

Returns a shallow, member-by-member copy of a set. For example:

```
a_set = {1, 2, 3}
b_set = a_set.copy()
```

After these statements are executed, b_set has the same contents as a_set, but they are two separate sets, so changes to one do not affect the other.

set_obj.difference(*other_set*)

Returns a set that contains all the elements in *set_obj* that are not in *other_set*. For example:

```
a_set = {1, 2, 3, 4}
b_set = {3, 4, 5, 6}
c = a_set.difference(b_set)
print(c)                        # Prints {1, 2}
print(b_set.difference(a_set))  # Prints {5, 6}
```

The **difference** operator, which uses a minus sign (-) for sets, produces the same results and is more compact.

```
print(a_set - b_set)            # Prints {1, 2}
```

set_obj.difference_update(*other_set*)

Performs the same action as the **difference** method, except that the results are placed in *set_obj* and the value returned is **None**.

The difference-assignment operator (-=) performs the same action.

```
a_set -= b_set       # Put results of diff. in a_set
```

set_obj.discard(*obj*)

Removes the element *obj* from *set_obj*. Returns the value **None**. Performs the same action as the **remove** method, except that no exception is raised if *obj* is not currently a member of the set.

```
a_set = {'Moe', 'Larry', 'Curly'}
a_set.discard('Curly')
print(a_set)                # Prints {'Moe', 'Larry'}
```

set_obj.intersection(*other_set*)

Returns the intersection of *set_obj* and *other_set*, which consists of all objects that are elements of both sets. If the sets have no elements in common, the empty set is returned. For example:

```
a_set = {1, 2, 3, 4}
b_set = {3, 4, 5, 6}
print(a_set.intersection(b_set))  # Prints {3, 4}
```

The intersection operator (**&**) performs the same action.

```
print(a_set & b_set)              # Prints {3, 4}
```

set_obj.intersection_update(*other_set*)

Performs the same action as the **intersection** method, except that the results are placed in *set_obj* and the value returned is **None**.

The intersection-assignment operator (**&=**) performs the same action.

```
a_set &= b_set       # Put the intersection in a_set
```

set_obj.isdisjoint(*other_set*)

Returns **True** or **False**, depending on whether *set_obj* and *other_set* are disjoint—meaning that they have no elements in common.

set_obj.issubset(*other_set*)

Returns **True** if *set_obj* is a subset of *other_set*; this includes the condition of the two sets being equal. For example:

```
{1, 2}.issubset({1, 2, 3})   # Produces the value True.
{1, 2}.issubset({1, 2})      # Also produces True.
```

set_obj.issuperset(*other_set*)

Returns True if `set_obj` is a superset of `other_set`; this includes the condition of the two sets being equal. For example:

```
{1, 2}.issuperset({1})        # Produces the value True.
{1, 2}.issuperset({1, 2})     # Also produces True.
```

set_obj.pop()

Returns a random element from the set and then removes that element. For example:

```
a_set = {'Moe', 'Larry', 'Curly'}
stooge = a_set.pop()
print(stooge, a_set)
```

This example prints, or rather may print, the following:

```
Moe {'Larry', 'Curly'}
```

set_obj.remove(*obj*)

Removes the specified element, `obj`, from the `set_obj`. This performs the same action as the **discard** method, except that **remove** raises a **KeyError** exception if `obj` is not currently an element.

set_obj.symmetric_difference(*other_set*)

Returns a set consisting of all objects that are a member of `set_obj` but not `other_set`, and vice versa. For example:

```
a_set = {1, 2, 3, 4}
b_set = {3, 4, 5, 6}
print(a_set.symmetric_difference(b_set))
```

This code prints the set {1, 2, 5, 6}.
The symmetric-difference operator (^) performs the same action.

```
print(a_set ^ b_set)        # Prints {1, 2, 5, 6}
```

set_obj.symmetric_difference_update(*other_set*)

Performs the same action as the **symmetric_difference** method, except that the results are placed in *set_obj* and the value returned is **None**.

The symmetric-difference-assignment operator (**^=**) performs the same action.

```
a_set ^= b_set          # Put the sym. difference in a_set
```

set_obj.union(*other_set*)

Returns the union of *set_obj* and *other_set*, which is the set containing all objects that are in either set or both. For example:

```
a_set = {1, 2, 3, 4}
b_set = {3, 4, 5, 6}
print(a_set.union(b_set))  # Prints {1, 2, 3, 4, 5, 6}
```

The union operator (**|**) performs the same action.

```
print(a_set | b_set)        # Prints {1, 2, 3, 4, 5, 6}
```

set_obj.union_update(*other_set*)

Performs the same action as the **union** method, except that the results are placed in *set_obj* and the value returned is **None**.

The union-assignment operator (**|=**) performs the same action.

```
a_set |= b_set          # Put the union in a_set
```

This operator provides an easy way to extend the contents of a set. For example:

```
a_set = {1, 2, 3}
a_set |= {200, 300}
print(a_set)            # Prints {1, 2, 3, 200, 300}
```

 # *Dictionary Methods*

This appendix lists the methods of the **dict** type. It does not cover functions that also may be used with this type, such as **len**. For those, see Appendix B.

In the syntax displays that head each section, square brackets are not intended literally but indicate optional items.

Table D.1. Most Commonly Used Dictionary Methods.

TO DO THE FOLLOWING TASK:	CALL THIS METHOD:
Add key/value pairs from another collection	update
Clear all contents of dictionary	clear
Copy all contents of another dictionary	copy
Delete a key and associated value	pop
Get a value by key; return a default value (such as **None**) if the key is not found	get
Get a sequence containing all associated values	values
Get a sequence containing all the keys	keys
Get all key-value pairs	items
Get the value of key if it exists; insert a default value otherwise	setdefault

dict_obj.clear()

Clears all the elements from an existing dictionary. Takes no arguments and returns the value **None**.

```
a_dict.clear()
```

dict_obj.copy()

Returns a shallow copy of a dictionary by performing a member-by-member copy. For example:

```
a_dict = {'pi': 3.14159, 'e': 2.71828 }
b_dict = a_dict.copy()
```

After these statements are executed, b_dict has the same contents as a_dict, but they are two separate collections, so changes to one do not affect the other.

dict_obj.get(key_obj, default_val = None)

Returns the value associated with the specified key within *dict_obj*. If the key is not found, the method returns *default_val*, which is **None** if not specified. For example:

```
v = my_dict.get('BrianO')
if v:
    print('Value is: ', v)
else:
    print('BrianO not found.')
```

The following use of **get** is an effective shortcut for creating histograms. Assume that wrd_list is a list of strings, each string containing a word. We can form such a list this way, along with an empty dictionary.

```
s = 'I am what I am and that is all that I am'
wrd_list = s.split()
hist_dict = {}
```

Now we can use the **get** method to produce the word count we're seeking.

```
for wrd in wrd_list:
    hist_dict[wrd] = hist_dict.get(wrd, 0) + 1
print(hist_dict)
```

These statements maintain word/frequency pairs in the dictionary. Each time a new word is found, it's added to the dictionary with a value of 1; otherwise, the existing value is incremented by 1. These statements produce the following output:

```
{'I': 3, 'am': 3, 'what': 1, 'and': 1, 'that': 2,
'is': 1, 'all': 1, 'am.': 1}
```

dict_obj.items()

Returns a sequence of tuples, in the format (*key*, *value*), containing all the key-value pairs in the dictionary. For example:

```
grades = {'Moe':1.5, 'Larry':1.0, 'BillG':4.0}
print(grades.items())
```

This code prints the following:

```
dict_items([('Moe', 1.5), ('Larry', 1.0), ('BillG', 4.0)])
```

dict_obj.keys()

Returns a sequence containing all the keys in the dictionary. For example:

```
grades = {'Moe':1.5, 'Larry':1.0, 'BillG':4.0}
print(grades.keys())
```

This code prints the following:

```
dict_keys(['Moe', 'Larry', 'BillG'])
```

dict_obj.pop(key [, *default_value*])

Returns the value associated with *key* and then removes that key-value pair from the dictionary. If the key is not found, this method returns the *default_value*, if specified; if that argument is not specified, a **KeyError** is raised. For example:

```
grades = {'Moe':1.5, 'Larry':1.0, 'BillG':4.0}
print(grades.pop('BillG', None))   # Prints 4.0
print(grades)                      # Prints grades, with
                                   # BillG removed.
```

dict_obj.popitem()

Returns an arbitrary key-value pair from the dictionary object and removes it. (This is not precisely the same as "random object," because the selection is not guaranteed to conform to the statistical requirements of true randomness.) The key-value pair is returned as a tuple. For example:

```
grades = {'Moe':1.5, 'Larry':1.0, 'BillG':4.0}
print(grades.popitem())
print(grades)
```

These statements print the following:

```
('BillG', 4.0)
{'Moe': 1.5, 'Larry': 1.0}
```

dict_obj.setdefault(*key, default_value*=None)

Returns the value of the specified *key*. If the key cannot be found, this method inserts that key, along with the associated value specified as *default_value*; this value is **None** if not specified. In either case, the value is returned.

For example, the following statement returns the current value associated with the key 'Stephen Hawking' if it is present; otherwise, it inserts a key-value pair and returns the new value, 4.0.

```
print(grades.setdefault('Stephen Hawking', 4.0))
```

dict_obj.values()

Returns a sequence containing all the associated values in the dictionary. To treat this sequence as a list, you can use a list conversion. For example:

```
grades = {'Moe':1.5, 'Larry':1.0, 'Curly':1.0,
          'BillG': 4.0}
print(grades.values())
```

These statements print the following:

```
dict_values([1.5, 1.0, 1.0, 4.0])
```

dict_obj.update(*sequence*)

This method extends the dictionary object by adding all the key-value entries in *sequence* to the *dict_obj*. The *sequence* argument is either another dictionary or a sequence of tuples containing key-value pairs.

For example, the following statements start with two entries in grades1 and then adds three more entries to that dictionary.

```
grades1 = {'Moe':1.0, 'Curly':1.0}
grades2 = {'BillG': 4.0}
grades3 = [('BrianO', 3.9), ('SillySue', 2.0)]
grades1.update(grades2)
grades1.update(grades3)
print(grades1)
```

These statements, when executed, print the following:

```
{'Moe': 1.0, 'Curly': 1.0, 'BillG': 4.0, 'BrianO': 3.9,
 'SillySue': 2.0}
```

 *Statement Reference*

This appendix covers a number of basic syntax issues in the Python language, except for operators, important methods, and built-in functions, each of which is covered elsewhere. The contents covered here include

▶ Variables and assignments

▶ Spacing issues in Python

▶ Alphabetical statement reference

Variables and Assignments

There are no data declarations in Python, not even for non-simple types such as multidimensional lists. Classes and functions are defined at run time, but otherwise, objects such as lists, sets, and dictionaries must be *built* rather than declared.

Variables are created by assignments. They can also be created by **for** loops. Within function definitions, arguments create variables with local scope. But assignments are still the basic tool for creating variables.

The simplest form of assignment is

```
variable_name = expression
```

You can also create any number of variables through multiple assignment.

```
var1 = var2 = var2 = ... varN = expression
```

Here are some examples of each.

```
a = 5.5
b = 5.5 * 100

x = y = z = 0            # Assign x, y, z the same val
var1 = var2 = 1000 / 3   # Assign var1, var2 the same val
```

587

Finally, tuple assignment is supported, in which the number of variables and the number of expressions must match, or one side or the other must be a variable representing a tuple.

```
x, y, z = 10, 20, 1000 / 3
```

In any case, a variable is created as a name referring to a value. More precisely, it becomes an entry in the symbol table at the global or local level. Each level of scope maintains its own symbol table as a dictionary. Consider the following program.

```
def main():
    a, b = 100, 200
    print(locals())

main()
```

The result is to print the data dictionary for the function's local scope.

```
{'b': 200, 'a': 100}
```

Now, whenever the variable a or b is referred to in an expression within this function, the corresponding value (which can be any type of object) is looked up in the table, and Python then uses the value associated with the variable name. If the name is not found, Python then looks at the global symbol table. Finally, it looks at the list of built-ins. If the name is not found in any of these places, a **NameError** exception is raised.

Consequently, Python variables are essentially names. They can be reassigned new values (that is, objects) at any time; they can even be assigned to different types of objects at different times, although that's mostly discouraged—except in the case of polymorphic arguments and duck typing. ("Duck typing" is discussed in *Python Without Fear* and other books.)

Variables, therefore, do not occupy fixed places in memory, unlike variables in other programming languages such as C and C++. A variable has no attributes of its own, only those of the object it refers to.

Variables work like references to objects. Assigning a new object to an existing variable replaces its entry in the data dictionary, canceling the old association. A counterexample would be the use of an assignment operator, such as **+=**, on a list, which works as an in-place modification. See Section 4.2.3, "Understand Combined Operator Assignment (+= etc.)," for more information.

A valid symbolic name begins with an underscore (_) or letter. Thereafter, every character must be a letter, underscore, or digit character.

Spacing Issues in Python

Spacing and indentation are highly significant in Python. Every time a line of code is indented relative to the previous line of code, it represents another level of nesting.

Top-level lines of code must be flush left, starting in column 1.

The indentation of a line of code must be consistent relative to the lines that are part of the same block. This means, for example, that the following is valid:

```python
a, b = 1, 100
if a < b:
    print('a is less than b')
    print('a < b')
else:
    print('a not less than b')
```

However, the following is not.

```python
a, b = 1, 100
if a < b:
    print('a < b')
  else:                         # ERROR!
    print('a not less than b')
```

The problem in this case is the position of **else**. It does not align with the corresponding **if** statement before it, which it must do to be valid.

You can do the following, although it's not recommended.

```python
a, b = 1, 100
if a < b:
        print('a < b')
else:
            print('a not less than b')
```

In this case, inconsistent indentation is used, but the logical relationships are clear. However, it's strongly recommended that once you choose a number of spaces for indentation, you stick with it throughout the program. Consistent use of four spaces per level is recommended by the PEP-8 standard.

Note ▶ Be careful about tab characters, which Python does not consider equivalent to any number of spaces. If possible, direct your text editor to insert spaces instead of tab characters (\t).

◀ Note

As a general rule, statements are terminated by the physical end of a line. There are a couple of exceptions. You can use semicolons (;) to place more than one statement on a physical line. These are statement separators and not terminators.

```
a = 1; b = 100; a += b; print(a)
```

You can also place an entire **for** or **while** loop on the same line, as explained in Section 4.2.17, "Use One-Line 'for' Loops."

Alphabetical Statement Reference

The rest of this appendix describes the statements supported by the Python language. This does not cover built-in functions, which are covered in Appendix B.

Table E.1. Most Commonly Used Python Statements.

TO DO THE FOLLOWING TASK:	USE THESE KEYWORD(S):
Break (exit) out of a loop	`break`
Catch and handle an exception	`try`, `except`
Continue to next cycle of a loop	`continue`
Define a class	`class`
Define a function	`def`
Global variable, create or manipulate	`global`
Import a package	`import`
Print an error message if assumption is violated	`assert`
Provide a "for" loop	`for`
Provide a "while" loop	`while`
Provide if/else structure	`if`, `elif`, `else`
Return a value from a function, or just exit early	`return`
Yield a value (create a generator)	`yield`

assert Statement

This statement is helpful as a debugging tool. It has the following syntax:

```
assert expression, error_msg_str
```

Python responds by evaluating the *expression*. If it's true, nothing happens. If the expression is false, *error_msg_str* is printed and the program terminates. The purpose is to catch important assumptions that have been violated. For example:

```
def set_list_vals(list_arg):
    assert isinstance(list_arg, list), 'arg must be a list'
    assert len(list_arg) >= 3, 'list argument too short'
    list_arg[0] = 100
    list_arg[1] = 200
    list_arg[2] = 150
```

When an **assert** condition fails, Python prints the error message and identifies the module and line number where the assertion failed.

Python turns off **assert** statements when you turn on optimization (-**O** from the command line), because this statement is for debugging purposes only.

break Statement

This statement has a simple syntax.

break

The effect of a **break** statement is to exit from the nearest enclosing **for** or **while** loop, transferring control to the first statement after the loop, if any. For example:

```
total = 0.0
while True:
    s = input('Enter number: ')
    if not s:              # Break on empty-string input.
        break
    total += float(s)   # Only executed on non-empty s.
print(total)
```

In this case, the effect of the conditional involving the **break** statement is to exit the loop after an empty string is entered.

Use of **break** outside a loop causes a syntax error.

class Statement

This statement creates, or "compiles," a class definition at run time. The definition must be syntactically correct, but Python doesn't need to resolve all symbols in the definition until the class is used to instantiate an object. (Classes can therefore refer to each other if neither is instantiated until both are defined.)

This keyword has the following syntax, in which square brackets indicate an optional item: *base_classes*, a list of zero or more classes separated by commas if there are more than one.

```
class class_name [(base_classes)]:
    statements
```

The statements consist of one or more statements; these are usually variable assignments and function definitions. A **pass** statement, a no-op, may also be used as a stand-in for statements to be added later.

```
class Dog:
    pass
```

Variables created in a class definition become class variables. Functions in a class definition become methods. A common such method is __init__. As with other methods, if it's to be called through an instance, the definition must begin with an extra argument, **self**, that refers to the instance itself. For example:

```
class Point:
    def __init__(self, x, y):
        self.x = x
        self.y = y
```

Once a class is defined, you can use it to instantiate objects. Arguments given during object creation are passed to the __init__ method. Note that this method provides a way to create a uniform set of instance variables for objects of the class. (As a result of this method, all Point objects will have an *x* and *y* element.)

```
my_pt = Point(10, 20)    # my_pt.x = 10, my_pt.y = 20
```

Function definitions inside a class definition can involve decoration with **@classmethod** and **@staticmethod**, which create class and static methods, respectively.

A *class method* has access to the symbols defined within the class, and it starts with an extra argument, which by default is **cls** and refers to the class itself.

A *static method* is defined in a class but has no access to class or instance variables.

For example, the following code defines a class method, set_xy, and a static method, bar. Both are methods of class foo, and both are called through the class name. They can also be called through any instance of foo.

```
>>> class foo:
    x = y = 0   # class vars

    @classmethod
    def set_xy(cls, n, m):
        cls.x = n
        cls.y = m

    @staticmethod
    def bar():
        return 100

>>> foo.set_xy(10, 20)
>>> foo.x, foo.y
(10, 20)
>>> foo.bar()
100
```

See Chapter 9, "Classes and Magic Methods," for more information.

continue Statement

This statement has a simple syntax.

```
continue
```

The effect of **continue** is to transfer execution to the top of the enclosing **for** or **while** loop and advance to the next iteration. If **continue** is executed inside a **for** loop, the value of the loop variable is advanced to the next value in the iterable sequence, unless that sequence has already been exhausted, in which case the loop terminates.

For example, the following example prints every letter in "Python" except for uppercase or lowercase "d".

```
for let in 'You moved Dover!':
    if let == 'D' or let == 'd':
        continue
    print(let, end='')
```

The effect of this code is to print:

```
You move over!
```

Use of **continue** outside a loop causes a syntax error.

def Statement

This statement creates, or "compiles," a function definition at run time. The definition must be syntactically correct, but Python doesn't need to resolve all symbols in the definition until the function is called. (This enables mutual self-references as long as both functions are defined before either is called.)

```
def function_name(args):
    statements
```

In this syntax, *args* is a list of zero or more arguments, separated by commas if there are more than one:

```
[arg1 [,arg2]...]
```

For example:

```
def hypotenuse(side1, side2):
    total = side1 * side1 + side2 * side2
    return total ** 0.5    # Return square root of total.
```

Once a function is defined, it may be executed (called) at any time, but parentheses are always necessary in a function call, whether or not there are arguments.

```
def floopy():
    return 100

print(floopy())          # Call floopy, no args! Print 100
print(hypotenuse(3, 5))
```

Functions have some other features, explained in Chapter 1, "Review of the Fundamentals." Also, functions may be nested, which is particularly useful with decorators, as explained in Section 4.9, "Decorators and Function Profilers."

del Statement

This statement removes one or more symbols from the current context. It has the following syntax:

```
del sym1 [, sym2]...
```

The effect is to remove the specified symbol or symbols but not necessarily to destroy any other object, as long as there are references to it. For example:

```
a_list = [1, 2, 3]
b_list = a_list    # Create alias for the list
del a_list         # Remove a_list from symbol table
print(b_list)      # List referred to still exists.
```

elif Clause

The **elif** keyword is not a separate statement but is used as part of the syntax in an **if** statement. See **if** statement for more information.

else Clause

The **else** keyword is not a separate statement but is used as part of the syntax in an **if**, **for**, **while**, or **try** statement.

except Clause

The **except** clause is not a separate statement but is used in a **try** statement. See **try** for more information.

for Statement

This statement has the syntax shown below. It's essentially a "for each" loop. You need to use the **range** built-in function if you want it to behave like a traditional FORTRAN "for" (which you should do only if necessary or you're very stubborn). The brackets are not intended literally but indicate an optional item.

```
for loop_var in iterable:
    statements
[else:
    statements]  # Executed if first block of statements
                 #   finished successfully, without break
```

One effect is to create *loop_var* as a variable, referring to the first item produced by *iterable* (which is a collection or generated sequence). This variable continues to exist at the current level of scope. Upon completion of the loop, the variable should refer to the last item in *iterable*, assuming there was no early exit.

The **for** loop performs *statements* over and over, just as a **while** loop does; but it also sets *loop_var* to the next value produced by *iterable* at the beginning of each iteration (cycle). When the iteration is exhausted, the loop terminates.

Here are some examples.

```
# Print members of the Beatles on separate lines

beat_list = ['John', 'Paul', 'George', 'Ringo']

for guy in beat_list:
    print(guy)
```

```
# Define function to calculate 1 * 2 * ... n

def factorial(n):
    prod = 1
    for n in range(1, n + 1):
        prod *= n
    return(prod)
```

See Section 4.2.9, "Loops and the 'else' Keyword," for an example of using an **else** clause with **for**.

global Statement

This statement has the following syntax, involving one or more variable names.

global *var1* [, *var2*]...

The effect of the **global** statement is: "Do not treat this variable, or variables, as local within the scope of the current function." It does not, however, create a global variable; a separate statement is required to do that.

This statement is sometimes necessary because otherwise, assignment to a global variable, from within a function, is interpreted as creating a local variable. If a global is not assigned to, there's no problem. But if you assign to a global variable from within a function, the code creates a local variable instead. This is what we call "the local variable trap."

```
account = 1000

def clear_account():
    account = 0        # Oops, create new var, as a local

clear_account()
print(account)         # Prints 1000, this is an error!
```

This simple program ought to create a variable, reset it to 0, and then print 0. But it fails to do so, because the statement `account=0` occurs inside a function. When executed, the function creates `account` as a local variable and therefore not connected to the global copy of *account*.

The solution is to use the **global** statement, which causes the function to not treat `account` as a local variable; it therefore forces Python to refer to the global version.

```
account = 1000

def clear_account():
    global account    # Don't make account a local var.
    account = 0       # Reset global copy to 0!

clear_account()
print(account)        # Prints 0, not 1000.
```

if Statement

This statement has a simple version and a more complete version, included here (although redundantly) for ease of understanding. The simplest version is

```
if condition:
    statements
```

The *condition* can be any Python object—or expression evaluating to an object—or a chained series of comparisons, as shown next.

```
age = int(input('Enter your age: '))
if 12 < age < 20:
    print('You are a teenager.')
```

All Python objects convert to **True** or **False** in this context. The *statements* are one or more Python statements.

Here's the full syntax. Square brackets in this case show optional items. You can have any number of **elif** clauses.

```
if condition:
    statements
[elif condition:
    statements ]...
[else:
    statements]
```

Here's an example. This example features only one **elif** clause, although you can have any number of them.

```
age = int(input('Enter age: '))
if age < 13:
    print('Hello, spring chicken!')
elif age < 20:
    print('You are a teenager.')
    print('Do not trust x, if x > 30.')
```

```
else:
    print('My, my. ')
    print('We are not getting any younger are we?')
```

import Statement

The **import** statement suspends execution of the current module and executes the named package or module if it hasn't been executed already. This is necessary, because in Python, function and class definitions are executed ("compiled") dynamically, at run time.

The other effect is to make symbols in the named module or package accessible to the current module, depending on which version is used.

```
import module
import module as short_name
from module import sym1 [, sym2]...
from module import *
```

The first two versions make symbols accessible but only as qualified names, as in **math.pi** or **math.e**. The third version makes symbols accessible without qualification, but only those listed. The fourth version makes all symbols in the module available without qualification.

This last version is the most convenient, but it presents the danger of naming conflicts if the named module or package defines many symbols. For large modules and packages with large namespaces, the other versions of the **import** statement are recommended.

See Chapter 14, "Multiple Modules and the RPN Example," for more information.

nonlocal Statement

This statement has a syntax that is similar to that of the **global** statement.

```
nonlocal var1 [, var2]...
```

The purpose of the **nonlocal** statement is similar to that of the **global** statement, with one difference: **nonlocal** is used to deny local scope and to prefer an enclosing, yet nonglobal, scope. This only ever happens when a function definition is nested inside another function definition. For that reason, the use of **nonlocal** is rare.

See the **global** statement for more information.

pass Statement

This statement has a simple syntax:

```
pass
```

This statement is essentially a no-op. It does nothing at run time, and its major use is to act as a stand-in or placeholder inside a class or function definition—that is, it holds a place to be filled in later with other statements.

```
class Dog:
    pass            # This class has no methods yet.
```

raise Statement

This statement has the following syntax, in which square brackets are not intended literally but indicate optional items.

raise [*exception_class* [(*args*)]]

The effect is to raise the specified exception, with optional arguments. Once an exception is raised, it must be handled by the program or else it causes rude and abrupt termination.

An exception handler can rethrow an exception by using **raise**. Using the statement with no *exception_class* rethrows the exception without changing it, in effect saying, "I've decided not to handle this after all" and passing it along. Python must then look for another handler.

```
raise
```

See the **try** statement for more information.

return Statement

This statement has one optional part. Here the square brackets are not intended literally.

return [*return_val*]

The action is to exit the current function and return a value to the caller of the function. If *return_val* is omitted, the value **None** is returned by default. Multiple values may be returned by returning a tuple.

```
return a, b, c    # Exit and return three values.
```

If **return** is used outside all functions, the result is a syntax error. See the **def** statement for an example of **return** in context.

try Statement

This statement has a fairly complicated syntax, so we break it down into two major parts: first, the overall syntax. Square brackets indicate optional items.

```
try:
    statements
[except exception_specifier:
    statements]...
[else:
    statements]
[finally:
    statements]
```

The first block of *statements* is executed directly. However, if an exception is raised during the execution of that block—even during a function called directly or indirectly by one of these statements—Python checks exception handlers, as described later in this section. There may be any number of exception handlers.

The statements in the optional **else** clause are executed if the first statement block finishes without being interrupted by an exception. The statements in the optional **finally** clause execute unconditionally, after other statements in this syntax.

Each **except** clause has the following syntax:

```
except [exception [as e]]:
    statements
```

If *exception* is omitted, the clause handles all exceptions. If it is specified, Python considers an exception a match if it has the same class as or a derived class of *exception*—or if it is an object whose class is a match. The optional *e* symbol is an argument providing information. Python checks each exception handler in turn, in the order given.

The **Exception** class is the base class of all error classes, but it does not catch all exceptions, such as **StopIteration**.

Handling an exception means to execute the associated statements and then transfer execution to the **finally** clause, if present, or else the end of the entire **try/except** block.

```
>>> def div_me(x, y):
    try:
        quot = x / y
    except ZeroDivisionError as e:
        print("Bad division! Text:", e)
```

```
    else:
        print("Quotient is %s." % quot)
    finally:
        print("Execution complete!")

>>> div_me(2, 1)
Quotient is 2.0.
Execution complete!
>>> div_me(2, 0)
Bad division! Text: division by zero
Execution complete!

>> div_me("2", "3")
Execution complete!
Traceback (most recent call last):
  File "<pyshell#21>", line 1, in <module>
    div_me("2", "3")
  File "<pyshell#19>", line 3, in div_me
    quot = x / y
TypeError: unsupported operand type(s) for /: 'str'
and 'str'
```

In these examples, the last one shows what happens if an exception arises that is not caught. The program terminates abruptly and prints a stack trace, but the **finally** clause is executed no matter what, even in this case.

The next example shows how a **try/except** structure can have multiple exception handlers; in theory, you can have any number. If the one block doesn't catch the exception, another can. The narrower categories of exception should be handled first. In the following example, any error not caught by the first handler is caught by the second.

Remember that the **as e** portion is always optional, but it's helpful for printing error text.

```
try:
    f = open('silly.txt', 'r')
    text = f.read()
    print(text)
except IOError as e:
    print('Problem opening file:', e)
except Exception as e:
    print('That was a Bozo no-no.')
    print('Error text:',e)
```

while Statement

This statement is a simple loop that has only one version. There is no "do-while." Square brackets are not intended literally but indicate an optional item.

```
while condition:
    statements
[else:
    statements]   # Executed if first block of statements
                  #  finished successfully, without break
```

At the top of the loop, *condition* is evaluated: Any "true" value causes the *statements* to be executed; then control is transferred back to the top, where *condition* is evaluated again. A "false" value causes exit from the loop.

(The true/false value of a non-Boolean condition is determined by applying a **bool** conversion and getting either **True** or **False**. All Python objects support such a conversion. The default behavior for Python objects is to convert to **True**. In general, objects are "true" except for zero values, **None**, and empty collections.)

So, for example, the following example counts from 10 down to 1, printing the number each time. (Blastoff!)

```
n = 10
while n > 0:
    print(n, end=' ')
    n -= 1              # Decrement n by 1
```

As a consequence of the rules for evaluating conditions, you could also write the code as follows, although it is a little less reliable, because if n is initialized to a negative number, the result is an infinite loop.

```
n = 10
while n:
    print(n, end=' ')
    n -= 1              # Decrement n by 1
```

See **continue** and **break** for ways to control execution of the loop.

with Statement

This statement has the following syntax, in which the optional part is shown in square brackets.

```
with expression [as var_name]
    statements
```

The effect is to evaluate the *expression* and produce an object. Python executes that object's **__enter__** method. If that method is not defined by the object's class, Python generates an **AttributeError**. Assuming that this exception is not raised, the *statements* are then executed.

Finally, the object's **__exit__** method is executed. If execution terminates early—for example, because of an exception—that method is executed anyway.

A common use of the **with** statement is to open and close files. The **__exit__** method of a file object automatically closes the file upon completion of executing the block.

```
with open('stuff.txt', 'r') as f:
    print(f.read())    # Print contents of a file.
```

yield Statement

The syntax of this statement is similar to that for the **return** statement, but its effect is completely different.

```
yield [yielded_val]
```

The default setting of *yielded_val* is **None**. Using **yield** outside a function is a syntax error.

The effect of **yield** is to turn the current function into a *generator factory* rather than an ordinary function. The actual return value of a generator factory is a *generator object*, which then yields values in the way defined by the factory.

This is admittedly one of the most confusing parts of Python, because no value is actually yielded until a generator object is created. (Whoever said all language designers are logical?) In fact, this is probably the single most counterintuitive feature in Python.

For clarifying information, see Section 4.10, "Generators."

Index

Z

VIDEO TRAINING FOR THE **IT PROFESSIONAL**

LEARN QUICKLY

Learn a new technology in just hours. Video training can teach more in less time, and material is generally easier to absorb and remember.

WATCH AND LEARN

Instructors demonstrate concepts so you see technology in action.

TEST YOURSELF

Our Complete Video Courses offer self-assessment quizzes throughout.

CONVENIENT

Most videos are streaming with an option to download lessons for offline viewing.

Learn more, browse our store, and watch free, sample lessons at
informit.com/video

Save 50%* off the list price of video courses with discount code **VIDBOB**

the trusted technology learning source